Spring 74

ALCHEMY

A Journal of Archetype and Culture

Spring, 2006

SPRING JOURNAL
New Orleans, Louisiana

— About the Cover Art —

Useless Science, or the Alchemist by Remedios Varo

Useless Science, or the Alchemist (1955) is the work of the Spanish surrealist artist, Remedios Varo (born 1908, in Anglés, Cataluña, Spain). Even as a student in a Spanish convent school, Varo showed an affinity for drama, the imaginal world, and the dark side of human existence. Throughout her life, she was profoundly interested in the reality of the numinous. She studied both Western and non-Western mystic and hermetic traditions, and, according to Janet A. Kaplan, "turned with equal interest to the ideas of Jung, G. I. Gurdjieff, [Peter D.] Ouspensky, Helena Blavatsky, Meister Eckhart, the Sufis, legends of the Holy Grail, sacred geometry, alchemy and the *I Ching*—seeing each as an avenue to self-knowledge and the transformation of consciousness" [*Unexpected Journeys: The Art and Life of Remedios Varo* (New York: Abbeville, 1988), 164].

The influences on Varo's art were numerous. The earliest was her father, a hydraulics engineer, who gave her the task, as a child, of copying his professional drawings for his projects. Later, at the Academia de San Fernando in Madrid (which she began attending in 1924) she became acquainted with the Renaissance masters. Her art especially recalls the sensibilities of Hieronymus Bosch, but it also contains distinct echoes of the style of the modern Italian artist Giorgio de Chirico. However, the predominant influence on her work was the ideas of the Surrealist movement, in which she became actively involved after moving to Paris in the 1930s. In 1940, she and her circle of Surrealist friends were forced to flee Paris in the wake of the Nazi invasion. She eventually settled in Mexico, where she spent most of her years from 1941 until her death in 1963. In her early years in Mexico, she made a living illustrating war propaganda materials and decorating furniture, but she also developed an interest in the primitive art of pre-Columbian cultures. It was only during the last decade of her life that Varo began to paint the images of her inner journey, and it was then that her true genius emerged.

Useless Science, or the Alchemist is one of her extraordinary images from this era. It is interesting to note that Varo's original title for *Useless Science, or the Alchemist* was *The Mechanical Labyrinth*; in Varo's mind the alchemist and the labyrinth pointed to the same mystery. In this painting, the tower-like houses—which throughout her work suggest initiation huts—contain the mechanisms of energy, which are set in

---

Editor's Note: *Spring* extends its thanks to Jungian analyst Mary Wells Barron for writing this note about our cover art. Mary is a Diplomate of the C. G. Jung Institute in Zürich and has a private practice in St. Louis, Missouri. Long interested in art and alchemy, she has written and lectured on the work of Remedios Varo in the United States and Europe since 1994.

motion by the alchemist's hand. The alchemist is evoked by the image of the woman at a spinning wheel—an apt image, since the work concerns the thread of life. The wheels inside the tower houses provide the energy for the process under way, namely, the extraction of essence, which appears as drops of moisture falling from above. Recalling the alchemical axiom "As above, so below," the viewer realizes that these drops are the "dew" of the unconscious. As Jung wrote: "... [T]hese instructions are the typical alchemical procedure for extracting spirit or soul and thus for bringing unconscious contents to consciousness." (*Collected Works,* 14 § 180)

In *Useless Science, or the Alchemist*, Varo depicts the process of transformation symbolically through the black and white tiles on the floor. The rigid, flat surface becomes flexible, and rises to form the alchemist's robe. Is this not precisely what occurs when, through slow, constant, even repetitious work, rigid defenses or lifeless patterns dissolve in the *solutio* and give way to new life, a less complexed, more resilient way of being? Upon reflection, the viewer realizes that it is Varo, the artist herself, who has assumed the role of the alchemist, and now sits on a three-legged stool, like the Pythia at Delphi, bringing her unique feminine lunar consciousness to bear on the task at hand, supported in her work by Wisdom, the Divine Feminine.

Not only does this painting, with its two titles, suggest the artist's love of irony and ambiguity, but it reminds us that alchemy is art, even as art is alchemy. The great artists of every age create images that serve not only their own personal transformation, but bring to all humanity the fresh images that are needed to contain, compensate for, and transform the one-sided, unbalanced *zeitgeist* of the collective, and thus bring about individuation.

MARY WELLS BARRON

CONTENTS

FILM REVIEWS

BOOK REVIEWS

From the Black Sun to the Philosophers' Stone

STANTON MARLAN

> When the light of the Sophia had mixed with the darkness, it caused the darkness to shine.
>
> — Sophia's Prayer of Repentance from *The Apocryphon of John*[1]

> It will be a matter, then, of attempting to say things in a way that lets the shining of their stone be manifest, that lets be manifest what is gathered into that shining.
>
> —John Sallis, *Stone*[2]

Introduction

Alchemy is a vast subject, and the Philosophers' Stone is one of its most enigmatic ideas. Historically, alchemists argued with one another about the materials, procedures, and nature of the Philosophers' Stone, and nearly every alchemical treatise proclaimed

Stanton Marlan, Ph.D., ABPP, is a Jungian psychoanalyst and a clinical/archetypal psychologist in Pittsburgh, PA. He is President of the Pittsburgh Society of Jungian Analysts, and a training and supervising analyst with the Inter-Regional Society of Jungian Analysts. He is also adjunct clinical professor of pyschology at Duquesne University and Editor of the *Journal of Jungian Theory and Practice*. His books include *The Black Sun: The Alchemy and Art of Darkness, Salt and the Alchemical Soul* (ed.), and *Fire in the Stone: The Alchemy of Desire* (ed).

Editor's Note: Stanton Marlan's most recent book, *The Black Sun: The Alchemy and Art of Darkness* (2005), is reviewed by Murray Stein and David L. Miller in this issue at pp. 318-325.

its own recipe as the correct one for the achievement of alchemy's sought-after goal. Typically, there was very little overlap between the views of the adepts. It was not unusual at the beginning of an alchemical work for the writer to start out by mercilessly denouncing other adepts, calling them fools, charlatans, puffers and the like, and proclaiming that only he had achieved the secret of the "Great Work."

In contrast to this, I would like to begin my reflections on the Philosophers' Stone with words of respect rather than words of derision. I am indebted first of all to the remarkable work of C.G. Jung, who opened up a depth psychological way of understanding the mysterious goal of alchemy, and to his classical followers Marie-Louise von Franz and Edward Edinger, both of whom, with a sense of appreciation, clarified and further developed Jung's work. Many other analysts, too many to name for the purpose of this piece, have continued in this tradition—or have contributed to it by reformulating some of Jung's ideas.[3] Several of them have written for this special edition of *Spring* on alchemy, thanks to the vision of Nancy Cater who has created a forum in which many of us have an opportunity to contribute our latest ideas on alchemical themes.

In terms of my focus on the Philosophers' Stone, two contemporary analysts stand out as having opened up new trajectories in alchemical thinking about the Stone: James Hillman and Wolfgang Giegerich. Hillman's work on alchemy is prolific and his influential series of papers on alchemical themes is undoubtedly well known to the readership of *Spring*. His most focused work on the Philosophers' Stone, however, is in his seminal paper "Concerning the Stone: Alchemical Images of the Goal."[4] Giegerich, likewise, has contributed an innovative view of alchemical psychology and the Philosophers' Stone in his challenging book, *The Soul's Logical Life*.[5] Like the traditional alchemists, Jung, Hillman, and Giegerich each hold differing views of the Stone, though there is often more overlap among them than might be apparent in a quick reading.

One way to imagine the psychological work on the Stone is to follow in the steps of the old alchemists and claim that each thinker advances over those who came before, each representing a version of the best or truest vision of the goal. While such a perspective ultimately may prove to be true, I must confess that I am not yet ready simply to move past Jung's work. Rather, I am still at work trying to understand

Jung's alchemical vision *alongside* those of Hillman, Giegerich, and others. While there are many scholars who have presented a number of valuable contributions to the alchemical work, I will be focusing here on Hillman and Giegerich, both of whom offer astonishing insights into the psychic reality of the Stone. Each of their perspectives can be read independently or as contributing to a larger and subtler vision still being articulated. For me, reading Jung side by side with Hillman and Giegerich evokes an image of the alchemical stove: Jung in one alembic cooking on a back burner over a steady low heat, Hillman and Giegerich in differently shaped vessels, boiling up front, while I attempt to prepare my own concoction utilizing the vapors produced by them and others and seeking to further distill the essences and elixirs necessary for the difficult production of the Stone. (A more comprehensive outcome of these distillations, however, must await a longer work on the Stone, which is still in progress. Here I can offer only a glimpse at the work emerging from the alembics of my colleagues, each with his own ideas and his own compelling images of the Philosophers' Stone.)

Tinctures of Stone

For the moment I will leave Jung's vessel closed and on the back burner, to be taken up later. Peering into Hillman's alembic reveals a phenomenology of the soul's colors: an imaginal rainbow of black, blue, white/silver, yellow, and red. For Hillman, the Stone is first an "idea" of the goal, since the goal must be deliteralized from the beginning.[6] While the Stone has facticity and objectivity, duration and substantiality, it is too complex to be described simply in *senex* metaphors. The Stone is also sensual, soft, waxy, and wounded. It is tender and flexible, oily, rich, and fat. It is vital and combustible and, though emotional, it has a kind of stability and timelessness. It moves in a circular way, turning like a wheel, returning *telos* to itself — "to the subjective urge that has impelled the entire work from the start .... the snake eats its own tail"[7] — and the *rotatio* announcing "that no position can remain fixed, no statement can be finally true."[8] It is ultimately the objectification of our subjectivity, yet it oozes with libido. It is Freudian, pagan, neo-Platonic, Greek, and Italian — a pleasurable pull towards Beauty, toward Voluptas rather than the "mediocrity of ataraxic rationality."[9] Hillman's patron saints, Corbin,

Ficino, and Valla, among others, stimulate a reddened psychology dripping with an Aphroditic language, exalting, revivifying, and crowning matter. The goal is not growth, health, development or transformation "but the seeking and searching of the awakened mind … like a burning jewel in the stone."[10]

A look inside the Giegerich vessel suggests the need to refine the Stone further. Its inner essence emphasizes the *logical* rather than the *imaginal.* The work of the adept, for Giegerich, would be to liberate the Stone from the confines of "sensate intuition" and "picture thinking." With the dissolution of the imaginal and of sensate intuition, one might be left imagining the Stone as colorless rather then colorful. If Hillman's tincture leans toward "*coagula,*" Giegerich's move is toward "*solve*"—toward the freeing of Mercurius through sublation, through the dialectics of the Negative, the "NOT" or "ou" (from the alchemical saying "*líthos ou líthos,*" that is, "the not-stone stone").[11] For Giegerich, the highest mystery of the whole work is the physical dissolution into mercury, a movement out of the imaginal into the logical. Here I imagine Kundalini shedding her skin and Thales remarking that all is water (liquidity). Giegerich also notes that *aqua permanens* is "a solid ground that in itself is not solid, not 'ground' at all, but rather liquidity, pure movement, that ... *is* nevertheless solid ground."[12]

So, if Hillman emphasizes wax (the body of the image), Giegerich thinks water (the *solutio* of its body). If Hillman finds soul in the valley, Giegerich points to the peaks. If Hillman critiques sublation,[13] Giegerich considers it to be the *elixir vital.* If Hillman draws inspiration from the Italians, Giegerich finds his in the German Hegel.

However, if one has read Hillman and Giegerich carefully, one soon begins to see that all of the above caricatures are at best misreadings. Both thinkers are far more complex than such sketches suggest and, while there are crucial differences between them, there are also considerable overlapping themes that call for further study. Placing the above ideas into a double pelican and reheating the entire mixture will allow us to see their similar essences circulating and rising up. Both thinkers emphasize the importance of 'ideas,' and both see that it is essential to go beyond the physical and the literal. Both emphasize the intrinsic link between idea and image, peak and vale, *solve* and *coagula,* and both officiate at the puer/psyche marriage, although the way each tinctures his syzygy differs. And, most importantly for me, both emphasize some version of the 'death of the ego.' While both might be seen as privileging one side of the syzygy over the other, neither can be accused of disregarding the importance of that which is not given priority.

In order to understand their respective positions, it may be useful also to compare some of their mutual misunderstandings. For example, when Hillman critiques Hegel's notion of *Aufhebung,* what he seems to have in mind is spirit detached from soul, the puer drawn apart from psyche, or anima separated from animus—a procedure that he uses as a heuristic device in his essay "Peaks and Vales."[14] However, to read Hegel's or Giegerich's notion of sublation in this way does not do justice to the complexity of their ideas. Nor does it recognize that for both of them sublation should never be understood as an either/or. Giegerich clarifies his position on this by noting: "What I offer instead [of an either/or interpretation] is a psychology of interiority. There are not two, but only one, and this 'one' contains its own 'other' within itself."[15] In other words, for Giegerich, thought is not an external other to the image, but the very soul of the image itself. Put in this way, Hillman's critique of sublation, if it is understood as a "climb into the thin air of mountain peaks,"[16] does not hold. Giegerich's notion of sublation already assumes a puer-psyche, anima-animus syzygy. If his thought can be said to lean toward the animus, it is because Giegerich feels that "thought" has been underdeveloped under the weight of the image in imaginal psychology. Giegerich makes it clear that his "pleading for 'thought' [an appeal Hillman makes as well] is not a call to turn our backs on 'image' and on what archetypal theorizing ha[s] accomplished, 'but rather to continue it radically in an attempt to complete it …'."[17]

However, in spite of his desire to develop Hillman's thought, Giegerich actually misconstrues the way Hillman defines image. He believes that Hillman's understanding of image is based on "sensory intuition" and that it is a form of "picture-thinking" in contradistinction to "thought" or thinking proper.[18] But here, just as Hillman's critique falls short of Giegerich's idea of "thought," so Giegerich's critique of Hillman seems to miss Hillman's more radical understanding of "image." After all, in "Image Sense," Hillman writes: "… images are not the same as optical pictures even if they are like pictures. ... We do not literally see images."[19] He adds, giving credit to Edward Casey, that "An image is not what you see but the way you see."[20] That is, we don't see images but see through them. In fact, Giegerich knows that his critique is different from what archetypal psychology actually proposes and that its notion of image has a deeper and more fundamental meaning than he has attributed to it. Seeing images as pictures might be considered to be a remnant of a sensationist psychology that understands images and even the imagination as epiphenomenal to actual things. Although he claims that he does "not want to *reduce*"[21] archetypal psychology's understanding of image to this limited representationalist notion, his critique is primarily aimed at image and the imagination in the narrow sense just described. David Miller also alludes to this issue of "the nonperceptual and nonsensate 'image.'"[22] While Miller's view of image is closer to Hillman's and different from Giegerich's, this difference for Miller is very small and does not diminish his deep appreciation for Giegerich's contribution.

Likewise, Greg Mogenson is aware that Hillman's understanding of image is non-representational and that it functions, in some ways, not unlike the work of negative interiorization as described by Giegerich. This is clear from Mogenson's choice of quotes from Hillman: "The soul's life is not upheld as correct by virtue of exteriority"[23] and "What is reflection then when there is no subject reflected, neither emotion nor external object?"[24] For Hillman, the image is most clearly "a metaphor without a referent."[25] While in many ways I share Miller's sense that in a larger perspective such issues are trivial, and perhaps heuristic on Giegerich's part, they nonetheless point to matters that require further distillation and a "labor of the concept,"[26] as Giegerich might describe it. This is particularly true in the face of the provocative question raised by Mogenson at the end of his chapter "Different Moments in Dialectical Movement."[27] He acknowledges that Hillman, like Giegerich, conveys "the negativity of the image"[28]—but he then calls attention to an even more radical interiorization. Pointing beyond Hillman toward Giegerich's notion of logical form, he asks: "But what of the gold that is to follow?"[29] Here he alludes to Giegerich's view that "the 'gold' of true psychology is the further negation of the image's silvery negativity into the absolute negativity of a consciousness that can *think* the various moments of each image all at once."[30]

But just what does absolute negativity mean when it comes to Giegerich's 'gold,' which, like the 'stone that is not a stone,' is a subtler 'gold that is not gold,' a gold that is spirit? How is this subtle gold to be differentiated from Hillman's idea? Hillman, too, speaks of gold, not only of silver's imagination of it. What is the difference when we "think" gold in the context of absolute negativity versus when we see it from Hillman's standpoint—particularly when we no longer define the imaginal as simply representing the real? Once we have Giegerich's subtle view of 'gold' as totally liquefied Mercurius, can we still distinguish it from lead, silver, or mercury? Are all sublated concepts dissolved in the grand solution of the dialectic? Is 'the gold that is not gold' the spirit of gold, the ghost of gold, a tincture of gold or no gold at all? I suspect that these questions mistake what Giegerich means and that we can distinguish gold's particularity once we have a deeper understanding of the dialectic he proposes. However, just how his gold can be "thought" in comparison to Hillman's 'seeing' its sensuous particularity requires further elaboration. When Hillman sees through gold, pushes off from it, he does not go 'all the way,' according to Giegerich—and for which he faults him. While Hillman's gold is also clearly not the "vulgar gold"[31] but rather the "fantastical gold" of alchemy, his way of speaking about it retains the "golden touch,"[32] the sensate "heart of gold," the "winner's gold," images of gold as "permanently glowing and untarnished," visions of "a consciousness ever shining like dawn, like the sun, without fits of darkening," ever "able to be beaten and beaten yet never crack under the hammer, to be bent, thin as a leaf and so cover mundane things with the shine of glory."[33] Images such as these are ideas of gold released from simple physicality, but they retain a pigment recognizable to the metaphoric ear. While Hillman's move takes him beyond the physical, he stays with the material, the concrete, what I have called here the pigment, a certain impurity that for him saves gold from the "poisonous state of splendid solar isolation."[34]

Therefore, the question about the gold that is to follow (Mogenson's question) is also a question that ultimately applies to the Philosophers' Stone and to the goal of the work. In considering the vision of the Stone in Hillman and Giegerich, it will be important to place Hillman's most radical view of image and of the Stone alongside Giegerich's ideas of "absolute-negative interiority, spirit, thought."[35] For Giegerich, the goal of both alchemy and a "true psychology" is to go *beyond* a psychology rooted in images and the imagination to a psychology rooted in the logical life of the soul. Such a move, for Giegerich, is a true working through of the hierarchical possibilities present in the dialectic and is superior to a psychology that remains rooted in the flesh of images. Since Giegerich does not propose that we eliminate images, the question remains how to understand the similarities and differences between Hillman and Giegerich in a way that moves beyond a side-by-side view of simple difference.[36]

This brings us full circle to my image of the alchemical stove and to my own side-by-side placement of differing views of the Stone. Is it adequate simply to allow different views, perspectives, archetypal stances —or does the "labor of the concept" demand that all views be subject to a dialectic in which "Reason" will produce one position more developed than others? Following Hegel, Giegerich notes that "items that are 'simply different' (*verschienden*) are indifferent to the difference between them."[37] Here I take Giegerich to be calling for an engagement of ideas versus simply settling for alternative perspectives. He has done much to argue for his well-worked-through positions, and his critiques of imaginal psychology merit careful reading and consideration. Miller and Mogenson have done a masterful job of giving us strong readings of Giegerich's work and of helping us toward a careful consideration of his ideas. What follows is my beginning attempt to work through an interface between Hillman and Giegerich and to raise a number of concerns about any move that relegates images to a status secondary to thought. In opening up the problematic of moving from image to thought, it is not clear whether, or in what way, thought is more fundamental than image, particularly when the image is understood in its most radical way. In addition, a number of philosophers have resisted this move and raised critical questions that must be explored before we can consider abandoning the primary place of image in the work of Jung and Hillman.

Resistance of the Remainder

My own hesitation/resistance about a move to spirit/thought is rooted in my belief that Jung and Hillman brought about a major advance in consciousness by revisioning image and imagination, both of which had been in the shadow of Western thought and metaphysics since Plato. Jung's resuscitation of images was a return to soul and began a reversal of the dominant historical process that had depotentiated images and reduced soul to rational intellectual spirit. Hillman's archetypal psychology continued and radicalized Jung's reversal. Hillman has taken note of the hatred for image. The battle between spirit and soul, thought and image, is an old one and even now continues to be fought. The fear of the power of image and of the imagination is very deep in our culture. Giegerich himself has acknowledged that the work of Jung and Hillman was a major step from which "there is no way back."[38] Given that Giegerich's return to the "rational" and to "thought" *is* so powerful, I am concerned that his perspective may be too easily assimilated into the cultural undermining of image, especially since image is still in a fragile revival of its importance, if not its primacy. We must give Giegerich full credit for the complexity of his ideas and for his recognition of the rational. However, although his work does suggest that the rational and the soul are integrated notions, the idea of the rational is so emotionally and psychologically laden with profound cultural implications that Giegerich's perspective, in spite of its sophistication, may serve to continue the repression of the imagination and to turn readers away from the radical innovations of Jung and Hillman. While this in itself is not an argument against Giegerich's position as such, it is an expression of my concern about how his work may be heard and taken up by others.

A move to spirit is an earmark of Hegelian and post-Hegelian Idealism and neo-rationalist philosophies. An example of this, perhaps another misreading, can be seen in the work of Paul Ricoeur, who—in spite of his creative valuing of the symbolic—nevertheless ends up ultimately in a neo-rationalist position in which thought/philosophy transcends mythopoesis. This can be seen in his formulation "the symbol gives rise to thought,"[39] which privileges thinking and tilts the balance away from the primacy of the metaphoric toward the superiority of the rational and the philosophical. My concern here is with the dangers of logocentrism, with what happens when an interpreter, philosophical or psychoanalytic, gives primacy to thought over image, to the rational side of a metaphoric copula, to a formulation in which image and metaphor could be reduced to being simply instrumental, as literary critic Dominick Lacapra has noted.[40] Lacapra's analysis echoes both archetypalist and deconstructivist critiques of the traditional position with its roots in the whole history of thought that gives priority to logos over mythos. It is a position resisted as well by a number of philosophers who take a critical stance toward the Hegelian dialectic and post-Hegelian neo-rationalist thinking and toward Hegel's attempt to sublate the image into the rational. Martin Heidegger, for instance, has commented that the 'not' or 'negative,' referred to earlier as a moment in Hegel's dialectic, cannot be simply overcome or assimilated by reason. The "not" is more than a dialectical alienation on the way to a sublation. In fact, it resists assimilation into the movements of thought. The negation of a negation does not culminate in an unconditional "yes" (i.e., a full assimilation of the "not"). For Heidegger, Hegel's interpretation of negativity is an inauthentic modification of an insurmountable "not"—a "not" that can serve as an access point that transitions from a logical understanding of the soul to a poetic one. For Heidegger, the more important category is not rationality but Being.

Similarly, Edgar Morin, a renowned French thinker, "faults Hegel for considering contradiction a transitory 'moment' of the *Aufhebung*, a moment which is ultimately annulled."[41] Like Heidegger, Morin is arguing, in effect, that the "not" cannot be sublated by any movement of thought and that it represents an unassimilable difference that resists any form of engulfment.

In a spirit similar to Heidegger's and Morin's, Jacques Derrida also recognizes the problem of the unassimilable 'not.' For him, trying to undo Hegel is like trying to decapitate the hydra. He argues that Hegel's dialectic incorporates all contradiction, and that every attempt to refuse such engulfment is seen as an error to be overcome by the continuing dialectic. He asks: how then to interrupt the operation of *Aufhebung*, how to handle a negative that is more than just a moment in an all-embracing process? How do we escape the perpetual reversal entailed in any oppositional system of thought? What would bring the death knell (*glas*) or laughter (Nietzsche) to bear on Hegel's attempt to achieve absolute spirit without remainder? For Derrida, Hegel's insistence on absolute spirit implies a drift towards rationalism and idealism and requires the creation of a metaphysical edifice, which for Derrida is rooted in a "trembling ground of double entendre."[42] He describes this trembling ground as a "fabulous scene" which any metaphysics of certainty effaces and yet this scene remains, stirring beneath it.[43] For Derrida this scene provokes "an endless confrontation with Hegelian concepts, and the move from a restricted, 'speculative' philosophical economy—in which there is nothing that cannot be made to make sense, in which there is nothing *other* than meaning—to a 'general' economy—which affirms that which exceeds meaning, the excess of meaning from which there can be no speculative profit—involves a reinterpretation of the central Hegelian concept: the *Aufhebung*."[44] In order to engage Giegerich's particular vision of the Philosophers' Stone, and while realizing that Giegerich's thought is to be distinguished from Hegel's, I find myself struggling with the above critiques naming the unassimilable 'not' as a remainder rather than as a momentary hiatus in the dialectic. In my own work, an expression of the negative that is unassimilable showed itself as the image of *sol niger*, a darkness that refuses conscious assimilation.

The unassimilable darkness was a theme of my book, *The Black Sun: The Alchemy and Art of Darkness.* The alchemy and art of this darkness require a further exploration of the light of darkness as an expression of both *sol niger* and the Philosophers' Stone. My work began with the recognition of that which resists conscious assimilation, with a black sun that would not yield or be incorporated by an ego stance. It would not dissolve, go away, or be lifted up, and it challenged my own psychological narcissism to the core. While *sol niger* did not allow itself to be possessed by ego and the ego at times felt more in danger of being possessed by it, a perceptual awareness occurred. The wounded and by now somewhat emaciated ego noticed that what it called darkness had a shine that Jung called the shine of darkness itself, the *lumen naturae*. My book, *The Black Sun*, was the beginning of an exploration of this darkness and of its odd luminosity. This strange lumen was my impetus to explore the Philosophers' Stone as I imagined it, present in a darkness that is no darkness. Could the lumen of the Philosophers' Stone be an image in Hillman's sense—something that is not simply an object of consciousness but something we can see through? Could this darkness be called sublated?

My ongoing work on the Stone owes a continuing debt to Jung, Hillman, Giegerich, and others—and, as I have noted, is a work in progress. It began in *The Black Sun* with the blackness of *sol niger*, with the *mortificatio* of brokenness, incision, and wound, castration, cut, negation, with an ultimate 'No' to the ego, with what felt unassimilable. As the title of this paper indicates, my attention is now turning from the black sun per se to the Philosophers' Stone. To bring the Stone into focus is not to leave the black sun behind, nor to simply move to an *albedo* psychology. Rather, it is to pursue my suspicion that the Philosophers' Stone has been there all along in the shine of darkness itself and that darkness will be there at the end as well, perhaps as an indispensable *caput mortuum*, the dross or residue that remains in the retort after distillation. In some philosophical and alchemical views, this residue is ultimately eliminated, but my wager and anticipation is that the Stone—whether in the language of revivification and Aphroditic pleasure or in the sublation to pure mercurial liquidity —is always accompanied by a remainder. This remainder, while not best understood as a thing-in-itself, is nonetheless that which resists a consciousness that does not account for its differentiation. At times, to accommodate this difference, the Stone has been described as "the unity of the unity and difference."[45] Such a description attempts to address the complexity of the Stone, but even the idea of "the unity of the unity and difference" privileges unity, although at a higher "logical level." The "unity of the unity and difference" is still a tincture of the syzygy that emphasizes unity as the major trope. The syzygy can also be tinctured to emphasize difference. This would call out for the complementary idea of "the difference of the unity and difference," a difference that resists being lit up by consciousness and which protects the remainder that emits a mysterious light of its own as opposed to a light that consciousness would shine on it. This complementary idea is itself similar to one of the stages of the logical dialectic discussed by the Buddhist sage Nargarjuna. His formulation resists any transcendent unification and reinstates a darkness, a void (*sunyata*) that can also be said to shine.

My exploration here of the shine of darkness begins with two images of *sol niger*. A skeleton stands on a blazing black sun; the image reads '*Putrefactio*.'[46] A black Sun burns down on a primarily desolate landscape in the alchemical text *Splendor Solis* (1582). These are images of a place an adept must enter if anything is to be learned about the light of nature and the Philosophers' Stone. Jung writes about this light, the *lumen naturae*, in his *Alchemical Studies*, where he calls it "the light of darkness itself."[47] It is a light "which illuminates its own darkness ... [and] turns blackness into brightness." It is a kind of light that the "darkness comprehends." This light is not the light of our day-world sun, but rather the *lumen naturae* that shines in *sol niger*. It can be seen in the risen black Ethiopian and the reconstituted Kali, and is cultivated in Taoist alchemy. It shines in the Secret of the Golden Flower, and in the *filius philosophorum*, imagined by Paracelsus as a luminous vehicle and referred to by Jung as "the central mystery of philosophical alchemy."[48] It is to this mystery, to this "luminous vehicle," that we turn as we imagine a move from *sol niger* to the Philosophers' Stone. Just as this light is not separate from darkness, so the Philosophers' Stone is not separate from *sol niger* but is intrinsic to it.

Is it then the shining that is problematic? How can darkness shine? In my work on the black sun, it was the shining that seemed most enigmatic. Is it a question then of presence and absence, or of a present absence, or of absence itself? The negation and presence of light is at the heart of the archetypal image/idea of the black sun. The Sun King is mortally wounded by darkness and in the negation of negation, *sol niger* shines; a strange reversal takes place or perhaps is "logically" present from the beginning.

One could say that *sol niger*, the black sun, is already a sublated sun, a philosophical/ psychological sun, a sun that is not a sun (as the alchemists say of their stone). It is black and yet, at the same "logical" time, it shines. What is the nature of such a shining, such a consciousness? Is it an image, an idea, or both? Is consciousness too dull a word to express this complexity? Philosophers and psychologists have often found difficulty with words like consciousness, image, and idea, and have struggled to give expression to their meanings in a way not encumbered by the metaphysical and metaphoric prejudices of their times—a seemingly impossible task that on occasion has silenced the best of philosophers. How then to let be manifest what is gathered into the shining?

In our postmodern world, our efforts have often left us with a virtual apophatic orgy of dissemination, of a negation of master tropes (and in their place, sliding signifiers), and of neologisms that require another language to follow the discourse. Yet our simple common language won't do either. Our best efforts are marked by traces of darkness, perhaps penetrating to the core of language itself, into a darkness that matters—and still there is the shine. How then to speak of it, of what Roger Brooke has called the "fertile and hospitable emptiness within which the things of the world could shine forth"?[49] To speak of the shining is not only to speak in the context of the metaphor of light, but also to speak of the shining in a way that aims at expressing an insight that goes beyond the traditional divide between light and dark, and in a way that approaches a more primordial awareness closer to Jung's more mature vision of the psyche, a vision influenced by the alchemical tradition.

Sparks of Reiteration

In *The Black Sun,* I began a consideration of this shining, and wrote of it as an image of light at the core of ancient alchemical ideas. The aim of alchemy, according to Paracelsus, was to discover this light hidden in nature. It is a light very different from notions of light as simply separate from darkness and by extension different from any conception of a consciousness separate from its dark background. My strategy in *The Black Sun* was to hesitate before this darkness, to pause and then to enter its realm of corpses and coffins, of monsters and monstrous complexity, and to engage its most literal and destructive demons: narcissistic mortification, humiliation, delusion, despair, depression, physiological and psychological decay, cancer, psychosis, suicide, murder and death. Such experiences can traumatize and kill. They can also drive the soul toward the unthinkable, a condition which archetypal defenses seek to avoid. To experience the above means to be in the grip of the *mortificatio*, a condition the alchemists knew was essential to reaching the depths of the transformation process. Through illness and/or a shamanic-like initiation, the *mortificatio* drives the psyche to an ontological pivot point, to a desubstantiation of the ego, and to what Theodor Adorno might call an "emaciated" subject,[50] leading to a gateway that is both a dying and a new life.

The black sun is a complexity. Its 'blacker than black' dimension shines with a dark luminescence. It can open the way to some of the most numinous aspects of psychic life and can give us a glimpse of the miracle of perception at the heart of what Jung called the *mysterium coniunctionis* and of the Philosophers' Stone. One might imagine such a vision in the Tantric rites of Kali who was worshiped at the cremation grounds where she copulates with her consort Shiva on the body of a corpse burning on a funeral pyre. Kali worshipers enact ceremonials associated symbolically and ritually with the annihilation of the ego. These rituals often depict the death of the ego, out of which, it is said, the "human being arises shining."[51] How is it possible to embrace Kali, the darkness that kills? Who is left to embrace her? The poet May Sarton has stated that

> Kali, the destroyer, cannot be overthrown;
> We must stay, open-eyed, in the terrible place.[52]

Similarly, for Hegel, "only by looking the negative in the face, and tarrying with it," is it possible that the negative can be "the magical power that converts [darkness] into being."[53] Likewise, Sri Ramakrishna writes that we must "hug the form of Death, Dance in Destruction's dance" [and be able to say] "Come, O Mother, come!"[54]

For the Tantrics, if one's worship is successful, if one is able to stay the course open-eyed, to dance Kali's dance, to welcome her, then her blackness is said to shine. This shining can be linked to the alchemical ideas of whitening and silvering, with the proviso that we see this shining *albedo* as part of the complexity of darkness itself and not simply as a literal phase following blackness. From one perspective, the theme of renewal follows from symbolic death, but from another, archetypally and logically, death and renewal are at the core of *sol niger*, and this is expressed in the simultaneity of blackness and luminescence.

Mystical Death

How can we further our understanding of this mystical death? How to speak of it? The idea of ego death is a difficult one in the light of the acknowledged importance of the role of the ego in relation to the unconscious in our classical way of thinking. When we think of ego loss, our thoughts immediately go to the problematics of a weak, impaired, or non-functioning ego, to a concern with annihilation anxiety and the defenses of the Self against it, as well as to thoughts of psychosis. Ego psychology has a dominant hold on our everyday psychological culture. Yet, the notion of ego death is and has been in the margins of our tradition: in Jung's idea that "*the experience of the self is always a defeat for the ego*,"[55] in Hillman's "psychotherapeutic cure of me,"[56] in Rosen's "egocide,"[57] in Miller's views about the "no self,"[58] in Giegerich's 'death of the ego,'[59] etc. Each has contributed to our understanding of a psychology that relativizes and/or dismembers the ego, and each has a stake in the transformation of our psychological theory.

Giegerich, for example, states that "the Self is real only to the extent that the ego has been negated, overcome ... one might even say, it exists only as a reality 'over the ego's dead body'[60] ... as one who has long died as ego personality."[61] "The art of psychological discourse," he continues, "is to speak as someone who is already deceased."[62] Here Giegerich extends the notion of ego death into the core of psychological discourse itself. For Giegerich this is a necessary step toward the achievement of a "true psychology" and essential in understanding the goal of both alchemy and of a psychological life. For Giegerich, ego death also signifies the death of all positivity and serves as the gateway to a liquification of the subject and thus allows entrance into the logical life of the soul. There is a resonance between Giegerich's reading of Hegel and poststructuralist thought, both of which proceed toward if not a liquification of the ego, at least a displacement of the subject from the center of philosophical, linguistic, and theoretical activity.

Several postmodern philosophers have made this connection between ego death and philosophical activity. For example, philosopher Geoffrey Bennington has remarked that "today taking something philosophically, then, always involves this more or less hidden relationship with death, or, by a slightly violent contraction, whatever I take philosophically is death."[63] Surprisingly, Bennington ends his statement with an enigmatic image, but one which captures his point: "The philosophers' stone is an inscribed head stone." For Marla Morris, another postmodern thinker, what is true of the Philosophers' Stone is also true for the "psychoanalyst's stone."[64] She notes that for Bennington, at the end of the day, it is death that deconstruction is all about.

The philosopher Simon Critchley argues in a similar spirit, noting that "ancient Ciceronian wisdom says that to philosophize [and, in light of Morris' comment, to practice psychoanalysis] is to learn how to die."[65] Critchley's exploration echoes the theme of *sol niger* in that it seeks to "*de-create* narratives of redemption" and to "strip away the resources and comforts of story, fable and narrative."[66] Here Critchley sounds like Giegerich and, following the work of Samuel Beckett, he seeks to understand "the meaning of ... meaninglessness," what he calls "a redemption from redemption."[67] He notes how Beckett's work "frustrates our desire to ascend from the flatlands of language and ordinary experience into the stratosphere of meaning"[68] and comments: "As is all too easily seen in both contemporary New Age sophism, crude scientism, and the return to increasingly reactionary forms of religious fundamentalism, there is an almost irresistible desire to stuff the world full of meaning and sign up to one or more salvific narratives of redemption."[69] Critchley, like Beckett and in the spirit of Giegerich's "birth of Man,"[70] leads us away from the temptation to redemption and toward a Zen-like perception of the ordinary, the "sheer mereness of things."[71] He turns to a number of poets—Wallace Stevens, Rainer Maria Rilke, Ralph Waldo Emerson—to give voice to this perception of the ordinary, a perception not unlike Hillman's whose reading of alchemy seeks to move our understanding and our language outside of redemptive, metaphysical systems and salvationist programs. Like Stevens' expression of particulars, "pond," "leaf," "tree," etc., alchemy, in Hillman's view, speaks more phenomenally and particularly. Its substances stand out, they shine: "metals, planets, minerals, stars, plants, charms, animals, vessels, fires, and specific locales"[72] —and, I would add, stones.

So what kind of 'thing' is a stone? For Critchley, like Hillman, perception yields a simplicity of awareness in which the subject/object, person/world dichotomy is altered. In such an awareness, we are like a "thing among things," displaying a shining world of sheer "isness," or, as the Buddhists would say, of "suchness." In such a world, a 'stone is not a stone,' because stones are part of the alchemical white earth and of matter illuminated from within itself. Ordinarily we think of matter as illuminated by virtue of an external consciousness separate from its object, but matter, in truth, is better understood as part of the complexity of the materialized soul. Such a soul can alchemically be said to be a stone "cleared of moistures"[73] and objective in the "psycho-alchemical" sense as Giegerich has described.[74]

Hillman has noted that depth psychology, including Jung's, has had difficulty in finding a way to express the complex/simplicity of psyche's need to substantiate[75] or likewise of substance's need to speak. For Hillman, the problematic is in part rooted in the way conceptual language splits apart a fundamental unity, "abstracting matter from image."[76] When this occurs, there is a powerful psychic demand to heal the split, to substantiate psyche and to bring it back in touch with something solid. The problem of languaging the soul was present for Jung throughout his life and work. The need to substantiate, to go beyond words and paper, played a role in his desire to personify and in his urge to turn to stone.

Turning to Stone

Ultimately for Jung "words and paper ... did not seem real enough ...; something more was needed."[77] He had "to achieve a kind of representation in stone of [his] innermost thoughts and of the knowledge [he] had acquired." Or, to put it another way, he "had to make a confession of faith in stone." Jung's need to substantiate was responsible for the building of his tower at Bollingen where he felt he was "reborn in stone" and through which he was able to express a concretization of his ideas.[78]

Jung carved his way to self expression through architecture, sculpture, and his focus on alchemical language and poetry, but even more one might say that he opened himself to the call of stone—to its message, and to the way the world came to him. Jung reports the story of the cornerstone he had ordered for his garden when he was building his tower at Bollingen. When the stone arrived it was the wrong shape and measurements, and the stone mason, furious, wanted to return it. However, when Jung saw the stone, he claimed it as *his* stone. He felt he "must have it!"[79] even though, at the moment, he was not sure what he wanted to do with it.

In short, Jung welcomed whatever arrived unwanted and unexpected, unlike Faust who murdered Baucis and Philemon. In other words, Jung opened himself up to experiences the ego would often reject, seemingly in good sense. As Jung contemplated the stone, a verse from the alchemist Arnoldus de Villanova came to him and he chiseled it into the stone:

> Here stands the mean, uncomely stone,
> 'Tis very cheap in price!
> The more it is despised by fools,
> The more loved by the wise.[80]

Jung was aware that this verse referred to the Philosophers' Stone and, as he contemplated it further, he saw in its "natural structure" a sort of eye[81] that looked back at him, a living other, who appeared to Jung as "the Telesphoros of Asklepios," the healing figure of a child who was seen as roaming through the dark regions of the cosmos and glowing like a star out of the depths, a shining "pointer of the way."[82] In this image and in the stone, Jung captured something in the heart of darkness itself, something that he found in the depths of inorganic matter, something that looked back at him and made a stone a living stone, a Philosophers' Stone that shines. For Jung, stones speak a shining truth and such a truth touches the core of what we have come to call, inadequately, psyche and matter.

Jung's attempt to repair this split in his life and work led not only to stone but also to innovative formulations in the language of his psychology by which he attempted to embrace both sides of a linguistic divide—subject and object, spirit and matter—using terms such as "psychoid," "synchronicity," and "*unus mundus*."[83] Such terms expressed Jung's urge to go beyond the subjectivity of words and paper in order to express psyche's need to substantiate and the need of substances to speak.

For Hillman, however, such words not only fall short of Jung's goal but also actually "reinforce the splitting effect inherent" in the neurosis of one-sided abstract language.[84] If this was a problem for Jung, it is also one which is deeply rooted in our collective, historical, cultural, and linguistic consciousness. It is an issue that penetrates into the problematics of perception and language, and into the archetypal psyche itself. How then to express psyche's need to substantiate and substances need to speak?

In his book entitled simply *Stone*, philosopher John Sallis speaks of his desire to substantiate, to find a way to articulate philosophical ideas adequate to the powerful stone monuments he is drawn to investigate, and in and through which he finds a "shining truth."[85] In his book, he explores the power of stone in "the various guises and settings in which stone appears"[86]—in monuments, the complexity of Gothic cathedrals, Greek temples, and the tombstones of a Jewish cemetery in Prague; in fossils, stone houses, and the power and beauty of wild nature in the mountains of Haute Savoie, France. In his search, he attempts to give voice to the power he discovers in these profound expressions of stone. Sallis writes:

> I would have liked this discourse to be inscribed by a very skillful stonemason, by one who knew just the right slant at which to hold the chisel so as to cut obliquely into the stone and produce well-formed, clearly legible letters, chipping away the stone so as to leave the inscription both in place of stone and yet still in stone, practicing thus a kind of lithography. I would have liked the well-measured strokes of his hammer to be audible, as he practiced his venerable craft of making stone, in its silence, nonetheless speak.[87]

One might imagine both Jung and Sallis as such stonemasons, adepts who inscribe their *materia* of rock and word such that stone has words and words matter. In both Jung and Sallis we find stones that speak, living objective stones that shine, modern day expressions of the alchemists' quest for life in the heart of matter.

Must we turn to stone? The stone that is not a stone

The well-known alchemical saying "Beware of the physical in the material" provides us with a warning not to confuse what the alchemist is after with literal materiality—but it is also important to recognize that a simple psychological or spiritual abstraction misses the mark as well. "The precious goals of alchemy are neither physical achievements ... nor metaphysical truths. ... We are not in the realm of metaphysics or physics,"[88] says Hillman. Sallis makes a similar point, noting that when trying to give expression to what we mean by "stone" it is important to do it in a way that does not split off our subjectivity from the voice of stone itself, nor turn this voice into a projection onto stones.[89] To fall into either one position or another fixes thought into a false subject/object dichotomy. Either the stone that we seek is literally over there in a mind-independent world, or it is simply part of our subjective inner life projected outward. Jung's psychology of alchemy is usually understood in the latter way and, thus, the Philosophers' Stone is seen as a projection of the Self.

I submit that this is one plausible reading of Jung, but it remains unclear exactly what the nature of such a projection entails and just what it is that is projected. Ultimately, the Arcane Substance that Jung often spoke about remained as mysterious as his understanding of the unconscious, and to assume that this projected substance was simply inside our subjectivity misses Jung's deeper understanding of "psychic reality," even if it was not adequately developed. In addition, the problem of projection itself requires a number of philosophical and metapsychological presuppositions that are taken for granted in classical analysis. Going beyond these assumptions requires a fundamental shift in metapsychology if not ontology.[90] Schwartz-Salant deconstructs the notion of "projection" and concludes that using this idea as a framework for understanding what the alchemists are talking about is inadequate. Alchemical "experiences do not always, or even primarily, fit into an inside-outside structure."[91] In its place, Schwartz-Salant constructs a field theory, an intermediate realm between subject and object, mind and matter. While he applies his field theory primarily to the analytic interaction, it is a move that also has consequences for how we understand both Jung's work with stone and the nature of the Philosophers' Stone.

Although Jung actually worked with literal stone, his more enduring corpus was what he produced through his imagination and with words and paper, that is, his ideas. And likewise it is with ideas and the imagination that Hillman finds a "rock-hard standpoint from above downward just as firm and solid as literal physical reality."[92] From this perspective, the Philosophers' Stone that is not a stone seems indestructible. It is solid, has objectivity, thing-likeness, facticity, and duration. It is an example of philosophical permanence. Yet, while its hardness wounds, it is also wounded, easily affected. The Stone is complex and resists one-sided descriptions and simple dichotomies. As David Miller has stated, "the course of wisdom consists in deferring one-sided judgment concerning meaning."[93] The *imaginatio* is as much a part of what is imaged as the world is itself the substance of imagination. Robert Romanyshyn makes a similar point:

> Imagining is not something which a subject adds to a merely perceivable world. On the contrary, we imagine and the world is imagine-able. To say one is to say the other. Each is the obverse of the other. In other words, imagining belongs as much to things as it belongs to us. Perception is always less certain than we naively believe it to be, and things are more shadowy than we often dare admit.[94]

In this passage, and throughout his analysis, Romanyshyn cautions us not to collapse the difference between perceiving and imagining. He underlines how the perceivable and the real exhibit a stubborn intractability which mark them as different from the imagination even if we have destabilized their absolute difference. Romanyshyn holds this distinction in place as he continues to subtly refine our understanding of the imaginary and the real. He demonstrates, following Merleau-Ponty and reminiscent of Schwartz-Salant, how perception and imagination are like mirrors "facing each other,"[95] forming "a couple more real than either of them"[96] would be independent of each other. For Romanyshyn "the imagine-ability of things is their very depth: that is the image of a thing, seen through other things, describes the depth of the real."[97] Romanyshyn's analysis gives amplification to Critchley's insight that things merely are and that we are things too. He sees into the complex materiality of the soul and into a substance's need to speak. For Romanyshyn, the "voice of things" is best served by the language of metaphor and imagination which "inhabits neither the brilliance of the day [spirit] nor the darkness of night [soul], but speaks simultaneously in light and shadow."[98]

If the imagination can be seen to be the voice of things, then one might also understand how "imaginal realities" exhibit a stubborn intractability. The Philosophers' Stone, as we have noted, exhibits facticity and thingness. It refuses to be altered by the manipulating ego subject, and yet subjectivity is part of its intrinsic reality, a subjectivity that appears as the ego subject dies, or is negated and relativized. It is a subjectivity that has been touched by ego death and therefore is no longer subjective. It is a subjectivity that is not subjectivity, a subjectivity in which the me-ness has been 'cooked out' —and redeemed from essentialist narratives of meaning.

As Hillman, making reference to Miller, points out, the stone "does not allow itself to be held in meaning"[99] and generality. "It does not yield to understanding." For Hillman, the alchemical process of *ceration* is "designed to obliterate a psychological *episteme* of … anything that would rigidify the idea of the goal into categories of knowledge."[100] And yet, as Sallis has noted, the stone exhibits a "shining truth,"[101] a truth discovered in a "suspension of the difference that otherwise separates the eidetic from the singular, a *peculiar* suspension in that its very force requires that the difference remain, in the moment of suspension, also intact."[102] If I understand Sallis correctly, such singular yet eidetic moments of "shining truth" recall the sheer 'isness of things' discussed above, the metals, planets, minerals, diamonds, pearls, stars and stones, the shining particularities that are also oddly universal but which can "never simply be assimilated to the purely eidetic."[103] Such singular moments of perception/imagination are neither inside nor out and must show themselves, be exhibited like pearls so as not to lose their luster, again to use Hillman's metaphor.

The bringing forth of such particulars allows them to shine, and this shine is for Hillman the revelation of Beauty, a term Plato used as well for that "shining truth" which he considered "the most radiant, that which most shines forth amidst the visible, in the singular things that come to be and *pass away*."[104] The Philosophers' Stone is such a radiant truth, but it is a truth that must as well remain in touch with negativity, death and darkness. It is "not enough," Hillman reminds us, "to shine in the dark."[105] The Philosophers' Stone is linked intrinsically with *sol niger*, "no matter how exalted the stage of any process in life, that stage lives within the context of whatever despair and failure accompanied its creation."[106] Thus, it is not surprising that Schwartz-Salant observes, in relation to the last image of the Splendor Solis, that there are "two states—a created self and its purified consciousness ... joined not only with life and body but also with a history of despair and failure."[107]

Likewise, as Hillman notes, in alchemical psychology "sorrow, solitude and misery can break even the most indomitable spirit."[108] The Philosophers' Stone requires a relationship with the ongoing deconstructive principle of the black sun. Perhaps this recognition of *sol niger* is related to why, for Giegerich, the imaginal requires continuing negative interiorization. But if this is so, just as Giegerich deconstructs the literal residues of the imaginal, so imaginal psychology continues to give flesh to the unseen. *Solve et coagula*, say the alchemists. In Hillman and Giegerich we have two moments of the Stone that not only can live together but also belong together in the same living mosaic—or do they? Jung has noted: "sometimes Mercurius is a substance like quicksilver [image], sometimes it is a philosophy [thought]."[109] To put it yet another way, if Paul Ricoeur is correct that the symbol gives rise to thought, then perhaps it is also the case that thought gives rise to symbol. What has priority may well be, as

Giegerich has noted, a matter of personal and philosophical conviction "of the psychology that one *has*," "that one *is*," "that one lives."[110] Perhaps in the end, thought and image may best be spoken of in a variety of ways: as an alchemical *circulatio*, or in a monstrous *coniunctio*, or as a trembling ground of poetic undecidables (Derrida). Perhaps all of the above might be thought/imagined as metaphors that attempt to speak the unspeakable, an idea perhaps captured in the title of Paul Kugler's latest book, *Raids on the Unthinkable.*[111] The struggle with these two seemingly irreconcilable moments is well articulated by Alain Badiou who gave expression to the importance of attempting to speak the unspeakable when he stated:

> Let us struggle then, partitioned, split, unreconciled. Let us struggle for the flash of conflict, we philosophers, always torn between the mathematical norm of literal transparency and the poetic norm of singularity and presence. Let us struggle then but having recognized the common task, which is to think what was unthinkable, to say what it is impossible to say. Or, to adopt Mallarme's imperative, which I believe is common to philosophy and poetry: "There, wherever it may be, deny the unsayable—it lies."[112]

In our attempt to express psyche's need to substantiate, we have come to see that the Stone to which we have turned is a "stone that is not a stone." It is rather a Philosophers' Stone. It is a Stone linked to the *lumen naturae* of *sol niger*, a luminous vehicle, a central mystery of alchemy. It is an alchemical achievement involving the death of the ego out of which something emerges shining and yet the shining was already there at the core of darkness. It is a part of the complexity of darkness itself, reflecting the death and shine of a positivity that is perhaps no positivity at all, but rather an image/idea requiring a liquification and/or displacement of the subject. The Stone requires learning how to die, how to decreate narratives of redemption, and thus allowing one to see, with Zen-like astonishment, the perception of the ordinary, the sheer mereness of things. As the poet Theodore Roethke once wrote:

> Near the graves of the great dead,
> Even the stones speak.[113]

NOTES

1. Quoted in June Singer, *A Gnostic Book of Hours* (San Francisco: HarperCollins, 1992), 16.

2. John Sallis, *Stone* (Bloomington: Indiana University Press, 1994), 4.

3. Renos K. Papadopoulos (ed.), *Handbook of Jungian Psychology: Theory, Practice and Applications* (London: Routledge, 2006).

4. James Hillman, "Concerning the Stone: Alchemical Images of the Gold," *Sphinx* 5, 1993, 234-265.

5. Wolfgang Giegerich, *The Soul's Logical Life: Towards a Rigorous Notion of Psychology* (Frankfurt am Main: Peter Lang, 1998).

6. The description which follows is a condensation of Hillman's ideas drawn from his essay "Concerning the Stone."

7. Hillman, "Concerning the Stone," 260.

8. *Ibid.*, 259.

9. *Ibid.*, 262.

10. *Ibid.*, 253.

11. Giegerich, *The Soul's Logical Life*, 111.

12. *Ibid.*, 148.

13. For example, Hillman argues that the goal is "not the lifting, the *Aufhebung,* of material worldliness, but the full realization of desire for the world that pulsates in the materials of the elemental psyche, those substances that compose the stone and give its enduring life..." James Hillman, "Concerning the Stone," 261.

14. Hillman, "Peaks and Vales," in *Puer Papers* (Irving, TX: Spring Publications, 1979), 54-74.

15. Giegerich, "Afterword," in Wolfgang Giegerich, David Miller, & Greg Mogenson, *Dialectics and Analytical Psychology: The El Capitan Canyon Seminar* (New Orleans: Spring Journal Books, 2005), 109.

16. *Ibid.*

17. *Ibid.*, 108. Portion of quote in single quote marks is attributed to David Miller, "Introduction," in Wolfgang Giegerich, David Miller, & Greg Mogenson, *Dialectics and Analytical Psychology: The El Capitan Canyon Seminar* (New Orleans: Spring Journal Books, 2005).

18. Giegerich, *The Soul's Logical Life,* 107.

19. Hillman, "Image Sense," *Spring* (1979), 130.

20. *Ibid.*, 134.

21. Giegerich, *The Soul's Logical Life*, 107.

22. David Miller, "The End of Ending: A Response to Wolfgang Giegerich," *Journal of Jungian Theory and Practice*, Vol. 6, No. 1, 2004, 85.

23. James Hillman, "Silver and the White Earth (Part Two)", *Spring*, 1981, 49; quoted by Greg Mogenson, "Different Moments in Dialectical Movement," in *Dialectics and Analytical Psychology: The El Capitan Canyon Seminar*, 106.

24. Hillman, "Silver and the White Earth, Part Two", *Spring*, 1981, 49; quoted by Greg Mogenson, "Different Moments in Dialectical Movement," in *Dialectics and Analytical Psychology: The El Capitan Canyon Seminar*, 105.

25. *Ibid.*

26. This is a phrase used by Hegel and borrowed by Giegerich, and here refers simply to the process of working through.

27. Greg Mogenson, "Different Moments in Dialectical Movement," in *Dialectics and Analytical Psychology: The El Capitan Canyon Seminar* (New Orleans: Spring Journal Books, 2005).

28. *Ibid.*, 106.

29. *Ibid.*

30. *Ibid.*

31. Hillman, "Concerning the Stone," 239.

32. *Ibid.*, 240.

33. *Ibid.*, 241.

34. *Ibid.*, 243.

35. Mogenson, "Different Moments in Dialectical Movement," 106.

36. Wolfgang Giegerich, "The End of Meaning and the Birth of Man: An Essay about the State Reached in the History of Consciousness and an Analysis of C.G. Jung's Psychology Project," *Journal of Jungian Theory and Practice*, Vol. 6, No. 1, 2004, 115.

37. *Ibid.*

38. Giegerich, *The Soul's Logical Life*, 104.

39. Paul Ricoeur, *Freud and Philosophy: An Essay on Interpretation* (New Haven: Yale University Press, 1970), 38.

40. Dominick Lacapra, "Who rules metaphor?" in *Dialectics* (Baltimore: John Hopkins University Press, 1980, 15-28.

41. Edgar Morin, *Science avec Conscience* (Paris: Fayard, 1982), 289. Quoted in, and citation provided, by Sean Kelly, "Transpersonal

Psychology and the Paradigm of Complexity," retrieved December 26, 2005 from http://www.purifymind.com/TranspersonalPsy.htm.

42. Quoted in D.T. O'Hara, "The irony of being metaphorical," *Journal of Postmodern Literature* 8(2), 324.

43. Jacques Derrida, *Margins of Philosophy* (Chicago: University of Chicago Press, 1982), 213.

44. Alan Bass (translator) in Jacques Derrida, *Margins of Philosophy* (Chicago: Univeristy of Chicago Press, 1982), 19-20, n. 23.

45. Giegerich, *Dialectics and Analytical Psychology*, 3.

46. C.G. Jung, *Collected Works*, Vol. 12: *Psychology and Alchemy*, p. 88, Taken from Mylius, *Philosophia reformata* (1622).

47. C.G. Jung, *Collected Works*, Vol. 13: *Alchemical Studies*, p. 160, § 197.

48. *Ibid*., p. 126, § 162.

49. Roger Brooks, *Jung and Phenomenology* (London: Routledge, 1991), 99.

50. Donald Kuspit, "negatively sublime identity: pierre soulages's abstract paintings," retrieved January 23, 2002 from http://www.artnet.com/magazine_pre2000/features/kuspit/kuspit10-7-96.asp.

51. Indra Sinha, *Tantra: The Cult of Ecstasy* (London: Hamlyn, 2000), 52.

52. Quoted in Rachel Fell McDermott, "The Western Kali," in *Devi: Goddess of India*, ed. J. Hawley and D. Wulff (Berkeley: U. of California Press, 1966), 290.

53. G.W.F. Hegel, *Phenomenology of the Spirit* (Oxford: Oxford University Press, 1977), 19, quoted in Greg Mogenson, "Different Moments in Dialectical Movement," 97.

54. Swami Vivekananda, *In Search of God and Other Poems* (Calcutta: Advaita Ashrama, 1968), 25.

55. C.G. Jung, *Collected Works*, Vol. 14: *Mysterium Coniunctionis* § 778.

56. Hillman, *Stone,* 259.

57. David Rosen, *Transforming Depression: Healing the Soul through Creativity* (York Beach, ME: Nicolas-Hays, 2002).

58. David Miller, "Nothing Almost Sees Miracles! Self & No-Self in Psychology & Religion," *Journal of Psychology and Religion*, 4-5, 1995, 1-25.

59. Giegerich, *The Soul's Logical Life,* 18-24.

60. *Ibid.*, 18.

61. *Ibid.*, 24.

62. *Ibid.*

63. Geoffrey Bennington, "RIP," in R. Rand (ed.), *Futures of Jacques Derrida* (Stanford University Press, 2001), 3; Quoted in Marla Morris, "Archiving Derrida" in *Derrida, Deconstruction and Education: Ethics of Pedagogy and Research*, ed. by Peter Pericles Trifonas and Michael A. Peters (Malden: Blackwell Publishing, 2004), 44.

64. Marla Morris, "Archiving Derrida," 44.

65. Simon Critchley, *Very Little: Almost Nothing* (London: Routledge, 2004), xvii.

66. *Ibid.*, xxiii.

67. *Ibid.*

68. *Ibid.*

69. *Ibid.*, xxiii-xxiv.

70. Wolfgang Giegerich, "The End of Meaning and the Birth of Man: An Essay about the State Reached in the History of Consciousness and an Analysis of C.G. Jung's Psychology Project," *Journal of Jungian Theory and Practice*, Vol. 6, No. 1, 2004.

71. Simon Critchley, *Very Little: Almost Nothing*, xxiv.

72. James Hillman, "A Note for Stanton Marlan," *Journal of Jungian Theory and Practice*, Vol. 5, No. 2, 2003, 102.

73. Hillman, "Concerning the Stone," 252.

74. Wolfgang Giegerich, "The Ego-Psychological Fallacy: on 'the birth of the meaning out of the symbol,'" *Journal of Jungian Theory and Practice*, Vol. 7, No. 2, retrieved from http://www.junginstitute.org/journal/JungV7N2p53-60.pdf.

75. James Hillman, "Therapeutic Value of Alchemical Language," *Dragonflies: Studies in Imaginal Psychology*, Fall 1978, 40.

76. *Ibid.*, 41.

77. C.G. Jung, *Memories, Dreams, Reflections*, recorded and ed. by Aniela Jaffe (New York: Pantheon, 1973), 223.

78. *Ibid.*, 225.

79. *Ibid.*, 226.

80. *Ibid.*, 227. This carved stone became a monument for what his tower meant to him.

81. *Ibid.*

82. *Ibid.*

83. Hillman, "Therapeutic Value of Alchemical Language," 41.
84. *Ibid.*
85. Sallis, *Stone*, 2.
86. From back of book jacket.
87. Sallis, *Stone*, 1.
88. Hillman, "Concerning the Stone," 241.
89. Sallis, *Stone*, Chapter 1.
90. Nathan Schwartz-Salant, personal communication, 2000. Quoted in Stanton Marlan, "Alchemy," in *The Handbook of Jungian Psychology*, 280.
91. Nathan Schwartz-Salant, personal communication, 2000. Quoted in Stanton Marlan, "Alchemy," in *The Handbook of Jungian Psychology*, 281.
92. Hillman, "Concerning the Stone," 242.
93. David Miller, "The 'Stone' Which Is Not a Stone," *Spring*, 1989, 116.
94. Robert Romanyshyn, "Voice of Things," *Dragonflies: Studies in Imaginal Psychology*, Fall 1978, 79-80.
95. Robert Romanyshyn, "Voice of Things," *Dragonflies: Studies in Imaginal Psychology*, Spring 1979, 73.
96. Maurice Merleau-Ponty, *The Visible and the Invisible*, 139. Quoted by Robert Romanyshyn, "Voice of Things," *Dragonflies: Studies in Imaginal Psychology*, Spring 1979, 73.
97. Romanyshyn, "Voice of Things," *Dragonflies*, Spring 1979, 73.
98. *Ibid.*, 79.
99. Hillman, "Concerning the Stone," 250.
100. Hillman, "Concerning the Stone," 255.
101. Sallis, *Stone*, 2.
102. *Ibid.*, 4.
103. *Ibid.*
104. *Ibid.*, 2-3.
105. Hillman, "Concerning the Stone," 239.
106. Nathan Schwartz-Salant, *The Mystery of Human Relationship: Alchemy and the Transformation of Self* (London: Routledge, 1998), 216.
107. *Ibid.*
108. Hillman, "Concerning the Stone," 239.
109. C.G. Jung, *Collected Works*, Vol. 9ii: *Aion*, p. 155, § 240.

110. Giegerich, *Dialectics & Analytical Psychology*, 108.

111. Paul Kugler, *Raids on the Unthinkable: Freudian and Jungian Psychoanalyses* (New Orleans: Spring Journal Books, 2005).

112. Alain Badiou, *Theoretical Writings* (New York: Continuum International, 2004).

113. Theodore Roethke, *Words for the Wind: The Collected Verse of Theodore Roethke* (Bloomington: Indiana University Press, 1970), 208.

Closure and Setting Free or The Bottled Spirit of Alchemy and Psychology

WOLFGANG GIEGERICH

Before I can begin, I must clarify the position from which I speak about alchemy and "which" alchemy I am speaking about. As to the first point: I am speaking as a psychologist and with a definitely psychological interest. And the alchemy I am speaking about is basically the picture of alchemy that emerges from Jung's description of it. So what I can say cannot lay claim to providing a historically and philologically correct assessment of the actual historical phenomenon of alchemy with all its incredible individual diversity and with its linguistic as well as ideational obscurity. My purpose in the first place is not to understand alchemy proper in its own terms and in terms of

Wolfgang Giegerich, Ph.D., is a Jungian psychoanalyst in private practice in Worthsee, Germany, who has lectured and published widely. His books in English include *The Soul's Logical Life: Towards a Rigorous Notion of Psychology*, Frankfurt/Main *et al.* (Peter Lang), 3rd ed. 2001; *Dialectics & Analytical Psychology: The El Capitan Canyon Seminar* (with David L. Miller and Greg Mogenson), New Orleans: Spring Journal Books, 2005: and, most recently, *The Neurosis of Psychology: Primary Papers Towards a Critical Psychology, Volume One, Collected English Papers of Wolfgang Giegerich*, New Orleans: Spring Journal Books, 2006.

its own time, the Middle Ages. Rather, I want to see how psychology relates to that alchemy (that foreign body within the corpus of psychology) that through Jung has already been appropriated for and incorporated into psychology. I could also say: I want to look at Jung's version of alchemy and its implications for psychology.

It is of course highly significant, and very characteristic for Jung's work, that Jung felt the need to make something as alien to psychology as alchemy a constituent element of his own psychological theory. The foreignness of alchemy is at least twofold. It is concerned with chemical substances and processes, with matter, rather than with people and *their* feelings, ideas, conflicts, etc. And it is completely obsolete for us, has been obsolete for several centuries; we are divided from it by a fundamental historical gap; the consciousness that gave rise to alchemy and provided the framework for the alchemical practice in laboratory as well as oratory can at best be reconstructed by us in the mind, but it can never become ours again. The interesting thing for us is to realize that it was, besides other aspects, precisely the foreignness of alchemy that made it so precious for Jung. In contrast to probably all other psychologists, he was not satisfied with clinical observation (with studying what was going on inside people) as the ground upon which psychology was to be based. Jung obviously needed to go away from immediate psychological experience, turn his back on psychology in the narrower (personalistic) sense, in order to find something *really* other that at first sight could not possibly be seen as psychology or psychologically relevant.

Psychology in Jung's view, so we can interpret this finding, *requires* otherness, difference—though not an utterly external other, something totally irrelevant, but its own internal other. Psychology must reflect itself in and base itself on a true (even if ultimately internal) other. For this reason Jung appropriated alchemy for psychology. It was foreign enough to be truly removed from modern psychology and at the same time open enough to be given a psychological interpretation of sorts. The reason for this need on the part of Jung is, so we may conclude, that he was instinctively open to the "psychological difference," to the insight that true psychology cannot be immediate psychology, but must be *sublated* immediate psychology. This is one of the features that sets his psychology apart from all the other psychologies of his time. And the objective, theoretical reason for this internal otherness is psychology's own necessity to overcome all naïve empiricism (the tendency to immediately turn to its object) which would unavoidably be fatal in that discipline which is characterized by the fact that in it the psyche observes *itself*. Because such a position of naïve immediacy makes it structurally impossible to make, within itself, allowances for the pitfalls of the "psychological equation." Jung was keenly aware of this problem.

At any rate, through alchemy Jungian psychology has, on a theoretical level, its own other or foreign body within itself. It thus exists as an internal tension. This tension can become productive if we compare both extremes, in two directions: (1) does psychological theory do justice to the spirit of its own internal other? Did what it discovered in the latter really come home to and permeate the constitution of the former? (2) Is this other, alchemy, conceived, comprehended, and described by this theory in such a way that the "alchemical impulse" (the inner motif power of alchemy) can really find its fulfillment? Mind you, the question here is not about the relation between historical-factual alchemy and psychology's description of it, but immanently about whether psychology's understanding of what it itself reports about alchemy is up to what is contained in this its own report. Obviously, the two questions are two sides of the same coin.

Jung held that alchemy was a "groping precursor of the most modern psychology" (*CW* 7 § 360), i.e., an unwitting precursor of his own psychology of the unconscious, as well as the historical link that connected his own psychology with Gnosticism. In this sense he thought, as he explains especially in *Memories, Dreams, Reflections*,[1] that his own psychology was the living continuation of an age-old tradition, a new link in the *aurea catena* of historical manifestations of the soul's truth. According to this thesis, alchemy was already in itself an implicit psychology, but "hampered by the inevitable concretizations of the still crude and undifferentiated intellect," so that it "never advanced to any clear psychological formulation ..." (§ 361). What in alchemy had still been merely implicit and hidden under the jumble created by a crude, undifferentiated intellect has now, in modernity, in Jung's own work, had a chance to become explicit.

* * *

What is it that makes alchemy, as Jung sees it, a precursor of psychology or even an implicit psychology? It is the sameness of purpose and concern. "But its 'secret,' too, was, just as that to be found in the process of individuation, the fact of the transformation of the personality through the blending and bonding of noble components with base ones, of the differentiated with the inferior functions, of the conscious with the unconscious" (§ 370). Although this statement does not come from one of Jung's later works, the thesis it expresses is one that he supported to the end of his life: the thesis that it is ultimately the interest in *the transformation of the personality* that alchemy and psychology have in common.

This is a thesis that invites a comparison, in the sense indicated, between the interpretation of alchemy in Jung's psychology and the report about the factual data of alchemy given by the same psychology. Is what psychology claims to be the inner telos of alchemy borne out by what we learn about alchemy from psychology's own description of its phenomenology?

What the alchemists were striving for was the philosophers' stone, the panacea, the red tincture, the life elixir, the *aqua permanens*, the philosophical gold, to mention only the most frequent names for the ultimate goal of the alchemical opus. It is clear that all these substances, whose description is highly paradoxical in all cases, indeed self-contradictory, do not refer to literal entities to be found or produced in the sphere of positivity. Jung interprets them as "The Projection of Psychic Contents" (*CW* 12, p. 242 ff.) and as mythological symbolizations (*ibid.*, § 342). It is true, his point that they are symbols, we could also say metaphors, is well taken, and his interpretation of alchemy as projections (of some ideas upon matter) *prima facie* makes a lot of sense, too, inasmuch as it is obvious that the alchemist in his expectations sees something in or into matter that cannot really, not literally, positivistically be found in matter. But his thesis becomes highly problematic when we look at *what* Jung says is that which is projected: "In order to explain the mystery of matter he projected yet another mystery—his own unknown psychic background—into what was to be explained ..." (§ 345). About projection in general Jung states, "In the darkness of some external reality I find, without recognizing it as such, an interior or psychic content that is my own"

(§ 346, transl. modif.). The alchemist "experienced his projection as a property of matter; but what he was in reality experiencing was his own unconscious" (*ibid.*).

"*His own* unknown psychic background," "an interior or psychic content that is *my own*," "*his own* unconscious"—from where does Jung get these ascriptions? Certainly not from the alchemical texts or from the spirit of alchemy as it is to be found in these texts. Quite obviously, the alchemists were not interested in their own personal development, their individuation or transformation. It is true, usually each adept worked by himself, but the *arcanum* he sought was never "his own." The *lapis* was explicitly the stone *of the philosophers* in the plural. The red tincture would have been the elixir of life for life as such, not for the adept's personal psychic life. The panacea was likewise not understood and intended as a means for his personal cure or salvation; as *pan*-acea (cure-*all*) it was conceived, much like a vaccine discovered in modern medicine, as something that would as a matter of course have belonged to the generality. The point of a vaccine or of medication or of methods of treatment for all sorts of health disorders is that they are the solution to objective problems that in principle threaten humankind at large, regardless of which individual happened to discover or develop the cure. Medicine as a field of study is not a private, subjective undertaking. Like science it struggles to find answers to general problems and is fundamentally a communal effort. In the same way, the alchemists, as lonely as they may have been in their laboratories, participated in a collective project that extended across the ages, and they all shared the same purpose of finding *the* (not each their own, personal) "philosophers' stone" (or whatever particular symbolic name they might have given to this ultimate goal). In sum, alchemy was trying to find something that had the logical status of objective knowledge, a universal "truth." The transformation of the individual was absolutely no theme or concern of theirs, and it could not possibly have come into their focus.

Interestingly enough, the very texts that Jung cites in support of his thesis that what the alchemist experienced was his unconscious clearly show the alchemist's nonpersonalistic, nonsubjective focus and could have opened Jung's eyes to the inadequacy of his individualistic premise:

> ... and you will see with your own eyes one thing after the other appearing by and by on top of the water, how God created all things in six days .... (§ 347)

The prospect was to gain an immediate insight into, and, as it were, to witness, *God's creation work.* No doubt, the general horizon of the alchemical work was cosmic, in a certain sense of the word even "theological." There is no trace of an interest in oneself, no self-centeredness. Alchemy's interest was one that belongs to the wider sphere of a general natural philosophy in the Hermetic tradition. The *Novum lumen* is quoted by Jung, in the same chapter on the projection of the psychic contents, with the following passage:

> To cause things hidden in the shadow to appear, and to take away the shadow from them, this is permitted to the intelligent philosopher by God through nature. ... All these things happen, and the eyes of the common men do not see them, but the eyes of the understanding [*intellectus*] and of the imagination perceive them [*percipiunt*] with true and truest vision [*visu*].

To be sure, it was each adept's personal longing to personally have such experiences and personally see "these things" with the eyes of the *intellectus* (which in medieval contexts is not to be confused with what we moderns mean by the [usually derogative] term intellect [cf. "intellectualism"]; it was the highest faculty of the mind, originally belonging only to God and only derivatively also to man). But just as when we today want to personally see the Egyptian pyramids or the Grand Canyon, or when we wish to personally acquire some of the knowledge produced by the great minds of our tradition, we are not primarily concerned with the transformation of our own personality, but with something in the real world out there, so his own individuation was not the purpose of the adept's hope to see the things he wished to see. His self was no topic. The topic and interest was, to say it with the words of Faust, to get to know and connect with "*was die Welt im Innersten zusammenhält,*" i.e., the innermost mystery or logic of the world or, in alchemical imagery, the *mysterium coniunctionis* as the separation-and-union of the opposites. It is the secret of the creation, the creation not as a primordial event in the past but as its ever-present ongoing living truth. An analogy may be helpful here. Each Roman-Catholic priest has to personally perform the ritual of the mass every day, but this does in no way imply that his goal in doing this is his own individuation. It is a fallacy to conclude from the personal nature of the aimed-for experience, insight, or effort that the focus of the effort and the content of the experience are one's personal development.

While the transformation of my personality is an absolutely private, subjective concern, ultimately (1) egoic and (2) "practical" (utilitarian: my progress and fulfillment), we see from the above quote that alchemy appealed to the understanding, which is fundamentally communal because it aims for knowing and truth (the "true and truest vision"). But the *person* who possibly happens to become aware of this general truth is *per se* of no importance or interest; only the truth of nature or the world itself is. The alchemist did not search for *his* self, but for *the* spirit Mercurius as the mystery deeply hidden in the real.

So if Jung claims that the alchemist projected "his own unknown psychic background" and that his secret was the "fact of the transformation of the personality," he did not learn this from the phenomenology of alchemy as it presented itself to him in the alchemical tracts that he so diligently studied. Rather, it is a true projection on his part, more specifically: a retrojection of his own modern psychologistic prejudice. The idea of individuation in Jung's personalistic or individualistic sense is foisted on alchemy, smuggled into it.

The same applies to the idea of "the unconscious." Jung asserts that the visionary experiences that sometimes occurred during the alchemical opus "cannot be anything but projections of unconscious contents." (§ 350) We already briefly discussed the theme of "projection," but now have to take up another aspect of it. This idea entails serious presuppositions. Projection implies that there is in me a within which houses the contents that in "projection" are thrown out and then appear to the subject out there, either as apparitions in their own right or as the property of empirical things or persons. By entertaining this concept psychological theory does something very queer and contradictory. On the one hand, it asserts a hidden movement from inside to outside and, on the other hand, it logically performs what psychoanalysts might call a "reversal into the opposite," namely a movement from outside to inside, by claiming that that which, phenomenally speaking, is seen outside as something real or as the property of something real out there is actually the property of the inner psyche of the subject. But *both* movements are fantasized since we do not actually see that something that "before" was in the alchemist was indeed thrown out from his interior into the external world.

This is very different from Jung's own theorizing, where the ideas of "projection" and of "unconscious contents," etc. are indeed first elements of psychological doctrine and only thereafter "seen" out there in alchemy; first modern concepts, and then said to have already been operative in the distant past. Here the word projection is warranted by the phenomenology of what happens. But as far as the visionary experiences of the alchemists are concerned we could simply leave out this fictitiously assumed and self-cancelling idea of the double movement of projection and stay with the simple phenomenon that something was indeed seen out there.

The idea of projection, not being the result of an empirical observation, serves the psychologistic purpose of *positing* a "within" in the person and of tying to the person, and reducing to personal significance, what for the alchemist (as well as phenomenally, for the unprejudiced observer) is about the inner truth or inner nature of nature. It is a speculative kind of natural philosophy. The visionary and fantastic aspect of the alchemical descriptions of their experiences with matter could well be accounted for by the difference between their interest in the inner truth, indeed the *mystery*, of nature and the totally different interest of the modern natural sciences (and the modern mind in general) in the *positivity* of nature, in what we call the facts. If we understand the historical difference between the medieval and the modern mind with their fundamentally different ideas of what is real, we do not have to take refuge in psychologistic interpretations in terms of "projections of unconscious contents." For the medieval mind the truth about nature was *a priori* "metaphysical," essentially mysterious, not positive-factual.

Another problem with the "projection of unconscious contents" idea lies in the notion of "contents." The tacit suggestion here is that what is projected existed prior to the projection, was somehow already a finished entity. The fantastic experience is then merely a removal of ready-made items from the inside storeroom to outside: a theory about the experiences from the point of view of a reifying, positivizing thinking. But why could it not be that the alchemists' experiences were genuine first-time *productions*, on the spot inventions? In other words, instances of creative speculative thought? The products of an active, lively mind? Production instead of "projection of contents"? Living thought (as the activity or process of thinking)?

If so, if it is a process of thinking that we are dealing with in alchemy, we do not need the notion of the unconscious implied by the phrase "unconscious contents" (which here means as much as contents coming from the unconscious). The visions of the alchemists are conscious events, products of a visionary or visionizing consciousness, their images and ideas products of a speculatively thinking consciousness, their dreams the products of a dreaming consciousness. In addition to a rationalistic, to an empiricistic consciousness, there are all kinds of other styles of consciousness, an emotionalizing, a fantasizing, a sober, a paralyzed, a pedantic formalistic consciousness, etc.

It is the positivistic mind that posits "the unconscious." The logic leading to this notion is that if what the alchemists believed to see in the object did not really come from the characteristics of the object, it must come from some other (positive-factual) place—"the unconscious in them." In other words, the theory of "the unconscious" is *sensualism in reverse*. Sensualism insists that "nothing is in the mind that had not before been given to the senses." The psychology of the unconscious accepts this, except that it adds a second, alternate source from which the mind's contents can come: in addition to the world out there in front of the mind, also "the unconscious" in the back of the mind. The idea that the mind does not *get* all its contents (either from the sensual world or from an inner reservoir of unconscious contents), but originally produces some of them on the spot and thus is in itself poietic is taboo. The mind must not be a thinking mind. It must be a merely recipient and "*data*"-processing mind.

Whereas the world given to the senses is warranted by our experience, the notion of an "unconscious" *behind* the visions and ideas of the alchemists is a mystification of the phenomenal evidence, a dogmatic invention of a, as it were, "metaphysical" entity within the positivistically viewed world! The mind's activity of speculative and poietic thought is hypostatized as an entity, region, or reservoir behind the mind.

In stressing the production-invention aspect of conscious thought and its momentary nature, I do not want to suggest that the production is the work of that lonely ego-consciousness in which it surfaces.

Especially in alchemy we can see how the fantasies and ideas, even those emerging in an isolated adept, are not private concoctions, but collective, often quite conventional, ideas. The creative individual consciousness is not private here, but floats in and is supported by something that is not its own, an age-old intellectual tradition and atmosphere. It is the climate of this whole hermetic spirit, not the latter's ego, that is doing the productive speculative thinking through each individual adept. Jung once wrote that we always dream from within the relationship. We could extend this statement by saying we always dream from within the real psychological context that we are in as well as from the more superficial or deeper psychological reality level that consciousness is open to. But this applies not only to dream thoughts. It applies to all non-ego thinking. And (a) the less a person has psychologically emancipated himself as a true individual from his social group or intellectual tradition, but is rather in a *participation mystique* with it (as, e.g., the medieval alchemists were with the hermetic tradition), and/or (b) the more a person's roots, through his inner greatness and depth ("genius"), reach down into the foundations of the inner core or truth of that tradition (in that status that has in fact been attained by it in its historical evolution at the respective present), the more the productions of consciousness will not be the merely personal property of the ego-personality. In everything great, in poetry, art, philosophy, in (the rare cases of truly great) statesmanship, etc. it is the *historical locus* (all around the person) that thinks, not the individual as a lonely self.

(Here I must, however, add that concerning a single individual we cannot claim that it permanently belongs to this or to that level. A truly great thinker can at times say quite banal things that come only from his private ego-consciousness, and people who for the most part do not appear to be geniuses may at times produce a single great work or insight that comes from the depth. We may all phase into and out of various depth strata and psychological-intellectual climates and participate in them or are emancipated from them at different times to differing degrees. There is an alchemical text, *Aurora Consurgens*, that has been ascribed to Thomas Aquinas. If we accept this ascription merely experimentally for a moment, we can say that Thomas, when he was in his study or monk's cell, was the great theologian who wrote his *Summae*, but when he went, metaphorically speaking,[2] into his "laboratory-oratory," he at once tuned into or was absorbed by the hermetic tradition and could produce this great alchemical text.)

It is always consciousness that thinks; and that *thinks* whether it dreams, muses, fantasizes, is poetically or artistically creative, or whether it thinks in the narrower sense of the word. The delusional concept of "the unconscious" amounts to a mystification, be it that it is understood as a reservoir of repressed or archetypal contents or of instincts and desires, or as an agent behind the scene that produces dreams and directs our fate, or as a region of the mind. "The unconscious" is really a *metaphysical* presupposition, a dogmatic concept, in Jung's psychology, notwithstanding Jung's oft-expressed horror of metaphysical assumptions and his avowal of a strict empiricism. Inadvertently, it serves a certain *strategic purpose*, although it is consciously intended as a simple naming of an "obvious phenomenon." But this alleged phenomenon does not exist and this is why "the unconscious" is a mystification and a metaphysical hypostasis.

The purpose of the concept of "the unconscious" is first of all to support the idea of "*one's own* inner psychic background," that is, to tie the phenomenology of the soul to the person and enclose, lock it in the individual. This remains true although Jung also often states that we are in the unconscious, which he then says is all around us, an idea that of course is the very opposite of such an enclosure. But this other idea did not lead Jung to entirely revoke the idea of "one's own unconscious." He pays certainly more than lip service to the idea of the unconscious all around us, but he nevertheless did not unmistakingly break with the unconscious in us. This is underscored by the fact that consistently to the end of his days Jung held on to the idea that the *individual* is the makeweight that tips the scale, that he or she is the one important factor that makes history, the only place where the salvation or rescue of the world can take place (cf. *CW* 10 § 586, 315, 536). And of course his whole focus on individuation and introspection points the same way.

* * *

But more important and serious than this locking the soul in "one's own inner" or in the individual person is another kind of enclosure performed by the notion of "the unconscious." The one discussed so far still takes place in the externality of space or in the imagination, and therefore also imprisons the soul only in an external sense; the closure does not get to the soul's heart. By imagining things, the soul leaves its native land and moving out gives itself the form of alienation from itself. Even though our imaginings and fantasies usually happen within the mind and do not literally go out into the material reality "out there," they are nevertheless a kind of mind-internal "projection." But with the second sense of enclosure effected by the notion of "the unconscious" we stay on the soul's home territory and this is why the imprisonment now really hits home. I am referring to the very meaning of the word 'unconscious.' It *logically* exiles the soul from the sphere of knowing and thought and conscious awareness, as from what is its own nature and truth. The concept of "the unconscious" is a true "projection," the transposition of a subjective attitude or function into an imagined "something" out there in objective reality. For ultimately it is the hypostatization or objective representation of *one's will* to hold the nature of psychic reality down in darkness, in undisclosedness, in the status of material nature (in contrast to mind). This concept, rather than innocently naming an observed reality, is a *program* that, however, comes in the guise of an (alleged) fact. And this program is best formulated with Jung's quote from alchemy: *ignotum per ignotius*. It is true, neither for the alchemists nor for Jung was this phrase meant as a program. No, subjectively, consciously, it was perceived more like a resigned admission of our limitations. But objectively it expresses in Jungian psychology a move deeper down into unknowing with no hope of any light. It once and for all denies the possibility of some sort of exit from the dungeon.

In mythology Danae was imprisoned by her father Akrisios, king of Argos, in the darkness of an underground vault. But Akrisios' intention was foiled by Zeus, who having fallen in love with Danae penetrated to her into the darkness of her prison from the height of heaven after having taken the form of a rain of gold that impregnated her and, so we can assume, lit up her darkness *from within*. This is what happens to the dark in ancient myth. Similarly, the Gospel of John (1:14) tells us, "And the Word was made flesh, and dwelt among us, and we beheld his glory, the glory as of the only begotten of the Father, full of grace and truth." "And the light shineth in darkness" (1:5), where, however, in contrast to the course of events in the myth the continuation tells us that "the darkness comprehended it not."

But psychology is, in total contrast to Akrisios, fully successful in locking the soul in darkness and perfectly sealing its underground dungeon. "The unconscious" remains dark *by definition*. There is no better lock than the logical one of a definition. No rain of gold from the heavens could possibly seep into what is defined as the unconscious. The possibility of a true *coniunctio* is *a priori* precluded. How could there possibly be a *coniunctio*, how could there be some kind of heavenly light to fall into the darkness, if "the unconscious" has already from the outset swallowed and pocketed its own other, the very light of heaven that could possibly penetrate the dark and enter into a union with it, and "heaven" as such into the bargain? "Since the stars have fallen from heaven and our highest symbols have paled, a secret life holds sway in the unconscious" (*CW* 9i § 50). What Jung here states is not comparable to the rain of gold seeping down to imprisoned Danae. The falling of the stars is the equivalent to an abolishment of the very source of that rain, Zeus, and his Olympus. The very place for the light in the system of thought has not merely become temporarily vacant, no, it has once and for all disappeared from this thought, it has become undialectically canceled. There is now a hegemony of darkness. Although the stars may still shine within the unconscious, although a secret life may hold sway in the unconscious, it is now *fundamentally,* i.e., *logically*, no more than the secret light and life under a totalitarian regime of darkness. Even the *scintillae* in the unconscious, its very own, native sparks of light, remain forever enclosed in it.

Psychology's commitment to "the unconscious" amounts to the systematic closure of that opening and clearance that according to mythology was produced by a primordial culture hero when he pried apart the bodies of the world parents, Heaven and Earth, who had been in eternal cohabitation, lifting up Father Heaven. "The unconscious" as alleged empirical fact is the Earth that does no longer have a Heaven above itself, indeed is not even embraced by Heaven as before the hero's deed: it has swallowed Heaven with the stars and all heavenly light altogether. Now, the whole myth of the separation of the world parents is said to have come from the unconscious as its real source. The latter is the ultimate, all-comprehensive reality.

With the "psychology of the unconscious," the condition for the possibility *a priori* of a *coniunctio* has been abolished. The psychology of the unconscious is a clear avowal of fundamental darkness. A syzygy cannot be, because the unconscious has lost its other. The *ligamentum*, the *copula*, the *vinculum* have been cut. The mind has systematically immured itself in (psychological) darkness by locating soul and truth in "the unconscious" as their authentic and exclusive place and by having rid itself of "heaven above."

But is it not precisely this psychology of the unconscious that in the first place made us aware again of the forgotten ideas and realities of the *mysterium coniunctionis*, of the syzygy, of the *vinculum* as vital and existential psychological problems and that tries to bring a new light to "our benighted present" (*Letters* 2, p. 396, to Trinick, 15 Oct. 1957)? Is it not the purpose of psychology and analytical psychotherapy to make conscious the treasures in the unconscious? Do we not carefully observe our dreams, trying to understand them and to integrate them into our lives? Did Jung not—in contrast to Freud's wholesale dismissal of the *superi* (the upper gods) in favor of *Acheron* (the underworld)—attempt to reconnect us to the light contained in myths and symbols, in the great soul topics expressed in dogmas and rituals and to bring back the fear of God and gods? Did he not expressly state: "Instead of creating light, we conceal in darkness, instead of lifting up, we expose to ridicule and contempt" (same letter, p. 395) and thereby show what his own outlook and purpose was?

All true. But to no avail. It is all *a priori* superceded by the psyche's fundamental immurement in the unconscious. All our devotion to myths and archetypal images, our "dream tending," as they sometimes call it, our painting from the unconscious, all our attempts at making conscious belong to the sphere of behavior, are instances of acting out, ego-doings. They are empirical, semantic events and efforts that have not got a chance with the fundamental logical-syntactical sinking of all light in darkness. The archetypes are *defined* as archetypes of the collective *unconscious*. No empirical, behavioral "making consciousness" undoes this logical definition of that which is to be made conscious as belonging to "the unconscious."

"It is not a matter of indifference whether one calls something an 'addiction' or 'a god.' To serve an addiction is detestable and undignified, but to serve a god is full of meaning and promise because it is an act of submission to a higher, invisible, and spiritual being," says Jung *CW* 13 § 55 (transl. modif.). Likewise it is not a matter of indifference whether one calls something "the unconscious" or, e.g., "the absolute," for to name it "the unconscious" is an act of repression, a *decision* to have it *logically* locked away in darkness once for all. In our psychological innocence we usually think that what really counts is what we do, that we go into analysis, carefully observe our dreams, devote ourselves to myths and archetypes, etc. But *psychologically*, that is, for the soul, all this is pretty irrelevant. All this happens on the level of the ego and refers to no more than contents of ego-consciousness, its semantics. But psychology only begins where it is a question of the implicit logic or syntax of consciousness, the categories, concepts, definitions, tacit presuppositions that consciousness sight unseen operates with, the *way* it thinks and quite naturally, as a matter of course, apperceives and comprehends its semantic contents, its empirical feeling experiences. For this reason it is indeed a matter of the greatest psychological importance whether we allow ourselves the notion of "the unconscious" or not.

Jung confessed, "Hence I prefer the term 'the unconscious,' knowing that I might just as well speak of 'God' or 'daimon' if I wished to express myself in mythic language." The latter

> terms have the great advantage of encompassing and evoking the emotional quality of numinosity, whereas the [former]—the unconscious—is banal and therefore closer to reality. This concept includes the fact that it can be empirically experienced, that is, the commonplace reality the way it is familiar and accessible to us. The unconscious is too neutral and rational a term to give much impetus to the imagination. The term, after all, was coined for scientific purposes, and is far better suited to dispassionate observation which makes no metaphysical claims than are transcendental concepts, which are contestable .... *(MDR*, pp. 336f., modif.)

We see very clearly that Jung was aware of the great significance for the soul of which names we use. But we also see two other things.

First of all we see that Jung with full methodological awareness opted for the notion of "the unconscious." And why? Because he insisted on the positivism of the modern scientific outlook as his basic stance: on the systematic exclusion of the metaphysical and transcendental dimension. He presented everything that he said about archetypes and the mysteries of the soul as positive facts, nothing but facts.

Logically they were given the status of positivity, while *under* this all-overarching umbrella of a definition, and semantically, they were allowed to be mysteries, gods, *daimones*. What he was doing was, he claimed, natural science. He did not, he insisted, make any metaphysical statements and could get quite worked up when he sensed that what he said was taken as such. The metaphysical, transcendental dimension was *anathema*. Or rather, it was *anathema* only when it was a truly *psychological* question of the names used and the logical statuses, while on the subjective-experiential and semantic level (i.e., on the level of ego-consciousness and its contents), Jung favored a language that acknowledged the numinosity and transcendental nature of the experiences, e.g., "God" instead of "addiction." What he allowed or even demanded with the one hand he sternly forbade with the other. The psychological difference between the psychologically essential logical or syntactical level and the (psychologically already sublated, pocketed) subjective and semantic level was decisively operative in his thinking, but he did not become really conscious of it and what it involved. This will be the second observation about the above *MDR* quotes that I want to point to. But before I come to it, I have to interpret the present findings.

If what for want of a better term we call here the "metaphysical" and "transcendental" dimension is, and must be, systematically excluded from psychology's basic notion, "the unconscious," how can Jung hope that we might "create light" and "lift up"? The dungeon is *absolutely* closed, because heaven and the light of heaven have *logically* been done away with. Even his own wording in the quote I just alluded to shows that all is lost: "Instead of creating light, we conceal in darkness, instead of lifting up, we expose to ridicule and contempt." The point has never been to *create* light and to *lift* up. It was the other way around. Zeus let his golden rain *fall* into Danae's dungeon of his own accord, and "people that walked in darkness have seen a great light" (from above); Prometheus stole the fire *from* heaven or from the carriage of Helios and brought it down to earth. Since what in myths is told "did never happen but always is," (Sallustios)—where can Prometheus steal the fire from when the transcendental dimension has been canceled? How can a light fall into the darkness of our existence when the very *source* of any true light is thought to be "the unconscious," the dungeon itself? When heaven as the former source of light, of the sun, the moon, the stars, has once and for all been eliminated from our binding *knowing*, our "official" worldview, and when consciousness voluntarily settles in the "banality" (Jung) of "the unconscious," in the blindness of the positive-factual? It is the notion of "the unconscious," that is the very way in which *psychologically* (even if not behaviorally) "we conceal in darkness" and "expose to … contempt." Why to contempt? Because this notion withholds the open acknowledgment of truth from what it comprises. It has already logically stolen that entire dimension wherefrom alone Prometheus could steal the fire or wherefrom a heavenly light could possibly fall into our darkness.

The second observation starts out from Jung's statement that the terms God or daimon "have the great advantage of encompassing and evoking the emotional quality of numinosity." What we have here is a *metabasis eis allo genos*. "The unconscious" is a generic term or refers to a whole realm or region, whereas God and daimon represent individual contents, semantic items. As we have seen, "the unconscious" is a logical term that locks the contents it refers to in the *status* of an *ignotum* and fundamental unknowable, in the status of contents that our consciousness cannot and must never accept intellectual responsibility for by owning up to their truth (because otherwise the forbidden metaphysical dimension would instantly again come out of the box into which it has been sunk). But Jung reduces and belittles the problem of which names to use to a subjective emotional or experiential issue: "banal, neutral and rational" vs. "evoking the emotional quality of numinosity and inspiring the imagination." We see here confirmed what we saw earlier, that Jung escapes to the semantic level, relegating and delegating what is actually a question of *whether something is true* to the question of *what it does to us in positive*[3] *subjective experience*. This skotomization of the logical question of truth, stealthily covered up by the reductive substitution for it of the subjectively so impressive category of positive-factual *Erfahrbarkeit* (this is the word I rendered above in the quote from Jung as "the fact that it can be empirically experienced"), *is* in itself the very "the unconscious"— a logical, "metaphysical" self-castration, self-blinding, the soul's self-immurement in irreparable *logical, mental* darkness, no matter how many subjective experiences of light—stars and suns and *scintillae* in the unconscious—one may have and how numinous they may be.

The translation of the category of truth and knowing into the category of subjective emotional and imagination-inspirational quality is psychologism pure and simple, psychologism not in the usual superficial sense, but on the very highest or deepest theoretical level, in the very heart of the matter. "The unconscious" is at the same time the lever by means of which this translation constantly is, no, always already has been, performed—tacitly, invisibly, unbeknownst.

In alchemical terms we could express the same observation the following way: Jung locks and hermetically seals the spirit in matter. His is at bottom an *opus contra opus alchemicum*. One of the main general purposes of the alchemical work was to free the spirit Mercurius from his imprisonment in matter. The alchemists maltreated their prime matter, subjecting it to all sorts of destructive and painful operations: pulverization, corruption, incineration, *solutio*, fermentation, etc. The alchemical work was basically one great attack on the image, on the *natural imaginal shape* of the matter in which it came. The intact image and natural form, i.e., the *status* of "natural entity," had to be overcome so that the substance might attain its spirit (or essence) form. When a substance was pulverized or incinerated or evaporated, its imaginable form was gone. You had something else, a vapor, a distillate, an essence, at any rate something that no longer had a figurative shape. And the absolutely self-contradictory nature of the aimed-for end-product, water that was permanent, a stone that was not a stone, shows that the whole level of the natural imagination had in principle been left behind. (In principle only. For it was precisely the dilemma, if not tragedy, of alchemy that what it logically aimed for, and was obviously already claimed by, it made empirically impossible through its own still imaginal style of thinking and by operating within the material-natural horizon of the chemical. Its work was a clear case of "acting out" that work "against nature"—the work of the negation of the natural and imaginal—that could only have been achieved if it had been interiorized into itself instead of being literalized on the level of behavior and if it had been applied to itself instead of being acted out on literal matter out there.)

Jung, by contrast, is a downright materialist, just as above he showed himself to be a positivistic sensualist. *Of course not on the semantic, but on the psychological, syntactic level.* (On the semantic level and explicitly, he is obviously the opposite. But what he actually does and how he thinks, how his thought is structured is more important than what he explicitly teaches.) He prevents—again I must qualify: not on the phenomenological, practical, and semantic, but on the fundamental-theoretical level—the spirit from escaping, he *logically* stuffs the soul's issues back down into the form or status of "matter," namely the status of *natural events* and *empirical facts* and *emotional experiences.* He does not try to *release* them from their positivity into their truth, in which they would finally have come home to themselves and would no longer be on principle imprisoned in the person ("one's own psychic background"), on the one hand, nor sealed in the logical status of irrevocable positivity, that is, occludedness-in-themselves, on the other. The term "the unconscious," after all, as we heard from Jung, "was coined for scientific purposes, and is far better suited to dispassionate observation which makes no metaphysical claims than are transcendental concepts, which are contestable." On the theoretical level Jung needed and insisted on the unbridgeable gap across which the external dispassionate observer could make his neutral, i.e., intellectually noncommittal, statements about the *per definitionem* "*un*conscious" psychological phenomena that in themselves (but only in themselves, only yonder, on the other side of the gap, in the private experiential sphere) certainly were, were allowed to be, nay, were *supposed to be*, of a "metaphysical" or "transcendental" nature. The soul phenomena were to be given intensive attention, emotional appreciation, amplificatory understanding, ethical regard. But the one thing they really want was absolutely denied to them: intellectual acknowledgment as belonging to our knowing, the subject's (committedly, not "dispassionately") honoring them as having the status of truths.

* * *

I said that Jung's work was a work against the spirit of alchemy. But it seems that Jung has alchemy on his side when we listen to the following passage from the chapter "The Problem of Freeing Mercurius" in his discussion of the Grimms' fairy tale *The Spirit in the Bottle* in his essay entitled "The Spirit Mercurius." As is well known, in this tale the son who had found the well-sealed bottle in which a spirit had been imprisoned, finally, after some complications, let this spirit out of the bottle and was rewarded for it. Jung is critical of this freeing the spirit. He writes,

> What happens when this Hermes-Mercurius-Wotan, a pagan god, is let loose again? ... The *avis Hermetis* (the bird of Hermes) has escaped from the glass prison, and in consequence something has happened which the experienced alchemist wished at all costs to avoid. That is why he sealed the stopper of his bottle with magic signs and set it for a very long time over the lowest fire, so that "he who is within may not fly out." For if he escapes, the whole laborious opus comes to nothing and has to be started all over again. ...
>
> Be that as it may, the behaviour of the young man—successfully as it worked out for him—must be described as *alchemically incorrect.* ... The golden age of alchemy was the sixteenth and the first half of the seventeenth century. At that time a storm bird did indeed escape from a spiritual vessel which the daemons must have felt was a prison. As I said, the alchemists were all for not letting Mercurius escape, but for his staying inside and for the internal transformation of Mercurius .... (*CW* 13 § 250f., transl. modif.)

No doubt, Jung is right that the alchemists unrelentingly opted for the spirit's staying in the bottle. But it is not only a historically correct statement about alchemy. I also wholeheartedly concur *for psychology* with the alchemists and with Jung (who in citing the stance of the alchemists certainly gave us also his own view of things). The fundamentally evasive spirit must be prevented from escaping. The bottle must be sealed.

What does this mean concretely? The way I understand the work of the psychologist, it has to be uncompromisingly devoted to the "matter" at hand, regardless of what it may be: in the consulting room this dream today, this memory from the past that now has come up, this emotional reaction that has become a topic in today's session, and outside the consulting room any issue or image or text that one has taken up as a subject for study. Once it has been adopted as one's topic, our commitment to it must be *exclusive*, for the duration of one's occupation with it. "That's it!" *Closure*. Nothing else must divert us from this topic. Just as, e.g., in dream interpretation we have to "stick to the image," as Jung and Lopez-Pedraza demanded, that is, in a *qualitative* sense be confined in what we say about it by its precise phenomenology, without going off to the level of generalities and abstractions not backed up by its concrete appearance and "feel," so we must also in a quantitative sense dwell with our attention *only* on the matter at hand. The alchemical vessel and the hermetic seal on it are in psychology no longer physical objects, but a mental, methodological attitude, an attitude that was with respect to the fantasy image formulated by Jung in the following maxim which I have quoted many times and have to repeat here once more. This golden rule of psychology can *mutatis mutandis* be applied to any matter.

> Above all, don't let anything from outside, that does not belong, get into it, for the fantasy-image has 'everything it needs' [*omne quo indiget*] within itself. (*CW* 14 § 749, modif.)

The application of this methodological maxim must not occur pedantically and with a literalistic, formalistic mind. The difficulty in making use of it is that there are no positive-factual criteria for the decision about what belongs and what does not belong, what comes from outside (is truly foreign) and what merely supports and enhances what is already there. The decision cannot be operationalized. Rather, it requires that "finer intelligence" that Jung demanded, an intelligence which is probably 'finer' for the reason (among others) that it contains within itself what Jung might call a differentiated "feeling function" and a good intuitive, inner susceptibility to "the soul" of the matter under psychological investigation.

This methodological principle means that anything like free associations, subjective feelings, causal explanations of how the material might have come about, any speculation about better ways for the dream ego to have reacted in the given dream or about other possibilities or potentials for a (good) ending of the dream would be extraneous and probably ego-stuff. The phenomenon *is* the way it is. It has to be respected—and stay enclosed—in its being-so. Psychological work requires a discipline and skill in *abstraction* from one's own merely-subjective feelings and personal views and sudden ideas that might pop up in oneself in view of a given motif. Only then can it be hoped that we are open to the self-display and for the logical self-movement of the matter into its own inner depth, its truth.

The purpose of the hermetic closure is "the internal transformation of Mercurius." The matter needs to be enclosed in the alchemical vessel because the work is work on and with the same. One and the same matter is supposed to be interiorized into itself, intensified, heightened. It is a work of the matter upon itself. The carefully sealed "vessel" is necessary so that the matter is prevented from following the natural course, that is, from acting out its own nature, by just being and behaving as would be normal for it. There must not be any external influences on it, but also no effects from it outwards on other matters, no interaction whatsoever. It must not spend itself, waste its potential by just "doing its thing." Its self-movement, such as the natural putrefaction of certain materials, must, to be sure, not be prevented, but it must be caught and retained so as return again to itself, be applied to itself.

As a kind of pictorial illustration of this self-application and the concomitant intensification through interiorization into itself I mention a Taoist ritual practice in which this self-application is literally acted out in the form of a sexual technique. The purpose of the ritual is to nourish the "life principle" and ultimately to gain immortality. The procedure is as follows. The Taoist first copulates so that "the essence" (the semen) is intensely stirred up. But then, when it is about to ejaculate, he has to quickly grab and pull the penis in a certain way behind the scrotum while at the same time vigorously exhaling for a long time through the mouth and flashing his teeth. If then he lets the essence go, it cannot come out, but comes back from the penis and rises up (through the spinal marrow), ultimately entering the brain (according to ancient medicine the locus of the soul and as such the place where semen originates in the body). This is a procedure the immortals exchange among each other, but swear not to pass on to everybody.[4]

Let us have a closer look at this practice. The life essence is first stirred up so that it becomes somehow accessible. It is awakened from its dormant state. But then it is prevented from spending and wasting itself for the natural course of events (ejaculation) and its natural purpose (gratification of desire and possibly reproduction). The interaction with the partner is disrupted, intercepted and the self is enclosed within itself. The life essence is forced *contra naturam* to travel back up to its source, the brain as the locus of soul. This reversal of the direction becomes possible through two measures. First, the relentless closure of the outward passage and the prevention of an escape. Secondly, a "displacement from below to above" for the outward tendency and simultaneously an activation of the spirit dimension (breath), in place of the physical, substantial dimension. The intended result of a nourishment of the life principle as such comes about through the self-application of the life principle to itself. And in contrast to normal nourishment of the life principle through something else, through food or joyful experiences, this is a counter-natural nourishment. This practice prevents the life principle from continuing along the lines of the natural horizontality of its movement (sexual intercourse, relation to others, taking in food from outside, etc.) and forces it into verticality, namely to a fundamentally "higher" or "deeper" logical level or status, that of "immortality." Apparently, this revolutionary vertical movement that bursts the horizon of the commonplace is only possible through "self-application." And this self-application presupposes radical closure, the hermetically sealed alchemical vessel.

Instead of fathering a child "out there" and thereby reproducing himself on the same old natural level of life through otherness, the Taoist "fertilized" *himself*, or rather, he forced the "life essence" in him to fertilize and intensify *itself*. We also have to note that his ritual was *not* a psychological one of self-reflection, of moving his *attention* away from his sexual partner as an external other to himself, a shift from the *intentio directa* to the *intentio obliqua*. He did not give birth to an internal child but was catapulted into a totally new dimension or status. In other words, it was not an achievement in the realm of subjectivity. No, it was the sphere of the objective "matter" itself, of the life essence, underneath his subjective mind, on which this revolution was brought about.

The similarity and difference between this Taoist example and the alchemical opus are obvious. The main difference is that concerning the Taoist procedure Jung could probably rightly say that, although not in a modern psychological sense, it served the purpose of the transformation of the personality, whereas alchemy did not, as I argued, aim at the person of the alchemist. The similarity of the logic of the two techniques is striking. The alchemists, too, wanted to drive the prime matter into verticality, into its own inner depth and truth. The closure of the vessel served the purpose of preventing the natural horizontal development of the matter. When alchemy strove for the stone, the life elixir, etc., it did not seek *another* object on the same horizontal plane of commonplace reality, an object that was merely different because it had miraculous power. Rather, these objects are images for a new logical status, a fundamentally different level of consciousness. Just as the Taoist did not want offspring, but the new status of "immortality," so the alchemist did not want a thing, but a fundamentally, syntactically different level of consciousness, which expresses itself in such terms as fermentations, distillation, sublimation, evaporation. And his dilemma was that what was actually a different logical or syntactical status he had to imagine and express and *think* in the alienating and self-defeating *imaginal*, i.e., semantic language, the language of things, for which reason he had to take refuge in paradoxical formulations ("the stone that is not a stone").

A psychology and psychotherapy in the spirit of alchemy cannot have a therapeutic *program*. No wish for the self-development, improvement, growth, individuation of the personality, no wish for a cure and betterment of the patient, because the alchemical project is not person-oriented. But also no wish for the redemption of the world (which sometimes in archetypal psychology is in truly Manichean manner viewed as a "fallen world") because the alchemical one is not a salvation and Manichean project, despite the fact that its outlook is "cosmic" in the sense of being concerned with the concrete material world rather than with the individual (person). Its intentions are more modest.

(1) While any kind of program, any longing for something else or new is psychologically a reaching out for the future and thereby stays horizontally on the same old level of consciousness, psychology can be said to turn its back to the open future and its wished-for possibilities. It stays put and wholeheartedly concentrates on and single-mindedly attends to what *is already there*, immediately before it in the retort. In this sense psychology is logically situating itself in the perfect tense. It is, in a way, a looking backwards. What is in the retort is always something that is already an accomplished fact, has already happened. Psychology, psychotherapy have no interest in future potentialities and alternatives to the present. They are committed to the real and the real's own inherent necessity (*Ananke*).

It can and must feel this way because what is in the retort, no matter how corrupt, stinking, perverse it may appear, is for it from the outset defined as being "perfect" in itself, inasmuch as it contains everything it needs *within itself*, even its fulfillment. It does not need any "other" from outside, any correction, any improvement. But what it does need is to be cooked, incubated, absolute-negatively interiorized into itself. It needs its own *vertical* deepening into its truth, its going under or dying into its Concept. "Redemption" or "salvation," *if* one wants to use these terms at all here, would here only mean that the phenomenon in the retort finds its fulfillment and freedom through being *released* into its essence—a transformation which the alchemists expressed in the image of the freeing of Mercurius from his imprisonment in matter, i.e., in the material, natural, imaginal *form* of the phenomenon. We could say then that the ultimate goal is that the "mercurial spirit" which had been hidden in and subdued by the material form of the phenomenon finally comes out into the open and takes charge of the phenomenon.

(2) Psychology's commitment is to eachness: to *this* problem, symptom, situation, this dream, image, text, phenomenon at hand and only this. In this present Now this one phenomenon at hand is in the retort, and inasmuch as I am a psychologist, I therefore have my back turned to everything else around me and to the retort. This is my methodological stance. As therapist I forget everything else; nothing else exists for me—for the time of my occupation with the present matter in the vessel. Through this absolute closure of the vessel or, the other way around, through this absolute exclusion of what is not in the vessel, this one seemingly insignificant matter in this one small alchemical *vas* is now all that exists for me. It becomes, it *is* the whole world. Jung said about the *vas Hermeticum* of alchemy that "it was 'hermetically' sealed (i.e., sealed with the sign of Hermes); it had to be made of glass, and had also to be as round as possible, since it was meant to represent the universe [*Weltall*, the All] ..." (*CW* 13 § 245, modif.). But the point is that we must not think that it "represents" the universe. No, it has become, and now *is*, the universe, the All, through the radical methodological closure and exclusion. There is really nothing outside it, including the literal universe. The *vas* and its content is all there is now.

If we had not also completely forgotten about the literal universe around us, the retort would not be a retort, not be hermetically sealed, because then we would still hold on to something outside of it. The retort *is* only the *vas Hermeticum* if it ceases to be an object in the world and instead in itself becomes the whole and exclusive world for us. The seal does not only have the function of keeping the spirit Mercurius imprisoned *in* the bottle; it also, and perhaps more importantly, has to keep everything else, including the notion of the world around it, *out*. The hermetic sealing of the vessel is the imaginal or symbolic representation of the logical interiorization into the vessel not of the literal world, but of the *notion* of world. This is indispensable. For if the *vas* has not from the outset been absolute-negatively interiorized into itself so that it has the notion of outside totally inside and the very notion of exteriority is altogether gone, how could we hope to interiorize into itself the prime matter contained in it?

Since the whole purpose of the psychological work is the "redemption" of each matter that happens to have been taken up, in the sense of releasing it into its truth or concept, and since in each case the matter is hermetically sealed into itself so that it turns, for the time being, into the whole world with nothing around it, we could call the purpose indeed "the rescue of the world." But we immediately see that this notion does not have the grandiose sense that we otherwise connect with it. The sense of world has completely changed. It is intrinsically connected with "eachness." Instead of its spatial sense, the external sense of infinite *extent* and sum-total of the infinite *manifold* of things, it is now the internal wholeness, inner infinity and totality of each individual phenomenon *provided that* it is apperceived in the spirit of the hermetic closure described. 'World" here therefore refers to the *self nature* of the phenomena.

Inasmuch as "world," "wholeness," "self" no longer refer, on the semantic level, to particular entities, contents, or states, but now mean the logical, syntactical character of each individual phenomenon that has been hermetically sealed within itself, all the objections that many Jungians raised, often rightly raised, against Jung's notions of the self and of wholeness no longer apply. Now these notions are no longer the literal mega-notions loaded with "numinous" meaning that they used to be. They have been absolute-negatively interiorized into themselves, distilled, evaporated. One also no longer has to literally play the world out there, "the city," the cosmos against the consulting room. Each phenomenon is its own cosmos, and the literal cosmos and literal "city" as external reality is not a topic of psychology.

One sees that I myself insist, here concurring fully with Jung, that the bottle with the spirit Mercurius needs to be hermetically closed, and stay closed. If the evasive spirit were to escape, if *ille fugax Mercurius*, the *servus fugitivus*, would go off from the phenomenon at hand to other alternatives, to new possibilities on the same horizontal semantic level, or, again on the semantic level, wander from one idea to the next, as in the manner of free association, or, with Lacan, "metonymically" glide from word to word (*mot à mot*), the whole opus of the vertical interiorization of the matter into its own truth through its syntactical, logical transformation would fail.

* * *

And yet I cannot agree with Jung's rejection of the behavior of the boy of our fairy tale who set the spirit free. Here I seem to be guilty of a contradiction on my part. How can I insist on the absolute closure of the vessel and at the same time approve of the spirit's being let out? The answer is that precisely this is, I think, the challenge of our tale as well as of the notion of alchemical and psychological closure, a challenge that Jung did not master.

Jung's mistake is that he "fell for" the imaginal-pictorial mode of presentation and took it literally. The problem of a narrative is that it has to portray as a sequence of events (on the semantic level) what is actually the logical-syntactical unfolding of the internal dialectic of one concept. On the level of behavior the hermetic enclosure of the spirit in the bottle and the breaking of the seal in order to release him absolutely exclude each other. On that level we have to chose, either – or. Because Jung stayed on this level, his choosing "closure" and rejecting the "opening" of the bottle is plausible, consistent, one of the two possible choices.

But the problem is that a reading of the story on the semantic or behavioral level is psychologically inadequate. And this inadequacy of his interpretation is due to his prior and general failure to really *think through* the alchemical notion of the hermetic closure of the vessel. His was a literal, external, dogmatic understanding of closure, closure in the sense of commonplace practical reality and everyday life, where as a matter of course formal-logical consistency and unambiguity of the terms used is required. But "closure" in this fairy tale and in alchemy and psychology is *a priori* a *hermetic, mercurial* closure that requires a dialectical understanding. It is not the simple self-identical fact which Jung took it for. The notion of closure *itself partakes* of the living mercurial spirit of alchemy enclosed by means of it. You cannot approach a story about the spirit Mercurius imprisoned in a hermetically sealed bottle with a positivistic sense of closure. With a positivistic bottle, stopper and seal, the spirit Mercurius could not be contained in the first place. He would laugh at any such incommensurable attempt, or rather, he would not even exist for this mentality. Jung's mistake is that he comes to a hermetic notion with a positivistic conception of this notion. The logic of his style of thinking does not match the semantics that it is applied to.

"Closure" needs to be interiorized into itself, to be applied to itself. And then it will, within itself, *open* itself to release its own truth, or rather the truth that it encloses. Within itself: this means that what narratively appears in our tale as a consecutive (new, other) event on the same level with the prior fact, the closure, is to be taken as an internal moment of this (one and the same) prior fact. Our story explains what "hermetic closure" is actually about, what it involves if it is truly comprehended in its depth and ultimate truth and not merely viewed from an outside literal perspective (external reflection).

Instead of being the undoing of the closure (or a revoking of the "don't let anything from outside, that does not belong, get into it"), letting the spirit out is in the fairy tale the closure's own internal completion, conclusion, fulfillment. How is this to be understood?

If through the closure the *vas* with its content has to become the All for the alchemist, he cannot just have the vessel opposite to himself as a small object. As an object for a subject (the adept) this object would necessarily be a thing *within* the world, in other words, it would have the real world *around* itself, not itself *be* the whole world. For Jung the hermetic vessel was accordingly only *meant to represent* the universe: that is, it was only a symbol *of* the universe, it was looked upon *as if* it *were* the world. But of course, as such it was not *really* the universe for the alchemist. As long as the alchemical *vas* is merely supposed to represent the All, the hermetic closure is still fundamentally incomplete. It has not gone all the way. This is only the first half of the real closure. It is only the literal, positive-factual sense of closure.

The self-application of the notion of closure to itself requires a second step, namely that what is hermetically enclosed is not only the matter or content in the vessel, but also this enclosing vessel itself, not only the *omnitudo realitatis*, but also the whole *sense* of "closure" itself, the very *notion* of "world," of "around" (around the vessel) or "surroundings." The closure has to be absolute so as to include and enclose *itself*, its own concept. Only then does it include everything without reserve and can it be said to no longer merely be meant to symbolically represent the universe in the sense of an as-if, but really be it.

But this closure that has relentlessly integrated every notion of "outside" or "around itself" into itself is *ipso facto* tantamount to the freeing of the imprisoned spirit Mercurius. Pictorially speaking, the surrounding of the bottle is now inside the bottle, which means that the bottle has become infinite, comprising even the adept, who now is also enclosed within it and has the bottle all around himself. He thus can no longer be the dispassionate observer of what goes on. And inasmuch as the bottle has truly become the all-surrounding world even around him, and inasmuch as he is hermetically enclosed inside the same world that the Mercurius, too, is imprisoned in, he now has the spirit all around himself and that spirit is now free to roam throughout the entire universe.

Our fairy tale tries to present the *whole* dialectic of the idea of the absolutely closed, hermetically sealed vessel. Because it has to do this in a narrative and pictorial form, it cannot fully do justice to what it actually wants to demonstrate. But thought "helpeth the infirmities" of the pictorial representation. What we have to realize is that the second time around the young man no longer lets the spirit escape in the literal, positive-factual sense, but now sets him free from the bottle only within the bottle, which alchemically speaking meanwhile has turned into the fulfilled notion of the All. The freeing of Mercurius from the bottle does not undo the closure but surpasses it, by going through with it all the way. It is its, the closure's, own having become absolute.

It is obvious that Mercurius can only be freed from his imprisonment in the bottle *within* his absolute imprisonment. The absoluteness of his imprisonment in fact is the precondition for there really being a Mercurius at all. If there is no absolute closure, there may be "bottles," but no bottle will contain the spirit, regardless of whether imprisoned or free. Only within the hermetically, i.e., absolutely, sealed bottle can Mercurius be released, and only through his being released does he begin to exist in the first place. Such is the "crazy" logic of the soul. There is not first a Mercurius as a positive-factual entity or being who is then imprisoned and after that (maybe) finally released. Without the absolute closure, there is only positive-factual reality. You have to pay the full price. There is no other way.

It is naïve to imagine that by locking the soul and the Mercurius *positivistically* into the two vessels of psychology (the spatial imagination of the "within" of the person as well as the logical status of "the unconscious") what is inside these two vessels would still be the Mercurius and the soul. With that kind of locking, the soul and Mercurius always have already escaped prior to your locking, and what then will be inside the vessels is at best their semblance, their semanticized as-if replicas. You cannot get away with the half-hearted, positivistic sense of closure. Psychology has to have gone all the way to the end in order to be able to begin.

Our fairy tale is thus not really a story about a series of consecutive events. It is the logical explication of one single notion, the notion of the truly hermetically sealed bottle. Closure and release are the same.

Jung *had to* evaluate the behavior of the young man in this tale as alchemically incorrect and forbidden, although the tale itself with its happy end indicated the opposite. He had to construe "closure" and "setting free" as undialectical opposites, as (literalistic, positivistic) alternatives and to chose closure and with some passion reject the setting free. With his *ad hoc* comments about this fairy tale and his clear vote "for not letting Mercurius escape, but for his staying inside," Jung at the same time unwittingly revealed the unconscious deepest impulse and principle of his own psychological thought. It is the literalistic closure to which "the unconscious" ("our own"!) and "the psychic background *in us*" owe their existence. He needed the literal closure because the one thing that he really feared was the release of Mercurius, from out of his containment in personalistic experiences and in the status of positive fact (the status of the irrevocably *ignotum*) into the logical freedom of the sphere of truth and mind, which would have involved psychology in "metaphysics" and in the obligation of having to *intellectually* take a stand concerning the content of what was experienced. Outside, all around the psyche, a positivistic frame of mind. Inside numinous, archetypal contents.

So Jung's psychology was a psychology of the *bottled* spirit, in the commonplace sense of bottled—not in the sense of absolute hermetic closure. Other than Freud, he *wanted* the spirit, but the mercurial spirit[5] only safely bottled, as spirit prevented from being spirit, and so he trickily substituted our subjective "*experiences* from the unconscious" for what actually should be the official mind's mercurial *truths*. The problem, however, was not, as the reader will understand after what has been shown, the "bottle" and the "bottling" as such, but that the bottle was externally imagined as a positivistic bottle which had psychology as its dispassionate, neutral observer outside of itself. And the problem was further that Jung believed and pretended that the personalistic phenomena prioritized and observed by it (the subjective numinous experiences, dreams, etc.) nevertheless had a mercurial, soul, even religious, significance simply as empirical facts.

No, the "bottle" is not the problem. On the contrary. Psychology can only *be* if it is inside the bottle. If it, psychology itself, is *in* the bottle, the latter is *ipso facto* the bottle whose "enclosing vessel" character has truly been interiorized into itself, too, so that it has nothing outside of itself and therefore has become absolute. And only then can the spirit Mercurius be *freed* spirit. And only the *a priori* freed spirit is the spirit that can be found imprisoned in a bottle in the first place. Psychology needs a sense of *mercurial, absolute* closure to find this bottle. Only like can find like.

* * *

Looking back at the steps of the movement of our thought concerning the topic of closure and setting free we can say that the first step was a methodological decision for an uncompromising closure. As a methodological decision it is an ego move. By insisting on staying with this closure, Jung did not only try to freeze the movement as such, but also, while semantically (content-wise) being open to the mercurial mysteries, syntactically held on to "the ego." His closure is an ego behavior that is inflicted on Mercurius from outside. With the second step, Mercurius is let loose to be all around us and permeate "the world" (whatever "world" happens to be at stake at each present), thereby establishing the logical position of interiority. As I pointed out, this step does not amount to an undoing of the closure. Rather, the ego now gives up its initial idea of having to be in charge of this closure and instead commits, entrusts, the responsibility of closure to the spirit himself as his self-enclosure. The freed Mercurius is he who does no longer have to be enclosed in and restrained by an external vessel because he has come home to himself and is enclosed in himself: in his *concept*, his truth. Only now is he true spirit. What would a Mercurius be who needs to be restrained from outside? This his enclosure in his truth is his freedom, the fulfillment of his essence. This is why he can freely roam through the whole world without becoming dangerous: he will from now on always stay contained in what he truly is.

Here I stop. But it is clear that the movement itself has not come to a full stop, because something has been left behind: the ego with whose methodological closure the movement started. It, too, wants to be released into its truth and freedom. This is why there has to be another step beyond closure and setting free, the step we could call "emancipation." But this is another story for another time.

NOTES

1. Pp. 200 ff. E.g., "Grounded in the natural philosophy of the Middle Ages, alchemy formed the bridge on the one hand into the past, to Gnosticism, and on the other into the future, to the modern psychology of the unconscious" (p. 201). On the *aurea catena* see *ibid.*, p. 189.

2. Legend has it that Thomas dictated this work on his deathbed (and thus did not produce it in an alchemical laboratory).

3. 'Positive' in the logical sense (the sense that underlies the term positivism).

4. See H. Maspero, "Les procédés does 'nourrir le principe vital' dans la religion taoïste ancienne," in *Journal Asiatique* (1937) pp. 177–252, 353–430, here p. 385. Cited in Mircea Eliade, *Geschichte der religiösen Ideen*, vol. 2, Freiburg et al. (Herder) 1979, p. 361.

5. 'Spirit' must here never be confused with 'spirit' in the New Age sense of "spirituality," "spiritual movements and practices." It is not the spirit to be sought on the "peaks" in contrast to the anima's "vales" (Hillman), but the mercurial spirit in, the internal logic of, each matter, each real situation, phenomenon, symptom.

Psychoid, Psychophysical, P-subtle! Alchemy and a New Worldview

VERONICA GOODCHILD

But the moment when physics touches on the 'untrodden, untreadable regions,' and when psychology has at the same time to admit that there are other forms of psychic life besides the acquisitions of personal consciousness...then the intermediate realm of subtle bodies comes to life again, and the physical and the psychic are once more blended in an indissoluble unity....We have come very near to this turning point today.
— C. G. Jung, *Psychology and Alchemy*, *Collected Works,* 12 § 394

[The Persian Sufi mystic] Suhrawardi's otherworld was not an invisible aspect of the world we know....was also not a spatial extension of this world....It was not an upper world, high in the sky, as is heaven....Suhrawardi's other world was a different dimension or order of existence, whose mystery defied logical description and explanation. It was spatially both within a person's earthbound body and a distinct region of the cosmos. It was not simply upper, or nether, or invisible. It was distinctly other. — D. Merkur, *Gnosis,* p. 224

All changes of spiritual consciousness depend upon the heart.
— R. Wilhelm, *The Secret of the Golden Flower,* p. 23

Veronica Goodchild, Ph.D., is a core faculty member in the Clinical Psychology Program at Pacifica Graduate Institute where she teaches courses in Jungian Psychotherapy, Alchemy, and Imaginal Perspectives in Research. She is the author of *Eros and Chaos: The Sacred Mysteries and Dark Shadows of Love.* Her forthcoming book, *The Songlines of the Soul,* elaborates many of the themes in this article, and puts forward a new worldview based on acausality, *creatio continua,* and the recovery of the subtle body world.

Alchemy and the Subtle Body

Initiated into the study of alchemy through a dream, Jung claimed that it had a central significance as the cultural, historical link backward to Gnosticism and forwards to his own psychology of the unconscious. Psychologically, alchemy could be seen as the projection of the unconscious onto matter, and its images and texts usefully studied to help elucidate the transformative difficulties encountered in the individuation process. Von Franz emphasized how the myth of alchemy was important, in part, because it balanced the prevailing Christian myth by including the shadow, the body, and the feminine, areas of life denied and relegated to the margins by the orthodox religious view. The integrity of these perspectives, clinically involving the withdrawal of projections and the ethical embodiment of new knowledge, can be upheld and my wish is not to challenge them. Jung describes these two stages of the incarnation of the Self as the first and second *coniunctios* respectively, and these stages must be honored, particularly the differentiation of the shadow, which is an ongoing ethical endeavor throughout life.

A less developed view of alchemy, nevertheless alluded to by Jung and von Franz in their alchemy studies, and by von Franz more particularly in her book, *On Dreams and Death*, was that it returns to us the psychic realm of subtle bodies and the unity of the psychophysical background world of the *unus mundus*. This view is important not only theoretically and for understanding psychological processes, but also experientially, as an appreciation for the nature of the subtle body often involves intense levels of experience of a psycho*physical* nature, and has implications not only for embodiment processes but also for direct experiences of another world in this one that are marked by profound levels of feeling and often bring about deep transformation and transmutation. This is perhaps more closely allied to what Jung refers to as the third *coniunctio*, union with the *unus mundus*.

Today, many of the accounts of extraordinary or paranormal experiences that have been well researched in recent decades since Jung's death seem to suggest the irruption of this subtle body world and its psychophysical intensity again in our times. A renewed interest in events such as near death experiences (NDEs), contact with "unidentified flying objects" (UFOs) or so-called extraterrestrial (ET) encounters, the recovery of shamanic techniques in analytical psychology, altered-states or non-ordinary consciousness research, crop circles and their hieroglyphic communications (sometimes using alchemical imagery), the Marian visions, which have increased significantly since the 1940s and particularly since the *Assumptio* in 1950 (along with our interest in UFOs), and all kinds of unpredictable anomalous events that nevertheless are reported by thousands of people all over the world, point in the direction of a reality which can no longer be regarded only as metaphorical and symbolic but rather, as the 12th century Persian Gnostic Ibn al-Arabi acknowledges following his mentor Suhrawardi, a reality that is "both symbolic and nonsymbolic simultaneously."[1] The suggestion here is that metaphor conceals a true event, and this is precisely what Jung's colleague, Henri Corbin, writes of the *mundus imaginalis* and its ontological reality.

In his alchemy studies, and additionally in his observations of the complex dynamics of synchronicity and its collective expression in the "flying saucer" phenomenon, Jung invites us into a late development in his creative work, which paradoxically can be viewed as an updating of features already present in the alchemical mysteries, yet now asserting themselves in contemporary forms. However, the full implication of what Jung begins to hint at, and even describes in the title of his "Flying Saucers" essay as "a new myth," has yet to be explored. My hope is to contribute some reflections to this inquiry. In so doing, I wish to be very careful about any claims about what the above anomalous experiences 'really are.' At this point, I stay with Jung and his comment that "*something is seen*,"[2] but we cannot know precisely what this is. Nevertheless, we can take the phenomena seriously and be guided by what credible individuals actually report of their experiences.

My own view is that the "something" possibly relates to the symptoms, signs, and sparks of a new worldview beginning to constellate as archetypal dominants shift as we move from one Platonic month to another—Pisces to Aquarius—the *psychological* ramifications of which Jung exhorts those in the healing professions to consider. According to both quantum physics and synchronicity, the new coordinates of reality (in addition to our achievements in rational consciousness) include the reunion of psyche and matter as a One world, the erosion of ordinary time and space, the participation of the individual in creating reality, the movement toward the *kairos* or 'right or propitious moment,' the notion of *creatio continua*, continuing creation, that arises out of a reciprocal, ongoing relationship between the individual and the *unus mundus,* or (in Bohm's term) implicate order, and the breakthrough of Eros awareness to a sense of oneness that does not sacrifice differentiation and distinctness.

All these features were characteristic of the sacred art of alchemy whose initiates, experimenting with meditation and the forces of *imaginatio vera*, 'true imagination,' also eroded the barriers between the seen and unseen worlds to arrive at the mysteries of the unitary background world, a third domain comprised of a subtle psychophysical reality and its inhabitants. The path to this gnosis was through the ancient, precarious, and unavoidable initiatory processes of death and rebirth. Today, we are again called to this difficult work, for like the sparks fallen into matter in alchemical imagery, these symptoms need our own creative imagination and discernment to participate in helping to make their treasures more conscious.

Quantum physicists and cosmologists have been less bashful than depth psychologists in attempting to describe a new reality, but these new visions can benefit deeply from the insights of analytical psychology, which holds to the "reality of the psyche" as an *a priori* reality, and to realms of consciousness beyond the personal, even, as Jung suggests in *Mysterium Coniunctionis*, beyond the transpersonal to a transpsychic realm that feels "outside the body," even "alien,"[3] yet nevertheless imprints us with its profound levels of mystery, depth, and silence that subjectively have deep implications for the stranger that we are, and usually have untold consequences of a fateful and vocational nature. Too, in accordance with one of the features of the Aquarian age, typically, 'extraordinary,' and 'non-ordinary' experiences link individuals to the cosmos, to time as deep time, to knowledge from the Source (Jung calls this "absolute knowledge" or "foreknowledge" in his synchronicity essay), and to the macrocosm and its inhabitants. Alchemists, mystics, and shamans of all time cross-culturally have suggested we are a part of this broader cosmic field. Here, our individual and local lives are restored to their proper place, beyond history to those sacred realms and Invisible Ones from which we have been too long estranged. Then, in accordance with the *aurea catina,* or golden chain tradition, of which mystic alchemy was a part, we are required to bring back the stories and share them with our community, to try to sort out how we are being addressed, and to try to give voice to that part of the collective problem of our time that has been given to us to struggle with.

Jung's References to the Subtle Body

Jung wrote of the individuation process, especially through the metaphors of alchemy, as an initiatory ordeal of descent and renewal. However, the relationship of this ordeal to the creation and establishment of the subtle body as the *telos* of the opus is a less commonly acknowledged aspect of this transformation process. In my view, this is an unfortunate omission and leads to continued misunderstandings, most notably in the preservation of the split between body and psyche, which the creation of the subtle body aims in part to overcome. While the various operations in alchemy aim at spiritual transformation (psychological change from insight), the deepening effect of these operations, over time, through the alchemical mixture of making spirit matter and matter (complexes and their affective charge in the body) psyche, is the creation of a third body, a subtle body made of spirit *and* matter that is symbolized by various images such as the *filius*, the divine or golden child, the philosophers' stone, the elixir, the golden germ, and so on.

The linking of individuation to the development of the subtle body is recalled by Jung explicitly when he received in the post from Richard Wilhelm the translation of a Taoist alchemical text called *The Secret of the Golden Flower*. Jung relates how between 1918-1919 at the end of WWI he had been reflecting on *mandala* symbolism and its relationship with the transformative path to the center or Self, and had just painted a picture with a golden castle in the center, which struck him as having a Chinese quality. Soon afterwards, he received the manuscript from Wilhelm. Not only was this a momentous synchronicity that confirmed many of his own ideas, but also in honor of the event, he wrote under his picture what had happened, noting how the image of the yellow castle—(in the Taoist text there is mention of the *Book of the Yellow Castle* and the 'golden flower' is the elixir of life)—represents "'the germ of the immortal body.'"[4]

Further, in his volume *Psychology and Alchemy* (*CW* 12), Jung indicates that the sacred art can be understood not just in contemporary scientific psychological terms of the projection of the collective unconscious onto or into matter, but can also be appreciated as taking place in the in-between realm of subtle bodies. In fact, alchemy is full of images of a subtle body nature, and we need mention only the "philosophers' stone" to glimpse a paradoxical reality that is made up of both psyche and matter, yet curiously transcends either the one or the other. Other terms, such as the "resurrection body," the "elixir", or the "*aqua vitae*"—also sometimes associated with the philosophers' stone—as psychophysical images of the goal of the work that can bring health and healing to the adept, are mentioned by Jung in his alchemy texts and his work on the psychology of the transference.[5] Too, alchemical terms such as the *lumen naturae* as well as the *unus mundus*, terms that Jung wishes to bring back into contemporary usage, also guide us in this direction of a subtle reality.

Jung, in the *Nietzsche Seminars* delivered between 1934 and 1939, writes specifically on the nature of the subtle body—a body formed out of suffering intense affect and emotions that burn up superfluities, according to the alchemists—as a kind of invisible somatic unconscious. This 'incorruptible' body as St. Paul describes it (as opposed to *sarx* or our biological flesh) is difficult for the mind to grasp as it is a transcendent concept outside of time and space. Yet our psychological knowledge, both conscious and unconscious, is embedded in our bodies so that, as Jung explores later with the nature of synchronicity and the tantalizing appearance of UFOs that also seem both psychic and concretely real and which led to his reformulation of the archetype as psychoid, we cannot know precisely where matter becomes psyche and psyche becomes matter. The new physics was also faced with these difficulties, yet the concept of nonlocality—which also points beyond time and space—has now been included in our vocabulary.

Individuation as the creation of this subtle body, variously called the "resurrection body," "immortal body," or "diamond body," here in this life, was a subtle body thought to survive physical death, and it would be the body—a kind of psychic body that nevertheless had 'substance' and contained your essence, or quintessence, also imagined as the *rotundum,* suggesting roundness and completion—that you would take with you when you sloughed off your earthly form. The notion of the subtle body is perhaps more familiar to us from Eastern religions, but there are mystic and metaphysical traditions in the West in addition to alchemy that preserve this reality for us. These would include the Platonic and Pythagorean schools, which reach back to Orphism, as well as Neo-platonic thinkers such as Proclus and Plotinus. G. R. S. Mead has written on the history of the subtle body in Western civilization, and in this work clarifies the distinctions between the spirit-body, the radiant body, and the resurrection body, which is particularly familiar in alchemy and the mystical traditions.[6] He stresses, however, that the notion of our physical forms being the expression of an invisible subtle essence is an extremely ancient belief, eclipsed only by the materialist and rationalist prejudices of our times which, even as he writes in 1919 with words that echo Jung's, are beginning to erode as science and psychology begin to penetrate more deeply into the invisible mysteries of matter and mind.

A more recent exploration of this in-between realm that is neither precisely waking nor dreaming can be seen in Peter Kingsley's original translations of ancient Greek texts in which he recovers for us the spiritual tradition that lies at the origins of western civilization. He writes of the pre-Socratic philosophers' dream incubation techniques that refer undeniably to journeys to another reality while keeping quiet and still, and their bringing knowledge back from a real but subtle world. The dream and meditative practices of these philosophers (in the original sense of "lovers of wisdom" — not the rational thinkers of the last few hundred years—) contributed to building the immortal body created by being true to your deepest reality, a journey described by Kingsley as "dying before you die,"[7] comparable to the dark night of the soul in mysticism, the *nigredo* or *solutio* in alchemy, and the descent into the shadow in the individuation process, which usually precede the deeper levels of access to the guides of the soul and their wisdom. Interestingly, recent research on UFO/ET encounters also indicates that abduction and traumatic experiences can precede erotically spiritual encounters, as if the template of the initiation mysteries is behind some of these unusual claims.

In addition to Jung's alchemy studies, his colleague Henri Corbin's research on the science of imagination among the 12th century Sufi Gnostics also recovers the subtle body world as an ontological reality.[8] This other world, or "lost continent," is an intermediate and intermediary world between spirit and matter, a third area that was of such importance to the alchemists. Corbin speaks of the psycho-spiritual landscapes of true imagination (amongst many other names) as the Eighth Climate, the *mundus archetypus* or *imaginalis*, and Na-Koja-Abad, "the country of non-where." In Sufi mysticism (as well as in other spiritual traditions), these landscapes are well documented and have particular names, for example, Hurqalya in Sufi Gnosticism, Shambhala in Tibetan lore, Avalon in stories of the Grail, and Olmo Lungring in Bon Buddhism. It is important to stress that these domains are not considered utopias, which is an abstract notion, a fictive fantasy not belonging to any place, but rather landscapes "between waking and sleeping" in which the sojourner has penetrated so far into the interior that she or he finds themselves in a new external, but not ordinary, outside. Here the spiritual state defines the *topos*, so one is no longer any*where*; rather, the *where*, usually related to sensory space, is an *everywhere,* the non-local topography of the mystical or emerald cities of the soul, a world as ontologically real as the world of the senses and intellect, a world accessed by true *imaginatio,* as in alchemy, in order to distinguish it from the self-aggrandizing fantasies of the ego. I draw attention to these facts because many of those experiencing anomalous encounters also struggle to describe a world that is neither dreaming nor waking and which seems "really real."

This true imagination, which Jung considered "the most important key to the understanding of the opus,"[9] is a spiritual creative force often connected with the feminine figure of Sophia, or Fatima in Persian mysticism, and it is also a subtle organ of visions and new creations. The use of *imaginatio*, together with the *meditatio*, which were conversations that took place with an invisible guide or 'good angel,' were the two faculties needed in the alchemical *processus* for the establishment of the subtle body. Jung of course updated the *meditatio* in his technique of active imagination, which remains one of the major contributions of analytical psychology to the therapy process. These two faculties are also required in taking synchronicities seriously, and they seem to be activated in paranormal events also. We will return to this below.

Jung's Experiences of the Subtle Body World

In a passage in *Mysterium Coniunctionis*, Jung writes of the possibility of an intense non-ordinary state:

> It may well be a prejudice to restrict the psyche to being 'inside the body.' Insofar as the psyche has a non-spatial aspect, there may be a psychic 'outside-the-body,' a region so utterly different from 'my' psychic space that one has to get outside oneself or make use of some auxiliary technique in order to get there.[10]

Jung records many of his dreams, visions, active imaginations, and encounters as direct experiences of another world in this one (or, alternatively, similar to Suhrawardi's claims, as a journey to another realm while remaining here), and he describes the reality of the psyche as an autonomous other world that is not created by us. Visionaries, shamans, mystics, and alchemists from east and west throughout history have always known these altered states of awareness too.

Of the many examples from Jung's own biographical accounts, from his terrible war visions to his peripatetic conversations with Philemon, his "ghostly guru," there are two particularly striking examples of an experience of this "crossing over" to another reality and its effects on consciousness. One is an account of Jung's second visit to Ravenna in 1933, and the second is his alchemical vision of Christ a few years later. I will summarize the features of these experiences that pertain to Jung's direct experience of the subtle realm and its effects.

Jung's Ravenna Vision

In Ravenna, Jung mentions falling into a strange mood once again at the tomb of Galla Placidia. Even during his first visit (in 1913) the place had a compelling aura for him. On this second visit, Jung and his traveling companion, Toni Wolff, move on to the Baptistery, which Jung describes as being filled with a strange blue light whose source is not visible.[25] There they come across four extraordinarily beautiful mosaic frescoes that Jung had forgotten about from his first visit. The frescoes depict various water scenes from the Bible, the most notable one being Christ holding out his hand to Peter who was sinking beneath the waves. Jung notes that a fairly lengthy discussion then ensues about the original meaning of Baptism as a treacherous death and rebirth ritual. He remembers, too, with great clarity the details of the mosaics, but is unable to find photographs of them afterwards. Later in Zürich he asks an acquaintance who is going to Ravenna to pick up the photos for him, but the colleague is unable to oblige as the mosaics *did not exist*. By this time, Jung had already lectured on baptism and the Ravenna frescoes, and Toni Wolff also remained equally convinced of their reality.

Jung comments that this story was among the most curious in his life. Acknowledging the cultural level of archetypal experience, he suggests that a strong identification with the highly cultivated Galla Placidia (d. 450) as an anima figure may have been responsible for this event, mentioning that the anima has a strongly historical character. Galla herself had survived a stormy boat crossing from Byzantium to Ravenna and had fulfilled a vow to build the Baptistery and mosaics if she survived her dangerous journey. The mosaics were destroyed in a fire in the Middle Ages, but a sketch of Galla in a boat remains in the Ambrosiana in Milan.

Jung continues that he, too, had suffered a near drowning in the waters of the unconscious, but his ability to integrate and realize their contents adequately saved him from this fate. His baptism in the waters of the psyche was an example of an initiatory process, a submersion in a perilous underworld journey that linked him with all *mystes* or initiates of the death and rebirth mysteries. The sinking Peter with outstretched hand to the Christ—the one fresco that had particularly drawn Jung's attention—could be a quintessential image of his psychology of the unconscious. It was, then, the constellation of the archetype of Initiation that lent a numinous quality to his visit. All very good 'Jungian' observations!

But these interpretations, correct as they may be (or not), do not account for the peculiar nature of the *experience itself* that Jung and his friend knew for certain they had gone through. He writes:

> Since my experience in the baptistery in Ravenna, I know with certainty that something interior can appear to be exterior, and that something exterior can appear to be interior. The actual walls of the baptistery, though they must have been seen by my physical eyes, were covered over by a vision of some altogether different sight which was *as completely real as* the unchanged baptismal font [emphasis mine].[11]

Here Jung impresses upon us the 'objective' reality of the visionary realm as another world as equally real as the empirical world of the senses. Yet he also describes the event as "deeply stirring." Other characteristics include the "incredible beauty" of the four mosaic frescoes that had replaced the windows he remembered from his first visit. He could not believe his memory had been so unreliable. And then there was the lovely quality of the light—the blue light that had no source, yet about which he did not question at all.

Jung comments on the vision as a "new creation by the unconscious,"[12] occasioned by unknown factors pertaining perhaps to previous integrations of unconscious material, but in the end relating to deeply felt sensibilities about oneself and to the mystery of one's nature. He goes on to say that such an event is completely unexplainable in rational terms, and adds, sadly, because of its astounding subjective importance, "finds no place in the official view of the world."[13] In spite of its extraordinary significance, the mystical event and its repercussions have no home in our culture anymore.

What Jung describes here is very similar to two features of Corbin's account of a journey to the *mundus imaginalis*: there is a break or discontinuity with ordinary space and time, and at the same time, though the beholder of this realm returns, and he or she *knows* they have been elsewhere, it is impossible to describe the way to anyone else. It is also often impossible to describe the journey itself. Even with synchronicities, people often do not speak of them because they fear being misunderstood. In addition, descriptions of the *mundus imaginalis*, or disclosures of the mystical cities, often include intense feelings of beauty that stir the imagination toward a deep pathos and an opening of the heart.

This sense of penetration through a veil to another reality—or alternatively, the irruption of another world into ours—while remaining grounded in this world is pictured well by the image reproduced in Jung's "Flying Saucers" essay, a woodcut captioned "The Spiritual Pilgrim Discovering Another World."[14] In this picture, the pilgrim, circumscribed by the arc of a circle representing this world, leaves ordinary space-time behind and gazes through the *fenestra aeternitatis* into the timeless eternal world. In the other world, the double wheels of Ezekiel's vision are present, suggesting that visionary events, or events in the *mundus imaginalis*, are an experience of the synchronistic union of the eternal and the temporal, the timeless with the time-bound, the meeting point at the mystical center where psyche and matter are one. Temporarily, the *unus mundus* breaks through, and the pilgrim feels close to a miracle, while her heart opens in awe to the full intensity of divine Presence. Afterwards, the 'window' closes, and the flow of events resume their ordinary patterning.

Such a description is very close to some reports of synchronicities, UFO encounters, and similar events to which I shall return.

Jung's Alchemical Vision of Christ

The second visionary experience of Jung's that I wish to recall occurred in 1939 while he was working on the studies for *Psychology and Alchemy*. At the time of the vision, he was also giving a seminar on the *Spiritual Exercises* of Ignatius Loyola, and was preoccupied with the *Anima Christi*, one of the meditations of the *Spiritual Exercises*. He writes: "One night I awoke and saw, bathed in bright light at the foot of my bed, the figure of Christ on the Cross … and I saw that his body was made of greenish gold." He adds that though experiencing visions was not unusual for him, this one (using words similar to those he used to describe his Ravenna vision) was "marvelously beautiful," and he was "profoundly shaken by it."[15] It was, as he notes, essentially an alchemical vision of Christ.

Jung had already made links between the psychological figure of Christ and the central symbol of the alchemists, the *lapis*, or stone. Here, the "green gold" referred to "the analogy of Christ with the *aurum non vulgi* ["not the common gold"] and the *viriditas*," the greenness of manifested life, of the alchemists. Hildegard of Bingen also uses the term *viriditas* to express the manifestation of cosmic energies in the created world and in the individual human soul. Jung understood this image, then, as referring to the divine spirit poured out in all of nature and the cosmos, as well as in us. His vision pointed to the necessity for the recovery of the *anima mundi*—also called the Anthropos or *filius macrocosmi* in alchemy—the animating principle of the *unus mundus*, the subtle world behind this world (expounded by Paracelsus' pupil, the mediaeval philosopher and alchemist Dorn), radiating as a life force throughout the whole of creation.

In his vision of the green gold Christ, Jung in effect recovered an alchemical gnosis for our times in the image of Christ as a mystical union of "spiritually alive and physically dead matter."[16] The history of Christianity recalled a story of the gradual separation of the spiritual from its home within the body, and the extrapolation of impersonal ideals at the expense of valuing the instinctual life, the wisdom of the creative feminine, and living in close harmony with one's feelings and the natural world. Matter and spirit were increasingly split off from each other. Indeed, the developing power of ego consciousness as an autonomous force of will separated from its instinctual roots in a psychic non ego left matter with no life at all, and consciousness at the mercy of its own driven power motives. The violence of our times mirrors back to us the destructive effects of rationalism divorced from spiritual values centered in the heart.

By contrast, Jung's alchemical vision restored matter as sacred, and *physis*—nature, the physical world, and our bodies—as infused with the divine, correcting the dissociation of Christianity and inviting the evolution of a different kind of consciousness, one informed with wisdom and eros awareness that aims to reunite thinking and feeling, passion and vision, spirit and matter. In his vision, Jung had glimpsed the psychophysical background to the world, an event which eventually led him to revise his notion of the archetype as psychoid, that is, at bottom unknown, yet extending into matter.

Jung's alchemical vision gives us a hint of how in the union of psyche and matter our exposure to the reality of the subtle world of the *mundus imaginalis* is aiding us in this transformation of consciousness demanded of our times. I should like to draw attention once again to the affective and numinous nuances of this vision for Jung. Not only is Jung describing another event belonging to that psychic landscape "outside the body," but he is also remarking on both the beauty of the Presence in his room and the emotional impact of this experience upon him. We are left with the deep impression that in being "profoundly shaken," his heart was penetrated and that this transpersonal vision not only gave rise to developing his thoughts further about the relation of the Christ figure to his alchemical psychology, but that his body was infiltrated by the feeling values of an eros consciousness arising directly out of the collective unconscious, or objective psyche. What burns through in mystical or visionary or imaginal perception is the conscious recovery of the *a priori* unified world, the *unus mundus*, a subtle world behind and infusing this one, held together by the numinous energies of love.

Similar to the visionary events of mystics and shamans the world over, this exposure to a transpsychic sphere is deeply transformative to body and psyche through the intense power of beauty, feeling, and an opening to the divine. At the same time, access to this realm far beyond the limitations of ego consciousness encourages a creative furthering of one's own work; logos and eros are brought into a new synthesis. This is simultaneously felt as a healing balm for the embodied soul and has an all-round deepening effect on our nature that penetrates to the core of our being. The feeling, too, of being initiated into a cosmic secret or divine disclosure endows our life with a sense of worth and meaning beyond the finite limitations of everyday reality. At such a moment we might also feel a sense of gratitude at having been granted such an insight and experience a paradoxical union of both humility and joyous devotion to a spiritual value beyond ourselves. For a moment we no longer feel so alone, but united with the forces of creation as one note in a cosmic symphony.

Yet in spite of the overwhelming significance of these kinds of events for the development of consciousness toward a *cardiognosis*, or heart knowledge, visionary or mystical perception is mostly undervalued, if not outright ignored, in contemporary psychology and psychotherapy. In the following example, Jung goes further with his exploration of the establishment of the subtle body which arises out of the inclusion of the four functions necessary for an individuated response.

Imaginatio, Intuition, and Heart Gnosis in the Creation of the Subtle Body

In his essay, "The Psychology of the Transference," Jung uses an alchemical text to describe the alchemical process of the embodiment of spirit, the spiritualizing of matter, and the emergence of the mystery of the subtle body as the "third" (the resurrection or "rebirth" body) in the individuation process. Far into the journey, he describes the events following the death-like depression of the *nigredo*, or dark night of the soul (which can never be circumvented, is repeated throughout life, and is, paradoxically, a spiritually positive state in which the dark radiance of God comes to pierce and purify our being), in relation to the alchemical illustration, *Purification.*[17] At this stage of the work, death and distress are left behind as life tentatively begins to slowly emerge again, showering its wet, dewy wisdom (*aqua sapientiae*) and divine gift of illumination on us like a balm. William Blake has a beautiful sketch of this moment in his watercolor series on Dante's *Divine Comedy.*[18]

Here Jung emphasizes the importance of a fully embodied individuated response to dream material. He notes that working through dreams must be not only an intellectual exercise, but also that an attitude must be elicited in the dreamer to include "heart knowledge," that is, feelings, as well as a sensation response, in other words, to bring the gnosis of the dream in some way into everyday, concrete reality.

But the dream work does not stop here. In order to further facilitate the soul's return to the body, Jung states that in addition to thinking, feeling, and sensation, a fourth stage is required. He links this fourth stage to the anticipation of the *lapis* (the goal of the alchemical *opus*) and describes it as "the imaginative activity of the fourth function—intuition, without which no realization is complete."[19] Jung's notion of intuition is here unequivocally linked to the forces of imagination, to the imaginal activity of the soul—an activity which creates the *lapis*—as an essential aspect of the processes of embodiment.

He also notes that this fourth stage of the anticipation of the *lapis*, the intuitive grasping of a possibility, is beyond the scope of empirical experience as it involves an obscure paradox, and he illustrates this by adding that in Greek alchemy, the *lapis* was called "a stone which is not a stone." In other words, Jung, and we too if we follow, are moving toward a consciousness no longer valued by Western scientific thinking, a mode of being and experience that values and embraces paradox and that cannot be verified or measured or repeated. Like synchronicities, we are moving toward the irrational, toward a mystery whose very unknownness completes our fragile, finite, human state.

As "a stone which is not a stone," the paradoxical *lapis* invites a radical transformation in sensibility. Specifically, it requires a metaphoric sensibility that not only reveals and conceals a true event, but also opens our awareness to the *unus mundus* as an ontological reality on its own terms, and as more than just a metaphor. Stone is an image of the beauty of the natural world that outlasts the fleeting reality of an individual's life; indeed, one might say, it lasts forever, certainly for millennia. The stone then is the perfect metaphor for something of lasting value, an abiding spiritual principle embodied in matter, and as the goal of the *opus*, both conceals and reveals that goal, which (as Jung emphasizes in this essay) is the establishment in this life of the subtle or rebirth body—a body that, like a stone, has substance—that was also thought to survive physical death. The key to the creation of this eternal body, the True Nature or Celestial I in Sufi Gnosticism, is the imaginative activity of the psyche, the fourth function of intuition.

Here, Jung's notion of intuition goes beyond his more conventional description of intuition as hunch or perceiving around corners or a direct knowing from the unconscious and becomes linked with the irrational yet indispensable values of spiritual imagination. This *imaginatio vera* ("the most important key to alchemy") not only exposes us to the visionary realm of transpersonal reality and its gnosis of the heart, but also is that spiritual faculty that contributes to the "new creation" of the subtle or rebirth body. In addition to spontaneous experiences of the imaginal realm, Jung's description of active imagination is perhaps the "auxiliary technique" that facilitates our journeys to those "utterly different" psychic regions "outside-the-body."

In relation to these observations, Jung also describes the fourth stage of intuition and its connection with the *lapis* in the following somewhat curious way:

> Intuition gives outlook and insight; it revels in the garden of magical possibilities *as if they were real* [my emphasis]. Nothing is more charged with intuitions than the *lapis philosophorum*. This keystone rounds off the work into an experience of the totality of the individual. Such an experience is *completely foreign to our age*, although no previous age has ever needed wholeness so much [my emphasis].[20]

The linking of intuition with the imaginative activity of the soul as "magical possibilities made real" reminds us of Jung's descriptions of the "reality" of the psyche, his imaginal meetings with fantasy figures like the wise Philemon, his terrible war visions, his ecstatic near death experience, and his visionary encounter in Ravenna. It is the recovery of the world of imagination as a really real domain, an external but not ordinary reality, that is so "completely foreign to our age." But the recovery of this ancient way of gnosis, the recovery of all that is now designated derogatorily as superstitious and unreal, is the road to our recovery of an irrational and intuitive wholeness, a world of beauty, healing, sorrow, and eros beyond the rational intellect.

In utilizing the technique of active imagination to promote the intuitive grasping of an impossibility made real, Jung emphasizes full emotional presence and involvement in this work so that conscious and unconscious become united, just as a waterfall links above and below. Both the ego's reality and the images produced by the unconscious are fully represented with the purpose of influencing each other and reaching a mediating or 'third' position. The activity involves the alchemical operation of the transformation or transmutation of consciousness in its intention to produce images ("magical possibilities made real"?).

In fact, Jung asserts the alchemical *imaginatio* is to be understood as "the real and literal power to create images (*Einbildungskraft* = imagination)—the classical use of the word in contrast to *phantasia*, which means a mere conceit in the sense of insubstantial thought."[21] Not only then is imagination to be distinguished from fantasy, but it seems clear also that *true* imagination creates a kind of reality that is quite real and not 'just imagination,' more like a visionary experience that is 'really real' (remember—"something interior as exterior and something exterior as interior", or a "psychic 'outside the body'" that Jung experienced, for example, in his near death visions), and a subtle body domain somewhat different from the hunches of intuition.

Again, Jung quotes Ruland who, in agreement with Paracelsus, says: "Imagination is the star in man, the celestial or supercelestial body."[22] We no longer have such words in our vocabulary for the subtle body or the suggestion of a resurrection body beyond our physical form, but in mediaeval alchemical esotericism and in the mystical traditions, as well as in Eastern thought, this idea is not foreign at all. We in the West, however, have lost knowledge of these other bodies, just as we have lost a sense of the reality of the psyche, the reality of imagination, and the reality of a visionary gnosis beyond all our empirical, scientific, measurable facts or our intellectual thoughts about them. Jung continues, commenting on Ruland's statement that imagination is the star in man:

> This astounding definition throws a quite special light on the fantasy processes connected with the *opus*. We have to conceive of these processes not as the immaterial phantoms we readily take fantasy-pictures to be but as something corporeal, a 'subtle body,' semi-spiritual in nature.[23]

Jung once again is unequivocal here in his response. That imagination is a star links it with something uniquely valuable for our new birth, our spiritual birth, our rebirth, and our transformed life under eternal time. And, imagination links us, not with fantasy ("immaterial phantoms"), but with suprasensible reality, a subtle body world. The *imaginatio vera* as star is that subtle body organ of knowledge that opens us to the invisible in things and makes visionary experience possible as "something corporeal." The act of imagining, then, is a focused concentration of both physical and psychic life forces. Such activity grants us access to the *mundus imaginalis*, the semi-spiritual realm of the soul, of the celestial I. This is the subtle domain that bestows double vision, opens the heart, and resituates us in the mystery of life. It is this kind of intuitive imaginal activity, then, that is "completely foreign to our age," and yet this recovery of our visionary ability and its participation in accessing an-Other world is inextricably connected to dreaming creation along, and is needed to make us whole.

Jung's notion of intuition as "imaginative activity" contains a radical recovery of the notion of imagination that we have lost. In this radical recovery, Jung goes beyond his earlier work in which fantasies are projections or images of unconscious contents or split-off complexes, and retrieves the subtle body of the world, the interworld of the *mundus imaginalis*. In alchemical thought, he notes, matter and spirit were not divided into an 'either–or,' but rather an intermediate realm between mind and nature—a domain of subtle bodies—was primary. Jung adds that with the exploration of quantum physics, on the one hand, and of transpsychic reality, on the other, an exploration that intermingles and con-fuses the physical and psychic realms that characterize our times today, we are enlivening the subtle body world once again.

It is essential to grasp what Jung means here by imagination as *imaginatio vera* in order to understand the relevance of the subtle world of alchemy and his alchemical studies to ongoing acts of creation, which, in turn, is essential to Jung's recovery and updating of the Christian myth as the ongoing act of God's incarnation in time. Jung's notion of imagination, the subtle body, the stages of alchemy, and synchronicity as examples of the subtle world, and his radical recovery of Christianity not as a petrifying *imitatio* but *creatio continua*, are all links in a chain. Specifically, without a proper understanding of imagination as a spiritual faculty that acts as an agent of the Holy Spirit or *anima mundi* in the ongoing creation, making what seems unreal realities real, the chain falls apart, and the subtle nature of the imaginal world becomes just another idea.

Synchronicities as Signs of *Creatio Continua*

Another area of research for Jung throughout his life was the phenomenon of synchronicity, which also combines "a mystical union of spiritually alive and physically dead matter." Synchronicity, in bypassing the time/space continuum, opens us to the subtle body of the world, points us toward evidence of continuing creation based on an acausal foundation, and relies on the co-creative contribution of consciousness through 'meaning' to this on-going creation. We might consider then that Jung's observations on the phenomena of synchronicity and the psychophysical unity of the world suggested by such unusual events were an effort to bring the mediaeval alchemical ideas on the non-local and con-fusing relationship between psyche and matter up to date. Indeed, in the linking of inner and outer worlds, Jung's synchronicity studies can be regarded as alchemy in modern dress, even 'alchemy with awareness.' We might even say that synchronicity made the more difficult and abstruse field of alchemy user-friendly!

The connection of synchronicity with alchemy unfolds in the following four ways. Once again, in synchronicity, as in alchemy, there is a connection of inner and outer events not linked to a cause. Secondly, this connection is experienced as meaningful beyond a purely personal level by a participating consciousness comparable to the alchemical visionary organ, *imaginatio vera*. Thirdly, synchronicities tend to cause a profound shift in attitude resulting from an emotional encounter that opens us to the subtle worlds of the numinous, like the direct experience of imaginal figures and the visions of the alchemists at various stages of the opus. Finally, these experiences, like the alchemical operations that serve as appropriate metaphors for and evocations of deep pools of affect that belong to the individuation process, reveal our life and our involvement with it as an ongoing creative process—a circumambulation—and not something that is fixed, linear, or determined from the beginning. Hence, Jung refers to synchronicities, whose nature is unpredictable and spontaneous, as "acts of creation in time;" they point not only to the sequential unfolding of reality but also to the possibility for quantum leaps that bypass conditioned reality and go directly to deep resources of inspiration and renewal. Jung's familiar story of his patient and the scarab beetle is emblematic here.

Like active imagination, experiences of synchronicity focus on the nature of our consciousness while we are awake, something that Jung begins to focus on—calling it a mystic consciousness with the color of violet when it is truly broadened into a union of instinct and spirit[24] —with his description of the psychoid archetype necessitated by these anomalies. Synchronicities tend to stop us in our tracks, slow us down, and move us into the present moment. This epiphany of the *kairos*, the union of the time and timeless realms (so important in alchemy), released by these spontaneous and nonlocal events temporarily takes us out of history, out of past and future, and opens our hearts to the numinous. The irruption of the *unus mundus* world into this one, a moment that supplements ordinary reality with the *irrational and impossible* that Jung comments is *psychologically* necessary for change, also inspires our creative work, and transforms us by direct contact with eros awareness from the collective unconscious or beyond. The atmosphere ripples around us, and we are deepened into a mystery that often involves thoughts we did not know we had access to from a source of knowledge beyond the ego, comparable to the subtleties of Jung's description of his Ravenna vision or his alchemical vision of Christ. This kind of knowing often requires language that is beyond our rational thinking towards a poetic sensibility that can try to capture the presence of the invisible in the visible.

"Flying Saucers" as Synchronicities on a Collective Scale and the Recovery of an Alchemical Gnosis

With the UFO phenomena, the process goes even further. Jung felt that if "flying saucers" were both expressions of an archetypal compensation *and* physically real, they would be examples of synchronicities on a universal scale, and hence point in the direction of a new myth constellating in our time due to changes in psychic dominants that accompany the move from Pisces to Aquarius. He urges us to contemplate the *psychic* consequences of such an astrological change. With "flying saucers" and comparable paranormal events (NDEs, etc.) we can observe the emergence of a new worldview based, as in alchemy and synchronicity, on acausality, space-time relativity and the numinous, the co-creative organ of *imaginatio vera*, and the principle of *creatio continua*.

But with such paranormal events, we go beyond a "myth of meaning" (that comes to a stop with synchronicity) toward a new paradigm of reality that includes the paradox of a union of symbolic and nonsymbolic realities simultaneously, and a new *psychophysical* basis to reality that must now include extraordinary or non-ordinary experience. The possibility of an Other world beyond the psyche was already alluded to by the Sufi Gnostics and alchemists, and is confirmed by indigenous cultures and shamanic initiatory tales cross-culturally. The mystery of this cultural and collective "psychophysical parallelism"[25] brought to us by the UFO, as with individual synchronicities, invites us to realize something new and to come up with a creative response to the archetypal and global changes before us. UFO encounters (and associated phenomena), through direct and immediate experience, are stressing the alchemical union of psyche and matter toward a subtle body reality, a third body comprised of new life, indeed, *a new creation never produced before*, arising out of 'meaningful coincidences' on intense levels. This new potential that tempers a clever, 'enlightened' intellect with a deeper feeling and ethical sense is to be realized through devotion and personal effort.

We might also anticipate that the new archetypal constellation will be associated with the intensification of 'irrational' elements (as in synchronicity), those indispensable ingredients of transformation when the conscious attitude is receptive to the reality of the unconscious. When the ego attitude toward the "incomprehensible" is dissociated from the creative potential constellating in the collective, then the destructive aspect of the archetype is activated, 'irrationality' becomes "acting out," the spiritual principle is replaced with power, and ideology, fundamentalism, and violence result. Too, as Jung comments in *Answer to Job,* once a psychic content enters consciousness it can never be *not* known again, and it creates a disturbance until the correct attitude can be found, until it is made fully conscious. As Jung writes in "Flying Saucers":

> It depends on us whether we help coming events to birth by understanding them, and reinforce their healing effect, or whether we repress them with our prejudices, narrow-mindedness and ignorance, thus turning their effect into its opposite, into poison and destruction.[26]

Anomalous experiences that usually also occur unpredictably (though they can be cultivated by various techniques), however, point to a more intensely felt subtle body reality that the true imagination experiences and the body registers as at once both psychical and physical. Here the new creation is not only predominantly spiritual through meaning (as in a synchronicity), it is psychophysical, even psycho-cosmic, as the initiate moves toward an intensified and potently transformed reality that is perhaps better served by the word transmutation. The individual recounts not only an altered sense of time in which past, present, and future are known as one (or other distortions of time), but also of moving or shifting into a different and heightened sense of space, a *topos* that feels intensely real, even "hyperreal," but is definitely not a dream experience.[27] The initiate travels from 'here and now,' which still feels more or less familiar, to 'there,' to a new outside, an outside that is *really real* but no longer in any sense familiar or ordinary.

In writing of the intensified reality of this other intermediate world, Corbin discloses it as a domain where interiority becomes the threshold to a new outside, a spiritual landscape where beings have extension and dimension but of an immaterial kind. The sojourner feels alive and awake in another world that feels intensely alive and inordinately strange. The experience is often that of Presence, a move out of history (because it is out of time as flow into deep or aeonic time) and out of myth (because it is no longer only a symbolic reality), a psycho-cosmic landscape, "celestial earth," where we can meet—as the alchemists record in their meditations and UFO or NDE 'experiencers' confirm—frightening forces that threaten to destroy, dismember, or distract us, or where we might also encounter the invisible guides of the soul who bestow wisdom, healing, advanced knowledge, or knowledge of earth changes from beyond.

As with a journey to the *mundus imaginalis*, the land of "non-where," you cannot quite pinpoint the moment of change or even how it happens, yet it is not possible to pass from the sensible world to the 'other' world without a break with ordinary reality, like that provided, for example, by a near death or encounter experience or intense meditative practice. When the beholder of this other realm returns, he or she knows they have been elsewhere, but it is impossible to describe to anyone else how to get there. This is different from individual synchronicities in which you know, more or less, when the epiphanic moment happens.

All initiatory journeys involve frightening as well as beneficent encounters, and this is no less true in the literature on UFOs or NDEs. Sometimes for those individuals who have repeated encounter experiences, there is a move from initially terrifying to more fruitful and life-changing experiences. Harvard's John Mack, who has interviewed hundreds of 'experiencers,' observes, similar to Jung's comments about how the face the unconscious shows toward us depends very much on our attitude toward it, that this could also be true of the type of experience UFO initiates undergo. Mack also writes about how the phenomena change and evolve according to the level of consciousness of the experiencer. He observes that initial indifferent, or even traumatic, contacts have led to meaningful connections over time, and even to profound love and ecstatic union beyond earthly forms of love.[28]

My own feeling is that one of the main purposes of the encounter phenomena is to initiate us to an opening of the heart chakra, to the compassionate life that unites us with all creation and leads us to live a creative life devoted to the harmony of the whole. A key feature of encounter experiences is their intensity, including intensely emotional states that have led to comparisons with kundalini awakenings. The intense psychophysical energies in alchemy were also linked with the energies of the stars, and union with the cosmos was the final stage of this process. These intense feeling states move the sojourner beyond thinking and ordinary feeling to profound levels of passion and vision, in which they "are addressed" by concerns beyond their own personal interests, and are led often to change their life's work to a vocational destiny beyond what they could ever have predicted. Beyond the invitation to a creative idea or psychological content characteristic of individual synchronicities, the 'calling' in the UFO encounter is a galactic one, emanating from the heart of the cosmos, and often involving concerns of planetary proportions, especially ecological concerns, and even earth's place in the galactic community. Experiencers are offered disclosures about how what we do here on earth effects levels of being way beyond our own sphere and far beyond our own planet.

Likewise, Jung writes of the third *coniunctio*[29] of the alchemists as the transmutation into a subtle body being, rejoining the "potential world" of being (insofar as psyche and physics arise from it) now with awareness, as in a *unio mystica*. He suggests that "far-reaching changes of consciousness" arise from this union, including the healing of organic and psychic ills, and compares this attainment with an enlightened or illumined consciousness—known from East and West from the distant past up to the present—impossible to define, yet linked with the wisdom of compassion and a kind of ecstatic joy. The individual's link with the greater universe is also a characteristic of the Aquarian age. Perhaps anomalous experiences are attempting to make this third *coniunctio* and its transformation of "the perishable into the imperishable" come into being on a collective level, though this seeming impossibility may be a millennial achievement of which we are merely on the threshold.

Concluding Remarks

In his later work, Jung corrects his conviction that paranormal activity is related to "exteriorized effects of unconscious complexes," and certainly not to the existence of real spirits. Now he writes with less certainty, doubting whether a "purely psychological approach can do justice to the phenomena in question." He suggests there may be yet another level of consciousness, a "transpsychic"[30] reality beyond the collective unconscious. Paranormal events may belong to a world of their own, neither explicable by 'my' psychology, nor by the deeper level of the collective unconscious or objective psyche. Synchronicity and quantum physics opened up the possibility of another domain of reality that is not 'of us' in any way, an invisible realm beyond the confines of the time/space continuum that nevertheless requires our participation to bring it into reality. A deeper understanding of the astounding power and intensity of the alchemical and gnostic *imaginatio vera* leads us to the knowledge that we can participate in, make a relationship with, be visited by, or otherwise find ourselves in its strange domains.

This *unus mundus* is comparable to Suhrawardi's 'other' world. Corbin writes that this imaginal landscape is populated by the mystical cities and our enlightened historical teachers, spiritual mentors, and angelic guides, all existing in a subtle state. Tibetan Buddhism would concur with this vision of what it calls the Pure or Noble Lands where the sacred knowledge is kept; it employs various meditation techniques to access its wisdom.

Jung also contends that a desire for union with this other world can only arise from a dissociated consciousness that feels orphaned from this other world and in that state is aware of its own suffering and distress. Like the mediaeval alchemists' dissatisfaction with orthodox Christianity, many people today feel a similar disturbance. Alchemists sought perhaps to heal the fracture between physical humans and their spiritual truths in the attempt to bridge the dissociation between spirit and matter upheld in conventional Christianity, but this attempt at embodiment was not realized on a collective level. Its 'failure' and the continued split led to great advances in science and particularly medicine (that can now prolong life indefinitely), though at the cost of spiritual values, especially the alchemist's acknowledgement of the divine spirit in matter.

Now that the spirit has been reduced to an epiphenomenon of the brain, and the materialist view of reality has all but extinguished it, and Matter (devoid of spirit) is the new God, we are suffering from the effects of this takeover, this logos consciousness without the wisdom and eros of Sophia, without the wisdom of the body, and this loss of psyche with its transpersonal values of imagination, vision, and dream that endow meaning beyond the "ticking of the clock." The soul is an endangered species, and so the guides from the soul of the world come to visit us once again, helping us to get back on track, awakening us to the mysteries once more, disillusioning us of our hubris and dis-ease that we are only historical beings in a desacralized cosmos. We need to "wake up" to our true identity as custodians of planet Earth who through the initiatory trials of the alchemical death and rebirth operations, can recover our relationship with the Invisible Ones and relearn the sacred history from those lands where the enlightened knowledge is kept. Only then will we recover the wisdom to live with humility on behalf of the macrocosm, and become citizens of the cosmos as a note in a score whose range vastly exceeds our current limited repertoire.

NOTES

1. Dan Merkur, *Gnosis: An Esoteric Tradition of Mystical Visions and Unions* (Albany, NY: State University of New York Press, 1993), 224.
2. C. G. Jung, *The Collected Works of C. G. Jung*, tr. R. F. C. Hull (Princeton: Princeton University Press, 1964), Vol. 10 § 591.
3. C. G. Jung, *Collected Works*, 14 § 410-411.
4. C. G. Jung, *Memories, Dreams, Reflections* (New York: Vintage Books, 1989), 197.
5. C. G. Jung, *Collected Works*, 16 § 486.
6. G. R. S. Mead, *The Doctrine of the Subtle Body in Western Tradition* (London: J. M. Watkins, 1919).
7. Peter Kingsley, *In the Dark Places of Wisdom* (Inverness, CA: The Golden Sufi Tradition, 1999), 61.
8. Henry Corbin, *Spiritual Body and Celestial Earth* (Princeton: Princeton University Press, 1977).
9. C. G. Jung, *Collected Works*, 12 § 396.
10. C. G. Jung, *Collected Works*, 14 § 410.
11. C. G. Jung, *Memories, Dreams, Reflections*, 287.
12. *Ibid.*, 286.
13. *Ibid.*, 287.
14. C. G. Jung, *Collected Works*, 10 Fig. VII, 404-405.
15. C. G. Jung, *Memories, Dreams, Reflections*, 210.

16. *Ibid.*, 211.

17. C. G. Jung, *Collected Works*, 16 Fig. 8, 275, & § 483ff.

18. See Charles Taylor & Patricia Finley, *Images of the Journey in Dante's Divine Comedy* (New Haven, CT: Yale University Press, 1997), 115, for an unfinished sketch by Blake (Tate Gallery, London) of this tentative moment, in which the guide is about to wash the pilgrim's face with dew, after the darkness of his terrible ordeals.

19. C. G. Jung, *Collected Works*, 16 § 492.

20. *Ibid.*

21. C. G. Jung, *Collected Works*, 12 § 219.

22. *Ibid.*, § 394.

23. *Ibid.*

24. C. G. Jung, *Collected Works*, 8 § 414.

25. C. G. Jung, *Collected Works*, 10 § 780.

26. *Ibid.*, § 731.

27. John Mack, *Passport to the Cosmos* (New York: Crown Publishers, 1999), 53-56.

28. *Ibid.*, 13, 18-19.

29. C. G. Jung, *Collected Works*, 14 § 762ff.

30. C. G. Jung, *Collected Works*, 8 § 600 & note 15.

Sulphur Dreaming

To James Hillman for his 80th

ROBERT BOSNAK

Like many of us writing in this issue, I owe my discovery of alchemy to Jung. When I went to the Jung Institute in Zürich in 1971 to train as an analyst, a member of the standing review committee overseeing my training, an old friend of Jung's, told me that one of the objectives of my training was to be the ability to read, without further outside help, Jung's *Mysterium Coniunctionis* (Jung's original depth psychology based largely on the medieval alchemical medley, the *Rosarium Philosophorum.*) This objective was considered by her to be on par with the other *desideratum*, a sufficient clinical training, both in practice and theory. For the latter requirement, I found myself working in psychiatric hospitals for close to five out of my six years in training, while studying myself into reading glasses. The former led to a continuous 35-year bafflement.

Robert Bosnak, Jungian analyst, grew up in Holland, trained in the Zürich of the 1970s, developed a method called 'embodied imagination,' and lectures worldwide. Currently living in Sydney Australia, he was in private practice for 25 years in Cambridge, Mass. His books include *A Little Course in Dreams*; *Tracks in the Wilderness of Dreaming*; and the forthcoming *Embodied Imagination*. He co-founded www.cyberdreamwork.com, and is past president of the International Association for the Study of Dreams.

Whenever I turn seriously to alchemy, as I had to do for this article, my mind unhinges, and I understand nothing of what I previously thought I had known about alchemy. It is a depressing occasion, similar to entering the unmanageable world of dreaming. If it isn't so exciting, whyever do it?

This moment in my alchemical unfolding—late 2005—finds me at odds with Jung's basic understanding of alchemy. James Hillman, whose 80th birthday we celebrate in April 2006, wrote one of his major works, *Re-visioning Psychology*, based on his 1972 Terry lectures at Yale, as—among a host of other matters—a fundamental critique of the prevailing Jungian dogmas of the time. While he deconstructed and re-visioned much of Jung's work, Hillman adopted Jung's alchemy dogma wholesale. He wrote: "The alchemist projected his depths into his materials, and while working on them he was also working on his soul. The means of this work was the imagination: alchemy was an imaginative exercise couched in the language of concrete substances and impersonal objective operations."[1]

I had always subscribed rather uncritically to this dogma of projected depth onto unknown physical materials, until the following passage shocked me into my nth crisis of alchemical faith. The following is a well-documented story recounted by Bishop Gilbert Burnet about his friend Robert Boyle, the great 17th-century Father of Chemistry, himself not an adept of alchemy. It is quoted by science historian Lawrence Principe in his remarkable book, *The Aspiring Adept: Robert Boyle and his Alchemical Quest.*

> A certain unknown man, dressed quite shabbily, once visited the illustrious Boyle and, after some discourse on chemical operations, asked him to have his servants (that is, the aforesaid Boyle's) bring some antimony with certain other quite common metallic materials, which being then (by good fortune) found in the most noble Boyle's own laboratory, he threw them into a crucible and placed the crucible in a furnace adapted for the melting of metals. After he had done so, and the contents of the crucible were seen to have melted, the unknown man then showed a little powder to the aforementioned servants, which they threw into the same crucible, and immediately thereafter he left, ordering that the crucible should be kept in the furnace until the fire had quite gone out, and promised that he would return in a few hours. But he indeed forgot his promise and was

> seen neither that whole day or the following day, nor on any thereafter, so Mr. Boyle, taking up the crucible from the furnace, saw within it a truly golden material that, after subjecting it to all assays, he was forced to declare good gold, although it was slightly inferior in weight. And it is that material of which I (not without admiration) saw a portion in the possession of that illustrious man who kindly communicated this account to me, as I said at the outset.[2]

A skeptic would say that Boyle either lied to his close friend, Bishop Gilbert Burnet, or was tricked, as so many have been, by a sleight-of-hand magician. But Principe recounts other instances in which Boyle observed transmutations, and tells of a transmutation performed before the alchemy-skeptical physician of the 17th-century Prince of Orange, assayed and checked by the mint master of Holland (then in its Golden-Age heyday as the richest nation on the globe, well advanced in science and paying close scrutiny to counterfeit), and investigated and verified by the meticulous rational philosopher Spinoza. All of this makes me suspend my disbelief.

Contemporary scientists have been able to transmute lead into gold since 1972, although not by way of chemistry, but through a physics process called nucleosynthesis. Using a particle accelerator, they can remove 3 protons from the nucleus of an atom of lead (which contains 82 protons) and thus turn it into gold (the atomic nucleus of which has 79 protons). This, however, requires a vast input of energy—costing far more than the value of the resulting gold.

If the medieval alchemists were actually able to produce the red tincture and make the gold they claimed they could, then the notion of alchemy as primarily a projection of unconscious material upon physical substances finds itself on very thin ice. In Boyle's experience, transmutation was happening *within* the *physical material*, not primarily in the *soul* of the alchemist he was observing.

* * *

In this section, I shall follow the preparation of the tincture as it is described in detail in the *Rosarium*, beginning with the treatise on Sulphur. The *Rosarium Philosophorum*,[3] the Rose-garden of the Philosophers, is a late-medieval search engine—descendent of the classical art of memory—in which an encyclopedia of ancient alchemical factoids stored in memory were organized around a primordial "song-line" landscape,[4] namely, a series of symbolic woodcuts called the "Marriage of Sun and Moon." The *Rosarium* comes highly recommended. The renowned Sir Isaac Newton read it frequently and called it one of the all-time great books on alchemy—or something along those lines, just a bit more formal.

The material I shall be working with spreads out along the sequential song-lines "Ablution or Cleansing," "Joy of the Soul, or Birth, or Sublimation," and "Fermentation." I will explore this material as a series of procedures for changing physical matter, called body (*corpus*) by the alchemist, in the hope that a new understanding of *the relationship between image and body* might emerge. In the treatise on Sulphur, next to the gloss on "ordinary sulphur,"[5] one Avicenna, so-called,[6] is cited as making the following observations in response to the often-heard alchemical statement that sulphur coagulates fluid material, making it curdle:

> ... [I]t [ordinary sulphur] does not enter into the masterwork (*magisterium*), because it is not born from it, since it always infects, blackens, and corrupts, no matter how skillfully it may have been prepared. It infects the fire with itself, and thus prevents melting. If it is truly calcined [subjected to great heat] it turns into an earthy substance, that is, dead dust. So in what way can it breathe life into something else? It obviously contains a double measure of superfluous elements, namely, a substance which breaks into flame, and a dross-like foulness (my translation of the original Latin text, here and hereafter, for all references to the *Rosarium*).[7]

In its ordinary form, sulphur is indeed highly flammable, bursting easily into flame and burning whatever it touches. However, it is not completely combustible, for when it has spent itself in flames, it leaves a residue that is completely inert, lifeless, uninspiring. Ordinary sulphur is like brief flaming infatuations, which generate momentary heat, then die away into uninspired inertia, like a shot of morphine. Ordinary (lower-order) sulphuric states do not generate anything but endless, changeless recurrence; a sulphuric explosion traumatizes one into shell shock and repetition compulsion. From ordinary sulphuric infatuation nothing can be generated or inspired. Ordinary sulphur leads only to inertia and burnout. Yet sulphur is needed for the work.

Without it nothing becomes solid. Apparently, it is not found outside what has first been accomplished by work. The excitement seen freely out in the open, publicly advertised and immediately accessible, the heat that makes bodies burn with glowing desire, leads to sinister clogging ("blackens," "foulness"), and ultimately corrupts and imparts to the body a foul stench. It is not the solidifying heat—a paradox, since heat is usually related to melting—the alchemist is looking for.

> These considerations lead us to the conclusion that ordinary sulphur is not the same as philosopher's sulphur, since philosopher's sulphur is elemental live fire (*simplex ignis vivus*), vivifying other bodies, which are dead, and maturing them, so that it completes the defect of nature with its own overflowing maturity—in accordance with the fact that it [elemental live fire] is perfect in its nature and is purified even further by being worked on.[8]

Philosopher's sulphur, live[9] fire, is alive as the generative passion for life inherent in all natural beings. For the alchemists, metals were *mineral, spirited, vegetative animals*. They declared it possible to extract vegetative spirit from these mineral animals, that is, their passion for living by which a germinating seed matures into a fully grown adult. Philosopher's sulphur is generative passion and agony. Thus, according to other alchemical texts, the first manifestation of philosopher's sulphur is in the innocent greenness of germinating springtime, which must inevitably be corrupted. In its concentrated, purified form, this generative force can raise the sick and complete what nature had left unfinished. By necessity, alchemy posits, nature strives towards fulfillment. In much the same way as an egg strives to become a chicken, all metals strive to become gold, for it is in gold that the force of generation reaches full maturity. Philosopher's sulphur is a concentrated and purified striving to mature, a striving that causes bodies to ferment. This striving towards gold is the dream of all metals: "When I grow up, I want to be gold!"—this is the body's inspiration. The alchemist strives to concentrate this embodied inspiration until it becomes a single focused fire, making the ferment coagulate into pure, solid striving to mature.

The best sulphur for gold-making is red sulphur—the most accomplished, the most mature. This is found in gold itself, in that striving which has been so powerfully inspired as to be able to create gold. The alchemist's task is to purify and activate this powerful inspiration, which fermented the inferior metal into gold in the first instance, and to concentrate the fermentation to an intensity so acute that it quickens the inferior metal, making it transmute spontaneously into gold. Red sulphur is a concentrated *will* to gold. Live fire, the striving ferment, is harvested from natural gold, for only the superior can improve what is inferior. The inferior can never create something better than itself.

The difference between ordinary and philosopher's sulphur is like the difference between the instantly accessible face value of a thing and the hidden qualities that give it intrinsic value. The alchemical texts are adamant: the husk needs to be shucked off first. Natural gold needs to be melted, shucked, pressed like grapes. Unto itself it is but coagulated, precious fermentation.

> On this matter, Avicenna says: Such sulphur [philosopher's sulphur] is not found on earth, but, nevertheless, it exists in these bodies, sun and moon (*sol & luna),* and in another, which is something that can be told to no man, unless it is revealed to him by God himself. In *sol* it is more perfect, because it is better digested and cooked. Thus, philosophers have subtly imagined how the sulphurs (*sulphura,* plural) in these more perfect bodies are drawn out, and how their qualities are refined by being worked on, so that in them [the sulphurs] is manifested, as a result of being worked upon by nature, a quality that at first did not appear, yet which they already had, from the very beginning, in all its fullness, yet hidden.[10]

Barring direct revelation, unreliable as that is ("unless it is revealed to him by God himself"), the creative fermentation of sulphur may best be harvested in bodies in which the dream of becoming gold has fully matured and grown solid. Once the sulphuric fermenting inspiration—the dream of becoming gold—has been extracted from its terminal by shucking its golden husk in the fire, what had previously existed in a hidden state now makes its radiant appearance. In gold the inspired striving of inferior metals reaches its full maturity, is fully digested and satiated. Not having any further to go, it becomes dormant and coagulates. It is the alchemist's task to melt, awaken, quicken, concentrate the somnolescent inspiring ferment to its highest potency, red sulphur. Such purified, refined, hyper-concentrated philosopher's red sulphur overflows with maturity. In it the striving towards gold is so potent that it can ripen vast quantities of base metal into its own golden maturity. *This* is the alchemical projection, the process by which a small particle of hyper-charged, highly concentrated embodied inspiration matures a relatively large quantity of inferior matter into something of supreme quality.

> And they concede that this can by no means be done without dissolving the bodies and reducing them into primal matter (*prima materia*), which is live silver (*argentum vivum*), from which they were originally made—and without any admixture of extraneous matter; for what is alien to the nature of our stone can in no way improve it, since nothing is suitable to it except that which is closely related to it, given that it is a medicine of an elemental [*simplex*] and excellent nature, produced from mercurous waters in which gold and silver have been dissolved.[11]

In the beginning, all metals were featureless live silver (a.k.a. 'our water'), or mercurius, pure fluid metal without properties. This was known as primal matter, which dates back to an age before time. Much like the Australian Aborigines, who believe that featureless land existed before the Ancestors created landscape, alchemists understood there to have been a primordial age, when metal flowed without specificity, like an empty, live mirror awaiting reflection. In this primal live silver, an inspiring fermentation, a live fire of sulphuric nature was believed to have entered, initially in a diffuse and contaminated manner, coagulating the live silver into the individual metals, each with its specific properties. It was held that the cosmic qualities embodied by the planets had planted their seeds in the featureless earth, reminiscent of the activity of the Aboriginal Ancestors. In lead, the seed of the planet Saturn, for instance, sulphur is thought to be so infected as to be rendered barren and impotent. Any attempt to gain live sulphur from lead is doomed: it is non-generative and barely alive. The alchemist has to make philosopher's sulphur from natural gold, in which the cosmic inspiration exists in its most vitally alive form. Some lucky alchemist might make red sulphur from some other material, a product of direct divine intervention, but that is pure grace, on which one should never rely. Short of divine intervention, gold is an alchemist's best bet for the extraction of red sulphur, since in it solar inspiration is fully embodied by nature.

After the ferment is extracted from gold, awakened from its dormant state through melting and the burning away of the passive live silver in which it has been dreaming until nothing else remains but the active awakened live fire, nothing extraneous should be added. Only the ferment of pure gold can be concentrated into the Midas touch, because, like a more mature sibling, it is closely related to the inferior fermentation of the lesser metals, which it can ripen into its own essence, coagulating the molten flow of inferior metals into gold.

As elemental live fire, red sulphur is the most purified, concentrated, activated heat of *life*. Thus, alchemy's identification as the precursor of chemistry is actually quite *erroneous*. Since alchemy understood metals to be *alive*, it is more properly a life science, in the tradition of *bio*chemistry. In fact, it is more akin to modern genetics than even to biochemistry *per se*. The contemporary field most similar to medieval alchemy is cloning. The remarkable similarity between the two is apparent in the explanation of the cloning procedure used in the creation of Dolly, the parthenogenetic sheep, in 1997, an explanation I lifted from the website www.scientificcage.com (Fig. 1).

In genetic terms, red sulphur as tincture might be considered the "nuclear genetic information" of activated gold. However, the difference between cloning and alchemical gold-making seems to be that while in cloning the receiving egg needs to be stripped of all its original chromosomal information, in alchemy the nuclear genetic information of gold is retained, and is in fact magnified to such a degree that it matures the genetic information of the lesser metals, an outcome that is possible only because gold is inherently related to the baser metals as a more refined form of the same substance.

We now turn our attention to a mythical tale involving a transmutation that was said to have been performed in 1382 by the famous alchemist and Parisian notary, Nicolas Flamel, and his wife Pernelle,[12] but not put into writing until 1600.

> The first time that I made projection, was upon Mercurie, whereof I turned halfe a pound, or thereabouts, into pure Silver, better than that of the Mine, as I selfe assayed, and made others assay many times. This was upon Munday, the 17 of January about noone, in my house, Pernelle only being present; in the yeer of restoring mankind, 1382 … I made projection of the red stone upon the like quantity of Mercurie, in the presence of

> Pernelle onely, in the same house, the five and twentieth day of Aprill following, the same yeere, about five a clocke in the Evening.[13]

What order of activity does this myth describe?

The word "projection" as used by Flamel has a very different significance from the word as used by psychologists of the 19th and 20th century. The 19th-century psychological usage comes from the world of the *camera obscura* and its descendants, modern photography and movies. It operates within the paradigm of a light source surrounded

Fig. 1: The Cloning of Dolly, the Sheep

Cloning is not as difficult as most people might think. In cloning procedures generally, nuclei are extracted from cultured cells that might have come originally from an embryo, a fetus (young of an human or animal while in the womb or egg) or an adult organism. The nuclei are inserted into egg cells which have had their original nucleus removed, a process called nuclear transfer.

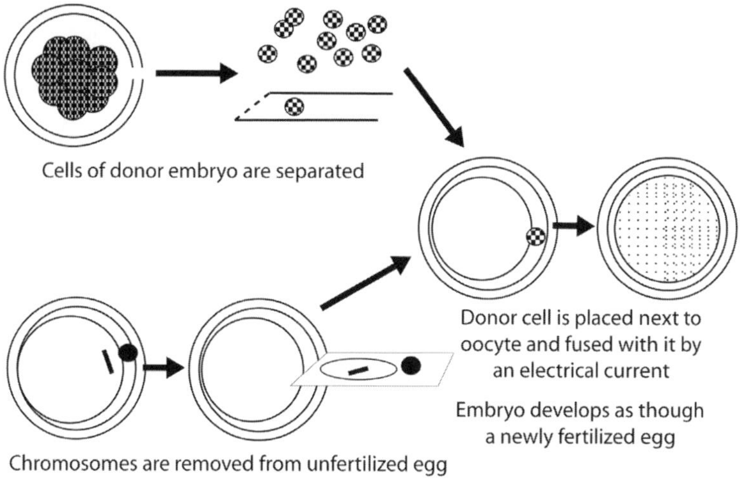

The technique used by Wilmut at the Roslin Institute uses adult cells as donors. He and his co-workers accomplished their feat by transferring the nuclei from various types of sheep cells into unfertilized sheep eggs from which the natural nuclei had been removed by microsurgery. Once the transfer was complete, the recipient eggs contained a complete set of genes, just as they would if they had been fertilized by sperm. The eggs were then cultured for a period before being implanted into sheep that carried them to term, one of which culminated in a successful birth. The resulting lamb was an exact genetic copy of the sheep that provided the transferred nucleus, not of those that provided the egg.

Recreated from http://www.scientificcage.com/doc/human_being_20010206.html.

by darkness casting its rays onto a blank screen. Under this paradigm, the statement, "The alchemist projected his depths into his materials" (Hillman), can be understood to be implying that the alchemist is the source of brightness, while the material, surrounded by the dark unknown, is the projection screen. The *alchemical* notion of projection, however, is completely different. As noted earlier, alchemical projection refers to the process by which a minuscule amount of live fire transforms a large amount of live silver. One proportion mentioned in the *Rosarium* is that of 1 to 100—when "one part [of the white tincture] is projected upon one hundred parts of live silver, it will color it into true silver."[14] Another, even larger, proportion is given in the account that "the Elixir transmuted nineteen thousand times its weight of lead."[15] Thus, far from drawing its inspiration from physics, medieval alchemical projection is informed by biology, and is in fact more akin to contemporary genetic nuclear transfer than to the science of optics. Unlike genetic scientists, however, the alchemist seems to have been able to activate the genetic nuclear material of gold to the point where it refines, rather than replaces, the genetic makeup of related materials.

Nevertheless, there might just be a process in alchemy that parallels the cloning procedure of getting rid of genetic information from the receiving egg cell. One injunction in the *Rosarium* (put into the mouth of Democritus) advises: "Cleanse (*mundifica)* tin with the principal ablution, extract from it its blackness and that which obscures it, and there will appear its dazzling whiteness."[16] To this, Hali (another mouthpiece) adds: "Take what has descended to the bottom of the vessel and purify it with hot fire, until its blackness is removed and its density diminishes, and evaporate from it its liquid components, until it becomes an excessively white limestone in which there is no blemish. Then truly is the earth fit and purified to receive soul."[17]

The word for tin, *stannum*, was used in Latin to describe an alloy of silver and lead. Thus, the text could be read to mean that the lead is separated from the silver, and that only silver remains, since silver is often described as white earth. But from Hali's remarks it becomes clear that we are dealing with a "whiter-than-white" quality in the limestone, an immaculateness ("there is no blemish"), which is often referred to as the snow-white "earth made of leaves," *terra foliata*. Alchemical etchings show the alchemist sowing red sulphur seeds in the foliated white earth.[18] I imagine *terra foliata* to be filmy white layers of dazzling full moon luminosity, piled up like the leaves of Fall. Through the process of cleansing with great heat, this white earth of leaves emerges out of hiding from under the pollution that initially obscures it. The material in the vessel looks like a polar landscape, without features, an immaculate primordial whiteout of snow upon snow. Thus stripped of all its features, like a blank mirror, this whiteout earth is finally fit to be animated. Red sulphur brings this white body to life, gives it soul.

This stripping away of blackness from base metals, this reaching back to the dazzling whiteness of primordial matter, *prima materia*, has a correspondence in the de-familiarizing effect our work with imagination has upon the human body. Like the various metals, our bodies are patterned in the habitual way which makes them *our* individual body with their own specific properties:

A timid man with narrow shoulders, who habitually dares not breathe or assert himself, and who walks with a hesitating step, has a terrifying dream. In his dream, he is attacked by a ferocious hulk, who throws him over his shoulder and runs away with him. The dream ego is scared to death.

In working on the dream, he feels his habitual fear magnified in his body by the abduction. In his sternum there is intense pain, as his heart beats rapidly, and he holds very still in order not to make things worse. He knows this body and its anxious pain well. It is his familiar, habitual embodiment. Through our work on absorbing the image environment, he enters into a full-fledged flashback of the dream experience. The scary world surrounds him. When I direct his attention to the broad shoulder of the man who abducts him, he can sense the bouncing of his body on the hulking muscles. After some time of focus, he becomes aware of the power in the muscles. An enormous force rages through this huge man, who breathes deeply and effortlessly. He hardly feels the load he is carrying. He runs as though he hasn't a care in the world. As the dreamer becomes absorbed in an identification with the abductor, he experiences an unfamiliar body from within. It is fearless, powerful, potent, forceful, and unfettered. The longer the dreamer is able to stay in the identification with the unfamiliar body, the more the habitual body is stripped away. In the final part of the work, he can, simultaneously, sense both the habitual body, concentrated in the pain in the sternum, and the unfamiliar body, focused in the hulking shoulder. This puts an even greater torque on his sense of his habitual body, which is stripped off even further. A few minutes after the work, his habitual body reclaims him, and I see him shrink before my eyes into his narrow-shouldered, collapsed, timid self. But for a moment, when he felt both his habitual body and the foreign condition, he had been in an unfamiliar state in between. In the work with images, this de-familiarizing of the body happens in an ongoing way. Over time, this ongoing de-familiarization can create a live silver body, stripped of its habits, fit to receive the simple elemental medicine, the refining live fire.

Upon writing this, after studying the texts about stripping away non-essential components in order to return to the featureless, primordial live silver, I notice that I am becoming unfamiliar to myself. In my work I had always thought that the focus should be on inhabiting alien bodies, such as that of the abductor, in order to expand the embodiment repertoire, much like an embodied version of what Hillman has called "soul-making." After all, the greater the number of embodied states that one has become familiar with (that is, the more embodiment patterns one knows subjectively, from within), the greater the freedom the soul has to stretch into ever more embodied life. But now I feel my focus shift to an unfamiliar position: suddenly I realize that building up a large repertoire of embodied states matters less than getting acquainted with the unfamiliar by being stripped of habitual patterns. The alchemists would say the husk that obscures the whiter-than-white, immaculate live silver needs to be stripped away.

I feel anxious and insecure. I'm losing my footing. Meeting live silver gives me vertigo and a sense of falling. I've lost my bearing. It feels horrible—and right.

* * *

As we all know from dreaming, the creative imagination is capable of presenting an entire world in a flash, fully formed. To me it is—as are love and logic—one of our golden faculties.

I find myself in a room where everything is real, the woman I meet is real, our relationship is real, our encounter is fleshed out to the very fragrance and touch. I live a life created by the genius of embodied imagination.

While concentrating upon the world from which I have just awakened, I can see again the room, the bed, the sheets. I see the wooden door as it opens to let me in. The atmosphere of anticipation takes hold of me again; I can feel heat rising, having returned to a world of desire. The more I let this atmosphere work on me, the more real the world becomes, as if the atmosphere creates itself a world. The atmosphere is the sulphur of the image, fermenting it, making it rise, like sourdough in leavening bread. It also makes image environments solidify, become more densely real. Whereas daydreams can be flimsy and transparent, night dreams are dense and solid, undistinguishable from physical reality. Perhaps red sulphur is what makes imagination solid, and the work with images is not only about the images themselves, but about *extracting sulphuric solidity* from their specific embodiments.

Over the years, my work with images has changed. I used to work on images for hours on end. The dreamer and I would enter into each detail, allowing it to work on us. Now I take less time, not exploring each detail of the image. Moving away from the photographic approach, my work has become more like Chinese and Japanese painting: a few brush strokes, and a mountain atmosphere pervades the silk screen. Then I wait for the atmosphere to mature into a solid embodied state, ripe in affect and sensation, like the timid man's experience of the hulking abductor, felt into its physical animation. The atmosphere is the ferment of the image, its sulphuric spirit.

* * *

Now that I have come to the end of four months of alchemical agony, seeing myself change, finding the central focus of my work drift towards stripping away habitual embodiments rather than gaining an ever wider visceral knowledge of the embodiment repertoire, and finding the solidifying embodying process more essential than the resulting specific embodiments, what has happened? Why is it important that alchemy be not merely a projection of unconscious imagination upon dark matter, but rather a process of transmutation within matter itself?

I am no closer to understanding the gold-making process itself, beyond the general insight that it is biochemical, a bit like cloning, that it activates and intensifies the fermentation abilities of gold, creating a golden dawn in material that has been fully cleansed of all its superfluous information, by first decomposing it into a black sludge, until the pure white shine of live silver emerges, as is described in the following statement about *citrinatio* (the yellowing that leads to gold):

> . . . Yellowing is nothing but completed digestion: when heat acts upon moisture it first generates blackness, and then leads to dryness, which causes whiteness; when fire transcends the thing it is acting upon, it mutates it into the purest yellow. All of this may be achieved through the calcination [subjecting to great heat] of lead.[19]

Heat corrupts the innocent dew of youth into black agony; heat dries the experience of age, making it mutable; heat turns the mutable into gold.

I understand that the live fire the alchemists talk about is not generated from outside, from the oven, but comes from within the material, as the fermenting live fire within the metal bodies, freed by the calcining heat. The ferment is the sulphuric dream of one day becoming gold, a dream inherent in all metals, and I shudder at the audacity of the alchemists, who place that day in the foreseeable future.

I now see that the important difference between psychological projection and alchemical projection is the *place* from which the generative inspiration arises. Psychology places it in the realm of unconscious imagery, where the projection is *outwards* upon the unknown. Alchemical projection, on the other hand, is generated *within* the core of the bodies themselves, where, after prolonged torture, purification, and concentration, generative spirits are released into the prepared surrounding body.

I may be beginning to fathom vaguely that the dream of becoming gold, this inspired striving to mature, is what gives bodies heat and makes them solid, and that the alchemist did not, in fact, project his inspiration upon the material, but coaxed inspiration out of the material itself in order to project the essence of this solidifying live fire upon infected matter so as to bring fulfillment to what nature had left sick with longing. From bodies thus arises the inspiration that can heal human affliction.

To the alchemist, bodies are the source of inspiration. Perhaps, psychological projection and alchemical projection are not antithetical after all, but co-exist in harmonious interaction, in which the alchemist's passionate belief that gold can be produced artificially is projected psychologically onto live bodies and elicits from these live bodies their inspiring ferment, which, when cleansed and concentrated to the highest degree, sets alchemical projection in motion.

NOTES

1. James Hillman, *Re-visioning Psychology* (New York: Harper and Row, 1975), 90.

2. Lawrence M. Principe, *The Aspiring Adept: Robert Boyle and his Alchemical Quest* (Princeton, NJ: Princeton University Press, 1998), 104-05.

3. The edition I am using here is: Joachim Telle, ed., *Rosarium Philosophorum: Ein Alchemistisches Florilegium des Spätmittelalters*, Facsimile of the Frankfurt 1550 Latin first edition (Weinheim: VCH Verlagsgesellschaft mbH, 1992).

4. Aboriginal song-lines form a musical score of song and dance across Australia, commemorating the landscape-creating exploits of the Ancestors, creating a mnemonic road map for travelers.

5. The Latin word here translated as "ordinary" is *vulgaris,* a word that connoted the common, the everyday, the ordinary, and implied an association with lower-order phenomena. Alchemy made a distinction between vulgar, ordinary (lower-order) sulphur and philosopher's (higher-order) sulphur. However, the modern English word "vulgar" (which is descended from *vulgaris*) carries a completely different significance, with its connotations of indecency, and would be quite misleading here.

6. This Avicenna is one of the authorities often quoted in the *Rosarium*. In all probability, he bears no relationship whatsoever to the renowned 11th-century Arab physician Avicenna.

7. *Rosarium*, 101.

8. *Ibid.*

9. I use the word "live" in the alchemical terms "live fire" and "live silver" in the way it is currently used in "live concert" or "live wire," to imply the quality of being vital and current.

10. *Rosarium*, 102.

11. *Ibid.*

12. Currently made famous through J. K. Rowling's *Harry Potter and the Philosopher's Stone*.

13. Principe, 109.
14. *Rosarium*, 84.
15. Principe, 104.
16. *Rosarium*, 78.
17. *Rosarium*, 79.
18. In the language of the Australian Tjukurpa, the foliated white earth is the featureless land before the Ancestors had their landscape-creating adventures. This primal material displays the pure white brightness of a cinematic projection through purely transparent film containing no information.
19. *Rosarium*, 103.

The Revelatory Nature of Alchemical Color in Flannery O'Connor's Short Story, "Revelation"

CYNTHIA ANNE HALE

The Relevance of Alchemy Today

The mystery and obscurity of alchemy pervades its two-thousand-year history in Greek, Arabic, and Latin cultures. Although substances, methods, and even the particular goals articulated in writings and drawings varied between cultures and even between individual alchemists, the common element was that of a quest to transmute a base substance such as lead into a higher and more precious form such as gold.[1] Alchemical processes worked with physical materials, yet usually incorporated a spiritual and philosophical perspective. "The union of the physical and spiritual," writes analyst Jeffrey Raff, "is a theme found in alchemy of all periods."[2]

Cynthia Anne Hale, LCSW, a depth psychotherapist with a private practice in California and New York, is a doctoral candidate in depth psychology at Pacifica Graduate Institute. She is writing her dissertation on the archetypal nature of the color red through its presence in ritual, myth, alchemy, opera, theater, film, and art. This article draws on material from that work. Further information can be found on her website: www.imaginalways.com.

The integration of the physical and spiritual in alchemy parallels the integration that C. G. Jung sought in his theoretical development. After reading the Chinese alchemical text, *Secret of the Golden Flower*, he was attracted to the richly colored baroque texts of Western alchemy, although at first their meaning seemed indecipherable. Studying and cataloguing the phrases and images of these and other alchemical works for more than a decade as if they were an unknown language, Jung found parallels with his psychological theories of the unconscious. This historical validation led him to deepen his research into primordial images and the nature of the archetype. He writes in *Memories, Dreams, Reflections* that what had begun for him with an investigation of myths was furthered by alchemy's reach beyond consciousness into a psychology of the unconscious.[3] Ultimately, he interpreted the chaotic and often inconsistent symbols of the alchemists as patterned representations of psychological change that reveal the process of inner transformation, or what he later called individuation.

Alchemy is relevant today in other ways as well. In addition to the parallels between alchemy and the framework of Jungian analytic theory and practice, James Hillman[4] proposes that alchemical language itself is therapeutic, giving us concrete, materially-oriented words that describe states of soul otherwise lost in contemporary psychological terms. Alchemy's words and images, such as "sulphur and salt, buried in horse dung, putrefying or congealing, turning white or green or yellow, encircled by a tail-biting serpent, rising on wings," cannot be taken literally, yet they are "accurate, descriptively true." Engaging with this language restores an "alchemical mode of imagining"[5] that rational thinking pushes aside.

Hillman's later essays on color explore the way alchemical language and the language of color combine to form images meaningful not only to the alchemists long ago, but also to us today. In "Notes on White Supremacy: Essaying an Archetypal Account of Historical Events,"[6] "Silver and the White Earth,"[7] and "The Seduction of Black,"[8] he recognizes and explores the archetypal and alchemical aspects of white and black as colors. Based on what he calls an alchemical appreciation of color, he writes that although each of the main hues may be interpreted symbolically, it is more important that they are perceived "*in imagistic context,* as colors in a painting derive their values from their relations with other colors."[9] This combines the characteristics of a color with all that relates to it. Viewed as much more than symbols having specified cultural meanings, color images reverberate on multiple levels.

In his essay, "The Yellowing of the Work,"[10] Hillman explores the significance of yellow for alchemy and psychology. Considering it as a necessary temporal quality of a transitional process, yellow (in its association with sulphur) can have the rotting, stinking properties of decay.[11] The old characteristics related to the darkness of *nigredo* must die, though, so progress can be made to the next phase. A transition from white (*albedo*) to yellow (*citrinitas*) indicates a change in thought as a clarifying intellectual illumination.

Hillman's "Alchemical Blue and the Unio Mentalis"[12] considers the importance of the alchemical blue transition as a phase between the black *nigredo* that leads into the white *albedo*. "Thus blue is the retarding factor in the whitening ... the element of depression, that raises deep doubts and high principles, wanting to settle things fundamentally ... . the effect can also appear in feelings of guilt and conscience." In this essay he points to poets and painters as the alchemists of our time: "The alchemical laboratory is in their work with words and paints, and psychology continues its tradition of learning from alchemy by learning from them." A footnote quoting the motto of the British landscape artist John Constable emphasizes the alchemical parallels: "The whole object and difficulty of the art (indeed of all the fine arts) is to *unite imagination with nature.*"[13] Anyone who works imaginatively—whether in art, science, agriculture, or business—strives for such integration.

Alchemy and Imagination

Alchemy's imaginings bring together concrete earthly images with more abstract psychic images. In his introduction to *Encountering Jung: Jung on Alchemy*, analyst Nathan Schwartz-Salant writes:

> In distinction to most of his other works, Jung's alchemical studies often present the self as having an embodied, material aspect. While Jung often takes references to the body in alchemical texts to mean the realization of consciousness in behavior or daily life, he follows another path of inquiry, that of the body and its transformations, and also that of the mental-spiritual self's

> embodiment. In alchemy the *lapis* has a 'spiritual' and a 'material' aspect.[14]

That the philosophers' stone is of a dual nature presents a challenge to our contemporary rational thinking. Whether their process defined the gold, the red stone, or the healing elixir as an ultimate goal, the alchemists infused their physical work with spiritual meaning through the imagination. The act of imagining gives access to spiritual and material realms simultaneously.

The imagination of the European alchemists, explains Raff, was expressed through their creation of emblems and drawings.[15] These images were not meant simply to accompany their writings, but were created to stand independently of the text. Through the use of the alchemist's meditative imagination, these images embodied the energies needed for the work, or the *opus*. By meditating on an emblem the alchemist engaged with the physical and the spiritual through "the wisdom and the puissance of the imagination." Thus the imagination was considered to be an indispensable "key to revelation."[16]

Different from fantasy, which is understood here to be more about the ego's needs and desires, such meditative imagination can be useful in this exploration of color in alchemical images and symbolism.

Color as an Alchemical Framework

Alchemical language utilizes arcane symbolic terminology that is, by design, often dense and difficult to access. Similarly, alchemical emblems are intricate and highly detailed depictions of imaginal enactments. Both language and images, however, often contain very specific references to colors. Color symbolism can indicate states of consciousness as well as change. Raff asserts that although alchemical images are indeed metaphors, "beyond that, they are symbolic expressions of states of consciousness and felt visions that are unique in themselves."[17] An alchemical engagement with the colors of images and their changes reflects the complexity of this mode of imagining.

As a way to engage with transformative processes, color is one aspect of a vastly complex system. Thus, it is more illuminating to consider it in context with other alchemical concepts such as those described in Edward Edinger's *Anatomy of the Psyche.*[18] Addressing the need to put what he calls the chaos of alchemy into order, Edinger focuses on seven major alchemical operations, or procedures, common to many of the ancient texts. While these operations are often discussed as occurring in a traditional progression, they can, in fact, occur in any order. Edinger finds that most alchemical imagery (along with the imagery of myth, religion, and folklore that also emerges from the archetypal psyche) can be ordered around these operations. This kind of approach, like one through color, enables an engagement with images that remains on a symbolic level.

Edinger offers the following quote from Jung to elucidate the paradox of working in this manner:

> Of course we all have an understandable desire for crystal clarity, but we are apt to forget that in psychic matters we are dealing with processes of experience, that is with transformations which should never be given hard and fast names if their living movement is not to petrify into something static. The protean mythologem and the shimmering symbol express the processes of the psyche far more trenchantly and, in the end, far more clearly than the clearest concept: for the symbol not only conveys a visualization of the process, but—and this is perhaps just as important—it also brings a re-experiencing of it, of that twilight which we can learn to understand only through inoffensive empathy, but which too much clarity only dispels.[19]

In his address to the 1990 Eranos conference, Hillman, too, cautions against trying to make linear, literal sense of alchemy, understanding it instead "as images of psychic conditions always available."[20] He emphasizes Jung's point that a person's engagement in the process, or the *opus*, is more important than creating the *lapis*, more of a search than an attainment. Discussing the goals of alchemy, Hillman writes:

> The precious goals of alchemy are neither physical achievements (they did not make physical gold) nor metaphysical truths (they did not redeem themselves). We are not in the realm of metaphysics or physics.[21]

Through the alchemical realm of the imaginal, the embodiment of psyche's images can be entered and experienced as the *opus*. This process is not solution-oriented. Uniquely, though, it is meaningful.

The alchemical hermeneutic methodology developed by Robert Romanyshyn and Veronica Goodchild also is not about solutions.

Rather,

> The circle of interpretation becomes a spiral in which the mutual engagement between 'text' and research is not only deepened; it is disrupted. In the hermeneutic spiral the progressive move toward the making of meaning in the circle of understanding becomes a move toward the continuous unmaking of meaning.... [In other words] presence precedes meaning.[22]

In this spirit and attitude, my attempt to engage with the relevance and meaning in alchemy is through color as an intrinsic aspect of images reflecting the process of transformation.

Color in Alchemy

Working to transmute a substance from one state to another, alchemists watched closely for color changes. Such transitions indicated that the material as well as its essence was transforming. We find such knowledge useful in practical, everyday aspects of the world today that are often taken for granted. Fruit changes color as it sweetens; the human body reflects sickness or health by changes in its color; and the color of the skies indicates the character of the weather, as Hillman[23] has observed. In the natural world or in a laboratory, an outer change in the color of something can mean its inner nature is reorganizing and transforming.

Through the correlation of alchemy with the individuation process, color changes may be understood as primary indicators of movement from one psychological state to another. Particular colors can symbolize stages within the process of change as well as particular emotional states of the individual engaged in the *opus*. Hillman notes, "transitions of color in our moods, tastes and dream figures reflect alterations in the material of the soul."[24] Manifestations of color changes can occur on many levels.

Jung defines the four stages of alchemical change characterized by colors as the blackening, the whitening, the yellowing, and the reddening.[25] These primary color terms, Hillman[26] contends, embrace the entire alchemical *opus—nigredo* (black), *albedo* (white), *xanthosis or citrinitas* (yellow), and *rubedo* (red). In this article, these phases of change will be explored as they appear in a contemporary short story about a woman's emotional journey.

Alchemical Color in Flannery O'Connor's "Revelation"

Fiction is an imaginal realm, often containing images and symbols within its text that influence readers on both conscious and unconscious levels. In examining the highly-acclaimed short story, "Revelation," by twentieth-century American writer Flannery O'Connor,[27] color can be interpreted alchemically as an indication of the protagonist's psychological process. Much like the alchemists, the author communicates a perception of the psyche's movement through the use of color. Here, though, the experience of color is activated through written words alone, themselves symbols that evoke images. Thought is transcended with these color-filled word images, opening readers to the archetypal realm while remaining grounded in the material world.

In O'Connor's story, color reveals a lopsided and rigidly judgmental figure, Ruby Turpin, whose own colored survey of the world is incomplete, ego-driven, and fragmented. Color moves the plot to suggest that Ruby needs to see more of the multi-hued and nuanced shades of the world than her limited vision presently allows. The title, "Revelation," braces readers for an intervention of consequence, a communication of truth, and the opportunity for a profound change of heart that reaches to the very core of psychological change.

O'Connor's Background and Influences

Like the alchemists of the Middle Ages who did not distinguish between the religious and practical nature of their work,[28] O'Connor did not write with an overtly religious emphasis. Yet the strong influence of her Catholic beliefs, evident in the themes of many of her stories, has been frequently noted. Literary critic Ted Spivey knew her personally and believes that her Catholicism exerted a more complex influence upon her work: "There was another, even more important tension in her nature—the tension between her conservative Catholic vision … and her modernist sociologically trained intellect." He concludes: "The struggle within her, partly conscious and partly unconscious, accounts for the strangely visionary quality of O'Connor's fiction."[29] Skillfully, she draws readers into an imaginal terrain populated by absurd, yet uncomfortably familiar characters who face crises of spiritual magnitude. Like it or not, their tensions—and O'Connor's—somehow resonate within us.

O'Connor's library included Jung's *Modern Man in Search of a Soul.*[30] Although "O'Connor hesitates to claim much affinity with Jung," Rebecca Rowley argues that the parallels between religious experience and the psychological process of individuation, along with the themes of many of her short stories, indicate that Jung may have influenced O'Connor more than she acknowledged.[31] Books on Jungian thought in her library (by Victor White and Josef Goldbrunner) and the marginalia within her copy of *Modern Man in Search of a Soul* suggest this influence as well. That she marked the following passage by Jung implies her interest in archetypes that are activated in artistic and poetic visions and work:

> When people go astray they feel the need of a guide or teacher ....These primordial images are numerous, but do not appear in the dreams of individuals or in works of art until they are called into being by the waywardness of the general outlook. When conscious life is characterized by one-sidedness and by a false attitude, then they are activated—one might say "instinctively" —and come to light in the dreams of individuals and the visions of artists and seers, thus restoring the psychic equilibrium of the epoch. In this way the work of the poet comes to meet the spiritual need of the society in which he lives.[32]

Primordial Images in O'Connor's Writing

O'Connor's imagery is rich and has been examined from many perspectives. Her images are sometimes called colorful, although her particular use of color as an aspect of the imagery has been explored very little. W.R. Martin's short essay, "A Note on Ruby and Revelation,"[33] proposes the color red as an indicator of divine presence in O'Connor stories. Literary critic Stephen Portch observes that her use of visual, realistic details, including color, is "an index to psychological truth," ensuring that readers can go beyond the stated and obvious into nonverbal and more convincing depth.[34] These critics' brief observations provide some suggestion of the importance of color, yet do not fully explore its depth.

Through color, O'Connor simultaneously evokes the physical nature of an image and its spiritual essence. Once activated, this image becomes more fully formed within the narrative context, where color changes reflect the psychological movement of the story. When the color imagery in "Revelation" is explored with this kind of alchemical imagination, its archetypal aspects become more apparent.

The Story

As the author introduces her, Mrs. Turpin does not appear to be aware of her need for transformation. Significantly, though, the story begins with her discomfort in the confines of a doctor's waiting room. Waiting there for the treatment of her husband's injury, she quickly judges the room and its inhabitants. Privy to Mrs. Turpin's unabashed mental observations, readers learn of her nature and character as she makes sweeping generalizations punctuated with a colorful description of all she sees even before she eases herself into a chair. Whether through a simple notation of a "well-dressed grey-haired lady" or the detail of her husband's bruise ("a purple swelling on a plump marble-white calf"), Mrs. Turpin neatly and thoroughly categorizes her environment.[35]

In this initial scene, Mrs. Turpin's values are emphasized by her associations to the hues of a single color. Her glance lingers on a plastic fern contained in a gold pot and is disturbed by the "white-trashy" woman with dirty, yellow hair, wearing a gritty yellow sweatshirt.[36] Through the contrast with gold and yellow, O'Connor indicates what Mrs. Turpin values and what she sees as beneath her. That gold, universally higher in value than yellow, appears on the same distasteful woman's sandals is clearly all wrong in Mrs. Turpin's view, a marked contrast to her accepting observance of the unchanging and artificial gold-potted fern. The gold she values here is like the vulgar gold warned against by the alchemists. Those who sought such gold remained strictly on a superficial level, missing the point of the true nature and value of the alchemical process. Mrs. Turpin misses the point with her narrow-sighted values.

Racial color, too, has a hierarchy in Mrs. Turpin's biased view. By seeing and judging the world in terms of literal as well as racial color, she soothes and distracts herself from anything that might interrupt and challenge her comfortable, literal, and self-serving perspective. Her world is colored by her need to put people into order—her order.

But Mrs. Turpin's rigid hierarchy and smug superiority are assaulted, literally, when she is hit directly over her left eye by a blue book with the ironic title, *Human Development.* This book, an image of truth and knowledge, along with the assailant's message, "Go back to hell where you came from, you old wart hog,"[37] interrupts the narrative of her bigoted thoughts and shatters her ordered and rigid defenses. As a catalyst for her emotional journey, the assault begins a psychological and, I propose, alchemical process that culminates in a powerful revelatory vision.

Prima Materia — The Beginning of the Work

An image of color is readily evoked with the full name of the protagonist: Ruby Turpin. But significantly, the given name—Ruby —is undisclosed until after the pivotal point when she is assaulted and hit with the book. Until then, she is referred to as Mrs. Turpin, as if hidden behind the formality of her surname. Alchemically speaking, it is as if the Ruby, the red stone, cannot yet come to life.[38]

An association can be made between the name, Turpin, and the substance "turpentine," a cleansing agent used for thinning or removing paint. By emphasizing this in the beginning of the story, O'Connor seems to be indicating that the protagonist needs to remove all that judgmental surface color to see what lies beneath it. In alchemical terms, this would be equated with the dissolution process of the *solutio*, with finding the *prima materia*, the first material that is deep within the chaos at the beginning of the work.

Von Franz associates red to the alchemists' *prima materia* and interprets it as the emotional quality related to fire: "The wingless bird, the red sulphur," she writes, "is an underlying factor of the inner psychic life and is always what one has first to unearth, for it is the *prima materia.*"[39] Applied to Ruby Turpin, this suggests that the emotions that ultimately lead her to a fiery revelation are unconscious until the assault shocks her into a different emotional state.

By joining the given name, Ruby, with the surname, Turpin, at the pivotal confrontation, the image emerges of a precious gem of supreme value that will be revealed only by dissolution through the chaos of the *nigredo.* O'Connor's conscious literary intentions would not have been likely to take her to this point, yet the depth of this image is powerful and indicates a life of its own—the ruby (or the red) as *prima materia*.

Experiencing Black, White, Yellow, and Red

Ruby Turpin's confusion builds from this point to the climax of the story, escalating as she psychologically absorbs the impact of the blow. Surprisingly, once she returns home, she shares her shock with workers on her farm, people she would typically consider beneath her. The black women sympathize too vehemently with the injustice of her described injuries, suggesting that what they are saying contradicts their true thoughts and feelings. Ruby has no patience for their insincerity, perhaps because this mirrors her own attitude prior to the assault.

O'Connor paints this exchange with the women beneath a sun that gets "whiter and whiter, blanching the sky overhead so that the leaves of the hickory tree were black in the face of it." This creates a contrasting image of radiant light that brings darkness into relief. Ruby reflects for a moment and O'Connor emphasizes the darkness that has descended upon her: "The dark protuberance over her eye looked like a miniature tornado cloud which might at any moment sweep across the horizon of her brow."[40] A state of blackness, Hillman writes, is a descent that occurs each time accomplishment falls apart.[41] In Ruby's case, the way she has constructed the world has fallen apart, and the *nigredo* of her dark wound indicates it should not be ignored.

Ruby's shock then turns to self-righteous anger. Questioning, or "mind's explanatory attacks on the soul," corresponds with the *nigredo* phase as a first level of psychological understanding. These attacks, Hillman writes, objectify events. "Something is being done to me beyond my doing. What is happening is a divine process; I am its victim."[42] Caught within the confusion and anger of the *nigredo*, Ruby questions the hidden message within her assault.

"With the look of a woman going single-handed, weaponless, into battle"[43] and as the sun changes from white to a deep yellow, she marches into the pig parlor on her farm where she turns a hard stream of water on the pigs. Hillman[44] calls the yellowing of the *opus* a necessary transition between white and red that sees each thing as it is, beyond subjectivity. Ruby does not yet see that her own bigoted subjectivity is wrong, but she no longer can self-righteously hold onto her singular view. Working up her fury at what she knows to be the divine source of the message, she challenges the contradictions that are undoing her once tidy sense of superiority. Where previously she conversed with Jesus to reinforce her thoughts and biases, now she fiercely roars at him, "Who do you think you are?"[45]

The landscape reflects a vivid response to her question: "The color of everything, field and crimson sky, burned for a moment with transparent intensity." For once, Ruby Turpin is silenced. She slowly gazes at the hogs, who seem to have something Ruby as yet cannot comprehend: "A red glow suffused them. They appeared to pant with a secret life."[46] The color of the sun and sky has changed from white to deep yellow to red—an alchemical progression of *albedo*, *citrinitas*, and *rubedo*. This, the red glow of the pigs, and Ruby herself indicate different stages of illumination. Jung explains that an external event can have the effect of illuminating consciousness:

> The illumination comes to a certain extent from the unconscious.... This dawning light corresponds to the *albedo* .... The growing redness (*rubedo*) ... denotes an increase of warmth and light coming from the sun, consciousness.... which now begins to react emotionally to the contents produced by the unconscious.[47]

Ruby Turpin is now able to lift her head toward the sky and follow a purple streak that cuts through the crimson field into the descending dusk. The vision she then beholds is a marked contrast to her rigid beliefs. Over "a field of living fire," a swinging bridge extends toward heaven. She still uses her judgmental language toward those people she sees as different from herself. But she cannot ignore that the "battalions of freaks and lunatics shouting and clapping and leaping like frogs" are leading the procession toward heaven. Surprisingly, white people like herself bring up the rear, despite their "good order and common sense and respectable behavior."[48]

As she looks more closely, though, Ruby sees something else remarkable about this group of people with which she identifies. Although "they alone were on key ... she could see by their shocked and altered faces that even their virtues were being burned away." The vision fades and as Ruby makes "her slow way on the darkening path to the house," she is left hearing the voices of the crickets as "the voices of the souls climbing upward into the starry field and shouting hallelujah."[49] The story ends here.

As one of the basic alchemical symbols, fire is associated with the emotion necessary for change. Marie-Louise von Franz writes that fire transforms, cooks, and brings light through emotion as the carrier of consciousness. "The fire has to burn the fire, one just has to burn in the emotion till the fire dies down and becomes balanced .... It must be endured .... until the last unclean element has been consumed."[50] The operation of *calcinatio* uses fire to act upon the black stuff of the *nigredo* by purging it and turning it white.[51] O'Connor does not reveal directly or through an image of whiteness whether Ruby Turpin has endured the revelation of the fire enough to be purified. She is subdued and quiet, though, still hearing the voices of revelation in the final image.

Perhaps O'Connor, with her Catholic beliefs, intended the story's revelation as one of divine grace that instantly alters Ruby's self-defined virtues. Dennis Patrick Slattery,[52] who introduced me to this story, argues that she is changed forever. The embedded images and processes in the story, however, lead me to a different interpretation which reflects more of an alchemical confluence of spirit and matter in color.

O'Connor leaves Ruby in the darkness with only the voices of the lingering vision. Although the fiery image of the heavenly procession holds many polarities and could represent the transformative energy of a fiery red *rubedo*, the falling darkness seems to indicate more of a continued *nigredo*. The alchemists point out that this phase must not be left too quickly and often must be returned to repeatedly.[53] Ruby's revelation represents a single encounter with the unconscious or the divine; although it has impacted her deeply, it may take repeated confrontations for her to embrace lasting change.

Whether or not this alchemical interpretation would resonate with O'Connor, insightful and visionary artists like her often seem to bridge consciousness and the unconscious. Viscerally through color, O'Connor has moved me into the more embodied experience of what it is to think and to feel like Ruby Turpin. Ruby's revelation is our revelation: an opportunity to hold and to feel the emotional tension between similarities and differences until these distinctions are united on a single multi-hued path.

NOTES

1. Jeffrey Raff, *Jung and the Alchemical Imagination* (Berwick, ME: Nicolas-Hays, Inc., 2000).

2. *Ibid.,* xvi.

3. C. G. Jung, *Memories, Dreams, Reflections* (New York: Random House, 1963).

4. James Hillman, "Therapeutic Value of Alchemical Language," *Dragonflies: Studies in Imaginal Psychology*, Fall (1978): 33-42.

5. *Ibid.,* 39, 40.

6. James Hillman, "Notes on White Supremacy: Essaying an Archetypal Account of Historical Events," *Spring*, (1986): 29-58.

7. James Hillman, "Silver and the White Earth, (Part One)," *Spring*, (1980), 21-48 and "Silver and the White Earth, (Part Two)," *Spring*, (1981), 21-66.

8. James Hillman, "The Seduction of Black," in S. Marlan (ed.), *Fire in the Stone: The Alchemy of Desire* (Wilmette, IL: Chiron, 1997).

9. Hillman, "Notes on White Supremacy," 48.

10. James Hillman, "The Yellowing of the Work," paper presented at the proceedings of the Eleventh International Congress for Analytical Psychology, Paris, 1989.

11. Analyst Robert Bosnak (personal communication, June 6, 2005) considers the fermentation of the yellow *citrinitas* phase, like other alchemical color phases, applicable to dream work. From the alchemical perspective within his approach (called Embodied Dream Imagery or Embodied Imagination), color can be considered a state of consciousness in itself as it appears in a dream image.

12. James Hillman, "Alchemical Blue and the Unio Mentalis," *Sulphur, 1* (1981), 33-50.

13. *Ibid.,* 36, 45, 50.

14. Nathan Schwartz-Salant, *Encountering Jung: Jung on Alchemy* (Princeton: Princeton University Press, 1995), 15.

15. Raff, *Alchemical Imagination.*

16. *Ibid.,* 83, 52.

17. *Ibid., xxvi.*

18. Edward Edinger, *Anatomy of the Psyche: Alchemical Symbolism in Psychotherapy* (La Salle, IL: Open Court, 1985).

19. Jung, quoted in Edinger, 15.

20. James Hillman, "Concerning the Stone: Alchemical Images of the Goal," *Sphinx 5,* 243.

21. *Ibid.,* 241.

22. Robert Romanyshyn and Veronica Goodchild, *Doing Re-search with Soul in Mind: The Alchemical Hermeneutic Method* (Unpublished manuscript: Carpinteria, CA, 2003), 36-37.

23. Hillman, "The Yellowing of the Work," 78.

24. Hillman, "Silver and the White Earth (Part Two)," 23.

25. Jung, in Schwartz-Salant, *Encountering Jung,* 104.

26. Hillman, *"The Seduction of Black,"* 45.

27. Flannery O'Connor, "Revelation," in *The Complete Stories* (New York: Noonday Press, 1971).

28. Raff, *Alchemical Imagination.*

29. Ted Spivey, *Flannery O'Connor: The Woman, the Thinker, the Visionary* (Macon, GA: Mercer University Press, 1995), 10.

30. Kathleen Feeley, *Flannery O'Connor: Voice of the Peacock* (New York: Fordham University Press, 1982); Rebecca K. Rowley, "Individuation and Religious Experience: A Jungian Approach to O'Connor's 'Revelation,'" *Southern Literary Journal,* 25. 2 (1993), 92-102.

31. Rowley, 92.

32. Jung, quoted in Feeley, 14.

33. W. R. Martin, "A Note on Ruby and Revelation," *The Flannery O'Connor Bulletin,* 16, 1987), 23-25.

34. Stephen R. Portch, *Literature's Silent Language* (New York: Lang, 1985), 117.

35. O'Connor, 488-489.

36. *Ibid.,* 490.

37. *Ibid.,* 500.

38. Stanton Marlan, "Fire in the Stone: An Inquiry into the Alchemy of Soul-making," in S. Marlan (ed.), *Fire in the Stone: The Alchemy of Desire* (Wilmette, IL: Chiron, 1997) presents a patient's dream that centers on the image of a ruby. He notes that the alchemical idea of the ruby as both the initial material that begins the process, the first matter, or *prima materia*—and as the ultimate goal, the philosopher's stone—was put forth by Katon Shual, *Sexual Magick* (1995), linking together the Indian alchemical and Tantric traditions.

39. Marie-Louise von Franz, *Alchemy: An Introduction to the Symbolism and the Psychology* (Toronto: Inner City Books, 1980), 127.

40. O'Connor, 504, 505.

41. Hillman, "Concerning the Stone."

42. *Ibid.,* 244.

43. O'Connor, 505.

44. Hillman, *The Yellowing of the Work.*

45. O'Connor, 507.

46. *Ibid.,* 508.

47. Jung, in Schwartz-Salant, *Encountering Jung,* 107.

48. O'Connor, 508.

49. *Ibid.,* 508, 509.

50. Von Franz, 252.

51. Edinger, 26.

52. Dennis Patrick Slattery, personal communication, 2004.

53. Hillman, *Concerning the Stone.*

Jung and Alchemy: An Interview with Thomas Moore

ROBERT S. HENDERSON

Thomas Moore was born in Detroit, Michigan. At age thirteen he entered the Servite religious order of the Catholic Church in preparation for a life of teaching and ministry. He left the order before being ordained and subsequently received his Ph.D. in religion from Syracuse University. His many publications include: *Care of the Soul, The Soul's Religion, The Soul of Sex, Dark Eros, Rituals of the Imagination, The Planets Within, A Blue Fire, Meditations, Soul Mates, The Re-nchantment of Everyday Life, The Education of the Heart, The Book of Job, Original Self,* and *Dark Nights of the Soul.* He and his wife, Joan, live in New Hampshire with their two children, Siobhan and Abraham.

* * * * * *

Robert Henderson: How did you get interested in Jung?

Thomas Moore: I had read *Modern Man in Search of a Soul* in my late twenties, but when I arrived at Syracuse University to work on a Ph.D. in religion, David Miller assigned the *Collected Works* as required reading. I read through them quickly and got an overview, completely

Robert S. Henderson is a pastoral psychotherapist living in Glastonbury, Connecticut. His forthcoming book, co-written with his wife Janis, is called *Living with Jung: "Enterviews" with Jungian Analysts,* and will be published by Spring Journal Books in the summer of 2006.

taken especially by the alchemy and phenomenology of religion. I read them a second time and became interested in a Jung behind Jung, not the system but the asides and the preparatory material for the system, the *prima materia*, so to speak. It was a time of awakening for me, and Jung played a major role. I remember being excited about his reading of the symbolism of the Mass. I wasn't long out of a monastery and appreciated Jung's depth imagination at work on material that was familiar to me. *Memories, Dreams, Reflections* taught me a lot about doing psychotherapy, about not interpreting with too much fire but connecting concretely with dreams and other kinds of imagery.

HENDERSON: Will you say more about the Jung behind the Jung that you became interested in?

MOORE: There are many Jungs, of course, maybe as many as there are readers of Jung. I find the systematic Jung beguiling but ultimately untrustworthy. His anima/animus/shadow/great mother are like Joseph Campbell's journey structure—too easy. Life is too particular and complicated to be reduced so far. There is a point in reduction where it serves simplification rather than clarification. I'm attracted to the Jung of *Memories, Dreams, Reflections*. I don't care if it isn't an authentic autobiography. It's the story of a life told with emphasis on the things that matter most, especially on the coalescing of a life story. It isn't confessional in the usual sense—it doesn't courageously offer secret details of the external life—but instead points to those places where emotion and fantasy come together to reveal the milestones of a life and its fundamental orientation. It is more subtle and complicated than the theory as reduced to Jungianism.

I'm drawn to Jung the alchemist. His writings on alchemy are a model for exploring traditional imagery with an eye on our own contemporary experience. I was recently told that the poet H.D. said, "I like my alchemy straight, so I don't read Jung." I don't agree. I like some help with difficult image systems, but I don't want any traditional system turned into modern theory. I find that Jung is quite moderate in applying his theory to alchemy, or reducing alchemy to it. I've read *The Psychology of the Transference* innumerable times, and each time I get something more out of it. I enjoy Jung most when he works as hard at preserving the mysteries as he does at clarifying them.

I appreciate Jung the religion historian and phenomenologist. I don't pay much attention, again, to those places where he psychologizes too much or Jungianizes the traditions. But, for me, he opens up archaic images so they can be appropriated and lived. My first reading of his essays on the symbolism in the Mass and his book *Aion* transformed by life. I didn't have to go out and Jungianize my world, but I could then address those received traditions in language that made them adoptable. I'm still doing that in my own work.

Most of all, I like Jung the Magus. I profoundly appreciate his reverence for magic, superstition, astrology, seance, and psychic abilities. Here is where he really departs from modernity and points a way back toward an enchanted life. The myth of modernism is killing us, dehumanizing us, and making us ever more arrogant. Jung's understanding of magic separates him from Freud and even those Jungian rationalists who are embarrassed by his esotericism. From the first time I read Jung, I wished he would not try to have it both ways and make his philosophy/psychology both rationalistic and esoteric. I wish he had trusted the spiritual and the magical even more. I'm also drawn to Jung the non-moralistic lover. Today I hear people judging him for the shape of his erotic life. I don't think we should criticize anyone for the sexual design of their lives. That is the most arrogant position of all. There are many more Jungs, but this is enough of a list for now.

HENDERSON: What is alchemy and why do you feel it is important?

MOORE: I'm not as knowledgeable about alchemy as I wish I were. I do know a few things. I'm especially interested in getting beyond the esoteric way of talking about it and seeing it in everyday life. For instance, I like to notice the coloring of moods and the shifting from one to another. I'm interested in the aspect of alchemy where you pay close attention and watch what is going on. You don't manufacture the process, but you further it with your care and skill. That sort of thing.

Alchemy is a form of imagination, a way of looking at certain qualities of experience and taking note of their transformations. Just as astrology uses the planets and their movements as material for a rich imagination touching on the whole of life, alchemy uses substances and their qualities for a similar purpose. And, just as we all practice astrology in simple ordinary ways, noticing the moon on an especially haunting night or commenting on the sun and even the weather, we also speak in alchemical imagery. He's a salty man. She has a will of iron. I'm steamed about what happened. My brain is fried. I feel blue. I'm in a black mood. Something is simmering in me. The point in speaking of alchemy seriously is to explore a rich image base for increased subtlety in our appreciation for developments in the soul. I have turned to mythology for many years for that kind of inspiration, but alchemy offers its own riches.

Jung shows how alchemy can help us understand the complexities of the transference in his book on that theme, and James Hillman has written many long and detailed essays on alchemical themes, such as salt, the colors white and blue, and the relation between Mars and anger, sulphur, and so on. I am curently writing a book called *OPUS*, using the alchemical word for the entire process of alchemy. My book is about finding your life work. So, alchemy is everywhere. Some of the alchemical themes we could discuss include vessels, processes, goals, heat, color, images, and the whole idea of personal growth, change, transformation, and development, as well as marriage, therapy, and family as vessels for alchemy.

HENDERSON: How do you see marriage and family as a vessel for alchemy? Do you see alchemic processes going on in marriages and families?

MOORE: When two people decide to marry, they take traditional ideas and forms, mix them with their own ideas and hopes and fears about a sexual life and living together, and go ahead, moved by even deeper, timeless fantasies and urges. They create an imaginal space in which their lives will unfold mutually and independently. That space is the first step in the alchemy of a marriage. It is the vessel. Into it they will pour their moments of happiness and their disillusionments. Maybe I shouldn't say that they will pour them in. Most of what goes on in a marriage is unconscious to the people involved. When people ask me, as they often do, what is the secret of a good marriage, as if I somehow knew the answer, I say: Tend to your partner's mystery. Tolerate it and appreciate and sometimes enjoy it. Then, learn from your experience to enjoy your own mysteriousness and unpredictability. I have never forgotten Jung saying that the biggest problem in marriage is one person assuming that the other has a psychological structure and dynamic similar to his own. So, in marriage an alchemy develops. The *prima materia* is the family histories, the cultural expectations, the individual anxieties and talents, the developing history of the marriage itself, and so on. The material is vast. And usually there is a lot of heat in a marriage. People are quick to anger and passion and perhaps revivified love. The vessel may be in constant danger of leaking and breaking, but that vulnerability seems to make the whole process intense. (This theme is a book!) One advantage in regarding marriage as an alchemical process is to get some of the ego out of it and to watch it from a distance with some objectivity. Marriage is a process you agree to participate in, not something you create and control. I remember playing at marriage and family when I was a small child. Those early fantasies are material for the present as well. The family alchemy is very similar. There isn't much choice involved in family matters. You find yourself in a huge tub of idealism, strong feelings, and generic detritus. There is love and there is frustration.

I have long thought that caring for the soul of a family means honoring the basics: blood ties, variety of personalities, histories, insanities and neuroses. I think what you get from a family is basic belonging, a fundamental narrative, and an imaginal space of identity. It's all alchemy. I see value in trying to help troubled families deal with their struggles, but I think it's a mistake to make it all rational and "therapeutic." People have to grow up and discover that family is not only literal. You find yourself in bigger, less literal "families" as your life complexifies. Yet that ur-vessel of your family remains as a factor forever.

HENDERSON: Some say that people have sexual thoughts many, many times each day. We have Viagra, affairs, and pornography. Masturbation is still seldom mentioned. Can alchemy help us understand sexuality?

MOORE: The first thing that comes to mind when I think of alchemy and sexuality are the many images of the king and queen lying on top of each other in the vessel. This suggests a theme that is important in all my work: Sexuality is one of the main dynamics in all that we do and are. Sex is not only part of physical life, it is also a major factor in the life of the soul and spirit. Only a materialistic viewpoint would allow us to speak of sex as "physical love." The alchemical images indicate that sex is part of the process by which the soul comes to life. In other words, alchemy works by means of erotic energy—not mind and not will. It helps us see that in some areas the soul is always in a certain phase in the process of its coming to life. One of those phases is the work of connecting elements that have been separate or alienated.

In my own life, I am always trying to connect my work world with the realm of family, or my love of solitude with my need for friendship, or my drive to be creative with my wish to relax and do nothing. These contraries all are filled with desire, but how do you get the competing desires to connect? Ultimately, it's a sexual matter. The sexuality of the soul. Alchemy shows that I have to find a vessel for this process, a way to keep it in solution, and some form where the two desires can copulate or couple. It's a process that takes time and won't be forced. It requires experiment and observation. It involves many ingredients: my past history, my ideals, my fears, my past failures, my passions. All this material somehow has to be gathered together in a suitable vessel and allowed to stew for a long time.

My sexuality is an important factor. How much do I trust my desire? What am I strongly attracted to? Where do my moralisms and anxieties appear? I don't think that sexual fantasies—whether individual and internal or cultural and pornographic—are usually about sexual behavior. I think they always represent a process in the soul whereby it is moving toward increased vitality. I would call sex, in a rather Jungian fashion, the archetype of life. It always represents an invitation for increased vitality, though the images for this important development may be confused, because taken too literally, with concrete sexual choices. I don't mean that we are never faced with decisions about sexual activity, but that more often erotic fantasy has to do with attractions and convergences of soul and spirit.

An example I often use, one I assume is familiar to most therapists, is the person who is happily married and yet is suddenly overwhelmed by an attraction to another person. The first therapeutic effort is to sort out the desires: Are they about actual relationships or about developments in the soul or both? Next, you have to read the sexual fantasies and emotions in relation to matters of relationship and tensions in the soul. Quickly, you shift from engineering life's arrangements to dealing with the soul's alchemy.

HENDERSON: Given the importance, for Jung and his creativity, of his relationship with Toni Wolff, a relationship where there was probably connection on all levels, including the sexual, what do you feel that the relationship revealed about Jung's soul?

MOORE: Let me say first that I am an admirer and a student of Jung, but I am not a Jung groupie. I don't know any secrets about his life, and I've never visited the holy places connected to him. I know very little about his relationships, though, of course, there is the gossip always about him and Toni Wolff. Let's say the gossip is true and Jung lived in a *ménage à trois* for a while. From his writings, Jung doesn't appear to have been a moralist. I mean someone who is always worried about the propriety of his private life, especially his sexual arrangements. Now, if you're not a moralist, how do you deal with your desires and fantasies for a wide-ranging scale of sexual experiences? The two extremes seem to be: Don't feel limited and do what you can to satisfy all your desires. Or, be committed to one person and never break those bonds. In between is a land of experiment and imagination. People try all kinds of formats from open marriage to serial monogamy. I don't think there is one right way of doing it. Much depends on the people and on the time in their lives.

Jung lived from a deep root-place and understood the connection between eros and sexuality. I mean that he didn't reduce the erotic life to sex. He lived from the soul. I believe he could come up with an arrangement that would be full of soul and flexible. I trust that his solutions to his sexuality were both ethical and thoughtful. Even so, I understand that women, especially those who have been betrayed in love, might find his ways objectionable. I understand that religious moralists would complain. Some men might think he was just creative at getting his own pleasures. But we are talking about some very thoughtful people—Jung, his wife, and his friends. It isn't my role to judge them. On the other hand, Jung is not only a father figure for many people, he is also a model of how to live the soul-centered life. Everyone has to deal with their sexual desires and fears and history, and many would like to know how Jung worked it all out. The point is, he directed all his ideas toward individuation, becoming a unique person.

We all have to find our way sexually and allow ourselves some room to experiment and fail. We have to forgive ourselves and others. Those who criticize Jung for his solutions probably are not comfortable with their own, or they have not allowed themselves to live. Those who want to copy Jung haven't heard his words about individuation. Sexuality is life. If you try to box it in too tightly, you don't live.

You die slowly. If you don't make the effort to give it a shape in your life, you're just living unconsciously. No alchemy. No soul. I think it's important to allow each other and ourselves opportunities to learn who we are sexually and to find forms that contain our passions without suppressing them excessively and while making the effort to give sex form. Jung found forms that worked for him and, one presumes, his lovers. Family, friends, and students may not approve, but that is the least of one's worries. To be alive, to be sexual, automatically means that you will not be approved by those who choose the death principle over the life principle. It's the calling of moralists to complain and of people of soul to live.

HENDERSON: That is most interesting, Tom. You had earlier mentioned moods. Moods can take over a person. Can alchemy help us with our moods?

MOORE: Alchemy shows that moods are sometimes a coloring. Alchemy speaks of blackening, greening, yellowing, whitening, blueing, and reddening. These are all moods or colors—states of soul. Alchemy shows that there are naturally many colors that follow one another, not in any prescribed order, but according to the dynamic that is taking place. A black mood may eventually lead to a white mood, after it has gone through another color or two. And white can then lead back to black. It helps to know the alchemy of our moods, or the mere fact that moods have an alchemical dimension. Then, we know that a mood will not last forever and that it has a job to do in the process by which we are gradually revealed.

Alchemy also give us a particular way of imagining moods. According to alchemy, qualities in the external world are mirrored in the interior world. The mist that settles over a pond is like a fog that muddles your thinking. A mood is like the weather. It comes inexorably on its own schedule, and it affects everything. A mood is a mode, as in music. The emotional tone of a major scale is a particular mood. A minor scale has an altogether different mood. There are other moods in the scales. Musicians call them modes and the music modal. It could be moodal or moodle, as in noodle. Anyway, the psyche is also modal. In music, the modes are "precompositional"; that is, they are the originating material, not the actual individual composition. Many pieces can be made up from the dorian mode, for example. Millions of songs have been made from the major modality. The same is true of the psyche's moods. They are vast materials out of which psychic material can be constructed. You can make a great deal out of your depression or your joy. The alchemy of a mood is very much like the modalities in music.

Alchemy is all about making something out of an originating stuff, or *prima materia*. The positive idea of a mood is to see it as raw material out of which soul things can be made. If you are in a blue mood, play some blues on the piano or guitar. Have a talk with a friend that will take its direction and content from the mood. For the most part, go with the mood, not against it. If you go against it, you can't use it as a resource. If a mood seems tenacious, and you wish you could get out of it, maybe the best thing is to do something constructive with it. I mean construct something. Use your depression (blue or black), let your anger make something (red), allow your sense of innocence or purity to construct your spirituality (white). Use up the material of the mood, and then it may relieve you of its oppression. But this is not the same as acting-out the mood: surrendering to depression, venting anger, becoming a religious fanatic. Then the mood persists as an underlying motivation that is never transformed by the alchemy of the psyche. Once in a while you can glimpse the chronic anger in a person devoted to power, or a chronic sense of oppression in a religious fanatic. The stuff of the psyche usually begins in a raw, ineffective form. It needs alchemy to make it accessible to the personality and for life. If it is repressed and left raw, it corrodes everything it touches. The processes of alchemy are essential for the care of the soul.

HENDERSON: A vessel is a container that holds something and was important to the alchemists. In terms of alchemy, how do you understand making and maintaining a vessel?

MOORE: If we understand a vessel as a container that holds stuff and allows us to see the stuff as it undergoes changes, then anything that contains our soul stuff can be a container at that level. I'm not saying that alchemy is always a psychological process and that the container is always psychological. It could be a social container or even a physical container. But I'm interested in the alchemy of the soul and so I focus on particular kinds of containers.

For example, as we discussed, a marriage can be imagined as an alchemical vessel. Few things in life have more of an alchemical quality than marriage. All kinds of stuff go into the process: personal history, wishes, fears, former relationships, family, children, sex, intimacy, work, home. The marriage has to hold all this stuff. I think the wedding ceremony could be important, depending how it is done, for establishing the marriage as a vessel. The great expense, the flowers and music, the costume, the food, the partying—they all help establish a strong vessel and give the marriage a lot of stuff for memory. Memory helps keep the vessel intact.

Friendship is another good vessel, but it, too, needs careful tending. You have to give it time and attention. A gift helps at times, conversation that is open and trusting, shared experiences. A classroom or a therapy office can be a vessel, as can the school or schedule or manner of engagement.

The vessel is usually both physical and imaginal. These letters are a vessel for these particular thoughts. Emily Dickinson bound her sheaves of poetry with ribbon, giving them a vessel aspect they wouldn't have otherwise. A file folder is perhaps less a vessel than a homemade book or ribbon-bound collection of papers. A book is a vessel, as is a tape or a CD. A conversation or a dinner party can be a vessel. The possibilities for vesseling the materials of the soul are infinite. You just need a container that holds and allows you to observe.

When you make a vessel, it pays to give special attention to its holding power. A conversation in a public place or with a person known to betray confidences may not be as good as lunch in a quiet spot or with a person you can trust. You can make the vessel tighter by asking for privacy and confidentiality. The vessel of confession in the Catholic Church was well known for its tightness. A vessel is also a thing of beauty. Notice some of the images of the vessel in alchemy. They are beautiful in form and color. The vessel can become precious because of its form. A letter beautifully written, on good paper, with special ink and calligraphy may be a more effective vessel than a sloppy note—but not always.

It takes art to make a vessel, and you can't put down rules for it. People have a tendency to moralize everything. They want to tell you with a stern tone how you should do it. I'd rather emphasize the pleasure and beauty of a vessel. You can have hundreds of them in your life, and you can enjoy them and take pleasure in them. One of my favorite physical/social vessels is a small room in a pub in Ireland. It's called a snug—a small, private place set apart from the activity of the restaurant or bar, where a small group of people or a couple can have a real conversation. The snug is not just a small space; it is a place of pleasure. A vessel is a thing to be enjoyed, not just used.

HENDERSON: I know you have some ideas distinguishing alchemical movements from personal growth and other forms of heroic and effortful change. Will you share them?

MOORE: The very point of turning to alchemy as an image system showing the dynamics of the soul is to appreciate the natural changes that take place chemically in the laboratory or in nature. The same is true of us: We go through changes naturally and in the laboratory of our reflection on experience. These changes can be observed and nurtured but not manufactured. The "work" of alchemy is the labor of nature and not the exercise of the heroic, intentional ego. The ego work in alchemy is art and religion, though the "and" in that phrase is probably not needed. When art is done well, it is a form of religion, and vice versa. At any rate, in the alchemical process we don't try to make ourselves into some ideal. We assume that nature has given us our goal and identity. We have to help it unfold and be revealed.

This is why, for me, Taoism is such a helpful aid in the spiritual life. Taoist sacred texts offer illumination on how to participate in the unfolding of life without pushing too hard or doing too much. I always have the *Tao Te Ching* within reach. The alchemy of the soul needs a cautious art of nurturing that is neither too passive nor too active. Every day life challenges us with invitations to pleasure and opportunities for suffering. Both kinds of experience have the potential of pulling us deeper into the alchemy of our souls. We tend to be afraid of both, perhaps even more fearful of pleasure than of pain. The alchemical process going on in our souls gives us the chance to become more of who we are and who we could be. Alchemy is an opportunity for an increase in vitality. But, as so many of the images from classical alchemy show, the process involves pain, mortification, little deaths, and dark moments. We tend not to understand that all of this is life, and all of it makes us into the fully alive people we can be. I have found that as a therapist it helps a great deal to embrace the persona of alchemist, among others, so that I can appreciate the autonomous processes of the soul that has presented itself to me. Therapy is not life management or ego training. It is the art and religion of caring for the soul, as, step by step, it takes form in life.

HENDERSON: In taking care of the soul, how can alchemy help?

MOORE: Alchemy offers a good model for dealing with the stuff of the soul: feelings, thoughts, memory, desire, fear, relationships, work. It also gives us a few particular strategies for working (*opus*) with the soul: making and sustaining a vessel; observing the stuff of life as outside yourself; artfully furthering the natural processes of change and development; using metaphors of the natural world for emotions and fantasies difficult to express; including a spiritual viewpoint in the work, instead of making it all psychological and analytical; not being heroic and controlling, but watching and making subtle moves. Alchemy is highly imagistic, which can be frustrating as we try to understand it. But the imagery teaches us to be poetic about the most important developments in life.

The traditional language for dealing with the soul is *therapeia*, which means service or nursing and is often translated into Latin as *cura*, or care. The word "psycho-therapy" means soul-nursing, or care of the soul. "Care" is a soft word, but it is substantial nonetheless. It is not heroic and ties in well with the processes of alchemy.

Just one example among hundreds of alchemical processes: I particularly like an image in alchemy of two men digging at the earth with picks and shovels. "Digging" is an alchemical process, and anyone who has ever conducted an hour of therapy knows what it means to "dig" for information and insight. Another good image shows the old king in a bathtub. Placing in solution, being in water, washing and soaking are all alchemical processes. I think we can be quite concrete about these images and see a comforting hour in a bathtub as an alchemical activity. The difference between taking a shower and taking a bath might be alchemical. Maybe the soul loves a long luxurious bath more than a quick efficient shower. There is more opportunity for fantasy and reverie in a bath. There, the imagination comes to life. But, of course, the bath is also an image for soaking our thoughts and memories, helping them break up (*solutio*) into their various sub-parts.

An alchemical imagination is useful in caring for the soul, just as a theological, astrological, and philosophical one offers a window onto a different aspect of the soul's life.

HENDERSON: This interview has been fun, Tom. How have you felt about it?

MOORE: I have enjoyed reflecting on alchemy from my very limited perspective. I have taken what I can from Jung and other sources. I have especially concentrated on the visual images used in alchemical texts. But, as I said, I am not by any means an expert on alchemy. Years ago, at the University of Dallas, I attended James Hillman's lectures on alchemy. His subtle reflections, written up in his remarkable essays on salt, the colors, and other aspects of alchemy blow your mind. I have done something very simple here, trying to show how an alchemical point of view can open up and educate the imagination for aspects of experience that otherwise may go unnoticed.

One theme we may not have discussed is something I take from Ralph Waldo Emerson, who is much more sophisticated about such things than people realize. In his essays on nature, the poet, and art and beauty, Emerson makes two points that align him with the aims of alchemy: 1) only the poet can know astronomy and the other natural sciences, because only the poet sees nature as full of "signs" 2) connecting with nature takes you in phases from sensual experience to various levels of perception. Emerson was a Neo-Platonist of sorts, and in his own way he was a magus. He didn't practice alchemy or use the imagery of the alchemists in any explicit way, and yet he saw nature in an alchemical light. He understood that nature stimulates the imagination in a certain direction and should never be taken literally. That is the basis of the alchemical work.

I mentioned that I am now completing a book I am calling *Opus: Finding Your Life Work*. The book was inspired by a lecture I was invited to give to career counselors. I decided to speak to them in alchemical terms about the process of uncovering your calling in life. Naturally, I didn't want to talk about the nuts and bolts of finding a job and a career. Not that these matters are not important, but my work lies deeper. I wanted to explore how each of us finds the activities that define us. In other words, what is the *opus* of our souls? The work that lies deep, reflected in the work we do on the job.

With its emphasis on signs and spiritual initiations, alchemy offers an alternative to the heroic attitudes dominant in the current culture. It invites us to reflect on our experiences, to foster the developments with subtlety and reserve. It acknowledges that human nature is nature.

We are natural beings who have the same kind of materials that the external world has. At the same time, as alchemy says, the work of the soul is a work against nature. That means that we take our natural circumstances, our "world," and consider them from the point of view of imagination. As James Hillman said in his earliest writings, we "see through" everything. Everything signifies *ad infinitum*. Without these significations, the heart of alchemy, literal experience means nothing to the human being, who lives a meaningful life and to whom imagination is everything. As William Blake said, save us from one-dimensional experience, from Newton's reductionism, which is still dominant in our culture.

Alchemy is as profound a development in human self-reflection as astrology, and these two methods have much in common: You look at the world around you and your see yourself. You use the minute details of that world to articulate your own "nature." Nothing could be more important, and when this "work" is ignored, we are left with acting out and one-dimensional analysis. Without alchemy, we are left with the absurdity and moral dangers of modernist science.

The Alchemical *Prima Materia* in Relationship

NATHAN SCHWARTZ-SALANT

> I have long held that our psychic situation is now being influenced by an irruption of the Oriental spirit ... analogous to the psychic change that could be observed in Rome during the first century of our era... The cult of Attis and Cybele spread throughout the Roman Empire.
>
> — C. G. Jung, *Collected Works,* 18 § 1287

According to C. G. Jung, the alchemical *prima materia*, the source from which the *lapis* (a new self-structure) will form, can be found in the myth of the Great Goddess Cybele and her son-lover Attis. Jung explained that this was because the myth compensated for the patriarchal dominance of Western culture.

> The historical shift in the world's consciousness towards the masculine is compensated at first by the chthonic femininity of the unconscious. ... [To achieve this] as alchemy shows, the unconscious chose rather the Cybele-Attis type in the form of

Nathan Schwartz-Salant is a Jungian analyst who trained in Zürich, Switzerland, and is a member of AGAP and IAAP. He is the Director of the Center for Analytic Perspectives and practices in New York and Princeton.

The ideas and examples in this paper are part of his latest book to be published in 2006/2007 as *The Black Nightgown: Tales of Madness and the Unlived Life.*

> the *prima materia* and the *filius macrocosmi.* ... The son type [Christ] does not call up a daughter as a complementary image from the depths of the "chthonic" unconscious—it calls up another son. This remarkable fact would seem to be connected with the incarnation into our earthly human nature of a purely spiritual God ....[1]

However, Jung's Attis (in his rendering of him as the *prima materia*) is a chthonic figure akin to the alchemical God Mercurius,[2] who possesses, among other virtues, instinctual, embodied power. Jung's choice is somewhat strange, for the Attis we know about from all the tales of his life with Cybele is anything but chthonic; Attis specifically lacks the chthonic dimension of embodied aggression. In a sense, Jung's Attis-Cybele myth is an updated version of the myth we know. I prefer to think of Jung as something of a trickster here, slipping in an individuated Attis rather than the weak and dependent Shepard of legend.

However, I think the myth in its original form(s) is indeed the *prima materia* that we must work with, and with a proper attitude towards it (which, as we shall see, is *not* that of the hero overcoming evil or disorder), the chthonic dimension of an aggressive and embodied shadow quality that is essential to break the magnetic spell of the Goddess may emerge. The *prima materia*, found in the ancient story of the Anatolian Great Goddess Cybele united with her son Attis in her entrance into Rome in the Third Century B.C.E.,[3] provides us with the best image we have of the alchemical *prima materia*.

Why the Roman authorities invited the dangerous and ecstatic Cybele into Rome and showed her great respect has been debated from many points of view.[4] The notion that the patriarchal collective consciousness was in need of renewal is certainly a major possible reason. Legend also supports this explanation, for a widespread belief existed then that an oracle demanded that Cybele be welcomed into Rome—perhaps one could say that the unconscious, as heard through the voice of the oracle, compensated for the state of the Roman collective consciousness. To their credit, the Roman authorities took the oracle seriously.

It would seem that they got far more than they bargained for, since the cult of Attis and Cybele became popular among all levels of society; but, how was a central facet of Her worship, namely the act of self-mutilation by her followers, the *galli*, to be understood? Scholars have done their very best to write this behavior off as acts of a disenfranchised group of slaves, homosexuals, or any number of other groups that were different, the scholars insist, from the ideals of the true Roman. This is not accurate. The cult existed in all levels of society. And Anneas, the founder of Rome, was himself a *galli*, whence his support from Cybele during his exploits in the *Anneid*. Virgil's description of Anneas is usually not focused upon by these historians, for the act of mutilation to gain Cybele's favor is so very difficult to accept in their view of Rome in the Third Century B.C.E..

The Attis-Cybele myth was devised by Ovid to explain the strange behavior of self-mutilation. I shall not go into the myth in detail. Suffice it to say that in the tale Attis is deeply bonded to Cybele, promising her his eternal allegiance. However, he falls in love with a nymph, Sagaritis, and the enraged Cybele kills her. Attis, in his grief (not for the nymph but for betraying Cybele), goes mad, castrates himself, and dies. Tales about Cybele from the Roman era emphasize her danger and her madness. In particular, the poet Catulus wrote: "Great goddess, goddess Cybele ... may all your insanity, Lady, be far from my house. Drive others to frenzy, drive others mad."[5] Attis is in the hopeless situation wherein separation from the Great Goddess leads to madness, yet if he stays with her he cannot individuate. His impossible dilemma is that he cannot stay with Cybele nor can he leave. I believe that dealing with these opposites, which can be denoted as fusion and separation—but especially in their psychotic form, whereby experiencing one annihilates experience of the other—is engaging the nature of the *prima materia* of alchemy out of which a new *self* in the form of an activated individuation process can emerge.[6]

I have developed the concept of the Fusional Complex to understand the clinical relevance of the Attis-Cybele myth as the *prima materia*. The Fusional Complex, drawing upon this archetypal core, organizes many dimensions of the field within a human relationship. For example, it engenders the experience of feeling bound to another's psyche, in extreme cases precluding any experience of space between two people, *and a simultaneous condition* of an absence of empathy or of any meaningful communication between them. In less extreme states, the opposites of fusion and distance are not as radical, *but in any degree of intensity, the two conditions are always contradictory opposites.*

In the domain of the Fusional Complex, fusion and distance cannot be both held at the same time in one's consciousness. The experience of one opposite does not continuously lead to the other. There is always a discontinuity, a jump rather than a smooth transition. We thus do not deal with a state of complementarity in which awareness of one opposite dampens our consciousness of the other. The situation is far more extreme. Each state is true, yet they are totally contradictory.

How can one be so completely entangled in a field experience with a person that one is engulfed in a welter of psychic and somatic states and, at the same time, feels no connection at all? One finds such states in philosophy as a problem of "true contradictories," for in being both totally fused and totally distant, A = -A, which is logically impossible.[7] To counter the pain and fears of madness that attend this state, people often enter into a form of symbolic castration in these kinds of relationships, whereby their own needs and life force are extremely diminished in service to another's containing safety, as long as they continue to behave in diminished ways. Here is an example.

A man had an affair with a woman, and he was worried that this woman would tell his wife of their affair. He both hated the woman and found her irresistibly attractive. Then, she became seriously ill, and he was even more frightened that she would confess their affair to his wife. In a grand heroic gesture, he decided to help her visit her ailing mother in a foreign country. He had very little money, yet with great energy and cleverness and spending everything he had, he managed to get her airline tickets.

She went on the trip, returned in a week's time, and he reported to me that he felt let down, for she showed hardly any appreciation. The night she returned, he dreamed that he had taken a knife and cut his finger to the bone, but was amazed that it didn't hurt.

This image perfectly represented his behavior and attitude. He mutilated himself to feel safe with this woman, and then, in hysterical fashion, didn't even feel the pain. In the process, he lost several important business opportunities and was even more in debt.

A person's Fusional Complex can be hidden for years under a compliant, false self or within any number of "disorders," such as borderline or narcissistic structures. The complex can hide in a subtle fabric, invisible to normal perception, that encloses the person. This fabric can be like the mythical tail-eating serpent, and the person is enclosed within it and terrified of leaving this "safe territory."

Separation from another person or thing can create extreme disorder and panic and feel unbearable. In this condition, *change of any kind*—paying a new bill, opening a letter from some authority, saying how one feels, having a sexual desire that has one iota of personal relatedness to it rather than a compulsive, impersonal quality, filling out a form, such as a tax return that would yield thousands of much needed dollars—is felt as dangerous. The slightest deviation from a terribly constricted "inner territory," which strangely feels safe and even warm, can threaten with one's insides falling out or with unbearable pain and anxiety.

The entire drama is equally played out on an inner level. Thus, a person can also feel bound to his or her unconscious feelings and fantasies with no capacity of separation and reflection possible. Within this condition, the person is also disconnected from the guidance or wisdom of the self.

A person with a strong Fusional Complex rarely leaves his or her constricted "territory" consciously or through an act of will. That is, he or she doesn't usually reflect upon what is needed and then proceed to act. An analysand described how her life was a series of circles that do not touch. Two never join, yielding a common, shared area. Instead, she lives in one and then, somehow, may make a jump to another. How this happens is unclear to her, but it may, or may not, just happen, perhaps through unexpected events. When it does, she can easily do a great deal in that other circle of possibilities and challenges, but only until she reaches a need to further expand, and then she is stuck again, frozen, unable to act.

A man who often languishes in this condition said to me, "Once I do something, I can do it forever. Doing it stops being a problem; it is beginning that's impossible, and I manage to forget about what I have to do in my daily life, like return phone calls, until I begin to drive to my appointment with you, and I then feel like a total wimp. Sometimes I'm too embarrassed to come."

So much shame accrues to potentials that cannot be actualized that a painful muteness is far more common. Images of powerful people acting aggressively in the best sense—stepping forward in word and deed in ways felt as serving one's deepest values—proliferate in the inner world of dream and fantasy. "What to do" in some situation is practiced over and over again in the secret confines of fantasy, yet when reality strikes and action is required, an awkward silence or barely spoken intent is all that is mustered. All, that is, except more shame and humiliation for, as the person experiences it, he or she fails yet again. Such failure can become so painful and recurrent as to create a very limited life, safe from the conscious experience of more shame. Yet compromises always fail; at times suicide beckons as the only way out of the agony.

The person's words can be extremely poignant: "It's not for me," a man, momentarily freed of his muteness, can say. Others can be aggressive and sexual, while he is banished to a world in which his best qualities seem unreachable in any real sense. They remain outside of him, inacessible. "I want to be sexual with my wife," he insists. He fantasizes about her, and when he isn't with her, he wants her. She excites him in his fantasies during masturbation. However, in reality, he says, "I go away, I'm not there, and I hate being this way." This state is often too painful to accept, and he spends time in a world of passive fantasy "spacing out" from the inner burden he would otherwise feel. All of this is painfully evident to him. His entire life has been ruled by knowing he has desires that he cannot actualize. Nor does he have the strength to be "in his body" and penetrate into the field between him and his wife and dare feel what he feels or see what he sees.

For some time, I blundered dealing with his dreams, for several depicted powerful men emerging from underground chambers, seemingly waiting for him to engage them, to "integrate" them into his more spiritual and mental ego. After all, why else would such imagery appear?

So often we find the hero struggling with dark, primitive forces that he finally overcomes and then reaps the benefit of their strength. Wasn't this urge in him, and wouldn't exhorting him to take hold of his strength be therapeutic?

However, in the suffocating embrace of his Fusional Complex such heroic impulses, which he so highly valued, not only failed to become real strength, but they led to more humiliation and despair. Over the course of several sessions, I learned that suggesting that he heroically overcome his fears and speak to his wife only added to his despair. It was possible that even thinking this way transmitted negatively, so acute was his suffering and so sensitive was the transmitting field between us. Thinking in terms of the heroic was my own defense against experiencing his and my own pain.

At one point, he had hired someone who was not showing up for work. He could not bring himself to confront the man. He then dreamt of a person he thought of as masculine and capable of standing up for himself. Still thinking along heroic lines, I urged him to consider that getting the work done was a goal that meant a great deal. Trying to tone down a pointed appeal to the heroic, I recast it by suggesting that the proposed confrontation was not against the other person, but something for himself. My encouragement was met with anger, as he forcefully said, "that is exactly what I tell myself, over and over again. Yet I can't do it, and I only feel ashamed of myself." His capacity to be angry with me was a glimmer of hope that he could own his aggression. At least that much came out of my wrongheaded approach.

A person's communications, when he or she is suffering in the domain of the Fusional Complex, are filled with contradictory opposites. Rarely do we hear a sentence that communicates a clear sense of pain. Rather, we experience a strange state of contradictory opposites while we hear of the terrible suffering and humiliation of a soul unable to get anywhere close to its beauty and potential. Whatever is said is subtly wiped out so that at the end of any attempt at listening, we feel like whatever we have thought or felt has drained out, as though water was held in a sieve. This alone could be helpful if we could realize that this absence of a container is exactly what the person suffers. However, our own confusion and pain at such times too often preclude such useful reflection.

The fusion-distance opposites in the Fusional Complex cannot be encompassed as an "inner," three-dimensional experience. Instead, as the following example shows, a higher dimensional structure is required.

During the first four years of my work with Suzanne, a sixty-year-old woman, an energy drain and a schizoid-like pull towards unconsciousness had dominated the field between us. Staying awake and focused was difficult, and letting down whatever focus I had in an effort to attain an embodied, imaginal mind-set seemed to only court my further dissociation into a trance-like state.

In every session it took an extreme effort to organize my thoughts and gather up an awareness of Suzanne's internal, psychic state and the ways in which it related to her maternal and paternal experience as well as to the transference. Suzanne had had over twenty years of Freudian analysis, some of it five times a week, and yet she had very few memories before she was ten years old. The Freudian model offered her very little consciousness or meaning.

When Suzanne would leave her "safe territory"—her home, for example, to do a simple errand—she would become very anxious and feel that she was like her anxiety-ridden mother. However, when she was back home, in predictable circumstances and thus in safety, she felt that she was nothing like her mother.

Suzanne fused with the maternal anxiety that she could introject in a semi-conscious way during childhood. This anxiety became a limiting but containing "skin," protecting her from becoming engulfed by her mother's deeper, more psychotic anxiety that she could not reflect upon at all, and instead unconsciously incorporated.[8]

I don't know why, but the session I will now describe was different; my imagination was more alive and I could focus upon the tangible nature of the energies and their images as they lived between us. Perhaps the "table was set" by Suzanne's own inner changes in which she embraced being an introverted-thinking type and was no longer pressuring herself to have feelings for people. Suzanne was also gaining more awareness of the affects upon her of her mother's rage and her father's extreme narcissism.

In this session, Suzanne wondered if she would ever feel an inner sense of having a self. Her question seemed to reach out towards me, and for a split second I could have avoided it because there was an expectation of avoidance. If I had done this, Suzanne's question would have receded, and she would never have complained and surely not shown the intense anger that we had just begun to realize lived deeply within her. I did not let her question slip away.

Instead, I explained that it wasn't that she had no self, but that it was not embodied or activated in her space-time existence. I also explained that when the self enters space-time life, it passes through a complex state, one characterized by the paradoxical condition of neither being able to join with an outer person nor to separate from that object. As I said this, I carefully watched to see if she dissociated or became only intellectually interested in what I was saying. Neither was the case. Suzanne was listening carefully, as though she sensed I was making sense.

Then I began to see our connection in a totally new way. I could now enter into a different relationship to the unconscious—now not receiving insights from a mental-spiritual level, from what Jung called the *psychic unconscious*, but instead allowing my awareness to shift more towards my body and away from anything mental. I felt in my body, as though my consciousness slid along a spectrum beginning with a mental-spiritual vantage point and then away from it and towards the body and the *somatic unconscious*.[9]

This offered me a different form of consciousness from the more mental-perspectival form of awareness that I had always felt to be my only option for relating to Suzanne. In this embodied state and seeing *through my eyes* rather than with them, I had the tangible and somewhat physical sense of the two of us being *linked* through a field. Then, like an epiphany, or—to use a metaphor Merleau Ponty suggests—as an animal appearing in a forest that never would be seen if one looked for it, I *saw* that strands of a nearly physical form linked to Suzanne's body were very hesitantly reaching towards me.

I then shifted from this body-centered state and moved more towards my mind and rational-awareness. This change felt abrupt and seemed to be part of the field experience, as though it had its own dynamics. Thus, at the previous time we were *in the field*[10] and subject to its dynamics, while now we oscillated to being subjects, as though we were now on the surface of a containing field. I could then sense that Suzanne and I were mentally relating, but the condition was tenuous. I have often known experiences with a person in which there was absolutely no empathy or understanding, no being "on the same wave length" or in "parallel universes," to dominate an interaction. With Suzanne, at this point, there was a mental connection, but it was not robust. I sensed our mental-link as part of a spectrum of states that could vanish into a nearly total, schizoid non-relatedness; for now it did not.

While the mental-link to her existed, the possibility to *experience* the body-oriented state departed. It was as though the experience had existed in one phase of being with her and was no longer tangible, but *it* (the experience) could now be talked about as though it was an object of memory that we had both known. Similarly, when connecting through the somatic unconscious, I could not simultaneously reflect from a mental-spiritual point of view or through the psychic unconscious. I could sense the growing contact of her subtle-body as it tentatively reached towards me, and I could *remember* the nature of our more psychic or mental connection, but not experience it.

The best image for containing these opposites is the mysterious alchemical *vas hermeticum* that Steven Rosen has shown to be topologically equivalent to the mathematical image known as a Klein bottle,[11] depicted in Fig. 1.

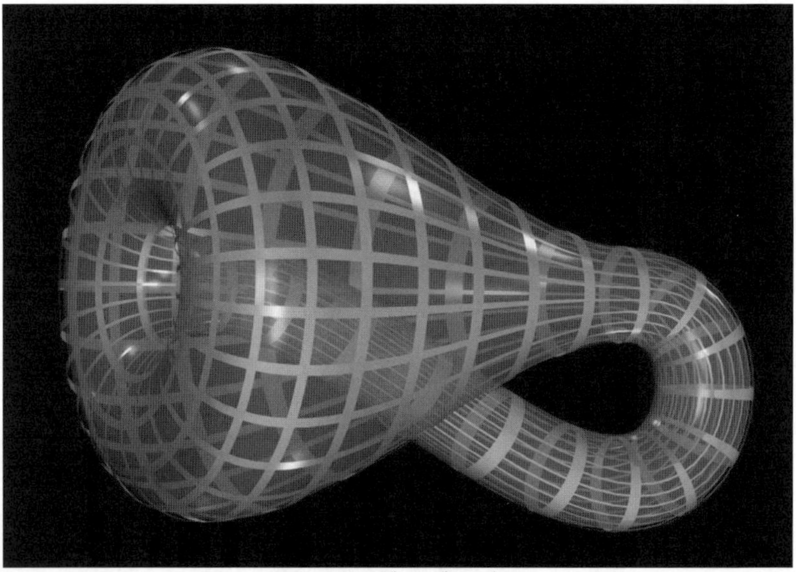

Fig. 1: Klein bottle

As one walks along the inside of the bottle, one eventually discovers one is on the outside of it. Thus, Suzanne and I could be *in it*, together, and then *on its surface,* looking at forms of our mental connection. When we were *in* the field we were *its* objects, experiencing a sense of Oneness that is the source of perceptions that appear like epiphanies. From this vantage point "in the bottle," what had been felt as psychic connections or various degrees of relatedness ceased to be perceptions in the here-and-now and became memories. When on the surface, so to speak, the mental connection was more palpable, and the somatic link only a memory.

This movement is not continuous. There is a discontinuity between the "outside" and "inside" of the Klein bottle.[12]

Suzanne noted that the two experiences were totally contradictory. When she felt the sensate-like link, there was no mental connection, and when she felt a mental connection, there was no "physical" linkage. Yet both were true. At any time if asked if we were we connected, the answer was Yes, but then, at the same time it was No. The situation is shown by the image of the Duck-Rabbit (Fig. 2), which captures the "true contradictories"[13] I earlier referred to. It is a duck. It is a rabbit. Both are true.

Fig. 2: Duck-Rabbit

Suzanne responded to this field experience with a solidity I had rarely known in her. She immediately could reflect upon many of her relationships in which a "person got too quickly and totally involved, when I allowed myself to come towards him in this sensate-like way," or else a person would sense her movement, "and he would instantly vanish." Her mother fit the first category, and her father the second, but numerous other people easily fell into one or the other, wanting to "eat me," as she said, or "totally abandoning me." Her previous husband, her friends, and her children fit into one or the other. What is remarkable is that Suzanne knew exactly what I meant by her subtle fibers reaching out or withdrawing in fear, and she could freely give these examples, which would never have been forthcoming if my own perception had not led the way.[14]

If Suzanne were to feel attached to anyone, as she had in several past relationships, all she knew was pain. She noted that she could become nearly glued to someone and could feel suffocated, yet also unable to separate. She could neither stay connected nor could she leave the relationship. For the person would either want to possess her or leave her, and she could negotiate neither state. Much of Suzanne's life was spent in avoiding this "impossible fusion state" by seeking a container for her thoughts and feelings through her mind.

Such a perception and experience of the Fusional Complex in the here-and-now is the doorway through which a self, and hence a sense of Being, incarnates into space-time life. In turn, this opens up extremely powerful issues, notably fears of madness, usually felt as "falling through" into nothingness and even being pulled towards that state, for the new order triggers disorder as well. The disorder breaks down defenses, and one often becomes aware of an internal, powerful rage or violence, along with other "shadow" qualities.

Suzanne had known this level of rage, but only in a very destructive form. Once, while in her forties, it actually came out at a person. Suzanne then attempted suicide. Yet, gaining some awareness and experience of the rage (which is archetypal and thus much larger than the ego) without acting it out is often the key to gaining the chthonic strength necessary to separate from fusion with objects that no longer serve one's individuation needs.

Experiencing her Fusional Complex led, as it so frequently does, to an unfolding of Suzanne's individuation process that had been dormant for much of her adult life. Over the next month of sessions the role of internal envy in her life emerged with one powerful example after another. In each session she carefully described how anything good in her life, such as a new job possibility or the beginning of a creative work, was immediately destroyed by actual physical accidents, some of them severe. The term "envy" made all the difference to Suzanne, for it became a container for a number of awful experiences that emerged whenever she came forth into owning her own power.

Suzanne could also experience her negative transference through which whatever I said during one session was destroyed by envy, leading to it being totally "forgotten." With that, Suzanne's individuation process, fortified with her "shadow integration" of envy, continued in remarkable ways.

A growing self, seen in several dreams as a new child that she saved from dangerous situations or seen in other dreams as an unknown, powerful woman, was forming. In turn, the field between us was gradually less dominated by dissociation and despair. Schizoid withdrawal ceased to be her main form of operation. Energy drain in the field between us greatly diminished.

Most significantly, Suzanne began to realize the extent of her mother's psychotic anxiety and how it had so ruled her own life. Imaginally perceiving her mother's uncontained and invasive anxiety acted like an exorcism. She could realize that at least much of the anxiety from which she suffered was not her own, and in a remarkable change, she could exclaim, "I am not my mother. I don't have to be afraid of everything." This was a genuine separation, not the pseudo-separation of dissociation.

The *prima materia* for Suzanne's process lay in perceiving the opposites in the Fusional Complex, with its archetypal core, the Attis-Cybele myth, organizing the energies of the field between us. Like the alchemists speak of the transformative power of a drop of their elixir, in a number of cases over the last ten years, since I began to recognize the existence of the Fusional Complex, I have witnessed the transformative power of a single session in which the Fusional Complex is *seen* and, by this vision, contained.

NOTES

1. C. G. Jung, *Psychology and Alchemy,* 2nd ed., *Collected Works* (Princeton: Princeton University Press, 1968), 12 § 26.

2. C. G. Jung, *Collected Works,* 12 § 529.

3. Lynn E. Roller, *In Search of God the Mother* (Berkeley, California: University of California Press, 1999), 263.

4. *Ibid.*, 263.

5. Cited in Lynn E. Roller, *In Search of God the Mother*, 304.

6. It is interesting that the Romans received Cybele in the form of a small, dark, sacred stone that had fallen from the sky (Roller, *In Search*

of God the Mother, 265). The stone is a common symbol of the *lapis,* the embodied self of alchemy.

7. Malcolm Bull, *On Seeing Things Hidden* (London-New York: Verso, 1999), 31-34.

8. It is beyond the scope of this paper to further discuss the central role of "substitute skins" in the realm of the Fusional Complex. The matter will be taken up in my forthcoming book, *The Black Nightgown: Tales of Madness and the Unlived Life*. Here, suffice it to say that the subtle body (see Schwartz-Salant, *The Borderline Personality: Vision and Healing* [Wilmette, IL: Chiron, 1989]) of the soul is a garment that contains the inner life and protects it from outer intrusions and from unbearable, archetypal energies. When trauma from such intrusions occurs, the subtle body is damaged, and "substitute skins" must form, else psychotic process becomes totally destructive.

9. C. G. Jung, *Nietzsche's Zarathustra*, ed. James L. Jarrett (Princeton: Princeton University Press, 1988), 441.

10. Schwartz-Salant, *The Mystery of Human Relationship: Alchemy and the Transformation of the Self* (London: Routledge, 1998), 63.

11. Steven M. Rosen, *Dimensions of Apeiron* (Amsterdam-New York: Rodopi (Value Inquiry Book Series, 2004), 185f.

12. *Ibid.*, 187.

13. Bull, *On Seeing Things Hidden*, 21.

14. See C. G. Jung, *Nietzsche's Zarathustra*, Vol. I, 443f. concerning the difficulties in conveying experiences of the subtle body, for these require images rather than rational discourse.

The Alchemical Attitude of the Analytic Mind: An Introductory Primer on *Prima Materia* for Initial Beginners at the Start

(Under the Guidance of Aureolus Philippus Theophrastus Bombast of Hohenheim, called Paracelsus the Great, and T. S. Eliot)[1]

RONALD SCHENK

To begin at the beginning — Dylan Thomas, "Under Milkwood"

In my beginning is my end.— T.S. Eliot, "East Coker"[2]

I receive a phone message from a prospective client. His voice is soft and deep, but something about it seems overly mature. His speech has an air of formality that feels somewhat forced, like something else is being held in confinement behind it. He mentions his referral source, and I feel gratified that this individual has thought of me. I am

Ronald Schenk, Ph.D., is a Jungian analyst practicing, teaching and writing in Dallas and Houston. He is currently President of the Inter-Regional Society of Jungian Analysts. He has written three books: *The Soul of Beauty: A Psychological Investigation of Appearance; Dark Light: The Appearance of Death in Everyday Life; and The Sunken Quest, the Wasted Fisher, the Pregnant Fish: Postmodern Reflections on Depth Psychology.*

feeling drawn in. The caller gives his phone number, but adds that he will not be available to answer the phone before 10 a.m. I ponder as to the reason—late sleeper? not working? Is there some kind of self indulgence here? ... But then I am an early morning person myself, and maybe my puritanical inclinations are intruding, my *senex* evoked by his *puer*, my pathology already part of the dialogue. When I call the number after the specified time, the man answers. His voice is soft, now seemingly effeminate, but again in a somewhat forced way. His language is formal, careful, protective, but he seems grateful for my ready response, knowledgeable about the location of my office and eager to get started. My trickster aroused, perhaps testing or maybe even provoking him, I give a time convenient for me but before his previous 10 a.m. boundary. I am a little surprised when he takes it. I am then taken aback when he mentions that his mother will be paying and asks if he should bring the check himself or have her pay directly. I had him pegged as anywhere from late 30's to early 50's, and now his mother is paying! I am wondering about what I am getting into as we end the conversation ... weird dependency? some kind of latent or passive aggression?

I have agreed to write a paper on alchemy. Where should I start? ... with an explanation and history of alchemy? ... an explication of the connection between alchemy and psychology? ... the place of alchemy in Jung's thought? As always, alchemy itself has an answer. Alchemy designates the beginning as the *prima materia* and elaborates on it. I think a quick explication will be easy. I have notes from classes and workshops, books, Xeroxed papers, tapes of lectures, etc., etc. Once into it, there will be a flow, a snap, no problem.

It doesn't happen. Time goes by; the deadline approaches. I find ways of distracting myself. Other concerns take on a larger importance, greater priority. I shuffle through my material, but I get pulled into going deeper into what was to be only the initial subject. I feel sluggish; the material is boring, and there is too much of it. I wrack my brain for examples. They don't come. Sliding around from one false start to the next, I remember a Laurel and Hardy sketch. The two are in a car packed to the gills, but with each attempt to start, accompanied by endless rounds of "good-byes," something goes wrong—the engine needs to be cranked, a tire bursts, something is forgotten, something doesn't work, somebody wants something, etc., etc. The entire movie is the attempt to get started. For alchemy, the *prima materia* is a world unto itself. I will have to limit my subject to just this—the beginning.

> So here I am, in the middle way, having had twenty years—
> Twenty years largely wasted . . .
>
> — Eliot, EC, V

The Bible commences with the words, "In the beginning," and talks of God and God's initial creations. The Greek poet, Hesiod, introduces his poem, "Theogony," calling upon the Muses, sources of inspiration, and Homer sets the *Iliad* into motion with anger and the *Odyssey* with the "many ways" of Odysseus. There is always a condition in the origination of any enterprise. It is dark, only chaos exists, there is no wind, the battle is at a standoff ... and there is something in us that continually draws us back to this beginning situation. We create stories, tales of origination, which are themselves originary. Eliot said that each new poem rewrites the tradition. All myths are in themselves creation myths, stories of beginnings. Every situation—a relationship, a class, the founding of a nation, the beginning of an organization, the germination of an idea—everything has an initial place to which the project continually returns.

> Through the first gate,
> Into our first world, shall we follow
> The deception of the thrush? Into our first world.
>
> — Eliot, BN, I

Alchemy

Alchemists dealt with concrete substances, *mater*. Alchemy thought of material as having a singular essence, subjectivity, or soul. Morenius wrote,

> Know that (the work) has but one (root), and but one matter and one substance of which and with which alone it is done, nor is anything added to it or subtracted from it.[3]

The substance itself suffers and rejoices, is mortified and energized. Further, each substance has a certain effect on each of the other substances—attracting, extracting, repelling, dissolving, coagulating, concealing, revealing. In addition, the matter and the alchemist were interchangeable. Morenius:

> Truly this matter is that created by God which is firmly captive with you yourself, inseparable from you, wherever you be, and any creature of God deprived of it will die.[4]

The dynamics of alchemy consist of matrixes of interacting subjectivities—alchemist and material, one material with another. There was no clean subject-object split, rather a constantly shifting emphasis between two entities as either subject or object. Alchemy gives a truly interpersonal perspective in that it views everything as both material (Basilius Valentinus: "Visit the interior of the earth; through purification thou wilt find the hidden stone"[5]) and subjective (Morenius: "This matter is extracted from you, for you are its mine."[6]). The substance is personalized, and human personality is of substance. The work is both a working upon and a being worked upon. The alchemist is cooked while cooking. The world becomes an infinite chain of signifiers between subject and object, worker and material, with no final resting place.

Paracelsus defines alchemy as "the set purpose, intention, and subtle endeavor to transmute the kind of the metals from one to another."[7] As Paracelsus' definition tells us, alchemy's work is one of change. Since alchemy sees the world as ensouled, it is already in flux, in process. Matter is always already changing under the sway of Nature's purpose. The alchemist's work is to help Nature change the world. The *Rosarium*:

> You should employ venerable Nature, because from her and through her and in her is our art born and in naught else: and so our magisterium is the work of Nature and not of the worker.[8]

The first part of the work prepares the material so that it will take its initial form, the *prima materia*, from which proper change can occur. The "first" step is actually a two-fold process — recognize the initial appearance of the matter and prepare it by bringing it to its initial form. The term, *prima materia,* originates with Aristotle for whom it meant "something that isn't there" (!). Paradox: a matter that isn't a matter. Right from the start, alchemy teaches us to see with a nonliteralizing, double vision. There is something, but also something else. The end is always something previous, so we are already beginners at the end point. Aristotle is referring to a potentiality which is not actualized because it has not taken on a particular form that will be imposed from without. For Plato, the potential form is that which lies latent within or beyond. Whether imposed or emergent, *prima materia* is a matter of inherent potential.

> And the bird called, in response to
> The unheard music hidden in the shrubbery,
> And the unseen eyebeam crossed . . .
> — Eliot, BN, I

The idea of a ubiquitous source or original state is itself a universal metaphor, the beginning as archetypal. The Greeks of antiquity thought that the entire universe started from one substance, the original stuff, a permanent unity, an underlying identity, unchangeable in the face of nature. The nature of the first matter depended upon the diagnostician. Anaximander saw it as an undifferentiated mass, the "boundless," and emphasized the latent conflict of the opposites, especially between hot and cold, and wet and dry. For Anaximenes, it was "air" ("mist," "fog"), for Heraclitus, "fire." Where the Greeks did agree was that in this source was the condition for transformation.[9]

Likewise, for the alchemists, in order to bring about change one had to first bring about the proper starting condition. "All error in the art arises because men do not begin with the proper substance."[10] As with the Greek philosophers, there were conflicting opinions among alchemists regarding the exact nature of the beginning. Some thought it had to do with mercury, others lead, water, fire, etc. Paracelsus considered "death" to be the start and end of all processes.

> From wrong to wrong the exasperated spirit
> Proceeds, unless restored by that refining fire
> Where you must move in measure, like a dancer.
> —Eliot, LG, II

Whatever it was, the *prima materia* was concrete material and also an attitude of mind, a way of being, a "philosophy." Olympiodoros elaborates on the sense of totality that lies in the notion of *prima materia* when he refers to "our lead" as distinct from common lead. Common lead was traditionally used to cover coffins and was black to begin with. By contrast, alchemical lead starts out a different color than black and must be darkened in order to achieve the proper beginning condition. Olympiodoros refers to Zosimov's notion of the "egg" as an image of the cosmos containing the four elements.[11]

> They call lead the egg—I mean the egg of the four elements—that is what Zosimos says, and by that he really always means lead. If they explain its shape (*eidos*), they really in secret allude to the whole thing, because as Maria says, the four elements are one.[12]

Lead as egg is a thing and a way of thinking, an ore and a mind, a metal and a world.

> At the still point of the turning world. Neither flesh nor fleshless;
> Neither from nor towards; at the still point, there the dance is,
> But neither arrest nor movement. . . .
>
> —Eliot, BN, I

From the standpoint of alchemy, material always implies a dynamic. Nothing is more enspirited than matter, nothing more material than spirit. Something appears in the beginning, but something is also not there, and whatever is there, is also not there, and whatever is not there is there. Change comes about as a process of the visible or lower form coming into alignment with the invisible or higher form, and the *opus* or work of alchemy is to help this change along.

Psychotherapy

Someone comes into therapy, and they are depressed or anxious or angry or can't function or have tears welling up or are afraid of intimacy or of abandonment or don't know what is the matter or don't know who they are or where they are headed or self-destruct in various ways. These are all states of soul with corresponding visibilities—boring job, distanced relationship, can't get up in the morning, tears in the eyes, bent body, etc. Visibilities are in the presenting problem, but also in the initial encounter, not just the first phone call or the first meeting, but in every session—the encounter in the waiting room, the first look on the face, the initial words spoken. What is the face saying today? the body? the first words?

Once into the therapy, clinicians put a great deal of focus on many forms of the beginning situation. We are curious and want to know when the presenting problem started and what was going on then. What were the originating circumstances in the patient's life? Where did it all begin? What was the family of origin like? How did the couple first meet? How did you get here? What brings you into therapy now? This initial stuff is important, because it is what is working on the patient and ultimately what will be worked upon by the therapy.

And last, the rending pain of re-enactment
  Of all that you have done, and been; the shame
  Of motives late revealed, and the awareness
Of things ill done and done to others' harm
  Which once you took for exercise of virtue.
— Eliot, LG, II

Alchemy helps psychology to see that the apparent starting condition, be it "diagnosis," "presenting problem," or "initial impressions," is a matter of substance. Through the eyes of alchemy, the presenting problem is matter appearing in an unfinished form, the ore—unrefined, the metal—imperfect, its soul in pain, ugliness or disquiet. Alchemy considers these external situations to have an internal correlative; nature is always doubled, both within and without at the same time. So the alchemical clinician sees the beginning situation with a metaphorical eye. Something is concretely there, but something else is also happening, and alchemy presents the psychotherapist with a multitude of complex images with which to imagine this dynamic.

In life, the appearance of an "other" brings up the first danger of the beginning condition: to make it something that suits one's own needs, rather than letting it appear in its raw form. I want to contain my own anxiety by imposing control or grasping the situation prematurely rather than to let it work on me. I want to take immediate action, to literalize, get on top of it, rather than simply imagine a metaphorical situation. "What you need is a good a, b, c, or f!" "You need to read this book, see this movie." "That's just because you are an x, y, or z type." "You have a this or that physical problem." "That's the Self speaking." When I have the "other" fixed, my own pathos recedes. I become comfortable in my control and don't have to feel threatened by the uncertainty, chaos, confusion, darkness, ugliness, messiness or terror of the beginning. As a clinician, a first tendency is to shrink back from the pathos of the beginning, to de-pathologize, normalize, simplify it, "I'm ok! You're ok!", or to overweigh the diagnosis,

"Another case of involutional melancholia!" or to refer, "You need medication," or "You need a therapist of x or y gender," or to ask for dreams—all as a means of displacing the problem.

As the old saying goes, "A sow's ear is a sow's ear." A sculptor is automatically Platonic, looking at the initial mass of wood or marble or clay, not from the standpoint of what she wants it to be, but through a sensibility for the autonomous life of the particular substance. She knows that the final form lies latent in the subject, and in order to allow it its autonomous presence, she has to avoid imposing a form which is comforting to her. The Zen master, Shunryu Suzuki, spent years teaching a simple idea, "In the beginner's mind there are many possibilities; in the expert's mind there are few,"[13] or Jesus: "Unless you turn and become like children, you will never enter the kingdom of heaven."[14]

Alchemy informs psychotherapy that after the initial appearance is encountered, a further starting place is needed, an essential, original condition from which to start the process. As in alchemy, so in psychotherapy, the need is to find the proper beginning point. Some clinicians want to go back to the originating place of "trauma" in the family, others want to get to initial feelings, but in one form or another, psychotherapists attempt to establish a proper place of beginning. With alchemy in mind, how can the *prima materia* of the psyche in therapy be distinguished?

Prima Materia in Psychotherapy

Our only health is the disease
— Eliot, EC, IV

1) It is chaotic. It seems out of control, irrational—an autonomous life that wants to devour anything and everything. "It's eating me alive." An alchemical image of Cerberus, the monster dog that guarded the underworld, depicts a three-headed monster, each head ready to devour a being while other figures are clutched in the paws and entangled in the tail.

A college-age male comes in for therapy. The son of parents who divorced when he was three and the object of each of their narcissistic needs, he has been depressed and anxious all of his life. His emotions came to a head during the past year when he was involved in an accident in which he was a passenger in a car struck by a drunken driver who pulled out of line and ran a red light killing a good friend who was driving. The young man is ridden with guilt, but also harbors a secret sympathy with the uncontrolled aggression of the offending driver.

2) It is ubiquitous—everywhere and anywhere. Wherever I go, there I am. Work, vacation, marriage, affair, friends, family—the same things come up in each situation.

> This Matter lies before the eyes of all; everybody sees it, touches it, loves it, but knows it not. It is glorious and vile, precious and of small account, and is found everywhere. … To be brief, our Matter has as many names as there are things in the world; that is why the foolish know it not.[15]

The Arabian alchemist Ab'l-Quasim al-Iraqi describes *prima materia* as being

> … found in a mountain which contains a measureless quantity of uncreated things. In this mountain is every kind of knowledge that can be found in this world. There is no knowledge, understanding, dream, thought, skill, interpretation, consideration, wisdom, philosophy, geometry, statecraft, power, courage, distinction, satisfaction, patience, discipline, beauty, inventiveness, travel, orthodoxy, leadership, exactitude, growth, command, authority, richness, dignity, counsel or business, which is not contained therein. But also there is no hatred, malevolence, deceit, infidelity, illusion, tyranny, oppression, corruption, ignorance, stupidity, lowness, despotism or excess, and no song, game, flute or lyre, or marriage, no jest, no arm, no war, neither blood nor homicide, which is not contained therein.[16]

3) It is inert in nature and therefore resistant to change. The patient says, "No matter what I do, I still feel the same way," or "All I've got today is what I've been talking about all along." The *prima materia* is indestructible, stone-like, cold and immutable. It gives the soul an experience of being held prisoner, reflecting spirit's imprisonment in matter, the incurable old king, or the mind's imprisonment in spirit.

A dreamer enters a Zen Buddhist monastery, walks through various rooms where people are in meditation and winds his way to the extreme back room where he finds the American head of the monastery sitting in a hot sweat box, head covered in sweat, face contorted in pain, body invisibly suffering in heat.

Energy is tied up in conflict, leaving a feeling of being stuck, unable to move, void of possibility, suffocated, helpless and hopeless, unchangeable. In therapy, the patient thinks an initial insight means "It's fixed!", but to his consternation, months and then years go by and the condition persists. The resistance and its analysis, or "working through," becomes everything. Inertia is represented in names— "lead," "our lead," "lead of the air," "Saturn," "Saturn's child." Maria Prophetessa considered lead to be the basis of the work, but Olympiodoros referred to the oracle Peasios who warned that lead was so "bedeviled and shameless" that those who want to learn about it fall into madness.[17]

A man in his late 40's with a soft, passive demeanor, comes into analysis complaining of a persistent ambivalence in his life. He has been married for over twenty-five years to an entitled, paranoid woman with whom he has little relationship except to take care of her considerable financial needs, and he spends a great deal of time, money and energy with a mistress and her children. He is a lawyer, dealing in bankruptcy, but finds himself cleaning up the messes of people he doesn't like, while his secret passion lies in writing. As a child his father absented the family while the patient served the needs of a histrionic mother and played fantasy war games by himself. At that time he had a recurring dream that a wolf was trying to get into the house. Recently he was forced to have eye surgery to prevent blindness, and his digestive system has been insistently problematic. As analyst in the first session, I immediately find myself feeling alternatively bored and unruly, and I mistakenly end the session 10 minutes early.

Dust in the air suspended
Marks the place where a story ended.
Dust inbreathed was a house—
The wall, the wainscot and the mouse,
The death of hope and despair,
  This is the death of air.

—Eliot, LG, II

4) It repeats itself; perseverating, appearing over and over, again and again. It's *deja vu* all over again one more time. The patient says, "I sound like an old record!" The "black pitch," like the tar baby, keeps sticking. I can't get away from it. "Haven't we been here before?" It won't let go. It's like I'm a sailor, "forever bailing." I feel compelled in my compulsion. I can't get this strange thought or silly song out of my head. There is a fascination about it. I feel like I am enchanted. It is irresistible, exquisitely seductive, "the whore of Babylon." There is a perpetual regurgitation, over and over creating, destroying, being created, and being destroyed.

A man in his fifties comes into analysis, anxious, depressed, angry, and questioning the meaning of his life. He is highly judgmental of himself and bears low self esteem punctuated with erectile problems. An insurance salesman, he finds himself unappreciated by his employer as has been the case throughout his career. He feels confused, can't find meaning in his life, and wants an answer to his life's suffering in an overarching philosophical system. As a boy he was equally influenced by a schizophrenic mother who consistently gave him mixed messages, and an abusive father who undermined his attempts at self expression before committing suicide. After several years of analysis in which he struggles through several jobs, finally finding one that seems to fit, and after achieving a sense of identity in relation to his wife, child and grandchildren, the patient develops prostate cancer and comes to his session anxious, depressed, angry and questioning the meaning of his life.

5) It is *increatum,* unformed, green, unripe, or prematurely pure. It is innocent, naive, rosy-cheeked, white-washed, or syrupy sweet, inviting violation.

A woman in her mid-thirties, a mother of two children and herself a housewife, finds little identity outside of her prescribed role, a "girl in a box." As a girl she suffered a great deal of emotional isolation while taking on the responsibilities associated with alcoholic parents. She reports a recurring nightmare of being chased by a dark figure.

"*No problema*!" "Cool breeze, man!" It is naïve, without fault. "I didn't realize ...," "Who ... me?" "Butter," "the milk of the virgin," or "virgin's milk," it is overly rich, fatty, creamy, hokey.

A man in his early thirties of artistic temperament and vocation who was raised in an abusive and chronically chaotic situation in which he was forced to take on a great deal of responsibility, finds himself having problems creating boundaries in a personal and professional life that is in perpetual turmoil. He smiles a lot, has a great deal of charm, and starts each session talking about how "great" things are in his life.

Increatum is unformed being, emptiness, a void, vacuum, or abyss —the black hole at the pit of the stomach of individuals with a lack in early attachment experience and an abundance of abandonment.[18]

> Dry the pool, dry concrete, brown edged,
> And the pool was filled with water out of sunlight,
> —Eliot, BN, I

6) It is called *turb,* a turbulence or storm which sweeps through creating havoc in the established order—affect, psychic energy, moods, tears, rage, fear, the "undisciplined squads of emotion" (Eliot, EC, V). Wallace Stevens wrote, "Out of nothing to have come on major weather." It is bi-polar, either afire with manic activity or stultified with *humiditas radicalis,* "moisture," "oily water," the "fatty water" of labile affect or moods or the perpetual weeping of patients whose profoundly tragic sensibility brings tears session after session, year after year. It is "the sodden, moist, fat, and muddy earth of Adam ... from which this large world, we ourselves, and our powerful stone were created."[19] On the other hand, it is the "red sulphur," a kind of drivenness—do something, get on with it, buy something, get out of here, do an active imagination. It is "lead of the air," a flurry of airy activity with a depressive foundation, the eagle tied to the toad.

A man in his mid-thirties has been working at a feverish pitch in the corporate world all of his career, but he feels himself stuck of late, his life void of relationship, direction, or identity. His mother is a new age artist and his father, an overly disciplined academic researcher. After spending a prolonged vacation practicing yoga and Tantric sex in India, he decides to move there to start a new business.

It is the "Muladara," or "salamander"— the instinct which provides the limits of efforts for socialization.

A promiscuous fifteen-year-old girl from an impoverished chaotic family says of sex, "Ah gots to have it."

On a summer midnight, you can hear the music
Of the weak pipe and the little drum
And see them dancing around the bonfire
The association of man and woman
In daunsinge, signifying matrimonie—
—Eliot, EC, I

It is—*ira*, irate, rage—the cultural shadow of a violent society where the beauty of anger is lost, and it is seen as only destructive. It is the "fire in the water," the anger underneath the tears, the energy underneath the boredom, the "hidden fire" of secret desire waiting for an adequate container in the world.

Water and fire shall rot
The marred foundations we forgot,
Of sanctuary and choir.
This is the death of water and fire.
—Eliot, LG, II

7) It is "other," alien, unwelcome, weird, odd, unrelated to, reviled, repugnant, denigrated, dis-ed—disliked, disowned, discounted, disregarded, in disrepair, or disguised. Its names are the "orphan," "accursed of God," "dung," and *vili figura*, the vile figure.

> The substance that we first take in hand is mineral. ... It is of great inward virtue, though it is vile to the sight. It is of venomous nature.[20]

This is the "identified patient" carrying the family sickness, the outcast or scapegoat in a group, as well as the part of the individual personality that is most shameful or carries the most guilt, the worst part of the most repugnant, the "*menstruum* of the whore."

A woman in her early forties comes to therapy due to the fact that her only daughter, a teenager, has suffered from an eating disorder. The mother would like to "work on her stuff." She divorced the father of her daughter eleven years previously, and in the intervening years the daughter has had a great deal of contact with the father. As the feelings of the mother start to reveal themselves, it becomes clear that she suffers from underlying guilt at not being able to "heal" her former husband's depression. She has been afraid that her daughter's illness is connected to the daughter's emotional care-taking of the former husband. Further, the mother, my patient, comes to realize that she also carries guilt associated with her inability as a girl to "heal" a schizophrenic older brother for her own mother.

> There is only the fight to recover what has been lost
> And found and lost again and again: ...
> —Eliot, EC, V

There is a bitter taste like vinegar, the salt of sea water, *amaritudo,* or the salt of tears, the "rhubarb water." A patient says, "I stood alone in the parking lot and cried, shedding scales of pain and loneliness." The alchemists bear witness to the bitterness, but see in it an eventual wisdom. Michael Maier: "There is in our chemistry a certain noble substance, in the beginning whereof is wretchedness with vinegar, but in its ending joy with gladness."[21] George Ripley: "Each thing in its first matter is corrupt and bitter. The bitterness is a tincturing poison."[22] "In the bitterness that is in its (the wingless bird's) throat the colouring will be found."[23] Mylius: "Our stone is endowed with the strongest spirit, bitter and brazen."[24] This is the venom-dripping pout, resentment, or the look of "silent sulking scorn" as one man described of his wife.

> O nature and of this wondrous thing, which transforms the body into spirit! ... When it is found alone it conquers all things, and is an excellent, harsh and bitter acid, which transmutes gold into pure spirit.[25]

It is a wounding remark, sharp, biting, a dart thrown out during conversation, a joke cutting too close to the bone.

It has a bad smell, "the stench of the graves," connected to the underworld, putrefaction, corruption, decay, decadence. "Something doesn't smell right here." Words come "out of the ass" or through *flatus voci.*

A young girl in play therapy starts each session by blessing the playroom with farts in each of the four directions, making herself complete by allowing her lower voice to be heard from all perspectives.

It is the "slime of the small world"— the little things, irritations, petty grievances, and annoyances.[26]

Garlic and sapphires in the mud
—Eliot, BN, I

8) It is associated with pain and called "Hades,"[27] or "affliction of the soul," which is applied to the substance and the worker at once, a dark tone of *nigredo*—dying, torture, devouring, suffocating, contorting, sinking, being skinned alive, shaven bare, stripped to the bone.

Who then devised the torment? Love.
Love is the unfamiliar Name
Behind the hands that wove
The intolerable shirt of flame
Which human power cannot remove.
—Eliot, LG, IV

A successful business man in his 50's, very thin and gaunt, a cyclist and spin instructor in his leisure, comes into analysis disgusted with his adopted adolescent son's gluttony and sloth. During the course of analysis he develops esophageal cancer for which he receives painful treatment and it recurs twice. He gradually becomes aware of his own needs which have been squelched in childhood when his family coped with a handicapped sibling. The work becomes a movement toward realization that he could, in fact, love himself, have his cake and eat it too.

9) It carries paradox, the experience of it and the opposite at the same time. It is "Mercurius,"[28] the "hermaphrodite," he of "two natures," who "runs round the earth and enjoys equally the company of the good and the wicked."[29]

> I am the poison-dripping dragon, who is everywhere and can be cheaply had. That upon which I rest, and that which rests upon me, will be found within me by those who pursue their investigations in accordance with the rules of the Art. My water and fire destroy and put together; from my body you may extract the green lion and the red. ... I bestow on you the powers of the male and the female, and also those of heaven and of earth ... father and mother, young and old, very strong and very weak, death and resurrection, visible and invisible, hard

> and soft; I descend into the earth and ascend to the heavens, I am the highest and the lowest, the lightest and the heaviest, often the order of nature is reversed in me … I am dark and light; I come forth from heaven and earth; I am known and yet do not exist at all ….[30]

"The fiery and perfect Mercurius" refers to synchronistic happenings, spontaneous combustions, out of the blue — "I don't know what got into me."

It is "Luna," moon mystery, moonshine, difficult to hold, constantly evaporating, vapor, "twilight zone," uncertainty, ambiguity, flux, fantasy, dead ancestors, half-life, limbo, things occult. The moon is the place where soul and spirit separate according to Plutarch, and under the moon arise suicidal thoughts, the spirit yearning for freedom.

It is "Word" as seed from heaven, "In the beginning was the Word," and all the mercurial qualities of language—Freud's slips of the tongue, Jung's association experiments, puns, metaphors and metonymies, words as images, words as worlds with histories, associations, etc. "I'm blocking!" "I can't think of the word." "It's right on the tip of my tongue." "It just popped out of my mouth."

> And so each venture
> Is a new beginning, a raid on the inarticulate
> With shabby equipment always deteriorating
> In the general mess of imprecision of feeling
> —Eliot, EC, V

10) It is the ground, fundament, parent—the "sea," *aqua permanence*, itself the container holding all forms, or the "tree" that grows on the surface of the world-sea branching out into all entities, or the "earth" which nurtures all beings, or the "red earth" which receives all elements.

> The parched eviscerate soil
> Gapes at the vanity of toil,
> Laughs without mirth.
> This is the death of earth.
> —Eliot, LG, II

A dreamer is toiling, taking down outhouses in the hot midday sun, shoveling dirt like mad into privy holes full of shit and piss ready to be incorporated back into the earth, and folding up the lumber of the outhouses to be moved on to another location.

It is the "Mother" or the "Father," not literal people back in all those Midwestern towns or in the Bronx, but the ideas or principles to which one always comes back—the *Unum*, "Adamica," "Adam," first man, original form, *ur*, "where it all began," "the root of itself."

A lawyer in his fifties comes to analysis complaining of the after-effects of successful prostate surgery. His sexual libido which has been prominent throughout his adult life has diminished. At the same time he has come to realize that he is quite dissatisfied with his work with a large firm cleaning up the legal ecological messes of corporations. The main focus of his analysis comes to be dealing with the anxiety in leaving the safe confines of his work both at the office and at home, care-taking his depressed wife and schizophrenic daughter, both derivatives of his job as a boy with a volatile and irrationally rageful mother and a shopkeeping father. His secret project is to build his own ecobusiness, taking care of Mother Earth in a unique and innovative way based on incentives for profit.

It is the body as carrier of turbulence, psychosomatic indicators—rashes, inflammations, infections, cancers, ulcers, infections, endometrioses, allergies, colds, headaches, autoimmune diseases, syndromes—chronic fatigue and Epstein bar.

> Yet the enchainment of past and future
> Woven in the weakness of the changing body,
> Protects mankind from heaven and damnation
> Which flesh cannot endure.
>
> —Eliot, BN, II

11) It has the quality of the divine, the "golden head," without beginning or ending, in need of "no second,"[31] having the nature of God, or "The One," *Unam, Unica Res*, "Monad," pure subject, "the infinite"—"It's all one, man!" "That from which things arise is the invisible and immovable God."[32] It is the identification with big questions—all black or all white—where are we going? Who am I? What is this all about?

A young man dreams that he is on the edge of a cliff in the middle of a hot day watching two giant bears, one black and one white, fighting a ferocious battle to the death. All of a sudden he feels something at his feet. A brown chipmunk is nibbling at his toes.

12) It is already the goal, the fruit of the work, the Stone (*lapis*), the "Redeemer," autonomous and eternal. What is "despised and rejected" is also the saving grace, the "Redeemer" (Isaiah). What starts in the stables, among the animals, becomes world savior. I may dislike my anger or be afraid of intimacy or be burdened by guilt and shame, or be confused about my identity or lack of direction, yet within these emotions lies exactly what will allow for change. That which is concealed wants to be revealed and integrated. The "gold" or "eternal water" or "joy with gladness" that marks the *prima materia* is the process of continually recognizing and incorporating what is already there.

> ... both a new world
> And the old made explicit, understood
> In the completion of its partial ecstasy,
> The resolution of its partial horror.
> —Eliot, BN, II

Paracelsus and the *Materia Prima* as *Principia Ultima*

For Paracelsus, the work of alchemy is to help Nature's or God's project of changing impurities (*materia prima*) into essences (*materia ultima*). Paradoxically, the first matter and the ultimate matter are, at the core, one and the same.

> The *first principle* with God *was the ultimate matter* which He Himself made to be the *primal*, just as a fruit which produces another fruit (italics mine).[33]

The primary matter is like a seed, which if treated with appropriate care becomes the plant or metal or creature it essentially is.

> The first matter of things, that is to say, the matter of principiating principles is begotten by Nature, without the assistance of any other seed; in other words, nature receives the matter from the elements, whence it subsequently brings forth the seed.[34]

"Nature begets a mineral in the bowels of the earth,"[35] and it, as "first essence," becomes potential life, a fetus hidden in the womb. In working with the matter, it is imperative to determine its actual content.

> It ought to be known what the primal matter is according to its essence. ... For the primal matter has in it such virtues that it will not allow the body which is born of it to go into consumption, but abundantly affords whatever is necessary for the supply of every requirement.[36]

The ultimate matter is a goal or state, alike in essence, but different in form from the *prima mater.*

> Whatever is to pass into its ultimate matter must become something different from what its origin was....In the beginning, it must be remarked, concerning the Primal matter, that it puts forth its predestination, to which it is foreordained, entire, and from its first origin to its final end well-defined and exemplified.[37]

This change is ultimately a renewal, an original form regenerated.

> For as the seed gives of itself the entire herb, with renewal of all its forces and consumption of the old essence, so that the former substance, nature, and essence have no further operation ... *we are born from one seed like something growing in the field according to its growing nature* (italics mine).[38]

Paraselsus thinks of the process of change to be "digestion," hence accompanied by a sense of torture and death. Bonus of Ferrara also sees alchemical transformation in terms of digestion and describes it as "the gradual development of that which is conceived by gentle outward heat,"[39] i.e., the evolution of a metal comes out of the digestive conjoining of one with another. Digestion implies a kind of death, and for Paracelsus, the entire process is "the transposition of the metals from one death to another,"[40] "Destruction perfects that which is good."[41] A seed in the ground must "putrefy" and "dissolve" in order to emerge eventually as that plant, metal, creature or form that it is meant to be in its visibility.

> The good is least good whilst it is thus concealed. The concealment must be removed so that the good may be able freely to appear in its own brightness. ... Each one of the visible metals is a concealment of the other six metals.[42]

Change is a matter of fluctuating revelation and concealment resulting in an ultimate appearance or emergence or extraction of a substance, "clear in its *esse*."[43]

For Paracelsus the cosmos is a matter of stones and stars. The stones or seeds of the earth reflect the stars as informing spirits. The threefold evolution of the seed or metal through the *opus* of alchemy is a matter of an evolving vision of imagination.[44] It starts in its gross appearance, is reduced to its place of origin, and then emerges in alignment with the stars as world soul.

A middle-aged businessman comes into analysis feeling "something dark underneath pushing upward like a force" and becomes tearful as he speaks of what he will call the "Mother of the Monster" after a figure in "Beowolf." After many years of analysis and life experience—loss of job, divorce, death in the family—he finally comes to experience the derivative of an inner rage that has been kept in check by admonitions of parental figures from an early age. A dream during this process depicts the patient alone at a campfire near a cliff wall, out of which emerge ancestral figures that have been depicted as petroglyphs on the wall. They dance around the fire and he joins with them.

The man ultimately finds himself at board meetings able to cut through bullshit in order to achieve an appropriate orientation to the different levels of process. Likewise, in his personal life, he finds himself able to be direct with others. At the same time, his fire for "business as usual" in work and "running the mill" of false attempts at relationship diminishes. He pulls back from business and social life, invests his time with family and devotes his energy and money to charitable causes.

Not the intense moment
Isolated, with no before and after,
But a lifetime burning in every moment
And not the lifetime of one man only
But of old stones that cannot be deciphered.
—Eliot, EC, V

Alchemy gives clinicians an image-based attitude of mind with which to approach the work of psychotherapy. The contents of psychological life can be thought of as substances. The substances are worlds of being with their own qualities which include the therapist, transference and countertransference always already in co-creation of a third realm. The work of therapy is a work upon the substance, but also the work of the substance upon the therapist and patient. The substance presents itself as a place to start from, a home of sorts, but also a dwelling of disaffection holding the rupture between meaning and experience. Each session becomes another new beginning, another delving into the inarticulate invisible, a new striving for a current revelation at hand. The work becomes a process of opening so that a surprise may occur and be received, shocking the old shell so that what one is and has been is seen in a newly darkened light. A fresh set of expectations and assumptions, hopes and loves emerges, largely for the wrong things again but this time closer to the mark while creating a different set of problems. With the new alignment comes a consciousness nearer the goal of being with the moment and a new faith—one in imagination as a mode of living ... out ... the same old stuff.

Inevitably there are times when the seed doesn't take, the resistance of soul too great. The man who had called for an appointment turned out to be a college dropout with a history of alcohol and drug abuse associated with parental divorce and a highly disruptive maternal presence. He was determined to give himself a new start, get into therapy, get a job, get back in school, etc., etc., and attended a few sessions, revealing a highly ambiguous, primitive tie to a dominating mother against whom he was struggling to separate. He did manage to get a job and shift some of his dependence to his father, but he didn't last long in analysis, dropping as well out of the therapeutic container unable as it was to hold his terrible mercury.

NOTES

1. This paper is inspired in part by a class on alchemy given by James Hillman at the University of Dallas, 1979.

2. Quotations from T.S. Eliot are from the "Four Quartets," each section of which is labeled as follows: "Burnt Norton" (BN), "East Coker" (EC), "The Dry Salvages" (DS), and "Little Gidding" (LG).

3. Lee Stavenhagen, ed., *A Testament of Alchemy* (Hanover, New Hampshire: The University Press of New England, 1974), 13.

4. Stavenhagen, 27.

5. Titus Burckhardt, *Alchemy: Science of the Cosmos, Science of the Soul*, translated from the German by William Stoddart (Baltimore: Penguin Books, 1971), 101.

6. Stavenhagen, 27.

7. Arthur Waite, ed., *The Hermetic and Alchemical Writings of Aureolus Philippus Theophrastus Bombast of Hohenheim, called Paracelsus the Great*, Two Volumes (Berkeley: Shambhala, 1976), I, 16.

8. As quoted from *Rosarium Philosophorum*, by C.G. Jung in *The Practice of Psychotherapy, CW* 16, trans. R.F.C. Hull (Princeton, N.J.: Princeton University Press, 1966), § 411.

9. For a complete discussion see *The Greek Philosophers: From Thales to Aristotle,* W.K.C. Guthrie (New York: HarperColophon Books, 1975).

10. As quoted by Jung from the *Rosarium* in *CW* 16 § 411.

11. C.G. Jung, *Alchemical Studies, CW* 13 § 109, n76.

12. As quoted by Marie-Louise von Franz in *Alchemy: An Introduction to the Symbolism and the Psychology* (Toronto: Inner City Books, 1980), 82.

13. Shunryu Suzuki, *Zen Mind, Beginner's Mind* (New York: Weatherhill, 1973), 21.

14. Matthew 18: 3.

15. As quoted from *Hermetic Museum,* by Edward Edinger, in *The Anatomy of the Psyche* (LaSalle, Illinois: Open Court, 1985), 11.

16. As quoted by Burckhardt, 100.

17. C.G. Jung in *Mysterium Coniunctionis, CW* 14 § 493.

18. Western consciousness particularly abhors the vacuum in contrast to Eastern consciousness which holds that each shape is determined by the particular emptiness around which a container is formed.

19. Henrich Kunrath, in "Theatrum sapientiae aeternae," as quoted by Burckhardt, 104.

20. As quoted by Edinger, 12.

21. As quoted by C.G. Jung in *Psychology and Alchemy, CW* 12 § 387.

22. As quoted by Jung, *CW* 14 § 245.

23. As quoted by Jung, CW 14 § 245 from *Rosinus ad Sarratantam episcopum.*

24. As quoted by Jung, *CW* 14 § 245.

25. As quoted by Jung, *CW* 14 § 245 from *Liber Alzer.*

26. In the myth of Inanna, it is dirt under the fingernails which gets the whole process going when it becomes stagnant in the underworld.

27. Another name for *prima materia*, "Lucifer," refers to the devil, but also fire in the stars, "light bringer," something from out of the blue, alluding to Heaven as Lucifer's first home.

28. Jung, *CW* 14 § 714.

29. As quoted by Jung, *CW* 13 § 267.

30. As quoted by Jung, *CW* 13 § 267 from *Aurelia occulta.*

31. Jung, *CW* 14 § 143.

32. As quoted by Jung, *CW* 12 § 431.

33. Waite, Vol. I, 91.

34. Waite, Vol. I, 293.

35. Waite, Vol. I, 36.

36. Waite, Vol. II, 40.

37. Waite, Vol. II, 39.

38. Waite, Vol. II, 39.

39. Bonus, Petrus of Ferrara, *The New Pearl of Great Price* (New York: Arno Press, 1974), 24.

40. Waite, Vol. I, 9.

41. Waite, Vol. I, 4.

42. Waite, Vol. I, 4.

43. Waite, Vol. I, 9.

44. Waite, Vol. II, 7.

True Imagination

SHERRY SALMAN

One way to define the goal of analytic treatment is that it is the well-functioning dialogue between ego identity and what lies beyond its margins. This on-going dialogue, whose 'to-ing and fro-ing' becomes more and more seamless over time, is what Jung imagined as analogous to the *lapis*, the invisible Stone. There seem to be at least three vectors rooted in alchemy which move toward this goal, all of which are integral to the individuation process. The first, the classical 'stone which becomes the Stone,' or 'squaring of the circle', is the work with opposites, differentiation, and wholeness. The second is the appreciation and analysis of 'field' phenomena such as resonance, synchronicity, and emergence, which have their feet in the alchemical notions of correspondences and the *unus mundus*. Third is the

Sherry Salman is a Jungian analyst practicing in NYC and Rhinebeck, NY. She is a founding member and President of the Jungian Psychoanalytic Association, and consulting editor for the *Journal of Analytical Psychology*. Her recent publications include "The Creative Psyche: Jung's Major Contributions," in *The Cambridge Companion to Jung*, 2nd ed. (2006).

This essay is a revised version of "Beyond the Margins: from Projective Identification to Active Imagination – the Question of Technique in Analytical Psychology," first presented in Barcelona at the 16th IAAP Congress, and available on CD in *Proceedings of the 16th International Congress for Analytical Psychology.* Zürich: Daimon-Verlag.

cultivation and animation of what the alchemists called 'true imagination'. While this study focuses primarily on true imagination, a close look at alchemy reveals these vectors as a unified whole, which have become somewhat fractured from one another, taking form in the various schools of Jungian theory and practice. Alchemy lays out many aspects of these clinical processes fairly clearly, but it is the non-literal perspective and the multi-valent language of alchemical images and practice which immediately pull any discourse firmly out of a reductive arena and introduce the possibility of transformation over and above a simple transmutation of symptoms. This is perhaps one of the reasons Jung favored alchemy as the mythology of psychological process. Just the phrase 'true imagination' speaks eloquently to this point.

In his on-going efforts to understand psychological transformation and the mechanisms of therapeutic action, Jung often privileged the imagination as the most important key to the understanding of the alchemical and analytic *opus.* Citing from the *Rosarium* in *Psychology and Alchemy*:

> Take care that thy door be well and firmly closed, so that he who is within cannot escape, and — God willing — thou wilt reach the goal. Nature performeth her operations gradually; and indeed I would have thee do the same: let thy imagination be guided wholly by nature. And observe according to nature, through whom substances regenerate themselves in the bowels of the earth. And imagine this with true and not with fantastic imagination.[1]

Jung understood 'true imagination' as the creation and evocation of images which have a life of their own and which develop according to their own logic, an "authentic feat of thought or ideation" which grasps inner facts and portrays them in images true to their nature. This is in contrast to 'fantastic' imagination (fantasy), a "mere conceit" of insubstantial thought, which "just plays with its objects," spinning groundless fantasies on the surface of things and concerned primarily with "conscious expectations."[2] The alchemists repeatedly cautioned that the work had to be done with 'true' imagination, with active, purposive creation, and not with fantastic imagination. This finds its analogy in analysis, which attempts to differentiate the defensive fantasies generated by complexes, which interfere with integration and reconstruction, from the trajectory of psyche's true imagination—the coherent synthesis of the real, the imaginal, and the mystery of what might be.

Many of the techniques and methodological assumptions in analytic work are oriented toward the activation of true imagination, and the alchemists had many formulas and procedures which enhanced this process. This study addresses some of these and also explores the relationship between the mythopoetic sensibility, true imagination, and the transference field. From the perspective of psyche's potential for true imagination, both a '1-person' (intrapsychic) and a '2-person' (intersubjective and transference-based) model of therapeutic action are understood as belonging to one unfolding psychological trajectory. The archetypal symbols of true imagination, with their ties to both subject and object, unfold simultaneously in both radical specificity and subjectivity (the intrapsychic dimension) and in numerous embodied avenues of experience and expression, including the transference field.

* * * * *

Jung began his speculations about technique in analysis with his typical concern and caution about focusing directly on technical methods. This appears to have been a reaction to what was perceived as Freud's dogmatic use of theory and method which, in Jung's view, negated the primacy of the individual.[3] In the next breath, however, he introduced the techniques of amplification and active imagination, which both derive from the idea of true imagination and which it seems he felt were both sufficiently tailored to the individual psyche and also opened-up into objective, and often collective, psychological experience.[4] Jung was prescient in his intuitions about intersubjectivity, field phenomena, and the interplay of subjectivity and objectivity. We now understand in more explicit ways that meaning and change in analysis are both created and discovered, both subjectively and objectively determined, and that all psychological mechanisms and techniques exist in a bi-directional field of inner-outer, self-other. As above, so below. Psychological process is mirrored and reflected in various fields of emotional, biological, interpersonal, social, and spiritual life, and these are not necessarily hierarchically determined. These correspondences and patterns, so central to understanding alchemy and archetypal processes, are both vertical and horizontal and form, in turn, the patterns of new emerging psychological dynamics and structures. Given the complexity and fluidity of these fields and the unfolding nature of healing narratives in analysis, what does it mean to practice techniques which 'observe and imagine' (as the alchemical text says) with true imagination?

Exploring altered states of awareness, our historical forbears experimented with automatic writing, hypnosis, spirits and seances, free association and word association in their efforts to get beyond the margins of the ego's psychology and activate true imagination.[5] Jung and the generation he trained were devoted to the techniques of amplification and active imagination, which were validated, Jung felt, by the historical precedent of alchemical tradition. They followed the mythopoetic trails of imagination and possibility found in dreams in their efforts to get beyond the margins. They believed firmly in the notion, reflected in alchemy, that all culture, including the culture of the individual psyche, originated from "incursions of the unconscious."[6] These incursions, these altered states of psychological process and alchemical procedure, were the secret doors through which our founders passed, and defined the craft of analysis at its beginnings. What so fascinated the early psychoanalysts was the observation of the mythopoetic sensibility of true imagination—whose psychopomps at the time were mediums, 'multiples', hysterics, and ordinary dreamers—and its constructive, healing function. But today we find ourselves in a 'twilight of the magicians', at the end of the road and at the edge of new experience, for the 'wise old men and women,' who seemed almost effortlessly at home 'beyond the margins,' are gone. Modern analysts have since explored self psychology, object relations, intersubjectivity, and modern psychoanalysis, pocketing, scavenging, and amalgamating various techniques which seemed of use.

At the same time, many have actively begun the process of deconstructing the reified structures of Jungian theory, looking both past its edges and into its essential core. While classical analytical psychology privileged the subject over the object, the inner over the outer, forays beyond that model privileged the object over the subject, the personal over the archetypal, and the 'real' over the imaginal. In a similar vein, attention was paid to the details and dynamics of transference and countertransference to a degree which the older generations would have found distasteful and, more importantly, of little use. Currently, we regard the idea that aspects of the transference are at best a nuisance as quite naïve, but has our focus on it led to downplaying the techniques of active imagination and amplification, which were the original and unique contributions of the Jungian method? A constructive deconstruction, or 'revisioning' as Hillman originally proposed it, is now underway, moving toward collapsing these oppositions. It is from this post-Jungian perspective of the "ever-present azure vault"[7] that the dynamics of the transference field and the techniques of amplification and active imagination may be bridged. Psyche's narratives and dramas of creation and destruction are liminal alchemical phenomena, which are readable with true imagination as mythologems, from splitting and projective identification through active imagination. Reading them and responding to them this way can help induce the imaginal processes so lacking in clinical situations where there are core archetypal identifications.

* * * * * *

One of the things I've been intrigued with is how we, as Jungians, can work analytically with so-called primitive mechanisms, like dissociation, splitting, and projective identification, from the perspective of our unique understanding of the role of imagination and emergent processes in psychological growth and reconstruction. As Jungians, we take it for granted that the language of true imagination is made up of symbols, which partake of both the perceptions and experiences of the already lived life and the emergent capacities of imagination. We are less used to thinking about clinical phenomena, like splitting and projective identification, as mythopoetic expressions of the emergent psyche, as vectors of true imagination with an individuating function, as generators of new meaning in an on-going story of individual development.[8]

These pre-Oedipal dramas are often so prejudiced in a clinical notion of 'primitivity' that their value as 'healing fictions' is hard to discern. But it is in just such states of mind that we participate in both the imaginal construction of reality, its deconstruction, and its reconstruction in the most 'real' and poignant ways. Here we are most in an alchemical process, intrapsychically, interpersonally, transpersonally. Within the ritual of analysis, emerging reconstitutive possibilities are often experienced in the transference field, which mirror the personified mythologems of alchemical process: *solutio, nigredo, mortificatio, calcinatio.* This is particularly true at early levels of process where the transference field stands in for the transcendent function. These alchemical mythologems in action, understood synthetically, are not personalizations, but rather personifications of emerging psychological process, the play of true imagination which orients the analysis in a specific matrix.

Images, and especially affects, spontaneously arise in treatment which serve to both express, to deconstruct ('compensate', in the older terminology), and to re-create what had been previously privileged and fixed. True imagination is the capacity to transform the material of what was and is into the real 'potential other', and liminal psychological states provide the opening for the true imagination of both patient and analyst. The depths of borderline states and identifications ritualized in the transference are often the substances "in the bowels of the earth"[9] from which psyche is being made. The challenge is to understand these clinical narratives as expressions of true imagination, and to evoke true imagination to get 'beyond the margins' of defenses and identifications in clinical processes where the fantasies of the complexes are very entrenched. For example, how does a field such as projective identification, or any of the transference dramas which begin by imaginally translocating dissociated splits into another, find its transformation in the field of true imagination so that emergent processes can proceed further?

In many respects Jung's entire constructive and synthetic method can be understood as based around the implicit notion of 'true imagination', the prospective, emergent, even prophetic capacity of unconscious psychological process. If one believed entirely in the exclusive efficacy of the reductive method, then *all* unconscious activity would appear to be merely infantile, or wishful 'fantasy', a house of cards divined by false imaginings going nowhere. It would appear, however, that contemporary scientific data from studies on the nature of mind and brain support the notion of psychological process which rests in a ground of imagination. Advances in neurobiology provide paradigms and data suggesting that synthetic, constructive processes are evident in the neural responses of the brain. As new experience occurs, neural mapping of all similar past experience and memory is re-encoded in light of the new data; and these neural maps are themselves continuously emerging and being updated, based both on objective experience and on what and how this has subjective value and meaning for the individual. It is tempting to imagine that these developments signify the edge of discovering the material substrate of what the alchemists envisioned as true imagination. If so, clinicians are justified, even mandated as therapists, to focus attention and understanding on those analytic techniques which, similar to dreaming, induce the most active, synthetic states of memory and imagination. So, we pursue the deliberate induction of both transference fields and the 'trance field' of active imagination, as these are where material, embodied transformation occur.

* * * * *

While Jung's method of dialogue between conscious and unconscious was initially conceived as an intrapsychic process, by the time he wrote "Psychology of the Transference"[10] he had expanded this view to include the analytic couple, and we now conceive of the entire analytic dialogue from within a multi-dimensional perspective. Practicing of true imagination is a dialogue, or meditation, with the unseen, with both the 'other' within, the so-called "coming-to-terms with the unconscious", and with what is manifest, incarnated, and experienced with others. What is unconscious, living in a state of projection, or simply 'other', is made manifest, 'perfected' in the alchemical sense, through the faculty of true imagination.

Both the alchemists and Jung endowed 'true imagination' not only with extraordinary powers of perception and creation, but also with a body. "Imagination is the star in man, the celestial or supercelestial body,"[11] said the alchemists; Jung imagined further that this supercelestial body was not a phantom, but corporeal, which he imagined as a 'subtle body' with ties to both subject and object, mind and matter. The expression "star" ("imagination is the star") refers in alchemical metaphor to what is also called the "*quintessence*". This implies nothing less than that imagination is the essence of life, both physical and psychological.

> The *imaginatio*, or the act of imagining, was thus a physical activity that could be fitted into the cycle of material changes, that brought these about and was brought about by them in

> turn. In this way the alchemist related himself not only to the unconscious but directly to the very substance which he hoped to transform through the power of imagination.[12]

True imagination is intimately connected to reality. It is the 'faculty of imagining the possible', of increasing adaptation to the possibilities which both exist and arise and acting to transform those realities—what Beverley Zabriskie refers to as "that which so submits to the realities of what was and is, that any breakthrough into what might be would occur on a continuum of true possibility."[13] True imagination speaks to the difference between compulsive 'plans', the fantasies generated by complexes which keep psychological process trapped, and genuine narrative reconstruction which reflects the integrity of an emerging psyche.

Imagination with a 'body' transcends the boundaries of subjectivity, opening up into the actual psycho-physical objectivity of others and the world. The dialogue with 'the other' is also just that: the forging of an empathic connection to others. It is in this sense that the imaginal peculiarities of many transference fields, which can often feel just as hallucinatory as the chemically induced visions of the alchemists, can be understood in their full significance as psyche's work of re-creating itself, its relation to others and to the world.

The archetypal symbols of true imagination arise spontaneously to heal splits. Affect-laden relational fields also arise spontaneously in response to splits[14] in order to regulate, but also to heal the splits by empathetic affective linking. In the transference, images and emotions are linked from the outset in an unfolding interactive field.[15] Image and affect may be better understood not as a continuum, such as Jung's original image of a red (instinct) to violet (image) spectrum, but rather as different facets of the same emerging psychological process, psychoid phenomena outside the margins of the ego complex. Images give form to emotions, and emotions give a living body to imagination; the expressions of new archetypal possibilities are often both poetic and dramatic. The poetics are most easily seen in the symbols of myth and dreams and evoked in the techniques of amplification and active imagination. The dramatics, the rituals, the affective component, are often more easily seen in the transference field, where the archetype has the autonomy and energy to significantly structure and restructure the field.

We are well aware of the contagion, psychic infection, and poisonous projections which can reach deeply into the psyche and body of both analyst and patient. Alchemical treatises are full of cautionary admonitions concerning deadly sulphurous or mercury-induced hallucinations, which have their psychological correlate in dismemberment experiences, both intrapsychic and within the transference field. We dwell less upon the other, more gracious side of this effect: the empathic connections forged by both imagination *and* shared emotions. The fluidity of unconscious process opens the psyche to both the subjectivity and objectivity of other selves and other realities. In this sense, the alchemy of emerging transference enactments may be understood as archetypal correctives which are very much alive and may have something of an edge over symbols in terms of their ability to effect therapeutic change. This is often hard to get at, however, due to both the 'altered state' nature of the field and to the 'attacks-on-linking' these fields also perpetuate through the projection factor. But a form of 'de-linking' may be just as evident in the production of those 'symbols' which are only images, a form of fool's gold, spun by defensive fantasies. The alchemists were fooled again and again by identifying with the fantasy that their goal had been reached. In analytic work, extreme caution is also warranted regarding the pull toward archetypal reductionism, a premature concretizing of psychological process into reified mythologems rather than seeing the true imagination of a mythopoetic psychodynamic process through to its end, which is often a surprise. The surprise element is due to the fact that the psyche's native language and mode of reconstruction, mythopoesis, doesn't function to just re-create ancient stories, but rather it pulls them apart, crunches them up, and creates new narratives, new variations on basic themes which point the way toward future psychological possibilities. Always dynamic and process-oriented, these variations are often at odds with prevailing collective mythology, which makes the mythopoetic sensibility a somewhat subversive sensibility and gives Jungian psychoanalysis its deserved reputation as a subversive art and craft, akin to the function served by the alchemical tradition. A mythopoetic psychological process often offers a critique of social norms through the individual psyche's on-going deconstruction of both personal and collective mythology.

* * * * * *

The heightened or lowered atmospheric changes which we experience during genuine reverie and imagination are often not unlike what we experience in affect-laden transference fields. All the alchemical warnings and procedures apply to both: close the vessel, tear down the house, remove the superfluous material, purify the stone. In *Mysterium,* Jung comments that the lapis is sufficiently purified when it is "led out of its proper house and *enclosed in an alien house.*" From the *Rosarium*:

> In the proper house the flying bird is begotten, and in the alien house the tincturing stone. Therefore pull down the house, destroy the walls, extract therefrom the purest juice with the blood, and cook that thou mayest eat.[16]

The image of 'houses' probably derived from astrology and the transit of the planets from their natal houses to their progressed placements. The "proper house" also refers to the matrix of a substance, its natural 'unconscious' home, its origin, the psychological 'givens', while the "alien house" is the alchemical vessel, the substance's new, *contra naturam* home. One gets a "flying bird", which is a gas which comes out of the matrix, from the proper house, but one gets the tincturing stone, the *lapis*, in the alien house. This typical recipe calls for pulling down the house, the dissolution of complexes and identifications, so that the extraction of the pure juice, the opening of true imagination, can proceed and create the tincturing stone. There then remains the all-important question of cooking and particularly "eating" and assimilating. Here, the issue of relationship and conscience becomes pertinent, for it is often within relationships with others "in the alien house" that we face and suffer the ethical imperative to make meaning manifest, to 'eat it', to bring the living symbol into engaged experience in distinction to increasing consciousness per se. Ritual enactments are often an attempt to do this, the beginnings of true imagination, but sometimes seen through a glass, darkly. The rubber-meets-the-road within the intersubjective field where the press to both evoke and resist psyche's true imagination is often greatest from both sides.

But the alchemists were ever optimistic:

> To cause things hidden in the shadow to appear, and to take away the shadow from them.... All these things happen, and the eyes of the common men do not see them, but the eyes of the mind and of the imagination perceive them with true and truest vision.[17]

The implication is that imagination opens the shadow, moving the ego beyond its margins into the reality of the psyche, into the heart of darkness of lived experience, into the shock of both internal recognition and of the ever-present other. The premise that the work of analysis is to make the unconscious conscious puts an inordinate burden on the ego, one which is often untenable, too much to stomach. Even more pertinent, the tensions and connections of emerging process enter the transference field long before they become conscious in either patient or analyst, and it is in this arena that the deep alchemical work of analysis, the "eating", is taking place, usually in ritual dramas beyond the margins of anyone's understanding. These processes need to be met on their own turf, metabolized through the vision of true imagination, and it is here that the amplification of alchemical mythologems often comes into play.

In active imagination, the "patient does not interpret what the image means but experiences what it means."[18] In transference fields where core archetypal affects are active, there is often just no space for a symbolic dialogue of interpretation, and attempting it may be experienced as synonymous with destructive identifications, defenses, and "invasive objects."[19] One does not so much interpret the affect, but rather experiences it as one experiences and is moved by the ritual enactments of any living mythologem. The experience is then further informed by the interpretive technique of amplification, which makes the implicit meaning of both affects and images more and more explicit, cutting a groove in the psyche and supporting the trajectory of true imagination. Amplification in analysis, carrying as it does the currents of collective imagination, experience, and possibilities, provides not just an enhanced 'high definition', transpersonal 'holding environment', but actually may open up new grooves in the psyche, creating new riverbeds for the flow of libido, akin to the healing *pharmakon*. Perhaps the mechanisms might be similar to those provided by psychotropic medications, which sensitize new pathways and connections capable of competing with those etched by trauma, depression, or the fantasies of complexes.

The song-like stories of amplification, their mythopoetic structure and their appeal to the non-rational psyche, can create an empathic resonance which reaches deeply into early levels of disturbance and process. This perspective may be particularly pertinent during those altered states of psychological process, where mythologems are being lived as alchemical dramas in analysis—the *solution, mortificatio, putrefactio*—where we participate most fully in the destruction and creation of old paths and new possibilities. This idea runs somewhat counter to the prevailing wisdom, which holds amplification not therapeutically effective at early levels of process and itself invasive. It may be, however, that a mythopoetic lens such as alchemy offers can provide the empathic links which are not possible through intersubjective analysis or analysis of the transference, as these require cognitive and affective abilities which postdate early levels of experience. In any event, effective use of amplification arises not out of the defensive or supportive needs of either patient or analyst, but out of the 'analytic third', from the true imagination of the analysis itself. Our reactions as analysts may be informed as much by the press of imagination as they are by countertransference enactments of various sorts, and seeing through this lens may achieve a truly functional neutrality, based as it is in the matrix of the archetypal psyche.

NOTES

1. C.G. Jung, *CW* 12 § 218.
2. C.G. Jung, *CW* 18 § 396-7.
3. Joseph Cambray, 2001, "Enactments and Amplification," *J. Anal. Psychol.,* vol. 46, no. 2.
4. Sherry Salman, "The Creative Psyche: Jung's Major Contributions," in *The Cambridge Companion to Jung* (Cambridge, UK: Cambridge Univ. Press, 1997).
5. Sherry Salman, "Beyond the Margins: from Projective Identification to Active Imagination – the Question of Technique in Analytical Psychology," Barcelona 2004, in *Proceedings of the 16th*

International Congress for Analytical Psychology (Zürich: Daimon-Verlag, 2006).

6. Erich Neumann, *The Great Mother* (Princeton: Princeton Univ. Press, 1955), 297.

7. James Hillman, "The Azure Vault: the Caelum as Experience," *Barcelona 2004: Proceedings of the 16th International Congress for Analytical Psychology* (Einsiedeln, Switzerland: Daimon-Verlag, 2006).

8. Sherry Salman, 1999, "Dissociation and the Self in the magical pre-Oedipal Field," *J. Anal. Psychol.,* vol. 44, no. 1.

9. C.G. Jung, *CW* 12 § 218.

10. C.G. Jung, *CW* 16.

11. C.G. Jung, *CW* 12 § 394.

12. *Ibid.*

13. Beverley Zabriskie, 2004, "Imagination as laboratory," *J. Anal. Psychol.,* vol. 49, no. 2.

14. James Grotstein, *Splitting and Projective Identification* (New York: Aronson, 1981).

15. See the illustrations in "Psychology of the Transference," in C.G. Jung, *CW* 16.

16. C.G. Jung, *CW* 14 § 180.

17. Johannes Fabricius, *Alchemy* (London: Aquarian Press-HarperCollins, 1976, 1989), 21.

18. Michael Vannoy Adams, *The Fantasy Principle: Psychoanalysis of the Imagination* (New York: Brunner-Routledge, 2004), 16.

19. P. Williams, 2004, "Symbols and self preservation in severe disturbance," *J. Anal. Psychol.,* vol. 49, 21-31.

Rosarium Revisited

AUGUST J. CWIK

Introduction

Jung's use of alchemy as a metaphor for psychological transformation continues to illuminate, educate, and fascinate even as it obfuscates, confuses, and repels. After acceding to demands to comment on the nature of the transference in psychoanalysis, Jung penned *The Psychology of the Transference*,[1] a commentary on an obscure alchemical tract, *The Rosarium Philosophorum*.[2] To add insult to injury, Jung provocatively states in it that, "The reader will not find an account of the clinical phenomena of transference in this book."[3] As Zabriskie notes, "If analytical psychology definitively left the discipline of psychoanalysis with Jung's assertions of the collective unconscious, psychoanalysis believed Jung left the world of sanity when he turned to alchemy as an earlier road to the unconscious."[4]

August J. Cwik, Psy.D., is a clinical psychologist, hypnotherapist and Jungian analyst in private practice in the Chicago area. He is Co-Director of the Clinical Training Program in Analytical Psychotherapy at the C. G. Jung Institute of Chicago and an Assistant Editor of the *Journal of Analytical Psychology*. He has published articles on supervision, dreams and active imagination and numerous reviews.

And yet Jung's genius is exactly his uncanny ability to see psyche alive and attempting to reveal herself in these ancient texts. Jung goes on to state that "it is only possible to come to a right understanding and appreciation of a contemporary psychological problem when we can reach a point outside our own time from which to observe it."[5] He elaborates on the creation of a "third thing" in the analytic field: once two people enter into a depth psychological process, the relationship itself becomes the focus of attention and both participants are impacted and changed. He anticipates and describes such clinical phenomena as projective identification in which one participant places unconscious contents into another in a desperate attempt to feel whole, communicate, and be healed—if only the receiver can grasp what is happening and to what end. Jung uses obsolete, affect-laden words like psychic infection, possession, and loss of soul to best describe states often lost in sanitized psychoanalytic jargon. He states,

> The difficulties of our psychotherapeutic work teach us to take truth, goodness, and beauty where we find them … they are hidden in the dirt or are in the keeping of the dragon. … In '*stercore invenitur*' (it is found in filth) … nor is it any the less valuable on that account … it does not transfigure the dirt and does not diminish the evil, any more than these lessen God's gifts.[6]

What Jung sees depicted in the series of plates from the *Rosarium* anticipates developments in the intersubjective and relational schools of psychoanalysis. This can be seen most obviously in Ogden's description of the "analytic third."

> [M]y experience of each analytic situation is to a very large degree a reflection of the specific type of unconscious intersubjective construction that the patient and I are in the midst of creating. The sort of unconscious engagement with the analysand to which I am referring results in the creation of a third subject, the 'intersubjective analytic third'. The experience of analyst and analysand in (and of) the analytic third represents an experiential base, a pool of unconscious experience to which analyst and analysand contribute and from which they individually draw in the process of generating their own experience of the analytic relationship.[7]

Jung's creation of a "third thing" in the analytic encounter resounds in this definition.

But, interestingly enough, Jung used only the first ten plates of the series in the *Rosarium* to demonstrate the workings of the transference. The culmination of this series is described as the creation of the White Stone, or *albedo*. There is second series of ten plates on which he does not comment. This is described as the creation of the Red Stone, or *rubedo*. McLean raises the question of whether Jung even had access to the second series.[8] However, Jung did analyze one plate (Plate 11) from the second series, but totally out of sequence. Also, toward the end of " The Psychology of the Transference," Jung discusses that the first sequence of ten plates focuses on the erotic aspect of the anima's role in masculine psychology and states that "the feminine unconscious produces a symbolism which, by and large, is compensatory to the masculine."[9] He goes on to state

> I must point out that a certain concession to feminine psychology is also to be found in the *Rosarium*, in so far as the first series of pictures is followed by a second—*less complete*, but otherwise analogous—series, at the end of which there appears a masculine figure, the "emperor," and not, as in the first, an "empress," the "daughter of the philosophers." The accentuation of the feminine element in the Rebis [Plate 10] is consistent with a predominantly male psychology, whereas the addition of an "emperor" in the second version is a concession to woman (or possibly to the male consciousness).[10]

So clearly, Jung had knowledge of the existence of the second series. But these are interesting comments, "less complete, but otherwise analogous" and "concession to woman," especially from the man who never met an alchemical plate or series that he did not like. By what standard outside of the series could it be deemed "less complete" or as a "concession to woman"? Alchemists practiced before the era of political correctness. The series is what it is; how could it be otherwise? One would have to have a preconceived notion of what the plates were attempting to describe to think differently. Even Schwartz-Salant, who has done considerable reflection and writing on both series, states, "The ten woodcuts of the *rubedo* [the second series] do not lend themselves to a field interpretation as readily as the first ten, although several of them, especially the eleventh woodcut,

'Fermentation' ..., can be seen as representing possible field dynamics."[11] Notably, this is the same plate that Jung artificially introduced into his commentary on the first series.

The second series is somehow portrayed as less interesting and less complete, at least as a portrayal of transference dynamics. It is this second series that is the focus of this paper.

Body, Soul, Spirit and the Three Stages of Coniunctio

Before discussing the dynamics reflected in the *Rosarium* series, some background of the alchemical opus is in order. The three basic entities of a human being, the *tria materia*, are body, soul and spirit. The fourth component could be thought of as the material world itself. The integration of these four areas of existence is the primary concern of the alchemist in the spiritual form of alchemy. At the risk of "operationalizing" these quite complex and esoteric concepts, let us attempt to define them for the purposes of this paper. The body houses the instincts—the animal nature in man. Soul refers to the non-material aspect of human beings as the core, heart or center.[12] But more importantly, Jung ascribes to sulphur that aspect of soul which is

> the motive factor in consciousness: on the one hand the will, which can best be regarded as a dynamism subordinated to consciousness, and on the other hand compulsion, an involuntary motivation or impulse ranging from mere interest to possession proper. The unconscious dynamism would correspond to sulphur, *for compulsion is the great mystery of human life.*[13]

In other words, at the deepest level of our being we are what we want. Yet this must be differentiated from the body's own desires. Von Franz points out how the body is often harnessed to get what the soul really wants.[14] This harkens back to Hillman's statement regarding addictive process in that you can't get enough of what you don't really want. Spirit is the non-material aspect of a living person and is conceived of as the opposite of matter.[15] Jung states,

> This higher world has an impersonal character and consists on the one hand of all those traditional, intellectual, and moral values

> (superego) which educate and cultivate the individual, and, on the other, of the products of the unconscious, which present themselves to consciousness as archetypal ideas.[16]

It also can be related to thinking and cognitive processes as these are completely non-material.

In the last chapter of his masterpiece, *Mysterium Coniunctionis*, Jung cites the work of Dorn on the three stages of the *coniunctio*.[17] Edinger expands upon this concept in his companion book, *The Mysterium Lectures*.[18] In the first stage, the soul unites with the spirit forming the *unio mentalis*, an interior oneness. What the soul wants must be separated from body desires, a *separatio* process. It should be noted that in this process spiritual principles are not necessarily considered to be of the greatest importance. Jung emphatically states,

> In the long run it does not pay to cripple life by insisting on primacy of the spirit, for which reason the pious man cannot prevent himself from sinning again and again and the rationalist must constantly trip over his own irrationalities. ... A permanent and uncomplicated state of spiritualization is therefore such a rarity that its possessors are canonized by the Church.[19]

This is an excellent reminder to help understand what is currently happening in our collective consciousness.

The incestual erotic aspect, complicated and fueled by the inadequate object relations of childhood, is experienced and analyzed in the transference so that the soul's true desires eventually become clearer. This amounts to an analysis of the shadow. Separation means withdrawing the soul and her projections from the bodily sphere and from all environmental conditions relating to the body, through introversion, introspection, meditation and a careful investigation of desires and motives.[20]

One can understand that the first series of the *Rosarium* relates to the establishment of the *unio mentalis*, the creation of the White Stone. This is probably why Jung saw the first series leading to the goal of analysis: it produces an individual capable of recognizing his or her own shadow and attempting to be and act in the world as a whole person. The individual, more or less, knows what are his or her intentions, while having some way to discern what is "right" for that individual. This does not mean that one always acts according to moral collective norms, but that one lives in harmony with the Self. More importantly, the individual can live with the consequences of decisions without going into complex.

In the second stage of *coniunctio,* the *unio mentalis* is reunited with the body. The product is called the *vir unus,* the unified man. This is the outcome depicted in the second series of plates leading to the creation of the Red Stone. The aware and reflective individual attempts to live life fully while coming to grips with its vicissitudes. This is the reddening, living the "full-blooded" life. The idea here is that a state of individuation is sought where the complexes do not necessarily lead the way—instinctually and affectivity are transcended.

In the third *coniunctio,* the body/soul/spirit integration of the *vir unus* unites with the world to form the *unus mundus,* the experience of a one, interrelated world. It is the unified field theory of alchemy and can be thought of as happening while approaching death. Glimpses of this totality are also found in ecstatic, visionary and synchronistic experiences. But, as we shall see, the last three plates of the *Rosarium* provide an approach to conscious death.

Review of the First Series Leading to the Creation of the White Stone

The plates from both the first series (Plates 1-10) and the second series (Plates 11-20) of the *Rosarium Philosophorum* are reproduced for reference at the end of this article. Due to space limitations readers interested in detailed analyses of the first series are referred to Allphin,[21] Edinger,[22] Jung,[23] Fabricius,[24] McLean,[25] Samuels,[26] Schwartz-Salant,[27] and Zabriskie.[28] Alchemical plates tend to draw out deep psychological reactions in those who reflect and meditate upon them. Because of this, they can be thought of as "psychic flypaper."[29] As William Blake emphatically states, "all things acted on earth are seen in them" and "every age renews its power from these works."[30] Some insights from these authors will be discussed as comparisons are naturally made between the imagery of the first series and that of the second.

Schwartz-Salant states, "psychoanalysis has seldom focused upon the transference relationship as an enlivened field quality characterized by passion."[31] The first series of plates in the *Rosarium* can be seen as embodying and representing the eventual fate of the erotic component of the analytic relationship, or of any deeply experienced relationship. The symbolic starting point, and end point, is the frontispiece of the series showing the mercurial fountain with its streams depicting body, soul, spirit and world and their potential integration (Plate 1, 'The Mercurial Fountain'). The initial diagnostic encounter of analyst and analysand is demonstrated with both its conscious communications and hidden unconscious incestual motives (Plate 2, 'King and Queen'). Their contract to be honest and genuine with one another and to speak of what matters is seen in the nakedness of the couple (Plate 3, 'The Naked Truth'). The creation of a space for and respect of unconscious material as an integral part of their experience together is reflected on their entering the mutual bath (Plate 4, 'Immersion into the Bath'). The joyous, yet potentially frightening, interpenetration and fusion of two personalities is seen in the *coniunctio*, the union of the opposites (Plate 5, 'The Conjunction'). Death and withdrawal of mutual projections necessarily follow an experience of conjunction with another (Plate 6, 'Death'). Then, there is an extraction of meaning from the whole experience as the soul unites with spiritual potentialities (Plate 7, 'The Ascent of the Soul'). An emotional purification and washing away of hurts and disappointments associated to things not being what they thought they were can then occur (Plate 8, 'Purification'). The reanimation of the couple in relationship with the meaning extracted earlier can then begin (Plate 9, 'The Return of the Soul'). Finally, there is the creation of an inner psychological structure which allows reflection through an observing ego depicted in the rather bizarre image of the Rebis, Androgyne or Hermaphrodite. This symbol demonstrates the conjoint union of the masculine and feminine principles (Plate 10, 'The New Birth'). This is a thumbnail sketch of a complicated psychological interactive process. Schwartz-Salant states that the series demonstrates,

> the realm in which *relations per se*, rather than the things related (for example, complexes belonging to one or both people) are the main focus. Concern over which parts of psyche belong to whom fades as both people become aware of a linking structure that has determined the nature of their interaction.[32]

Of Terminations and Symbolic Friends

One way of looking at the second series of plates from the *Rosarium* is that it portrays a dynamic that can only be lived outside of analysis. As Jung states, "when it comes to the question of real experience the analyst can no longer help him (the patient): he himself must put his hand to the work."[33] As long as the analytic relationship exists, one will necessarily be thrown back into the projective dynamics of the first series. One could think of the first series as the working through of the bad object relations of childhood in order to experience a unified personal self. The asymmetrical quality of the analytic relationship will always constellate a transference reaction—the analyst will continue to carry functions of the Self as an ordering and directing principle. Only termination with the concomitant working through of the transference allows the patient to become free of the analyst's influence. The patient has his or her own relationship to the unconscious and is able to navigate what life brings.

But as analyses grow in length and one experiences how patients change in relationship to the work, this idealized notion of termination comes into question. Some long-term patients clearly move into what I call *individuation proper*. Symptoms have either abated or become non-issues. And yet the patient—perhaps the terminology needs to change at this point—continues in the relationship in order to have a space in which to reflect on the conscious and non-rational components of his or her life experience. Or, as Tresan suggests, "one can only become fully human in relation to an other."[34] The role of the analyst becomes less interpretive and more like a co-amplifier of material, a witness to life's drama. Henderson describes this situation in the last chapter of *Thresholds of Initiation* as, "My own role is less that of an interpreter than a friend sharing their experience or a commentator whose knowledge of mythology may help to provide some amplification of the archetypal background from which the visionary images arise."[35] In a little-known earlier paper, Henderson attempts to describe a relationship that

> is not quite like any other since it has come into being as a product of the transference relationship but is no longer transference. I have been unable to think of a suitable term to express such a relationship and possibly it would be better to let it remain

> nameless. But perhaps I may hazard the suggestion that it could be called a symbolic friendship if it were understood that its being symbolic takes nothing away from the authentic feeling of friendship and that the friendship does not wrongly personalize the symbol.[36]

Tresan, in *Thinking Individuation Forward*, expands on this idea calling it a "continuing life education of the most profound and individualized sort." He notes that this type of continuation of analysis has not been thoroughly addressed in theorizing about the termination process.[37]

Schwartz-Salant uses the second series to extend the field dynamics of the analytic relationship, but he describes it as a stretch of the meaning of the plates to do so. One might consider that his description of the field dynamics in the second series is what psychologically is required to become a symbolic friend. The contention of this paper is that the second series of plates from the *Rosarium* describes the dynamics of the symbolic friendship and/or the intrapsychic dynamics of an individual "coming to grips" with life post analysis.

The Second Series Leading to the Creation of the Red Stone

Plate 11: Fermentation

Some of my own projections that stick to the "flypaper" of the *Rosarium* involve seeing Plate 4, 'Immersion in the Bath,' as the establishment of the *mundus imaginalis*. The *mundus imaginalis* is a concept put forward by Henry Corbin emerging out of his study of Sufism.[38] He posits that it is an "order of reality" that is an intermediate world between the world of cognition/intellect/spirituality and the sensible/sensate world. It can be seen as the realm of soul as it mediates the cognitive and sensate worlds. This realm can be thought of as an *a priori*, pre-existent field capable of facilitating psychological processes.[39] This is the psychic "ether" providing a medium for intersubjective experience and imagery. When two individuals enter into a depth psychological process, they allow a lowering of consciousness to occur, seen in the half-submerged couple, which allows access to the imaginal as an important informative source of what is happening at the unconscious level of the relationship. This is similar to the "imaginal couple" work described by Schwartz-Salant.

Thus Plate 11, 'Fermentation,' can be understood as a fully functioning *mundus imaginalis*. The winged nature of the figures suggests that what is represented is the outcome of a *sublimatio* process—the winged couple represent the thoughts and ideas of the participants. Also, they are no longer pictured as fully under the water. Analyst and analysand can now know the rhythm of a *coniunctio* process, which is a "third thing" that can be imaginally alive and sensed. It is more consciously engaged than the *coniunctio* represented in Plate 5.

Plate 11 is the plate that Jung inappropriately compared to the conjunction of Plate 5. Zabriskie suggests that Jung's intrusive introduction of the non-sequential plate is a blatant complex indicator. She suggests that he was "rationalizing" some of his intimate, and perhaps sexual relationship(s), as having a "higher" or more spiritual motive.[40] One has to agree that randomly including a plate from the second series seems totally out of place. McLean[41] and Fabricius[42] both take umbrage to Jung's using the plate out of context. Both stress the necessity of examining alchemical plates in the context in which they belong. 'Conjunction' (Plate 5) is not 'Fermentation' (Plate 11); although there are similarities, the differences are compelling.

The action reflected in the image in Plate 11 is often seen as the female taking the upper position in the couple. Other versions of the *Rosarium* series make this more apparent. But one thing is clear—the bottom figure is disrupting, preventing the penetration. Both the wingedness of the couple and the "*coniunctio interruptus*", if you will, speak to the fact that the plate portrays a different type of encounter than the unabashed conjunction of Plate 5. It is close, it is intimate, but it does not involve the full erotic interpenetration of the masculine and feminine principles. The heat is lower, but still hot. It is not just the erotic that is referenced, but the *eros* of a more spiritual encounter. Samuels reminds us that the *eros* in the series is much more than just genital sexuality. As an archetypal principle of psychological functioning, *eros* is concerned with connectedness, relatedness and harmony. He identifies five aspects of the "erotic": a reproductive element, a lustful approach, a caring and more romantic element, a spiritual dimension, which enhances the presence and impact of the other, and, finally, a wisdom component best defined as *Sapientia*.[43] It is not the physicality of the participants that is emphasized but their own symbolic representation. One could think of it as the "subtle bodies" of the participants. They represent interactions going on in the imaginal realm.

If we take the plate to represent the intrapsychic realm of an individual, Plate 11 is a good image of active imagination: an imaginal ego engages a personified aspect of the unconscious. Jung saw active imagination as the way to free the patient from the transference on the therapist. He strongly advocates the transcendent function (understood as active imagination), which:

> not only forms a valuable addition to psychotherapeutic treatment, but gives the patient the inestimable advantage of assisting the analyst on his own resources, and of breaking a dependence which is often felt as humiliating. It is a way of attaining liberation by one's own efforts and of finding the courage to be oneself.[44]

Plate 12: Illumination

McLean points out that Plate 11, 'Fermentation', closely compares to Plate 5, 'Conjunction', and that Plate 12, 'Illumination', actually has more in common with Plate 4, 'Immersion in the Bath.'[45] Indeed, they are very similar stylistically. But 'Fermentation' really has more to do with the ongoing use of the *mundus imaginalis*, hence depicted as interacting in the bath, or the medium of the *mundus imaginalis*. Plate 12, 'Illumination,' can be viewed as a conjunction of an entirely different order.

Plate 12 is extraordinary in that other than the fountain of the frontispiece, this is the first plate that is not anthropomorphic. It is a "beautiful" portrayal of annihilation anxieties. This winged *Sol* submerging into *Luna* as the mercurial tomb/womb is clearly archetypal in nature. Here solar stability and constancy are being totally dissolved by lunar changeability. It is rationality being inundated by the well of emotionality. And so, while McLean finds it closer to Plate 4, 'Immersion in the Bath', I think it represents a *coniunctio* of major proportions and is actually closer to Plate 5, 'The Conjunction', in its depiction of a powerful psychic process.

On one hand, this is a symbolic portrayal of cataclysm. Here one's notion, the wingedness again, of what is most important in life is defeated. This is the loss of a loved one, finding out one has cancer, losing everything in a hurricane. On the other hand, it can represent the slow degradation of mental and physical abilities in the aging process. What was once sharp and well defined becomes vague and diffuse. It is the loss of the dominant understanding of how one thought life was supposed to be—it never goes just like we want it to, and it is never suffering that we expect to find. This is the experience of being analyzed by life—being reduced to the *prima materia*, a return to the basics. Or, as Jung says, "the experience of the Self (here understood as nature or life) is always a defeat for the ego."[46] We are reminded that we are not captain of the ship.

A good example of this state is described by Jung after his major heart attack in 1944, a time when he had powerful dreams and visions and became profoundly disengaged from the things of life. He states, "I had the feeling that everything was being sloughed away; everything I aimed at or wished for or thought, the whole phantasmagoria of earthly existence, fell away or was stripped from me—an extremely painful process."[47] This is an excellent description of the annihilation experience of the submergence of the winged sun.

Schwartz-Salant, working the image of Plate 12 into field dynamics states,

> Solar rational awareness and illumination can be destructive and how they must often be sacrificed—also represent the same *nigredo* sequence seen in *albedo* phase—except the hermaphrodite is winged—more capable of being conscious to the participants and readily reflected upon than blindly suffered as is often the case in the albedo phase.[48]

Here solar awareness is both the sacrificed and the sacrificer; the analyst and analysand must consciously sacrifice what is known. This can be thought of as the creation of a symbolic friendship.

Plate 13: Nourishment

Here is a representation of despair. And yet, the joined hermaphrodite, a representation of the "third thing" of the relationship, remains winged. No small feat in the aftermath of cataclysm. A new *nigredo* of a spiritual nature is "born" in disaster yet experienced more consciously. There remains some consciousness in contrast to the

'*Mortificatio*' of Plate 6. The presence of the wings suggests that some measure of hope, or at least awareness, remains, even as the death experience inundates the psyche.

Plate 12, 'Illumination,' is the event and Plate 13, 'Nourishment,' represents the *sequela.* When a great notion dies, one feels lost as to how things are actually put together and why such a thing happened. The *mundus imaginalis* is broken and yields little of value to the working of the relationship. And yet, as Jung comments in the exposition to Plate 6, 'Death,' there can be "no new life without the death of the old,"[49] and Plate 13 is called 'Nourishment,' of all things, suggesting that something is growing in the tomb. In this "firing" by life, a new formulation is being sought unconsciously, bracing us for bodily death as the goal. A man, whose wife died of a rare form of cancer activated by pregnancy, said, "I thought I was made of steel, but this melted me to the core." This highly rational doctor eventually became extraordinarily more feeling and related as a consequence of this tragedy. Intrapsychically, this is the aftermath of trauma. Wildly emotional states can alternate with dissociative flatness. An individual considers either starting therapy, if not already in it, or of returning to it, if it has terminated. In a symbolic friendship, both participants tend to be deeply affected, not because projective identification is in play, but because the humanity of the situation is empathically sensed. There are no words to ease the pain of the experience, nor are words necessary. The need for the presence of the other is palpable even in situations where withdrawal is necessary or desired.

Schwartz-Salant states, "The importance of the transformation of consciousness cannot be over-emphasized—sacrificing consciousness on the part of the analyst can lead to a watery stage unless it is known that something is being given up for a greater goal."[50] Perhaps we can see in his approach what is involved in living a symbolic friendship. If the analyst pretends to know too much about these workings of nature, he or she will flip the analysand back into the dynamics of the first series. A new, more stabilized relationship to life and the world, even as it fades, is being sought in a move toward the *unus mundus.*

Plate 14: Fixation

Jung described the experience depicted in Plate 7, 'The Ascent of the Soul,' as a "schizophrenic dissociation." Similarly, the experience imaged in Plate 14, 'Fixation,' compares in its empty annihilation. Most notable here is that the hermaphrodite is no longer winged. No symbolic attitude can or should be maintained in the face of disaster. It prevents the full emotional experience of the loss. The analyst or individual should not rush in, trying to find meaning in a painful event before it is fully felt, fully "savored."

This plate is almost identical to Plate 7, with the major exception that the ascending soul bird/child is clearly feminine, whereas it is masculine in the first series. This is the reiteration of a *sublimatio*, similar to the final formation of the *unio mentalis*, except with feminine soul energies rather than masculine. In Plate 7, it is the active and penetrating aspects of the masculine that have to be separated and "tempered" by spirit so as to allow development of the related and reflective feminine capacities. Here the analyst's interpretations may prove more useful. *Logos* is needed to analyze projections from the parental complexes.

In Plate 14, the opposite occurs: the reflective and relational aspects of the feminine are given up as they are sacrificed to a *coniunctio* with the spiritual principles of the collective unconscious. Here it may be the amplifications of the analyst that prove most useful in extracting meaning from the destructive life event. It is *Eros* which takes the lead in finding connections and grasping patterns. A man with terminal cancer dreamt of entering a beautiful valley filled with hills and wild flowers on a sunny day. As he lowered himself toward the ground, he began to see underlying patterns that utterly terrified him. Here the image is of the dream ego "lowering" itself as it begins to see nature's "higher" forces, the archetypes and where they are leading him.

Schwartz-Salant points out that the journey at this moment moves from the image of the sacred marriage model to a *unio mystica* model, in which there is a solitary ascent of the soul to God.[51] But also, as Plates 7 and 14 suggest, this solitary journey involves a paradox—it can only be completed in the presence of an other. This is similar to Winnicott's notion that the capacity to be alone always involves a paradox, in that it can only be experienced in the presence of an other, the internalized good mother.[52]

Plate 15: Multiplication

I have always found it interesting that before the soul/spirit union—the sublimated product—returns, it is preceded by this watery, rain image. It also occurs identically in Plate 8, 'Purification.' It is almost as if an emotional watering is necessary before new meaning can be seeded into the desiccated hermaphroditic corpse. The realization and acceptance of the laws of nature bring a cool healing rain to the united dead couple—nature is "realized." This cleansing shower also brings a purifying relief to the pair. This shift is palpable when the emotional climate changes from one of despair to one of acceptance. Of course, many remain in this stage of deadness or turn to addiction, never to reemerge into life and individuate.

Being identical to Plate 8 leads to the suggestion that one might escape, i.e., regress, to the dynamics of the first series in a "chutes and ladders" kind of way. Then, being with the person of the analyst becomes the "cure" itself, and the Self becomes projected once again instead of leading to an experience of being in alignment with nature. The shadow of a symbolic relationship is that it conceals unconscious dependency on the analyst. The "relief" presaged in the image can easily be "transferred" onto 'the being with' the person of the analyst.

By referencing the alchemical process of '*Multiplicatio*', the image in Plate 15 suggests that this affective shift "fixes," a *coagulatio* process, a certain emotional quality in the participants or in an individual post analysis. This means that a strong and viable sense of self, or better yet, an ego-Self axis, is being created. This often has a "multiplying" effect on anyone who knows the individual. This is one of the powerful attributes ascribed to the Stone, the goal of the *opus*.

Plate 16: Reviving

The revivification of the hermaphrodite is heralded by the return of the soul/spirit girl. A new observational and relational attitude is returning to the situation, perhaps assisted by the amplificatory process of the analyst. This observing ego is now informed by life's possibilities and limitations. The goal of this process is to allow a new active engagement with life. Remember the dying man who dreamt of being terrified by the deep patterns he was beginning to find in nature? Later in the dream, an unknown man in a kiosk outside the valley selling postcards of the idyllic scene, the keeper of nature's images, helps to mitigate his terror. He was being schooled in the rhythms of life creating a *unio mentalis*, a unified mind, to face what was to come, thus becoming a *vir unus*. By the way, he managed to do this in an amazingly conscious manner that deeply affected all who knew him. In Jung's case, after his nearly fatal heart attack, he gradually reconnected to life and the living. At the time of his illness he had been working on *The Mysterium Coniunctionis*, which exactly deals with this phenomenon of the union of the opposites. He said that only after surviving the heart attack could he know the full reality of what he had been writing.[53]

This new meaning that descends allows one who has experienced life's slings and arrows to come to a stance not constellated by the complexes. One accepts a certain "isness" to life's vagaries. The neurotic way once again seeks understanding in the deficits of early life, as if the catastrophe could have been avoided if only he or she was good enough. A good example of this came while channel surfing. I happened upon an interview with two survivors of the tsunami. The first one said, "We must have done something very bad for God to have punished us this way." The second one said simply, "This is what the ocean does." The feeling sense of the second response might be the one suggested in Plate 16.

Plate 9, 'The Return of the Soul,' shows the surfacing of two birds, the fledged and unfledged. A single bird finally emerges next to the Rebis in Plate 10, 'The New Birth.' Plate 16, 'Reviving,' shows no such parallel formation. The presence of these birds seems to have generated some amount of curiosity in the literature. Even Edinger, who is rarely at a loss regarding anything symbolic, states, "I'm not going to say more about that bird. I don't know what it's doing there, except there's just one so maybe the two birds in Plate 9 got together—just as the body got together. But I don't know about that."[54] Zabriskie suggests that they reflect the new life emerging from the dead hermaphrodite.[55] Fabricius emphasizes the destructive aspects of the feminine in the "cruel beak" which devours the masculine in the act of copulation.[56] Jung himself was unsure of their significance, but hints that the black bird is always a harbinger of the *nigredo*, the dark beginning of an alchemical process. Following up on Jung's statement, I think the emergence of the birds heralds the forthcoming *nigredo* of the second series; the appearance of two things often suggests that something is coming into consciousness. While at one level they signify the creation of a new spiritual life, the black bird also represents the untransformed dross of the first sequence. The heroic masculine still needs to be transformed into a more lunar masculine, ready to accept and engage a life of decline and loss, to deal with shadow.

Plate 17: The Demonstration of Perfection

At the end of the first series a psychic integration is realized in Plate 10, 'The New Birth.' The grand opposites of masculine and feminine, solar and lunar, as king and queen are united in the image of a winged hermaphrodite. This figure holds in the right hand of consciousness the chalice or container of three plumed serpents and, in the left hand of unconsciousness, a plumed serpent. This demonstrates that a conscious to unconscious relationship is "grasped" by the individual regarding instinctual processes. The problem of the three and the four is reflected in the serpents. Basically, the idea is that when wholeness is conceived as a quaternity, whether typologically—as in thinking, feeling, intuition and sensation—or elementally—as in earth, air, fire and water—consciousness is only capable of holding three elements simultaneously. The fourth will tend to remain unconscious and be the doorway through which the unconscious manifests into consciousness.

The Rebis image of Plate 10 can be understood as a more enlightened understanding of the instinctual psyche. The erotic component of relationship can be acknowledged and felt but not necessarily acted on. Elements of this transformation are reflected in the wingedness of the figure and the plumes on the serpents. Both reflect that some form of "spiritualization" has occurred. The figure is firmly planted on a crescent moon image signifying a certain mastery of lunar forces. This idea is echoed in the thriving moon tree seen on the left side of the plate: a predominantly lunar reflectiveness is a "vegetative", hence living, aspect of the organism. The black bird on the right reflects this new consciousness, while also being untransformed shadow material, the dross, of the process. This raven is the "good omen" of the *nigredo* that follows, allowing deeper transformation.

This lunar consciousness means that a reflective stance has been established, suggesting the presence of an observing ego not totally in sway to the instincts. What is established is

> a border that one cannot cross without doing violence either to one's own soul or to that of another, and when one suffers the frustration of non-identification with those energies, then this shadow becomes more creative—the shadow then becomes the sacrificer of rigid structures.[57]

An intentionality is born that comes face to face with the vicissitudes of life.

The figure of Plate 17 is darker and therefore more complete. It is titled 'The Demonstration of Perfection.' It is symbolic of the capacity to be and live in fully human manner, the *vir unus*. The Rebis of the White Stone, while reflecting a very difficult integration, lacks a relationship to shadow's blackness and death. These darker aspects are alluded to in the bat wings, now capable of traversing spiritual darkness, and the figure's stand on a mound of earth with three dragons devouring themselves. This is a reference to the triadic unity of Mercurius initially observed in the fountain of Plate 1. This is "the chthonic, lower, or even infernal counterpart of the Heavenly Trinity, just as Dante's devil is three-headed" so "Mercurius is often shown as a three-headed serpent."[58]

Solar life is thriving in its vegetative aspects, seen in the sun tree on the left. This is a fully alive, reddened consciousness, especially in its ability to engage blackness. It is clothed, denoting a *persona* that can adapt readily to even the final stages of life. The pelican, replacing the raven of Plate 10, is shown feeding its young through the blood of its own breast. This is a common alchemical reference to Christ who sacrifices his own blood in order to redeem his people. It is a symbol of a "self-nourishing" process. But it is also a preeminent indication of the need for self-sacrifice, a hallmark of the beginning of the end. The end is presaged in the lion resting behind the figure. A solar symbol itself and yet heralding the final *nigredo* to come.

The state of consciousness related to this image is best described by Jung after surviving and integrating the experiences, visions, and dreams surrounding his near fatal heart attack. He learned something of extreme value from his initial experience of detachment from the material world. It transformed into what he described as objective cognition.

> The objectivity which I experienced in this dream and in the visions is part of a completed individuation. It signifies detachment from valuations and from what we call emotional ties. In general, emotional ties are very important to human beings. But they still contain projections, and it is essential to withdraw these projections in order to attain to oneself and to objectivity. Emotional relationships are relationships of desire, tainted by coercion and constraint; something is expected from the other person, and that makes him and ourselves unfree. Objective cognition lies hidden behind the attraction of the emotional relationship; it seems to be the central secret. Only through objective cognition is the real *coniunctio* possible.[59]

Plate 18: The Green Lion Devouring the Sun

I consider the final three plates to be dealing with physical death and the experience of the *unus mundus*. The interrelatedness of the world may be glimpsed at any time in life through visionary or meditative experiences. But death as the final goal of consciousness seems to be what is suggested at the end of the series. Other theorists seem to see this as another round in the *coniunctio-nigredo* sequence, but the imagery here is too dramatic and archetypal to be anything but a literal reference to the dying process itself. The last three emblems could be seen as illustrating the fate of body, soul and spirit in that order.

Plate 18 is a classic image of the *nigredo*. But being placed at this point in the series gives it a whole new perspective; this is not just any *nigredo*. The lion lurking behind in Plate 17 comes forward to devour the sun, consciousness and ego awareness. No winged symbolic sun dissolving in a contained bath here, but the sun itself being swallowed into the "belly of the beast." As McLean states, "The sun here represents all that the alchemist has so diligently won for his consciousness, through this process of inner development. The Green Lion is the devouring, dissolving aspect of the unconscious."[60] All of the hard-earned redness from the previous series flows down to be reabsorbed by nature herself. Marlan suggests that this "wounding" of the sun could lead to nourishment. "When psychological blood flows, it can dissolve hardened defenses. This then can be the beginning of true productivity."[61] Jung's most productive period followed his heart attack. The somewhat gruesome appearance of this process suggests that this task could be terrifying and painful. In visionary states, this is the loss of ego consciousness itself.

The lion is a solar creature so we have consciousness returning to itself. This presents one of those conundrums in alchemical imagery. We could look at this as a suggestion that the consciousness gained during individuation becomes added to the sum total of collective consciousness; it becomes an enduring addition to the archetypal psyche. This is certainly a Jungian notion that the work of an individual striving to develop consciousness affects collective consciousness in general and actually changes the nature of the collective unconscious. Plate 18 should be recognized as our collective funeral banner.

Plate 19: Coronation of Mary

The last two plates are prototypically Christian in nature. And, after all, it should be remembered that we are contemplating and meditating on the *Rosary of the Philosophers*. This alchemical series is literally based upon the picture rosaries created in the 1500's when it became possible to reproduce inexpensively woodcut picture prints for the first time. The Assumption of the Virgin Mary was a very important image to Jung. First of all, her elevation allows the Trinity of the Father, Son and Holy Ghost to become a quaternity as seen in the plate. As a quaternity, the God-head becomes whole and complete with its missing feminine counterpart. Since it is not just her soul but her actual body that is raised, materiality and matter become spiritualized psychologically.

But we must keep in mind that Jung's contention is that the processes depicted in alchemy are a collective compensation for a christian consciousness which tends to see matter, the body and the feminine as dark and sinful. So the "christianized" image we are confronted with really speaks, in a way, to its opposite—giving the highest value to matter, *mater*, itself. The Virgin Mary becomes equivalent to *anima mundi*, the world soul, and the principle of interrelatedness. As such, this dynamic often is sensed in synchronistic experiences. Synchronicity is 'an acausal connecting principle' which links inner psychic events with the material world.[62] And, while synchronicities can and are experienced at any time, there is some anecdotal evidence to show that they may increase in frequency as death approaches. In this manner the *unus mundus* may be comprehended.

But at a more "mundane" level, what is the fate of the soul after death? Or, in our project, what of feminine relatedness remains in matter, in the world, once body is gone? We know that we leave behind some traces of our material presence in the world through our "estates." As a psychoanalyst, I see the *remains of relationship* existing in the psyches of my patients everyday. Just the *memory* of those who have died creates very powerful affective responses, both positive and negative. Following the dreams of individuals who have lost a friend or loved one always proves quite informative. The previous relationships always have a here-and-now quality as the inner objects and imagoes begin to appear. Imagoes are images that are subjectively influenced. They are perceived and colored by the inner state of the subject.[63] In this way imagoes themselves reflect a *coniunctio* process because they are amalgams of both subject and object. Very often a dream series focusing on a person who has died moves along a certain trajectory. At first, encounters occur where nothing out of the ordinary is noted by the dream ego; there is no awareness that the person has died. Then the dream ego often notices that the person cannot be there because he or she is dead. This is usually interpreted psychoanalytically as a denial of the loss. But we could just as well hear it as compensatory to a consciousness that thinks it knows what the "truth" is regarding the nature of death. Jung makes some extraordinary statements about these experiences in *Memories, Dreams, Reflections* in the chapter 'On Life After Death.' As he says, "the figures from the unconscious are uninformed too, and need man, or contact with consciousness, in order to attain to knowledge."[64] And, likewise, consciousness needs to be informed by the figures of the unconscious. Again, the Jungian notion of a mutuality, a *coniunctio*, between consciousness and unconsciousness is emphasized.

There is an old Mexican saying that goes something like this: We all die three deaths. The first death is when we take our last breath, wounded by the green lion, if you will. The second death is when we are buried and lose all connection with friends and relatives, swallowed by the green lion. The third and final death is when we are forgotten.[65]

Plate 20: Resurrection of Christ

The last image is the most christianized of all: the resurrection of Christ from the tomb. It is emblematic of the eternal life of the spirit in its ability to overcome death. Experiences of the *Imago-Dei*, the God-image, whether in visionary states or dreams, are always deeply compelling and numinous in nature. It is a unifying and transcendent symbol of the Self, the totality, and the *unus mundus* as that totality.[66] Again, this type of "beatific" vision is not totally uncommon surrounding death.

But the tomb here looks suspiciously similar to our alchemical vessel in which the prior psychological transformations took place. Here Christ becomes the image of the *Anthropos*. This is an image of the original or primordial man trapped in matter; it is an archetypal image of wholeness in alchemy, religion and Gnostic philosophy.[67] Once again, the alchemical conceit reverses the traditional religious notion and attempts to reunite spirit with matter rather than have it return to heaven. Hillman phrases it this way, "resurrection would indicate not the confirmation throughout eternity of the personal subject and its body saved from the world and the devil of its flesh, but rather the resurrection of the body of the world with an idea to its eternity."[68] Or, as Schwartz-Salant puts it,

> This last wood cut, which represents the overcoming of death, suggests that one cannot truly live unless mindful of mortality. This woodcut also symbolically portrays the final but never-attainable goal of the work of the complete integration of the archetypal sphere into the human being, in which the transcendent Self and the individual self are identical.[69]

Again, at the "mundane" level, there occasionally is an interesting sort of dream in the series after the death of a loved one. A good example of this type of dream was demonstrated by an older man whose wife died an extremely painful and traumatic death from cancer. He was in a major depression and barely able to function. She and the circumstances had made many demands on him in the time leading up to her death. She often yelled at him for not doing enough. He could not prevent her from dying nor take away her pain. He had many dreams replaying these emotionally painful situations. He was beset by monstrous female figures set on destroying him. He was often portrayed as being angry, enraged and retaliatory. But, being a good Catholic of the old school, he could not possibly speak ill of the dead. He could not acknowledge the anger that blocked his mourning process. After a long period of analysis, his wife came to him in a dream. She was beautiful and radiant in a flowing gown. The action took place in a forest clearing, the place of fairytales. She gave him permission to listen to and believe what his therapist was telling him. The dream had such a completely different atmosphere than any of his other dreams which usually took place in his home surroundings. We both noted the palpable difference. It was as if we were transported to another realm of experience—crackling with energy and crystal clear. From that moment on he was able to express his feelings surrounding the traumatic experience. His depression eventually lifted and he returned to life.

The figure in this dream represents something more than a mere imago of his wife. It felt like her essence, her purified spirit. I have experienced similar occurrences in the dreams of other patients. There is a qualitative difference from usual dreams. I am not suggesting that this in any way proves the existence of actual spirits. But these are empirical phenomena of the psyche. These figures could easily be conceptualized as wish-fulfilling imagoes. But they seem to represent something very spirit-like that remains in nature after we are gone.

Visitation Hours Over

The differing dynamics suggested by the two series of the *Rosarium* do not occur in a linear manner. Life events hardly wait until we have worked out our relational issues. There is always a movement back and forth between the two and even numerous repetitions within each series. Many people in relationship simply look for another relationship when the disappointment of Plate 6, 'Death,' occurs, and they start the cycle over. But what is implied is that until we obtain some "objectivity," we will tend to personalize negative experience, experience things in a complex-ridden way. The attainment of the *unio mentalis*, the goal of the first series, allows us to know the "heights and depths of our own character." But Jung was very dubious of modern man's capacity for even reaching this aim. This may be why he only commented on the first series as depicting the goal of analysis.

And, since we can never know exactly what happens after death, the alchemical view suggested in this paper provides an interesting counterbalance to traditional religious thinking and doctrine. It does not negate but rather compensates the established Judeo-Christian spiritual view. It is a material spirituality or a spiritual materiality. If indeed things do work in the compensatory manner suggested by Jung, then the "truth" is probably some transcendent symbol that mediates both perspectives. I hope revisiting the "flypaper" of the *Rosarium* pulls out some of your own projections and reflections on the nature of life and relationship.

NOTES

1. C. G. Jung, "The Psychology of the Transference," in *Collected Works of C.G. Jung, Vol. 16, The Practice of Psychotherapy* (Princeton: Princeton University Press, 1966), 163-323. (Hereafter abbreviated as *CW*.)

2. Adam McLean, *The Rosary of the Philosophers* (Edinburgh, Scotland: Magnum Opus Hermetic Sourceworks, 1980).

3. *CW* 16, Foreword, p. 165.

4. Beverley Zabriskie, "Exiles and Orphans: Jung, Paracelsus, and the Healing Images of Alchemy," *Quadrant,* XXVI (1995), 12.

5. *CW* 16, Foreword, p. 166.

6. *CW* 16 § 384.

7. Thomas Ogden, "Reverie and Metaphor: Some Thoughts on How I Work as a Psychoanalyst," *International Journal of Psychoanalysis,* 78, (1997), 720.

8. McLean, *Rosary,* 118.

9. *CW* 16 § 518.

10. *CW* 16 § 520.

11. Nathan Schwartz-Salant, *The Mystery of Human Relationship: Alchemy and the Transformation of Self* (London: Routledge, 1998), 158.

12. Andrew Samuels, Bani Shorter, and Fred Plaut, *A Critical Dictionary of Jungian Analysis* (London: Routledge & Kegan Paul, 1986), 140.

13. C. G. Jung, *Mysterium Coniunctionis, CW* 14 § 151. (Italics added).

14. Marie-Louise von Franz, *Alchemical Active Imagination* (Irving, Texas: Spring Publications, 1979), 103 ff.

15. Samuels, et al., *Dictionary*, 140.

16. *CW* 14 § 675.

17. *Ibid.*, § 738 ff.

18. Edward Edinger, *The Mysterium Lectures: A Journey through C.G. Jung's Mysterium Coniunctionis* (Toronto: Inner City, 1995), 278 ff.

19. *CW* 14 § 672.

20. *CW* 14 § 673.

21. Claire Allphin, "Mutual Influence in the Analytic Relationship: Jungian and Psychoanalytic Views," in Mary Ann Matoon, ed., *Open Questions in Analytical Psychology: Proceedings of the Thirteenth International Congress for Analytical Psychology* (Einsiedeln: Daimon-Verlag, 1995).

22. Edward Edinger, *The Mystery of the Coniunctio: Alchemical Image of Individuation* (Toronto: Inner City, 1994).

23. *CW* 16 § 353-539.

24. Johannes Fabricius, "The Individuation Process as Reflected by 'The Rosary Of The Philosophers'," *Journal of Analytical Psychology*, 16, (1971), 31-47; *Alchemy: The Medieval Alchemists and their Royal Art* (Copenhagen: Rosenkilde and Bagger, 1976).

25. McLean, *Rosary*.

26. Andrew Samuels, "Symbolic Dimensions of Eros in Transference-Countertransference: Some Clinical Uses of Jung's Alchemical Metaphor," *International Review of Psycho-Analysis*, 12, (1985), 199-214.

27. Schwartz-Salant, *Mystery*; The *Borderline Personality: Vision and Healing* (Wilmette, Illinois: Chiron, 1989).

28. Beverley Zabriskie, "Fermentation in Jung's Alchemy," in Mary Ann Matoon, ed., *Open Questions in Analytical Psychology: Proceedings of the Thirteenth International Congress for Analytical Psychology* (Einsiedeln: Daimon-Verlag, 1995).

29. Jung describes how an inscription called the "Enigma of Bologna" managed to mystify anyone who tried to solve its riddle. "Let it be said at once: this epitaph is sheer nonsense, a joke, but one that for centuries brilliantly fulfilled its function as a flypaper for every

conceivable projection that buzzed in the human mind." I think of this metaphor whenever alchemical text or plates are approached. *CW* 14 § 52.

30. As quoted in Alexander Roob, *Alchemy and Mysticism* (New York: Taschen, 1997), 8.

31. Schwartz-Salant, *Mystery*, 195.

32. Schwartz-Salant, *Borderline Personality*, 109.

33. *CW* 14 § 752.

34. Personal communication, 2005.

35. Joseph L. Henderson, *Thresholds of Initiation* (Middletown, Connecticut: Wesleyan University Press, 1967), 202 n.

36. Joseph L. Henderson, "Resolution of the Transference in the Light of C.G. Jung's Psychology," *Acta Psychotherapeutica,* 2, (1954), 275.

37. David Tresan, "Thinking Individuation Forward," to be published in the *Journal of Analytical Psychology.*

38. Tom Cheetham, *The World Turned Inside Out: Henry Corbin and Islamic Mysticism* (New Orleans: Spring Journal Books, 2003); Henry Corbin, "Mundus Imaginalis: Or the Imaginary and the Imaginal," in Benjamin Sells, ed., *Working with Images* (Woodstock, Connecticut: Spring Publications, 2000).

39. Andrew Samuels, "Countertransference: The Mundus Imaginalis and a Research Project," *Journal of Analytical Psychology,* 30, (1985), 47-71.

40. Zabriskie, "Fermentation," 553 ff.

41. McLean, *Rosary*, 118 ff.

42. Fabricius, "Individuation Process," 31 ff.

43. Andrew Samuels, "Symbolic Dimensions," 208.

44. *CW* 8 § 193. (Parentheses added.)

45. McLean, *Rosary*, 123.

46. *CW* 14 § 778. (Parentheses added and "Self" capitalized).

47. C. G. Jung, *Memories, Dreams, Reflections* (New York: Vintage Books, 1989), 290-291. (Hereafter abbreviated *MDR*).

48. Schwartz-Salant, *Mystery*, 201-202.

49. *CW* 16 § 467.

50. Schwartz-Salant, *Mystery*, 204.

51. Schwartz-Salant, *Borderline Personality*, 119.

52. D. W. Winnicott, "The Capacity to be Alone," in *The Maturational Processes and the Facilitating Environment* (New York: International Universities Press, 1965, originally published 1958), 29-36.

53. Barbara Hannah, *Jung: His Life and Work: A Biographical Memoir* (New York: Perigee, 1976), 279.

54. Edinger, *Mystery of the Coniunctio*, 96.

55. Zabriskie, "Fermentation," 548.

56. Fabricius, "Individuation Process," 39.

57. Schwartz-Salant, *Mystery*, 196.

58. *CW* 16 § 403.

59. *MDR*, 296-297.

60. McLean, *Rosary*, 128.

61. Stanton Marlan, *The Black Sun: The Alchemy and Art of Darkness* (College Station, TX: Texas A & M University Press, 2005), 22.

62. Samuels, et al., *Dictionary,* 146.

63. *Ibid.*, 73.

64. *MDR*, 306.

65. Quoted on an *ofrenda*, an altar dedicated to a relative who has died. This installation was at the "Day of the Dead" exhibition at the Mexican Fine Arts Center Museum in Chicago, 2005.

66. Samuels, et al, *Dictionary,* 61.

67. *CW* 14 § 152.

68. James Hillman, "Concerning the Stone: Alchemical Images of the Goal," *Sphinx,* 5, (1993), 261.

69. Schwartz-Salant, *Borderline Personality*, 110.

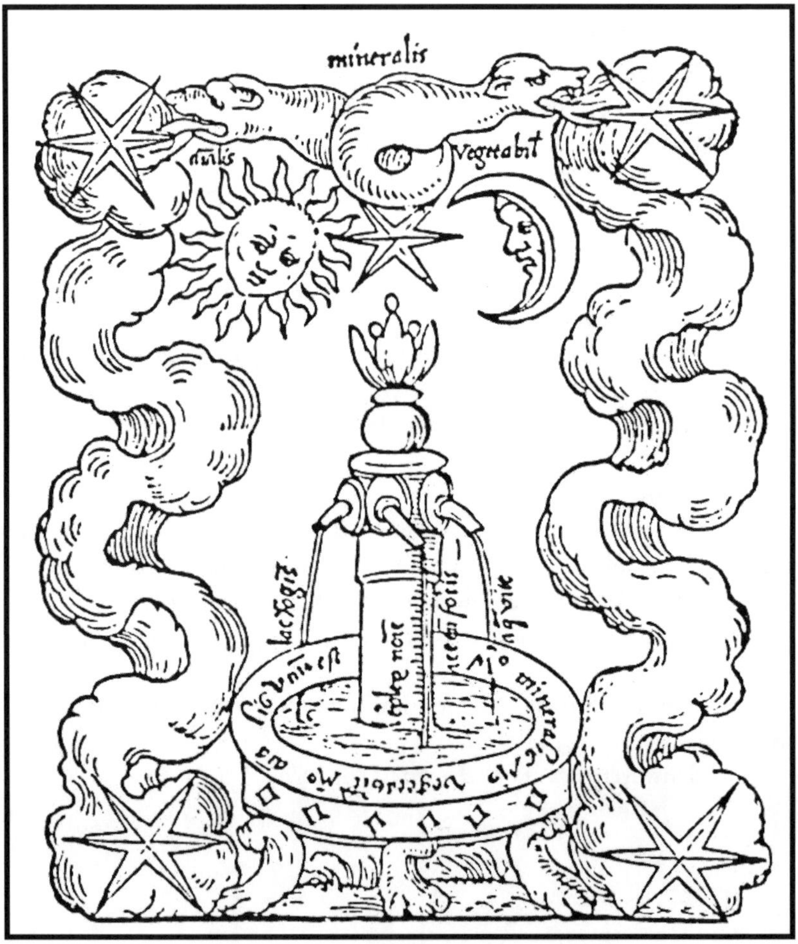

Plate 1: The Mercurial Fountain

Plate 2: King and Queen

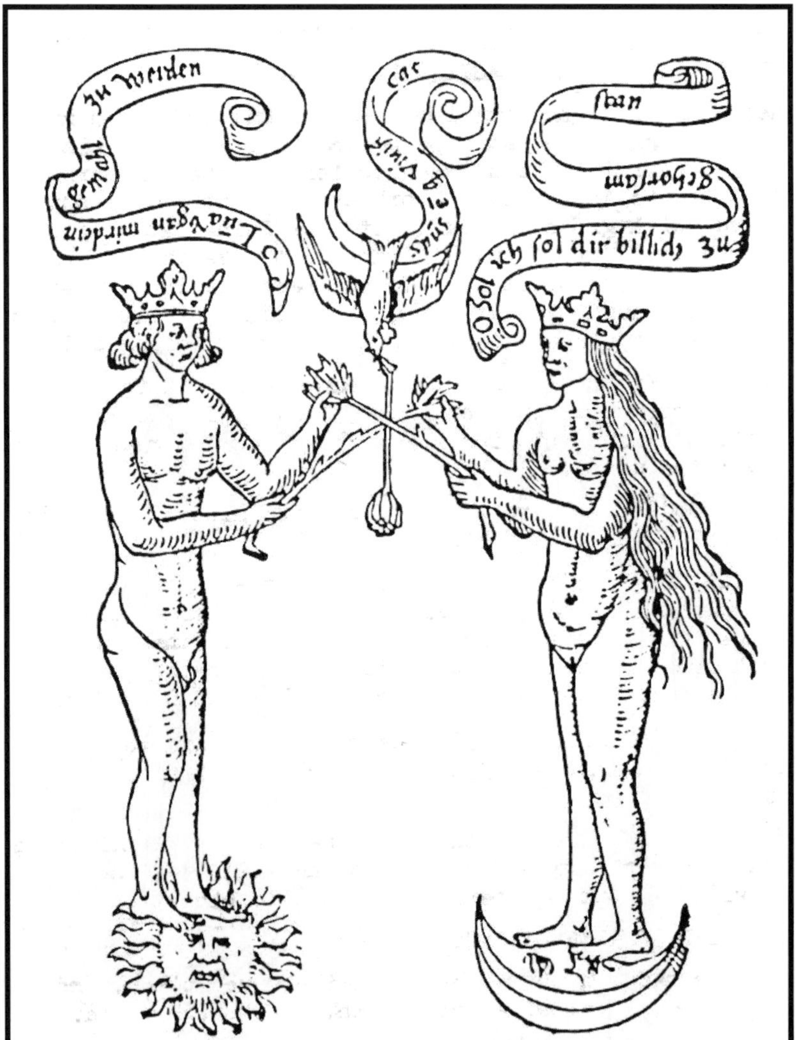

Plate 3: The Naked Truth

Plate 4: Immersion in the Bath

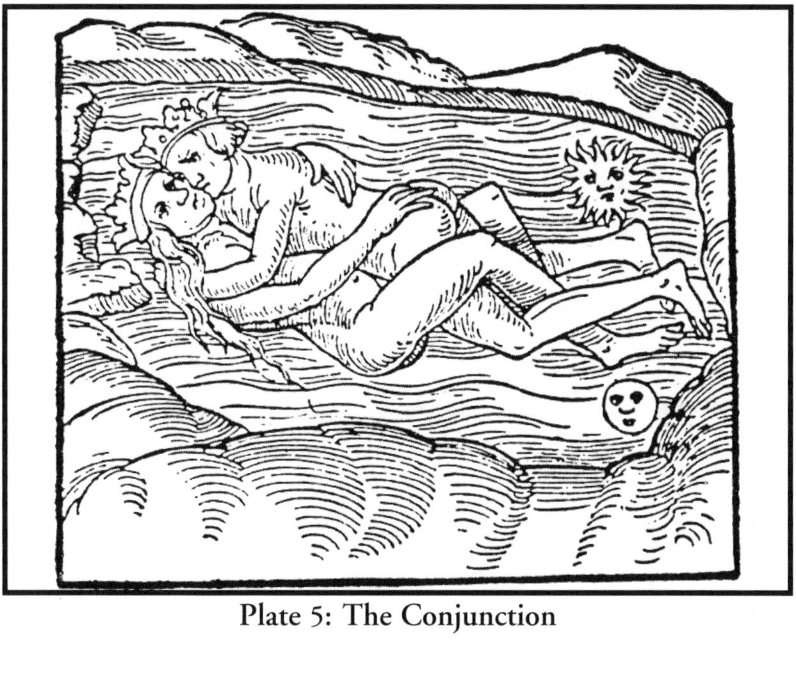

Plate 5: The Conjunction

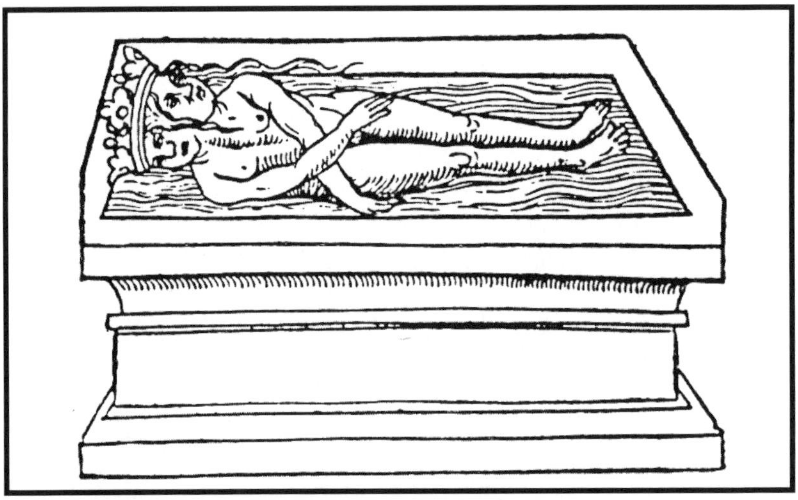

Plate 6: Death

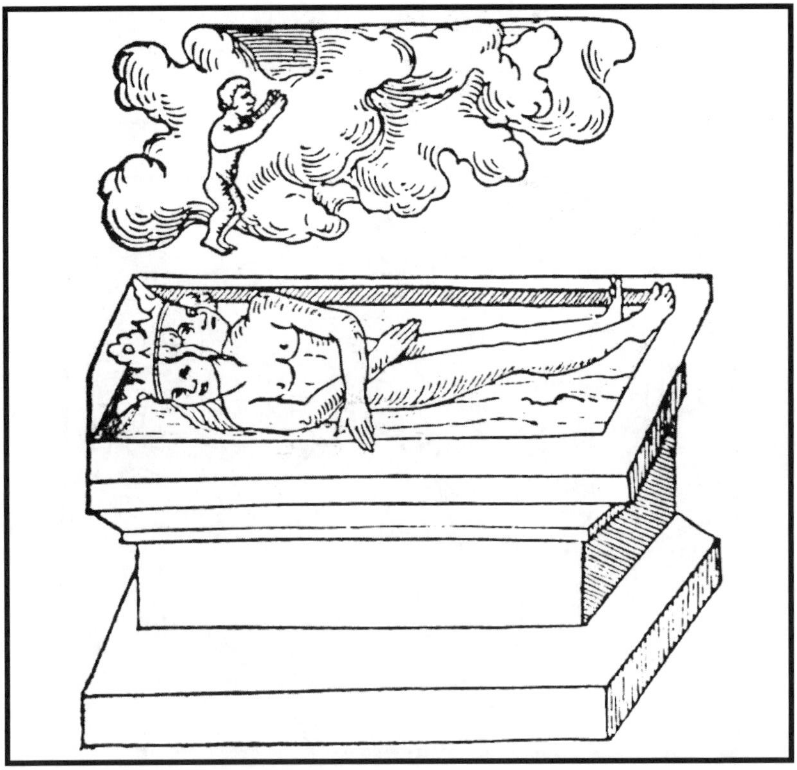

Plate 7: The Ascent of the Soul

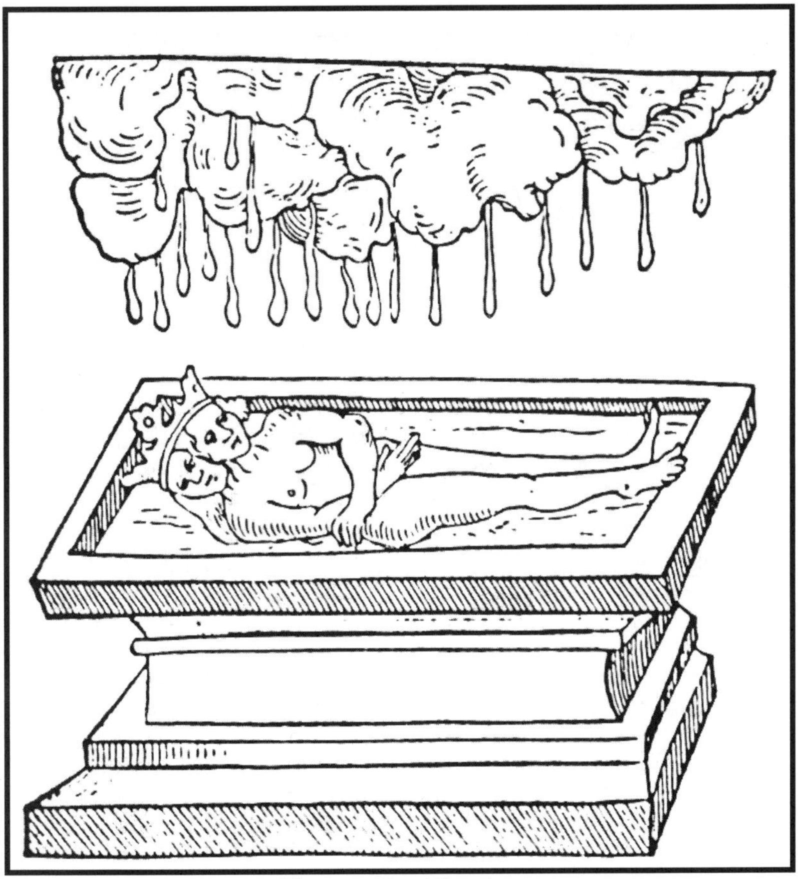

Plate 8: Purification

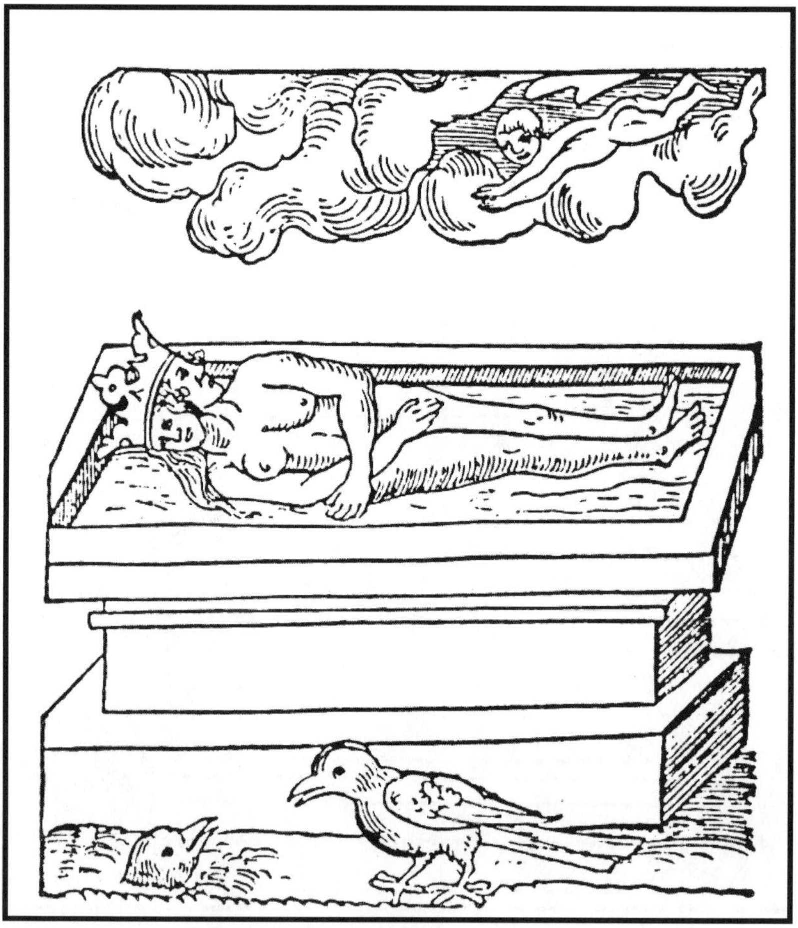

Plate 9: The Return of the Soul

Plate 10: The New Birth

Plate 11: Fermentation

Plate 12: Illumination

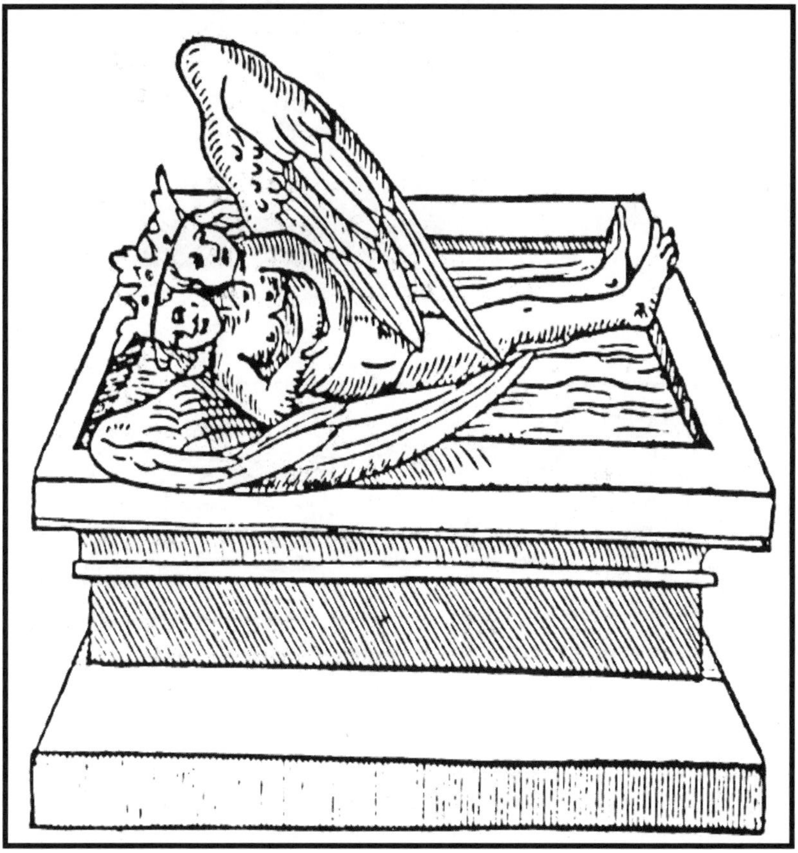

Plate 13: Nourishment

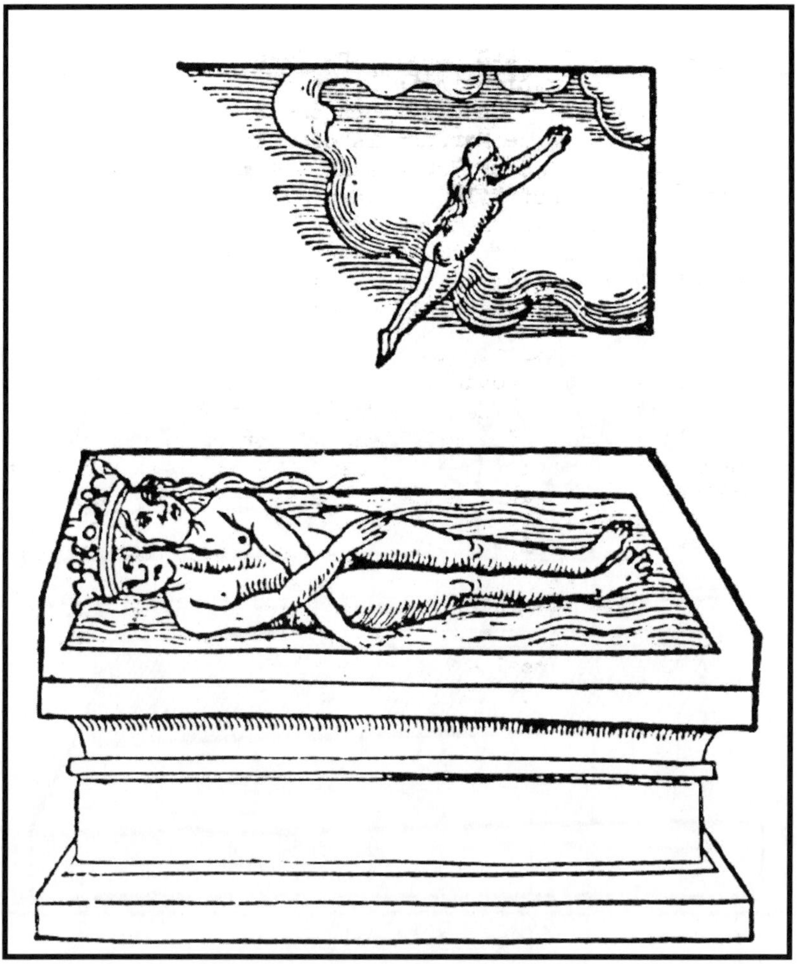

Plate 14: Fixation

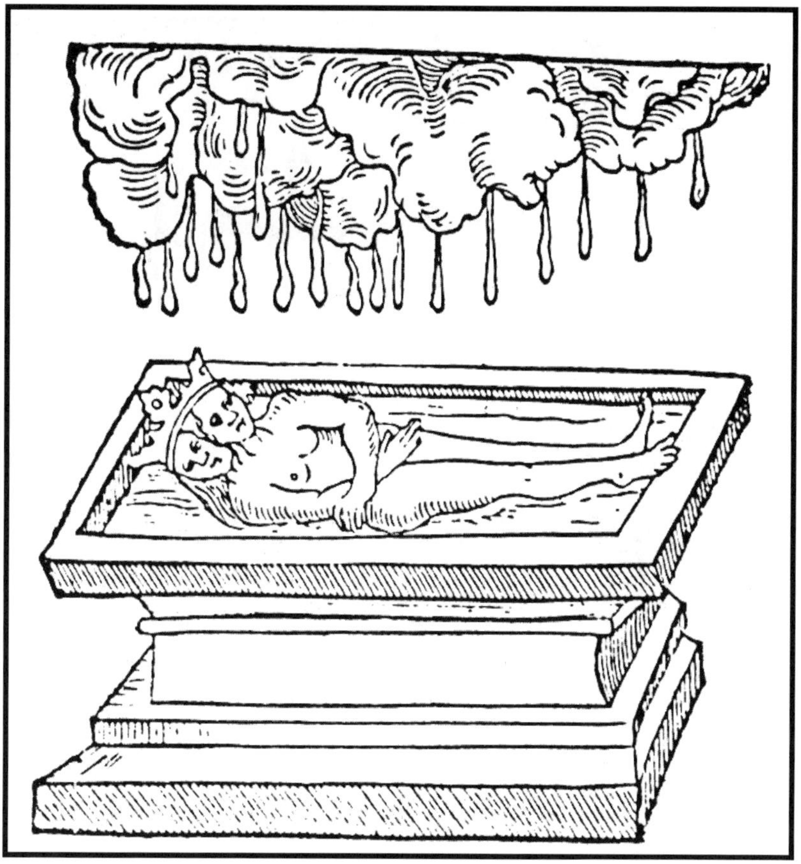

Plate 15: Multiplication

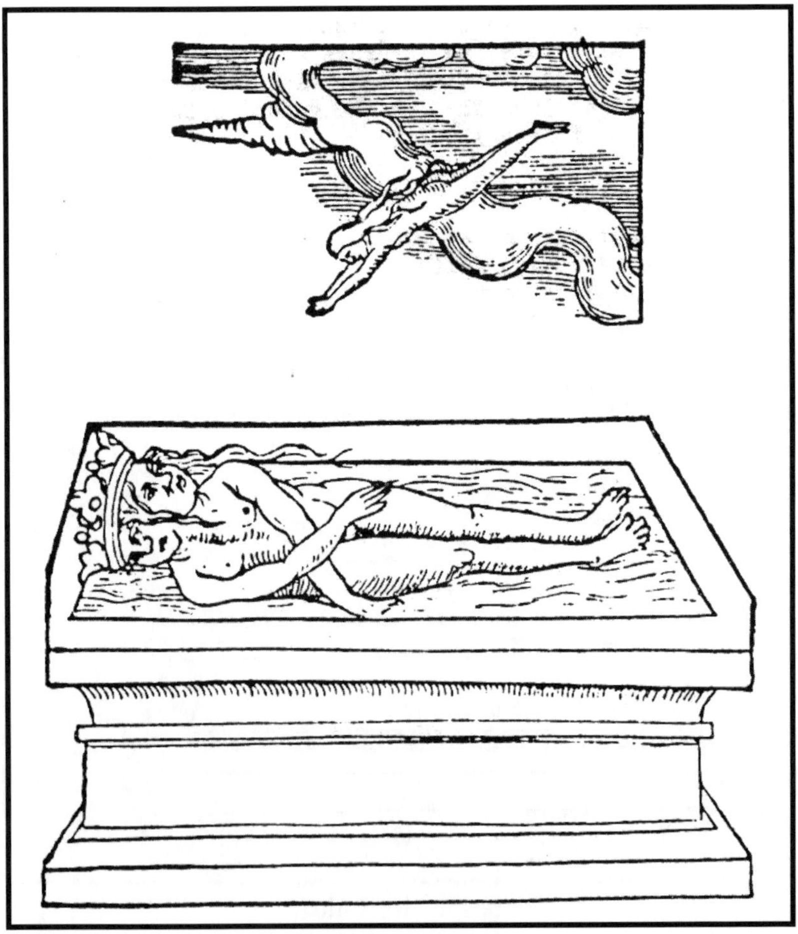

Plate 16: Reviving

Plate 17: The Demonstration of Perfection

Plate 18: The Green Lion Devouring the Sun

Plate 19: Coronation of Mary

Plate 20: The Resurrection of Christ

ALCHEMICAL IMAGES, IMPLICIT COMMUNICATION, AND TRANSITIONAL STATES

DYANE N. SHERWOOD

The symbols and images of alchemy, like Jung's view of the psyche, cannot be fully defined in conceptual or theoretical language. As Joseph Henderson said in a 1982 lecture, "You see, our psychological point of view is not just a rational, scientific procedure but one that evokes the nature of the unconscious and its corresponding imagery."[1] As I understand it, Jung's method relied less on abstraction, intellectually-derived concepts, or biological models and more on the symbolic function of the psyche and its capacity to represent itself. As Jung has shown, the psyche symbolizes itself to consciousness, for example in dreams, with an apparently self-regulating compensation or complementarity out of which a certain kind of objectivity can emerge. We refer to a dialogue between the ego and the Self or the

Dyane N. Sherwood is an Analyst Member and on the Teaching Faculty of The C. G. Jung Institute of San Francisco. She is the Editor of *The San Francisco Jung Institute Library Journal,* and the co-author of *Transformation of the Psyche: The Symbolic Alchemy of the Splendor Solis* (Routledge, 2003). From 1971-81, she studied invertebrate nervous systems using intracellular neurophysiological techniques, with a particular interest in the emergent and plastic properties of neuronal connections underlying basic sensory processing and simple behaviors. She also taught an upper division course on "The Neurobiology of Learning and Memory" in the Human Biology Program at Stanford University.

process of individuation, in which we become more who we are as an individual while being less in the thrall of personal complexes. At the same time, a person can become more objective in the sense of seeing more clearly while simultaneously feeling more deeply connected with other human beings, with nature, and with the mystery of life. The qualities and forms of experience that constitute this psychological objectivity cannot be explained discursively, nor taught by intellectual means alone. How, then, can we know whether this profound form of knowing is purely personal and idiosycratic, even delusional?

Early in his career, Jung used word association experiments to test his theory of "feeling-toned complexes."[2] As far as I know, this was the very first experimental work demonstrating unconscious influences on verbal responses. Looking back, this work is still impressive for its careful design, the number of measures used to study the response (including reaction time and galvanic skin response), the careful analysis of the many factors influencing the results, and the use of statistics.

Later, Jung began a search for comparative material, from other cultures and times, to test the generality of his observations about the nature of the unconscious as revealed in the dreams of his patients and the process of their analytic work. Jung's comparative method was not so very different from that of Charles Darwin, who compared morphological and functional similarities and differences among species and theorized that adaptation to the environment and competitive success of adaptations resulted in the extinction of some plants and animals and the survival of others (natural selection). Darwin's theory of evolution, then, relied on observations and comparisions for support. It later received support from experimental biology and biochemistry, which have elucidated the biological *mechanisms* of natural selection, for example, the structure of DNA, mechanisms of genetic expression, and the tracing of evolutionary maternal lineages through mitochondrial DNA.

Jung's search for comparative material eventually led him to the obscure images and text of the alchemists, and he hypothesized that the alchemists projected psyche onto the unknown in matter. His writings on this subject are difficult and complex, even for those who read him with interest. Jung had already been ostracized by the psychoanalytic community, and his fascination with alchemy was considered not only unscientific but also mystical and misguided. Jung's work was ignored by 20th-century behavioral, rational, and conceptual approaches to psychology in the academy, which for the most part was not interested in the unconscious *per se*. In the United States, psychiatric training was dominated by the superficially more scientific, authoritative, and developmentally-reductionistic approach of Freudian psychoanalysis, until that was displaced by psychopharmacology. Thus, it is a remarkable and unexpected development that a half-century after Jung's death we witness the confluence of scientific psychology and Analytical Psychology: neuroimaging techniques, which give real time observations of the neuronal activity in human brain, are yielding results that are consistent with Jung's views about the reality of the psyche, the nature of the unconscious, the Self, and the process of individuation.

This article will relate a series of alchemical illuminated paintings, which depict a process of transformation in depth, to recent work on the phenomenology and neurobiology of implicit communication and affective self-regulation. I see this as the beginning of an exploration into imaginatively and intellectually fertile new ground.

For sharing his deep connection to alchemical imagery, I am deeply grateful to San Francisco analyst Joseph L. Henderson.[3] Dr. Henderson analyzed with Jung and attended Jung's English lectures in the 1930s, when Jung was at the beginning of his researches into alchemy. In 1937, while attending medical school in London, Dr. Henderson came across a beautiful alchemical treatise in the rare manuscript collection of the British Museum. The colors in its illuminated paintings—made from actual gold and silver, from stones such as lapis, and from plant extracts—spoke to dreams about color that he'd been having, and he became intrigued with them. As he got to know them better, he found that they spoke to him rather directly about the work of analysis.

Dr. Henderson and I collaborated on a book, *Transformation of the Psyche: The Symbolic Alchemy of the Splendor Solis*,[4] which was published in 2003, when Dr. Henderson was 100 years old. In *Transformation of the Psyche*, we address the symbolism in the paintings and relate it to analytic process, including dream images. We tried to remain true to the spirit of both alchemy and analysis by presenting the material in a way that invites the imagination of the reader rather than attempting definitive interpretations. Recently, we completed a three-and-a-half-year-long seminar with advanced candidates at the San Francisco Jung Institute, where we gave the participants one image each month, without any written material, and asked them to contemplate it until the next meeting, responding to it in their own ways. It was a very vital experience, constantly fresh and full of discovery, evoking the nature of the unconscious and the creativity of the group.

Fig. 1: Paintings from the first series of illuminated paintings of the *Splendor Solis* (1582). 1a. (above) Plate I-4. Meeting of the King and Queen; 1b. (opposite page) Plate I-6. The Philosophical Tree.

THE HARLEY *SPLENDOR SOLIS*[5]

The illuminated manuscript belonging to the British Library was probably painted in Southern Germany in the late 16th century, but it has been speculated that the images in the *Splendor Solis* were well known and perhaps copied by students of alchemy during the early Renaissance.[6] Certain features, such as a knight with a scimitar, suggest to me that they could have an Arabic origin or influence.

In the *Splendor Solis*, an alchemical process of transformation is shown in three different series of images. In the first series, we see familiar alchemical symbols, such as the meeting of the Queen and King (Fig. 1a) and the Philosophical Tree (Fig. 1b), but in a much more

Fig. 2: Paintings from the second series of illuminated paintings of the Splendor Solis (1582). 2a. (above): Plate II-1. Under the sign of Saturn, the infant Mercurius in the alchemical vessel feeds the *prima materia* to a young dragon, while using a bellows to feed the fire in the heart of the dragon; 2b. (opposite page): Plate II-2. Under the sign of Jupiter, the outer world is in an order based on a hierarchy of roles, while within the alchemical, we find three birds in the colors of the alchemical transformation of black to white to red. Their imaginal nature is indicated by the way they interpenetrate one another, something not possible in the physical world.

expressive and sophisticated form than most of the alchemical images that have survived to this day. On the *tromp l'oeil* pedestal at the base of each painting, we see depictions of animals, Greek and Roman myths, legends, and Old Testament episodes.

The second series of paintings also depicts a process of transformation, but one that has more objective qualities. Each painting is of an astrological type, which shows a planet ruler in the sky above and related scenes in the world below. These paintings are unique,

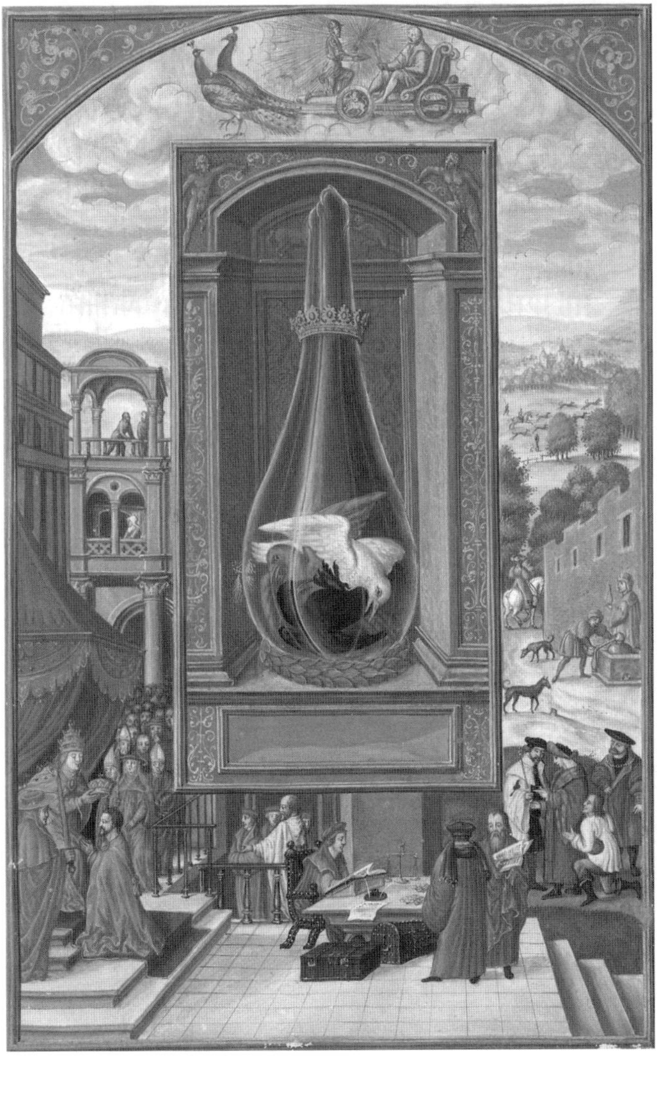

however, in that in the center of the painting is a large vessel containing symbolic images. One way to approach the vessel is to see it as an inner experience in compensation or response to the outer situation. The figures in the vessel could then be viewed as symbolic representations of psycho-physiological states of being, perhaps unconscious or at least not expressible in words. Such states are of particular interest to us as analysts because we attend to changes in the field or the emotional state of our patients and ourselves, and especially to the nature of transitions from one state to another.

The *Splendor Solis* has a final series of four paintings, which represents the whole process, and for me, these images convey the heart and soul of transformation in depth. I will discuss all four images in the last part of this article.

Implicit Communication by Alchemical Imagery

We cannot really know how the painter of the *Splendor Solis* related to its images, what was conscious and intentional and what was not. However, I am going to suggest to you that at least some aspects of the paintings can be read by us across time and cultures because they rely on universal and basic aspects of implicit communication, as well as explicit references to mythological and biblical stories.

Recent findings in the neurobiology of affective regulation support and enrich my appreciation of Jung's experientially-derived view of the psyche, including archetypes, complexes, and the importance of implicit communication in the transference and counter-transference, as well as the healing nature of expressive modalities within the analytic container.

I have been heartened to see that over the past two decades and especially in the past several years, psychoanalysts influenced by developmental psychology and neurobiology have formulated views about the nature of the unconscious and the process of analysis that are converging with those of analytical psychology. Allan Schore, a Los Angeles psychoanalyst, has been particularly active in studying and integrating the neurological literature in relation to attachment and trauma. His ideas have been stimulated in part by studies using imaging techniques, which allow the observation of brain activity in real time. Schore is making a strong and carefully documented argument for a radical revision of psychoanalytic theory and technique. He has even suggested that the analytic couch might need to be set aside in favor of working face to face!

Schore writes, "Instead of a repository of archaic untamed passions and destructive wishes, the unconscious is now seen as a cohesive, active mental structure that continuously appraises life's experiences and responds according to its scheme of interpretation."[7]

We might be inclined to say that it is not either/or but that the unconscious contains both. Schore continues, "And in contrast to a static, deeply buried storehouse of ancient memories silenced in 'infantile amnesia,' contemporary intersubjective psychoanalysts now refer to a 'relational unconscious,' whereby one unconscious mind communicates with another unconscious mind."[8]

We might compare Schore's viewpoint to Jung's "Psychology of the Transference," first published in 1946, in which he explored the unconscious-to-unconscious relationship between the analyst and the patient, referring to the alchemical images of the *Rosarium philosophorum.* Here we see the image of the King and Queen of the *Rosarium*, who join their left hands suggesting their unconscious union in the work (Fig. 3).

Fig. 3. The King and Queen from the *Rosarium*, as reproduced in Jung's "Psychology of the Transference."[9]

As Jung wrote,

> The left is inauspicious and awkward; also it is the side of the heart, from which comes not only love but all the evil thoughts connected with it, the moral contradictions in human nature that are expressed most clearly in our affective life. The contact of left hands could therefore be taken as an indication of the *affective nature of the relationship* (italics added).[10]

The Neurobiology of Affective Development and Self-Regulation

In addition to unconscious-to-unconscious or implicit communication, both Jung and Schore refer to improved self-regulation as an important parameter of analytic work.

We now have some clues about where in the brain higher-order processing of self-regulation may occur. Our bodies and brains have a bilateral form, with representations of the left side of the body's skin and muscalature connecting to the right side of the brain. Thus, the left hands of the King and Queen in our alchemical picture connect to the right side of their brains. Roger Sperry won the Nobel Prize in Medicine in 1981 for showing that the two halves of the human cerebral cortex are not simple mirrors of each other: areas responsible for higher-order processing in the right and left cortices are differentiated to perform specific tasks. The specialization of cortical functions continues to develop until at least puberty.

Allan Schore and others have focused on one particular region in the right hemisphere, the orbitofrontal cortex (Fig. 4), which they suggest is the brain region responsible for higher-order affect regulation. The orbitofrontal cortex—which, as its name implies, is at the front of the brain behind the orbit of the eyes—receives input from the limbic regions of the brain, meaning, literally, the parts of the brain that are on the edge, where things meet. The limbic system integrates input from the autonomic nervous system, the hypothalamus, and other areas involved in physical and emotional self-regulation, with information from the five senses. The orbitofrontal cortex is thought to support a more differentiated non-reactive response to one's affective circumstances, and it is a region that remains plastic—in other words, can change and develop—throughout the lifespan. This is important, because neuroscientists believed until fairly recently that the adult brain could lose nerve cells but not make new ones. These findings strongly suggest that higher-order regulation of affect may be more malleable than scientific dogma would have led us to hope.

Implicit Communication of Affective States

Let us now turn to one of the many ways that affect is communicated implicitly and may be experienced without conscious awareness by both the sender and receiver of the information.

Thirty years ago, when I was a student of ethology and neurobiology, I was very taken with Darwin's book, *The Expression of Emotion in Man and Animals*,[12] in which he explored species-specific emotional responses and communications through facial expression in much the same way that he compared morphology within and across species. In Fig. 5, you see some dramatic photographs of basic facial expressions, which appeared in the very first edition of Darwin's book.

Using more sophisticated techniques, Paul Ekman and others have confirmed and extended Darwin's observations that certain basic

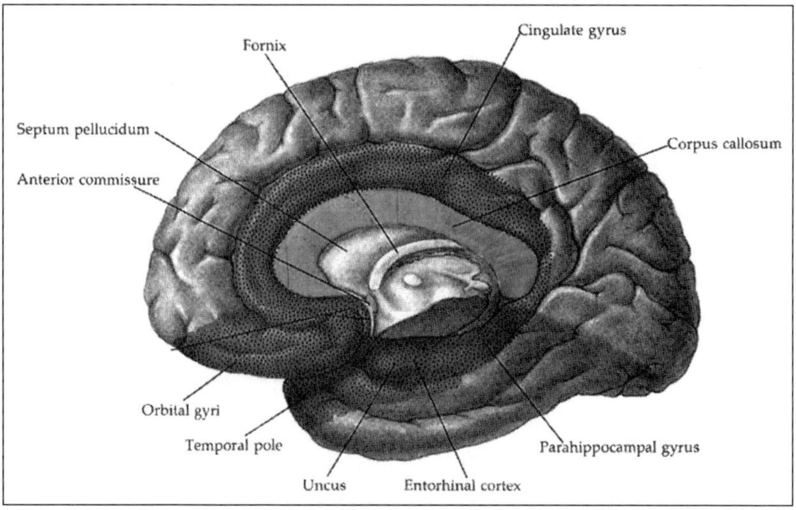

Fig. 4: A midsaggital view of the right side of the human brain, showing the cortical regions that process emotion and body state, which are indicated by stippling.[11]

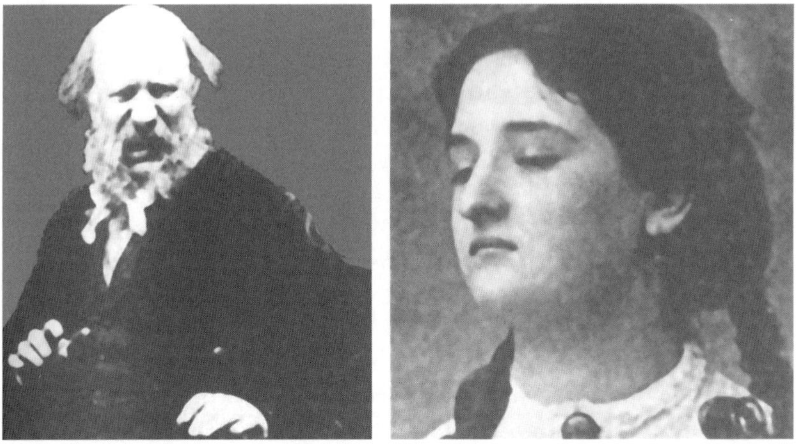

Fig. 5: Photographs used by Charles Darwin to illustrate the facial expression and body language expressing disgust (background flattened for clarity). 5a. Disgust; 5b. Contempt.

emotions and their facial expression are recognizable across cultures (Fig. 5). Among Jungians, Lou Stewart and Joan Chodorow integrated this work into their studies of affect and expression.[13]

Our faces, if uncensored, reflect our emotional state, and in turn, we each have the potential to respond to and perhaps make meaning of the emotional states of others as communicated through facial expression. However, the development of this capacity is shaped by dispositional factors and by our experience in relationships, which are personally and culturally influenced.

Recent neurobiological research has shown that a very slight change in a human facial expression is detected and processed by an observer within a tenth of a second,[15] long before it reaches consciousness. Facially-communicated state changes are often mirrored within three- or four-tenths of a second.[16] These reactions may or may not later come into conscious awareness (Fig. 6).

The role of face-to-face contact between mothers and infants has been of interest to developmental psychologists for many years, and it is known that human infants early on see most clearly at the distance from the mother's breast to her face. Experimental developmental psychologists have shown that infants prefer to gaze at drawings of faces where the eyes, nose, and mouth are in the normal configuration in comparison to faces where the features are rearranged. They

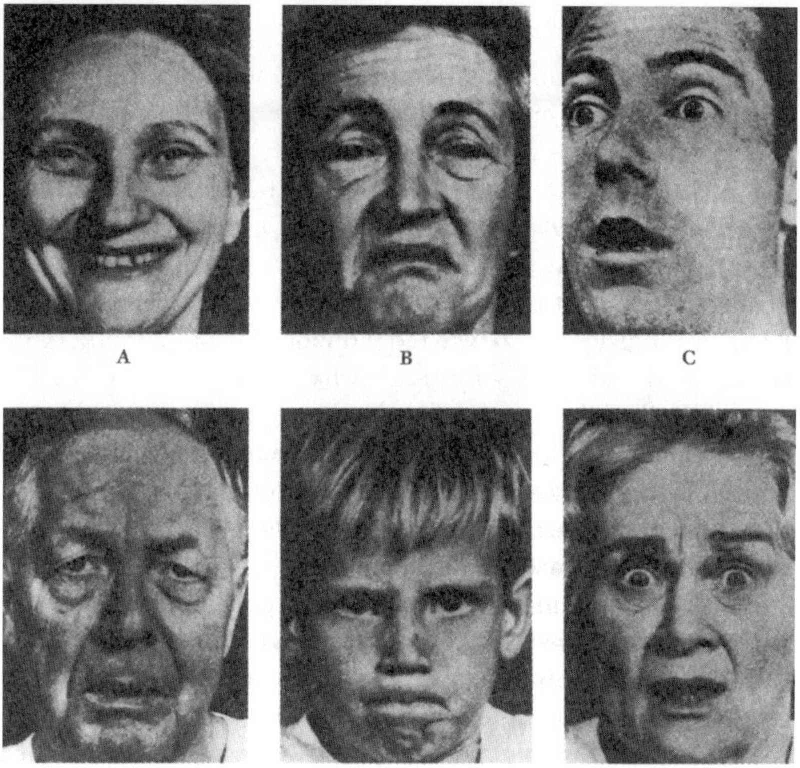

A B C D E F

Fig. 6: These photographs were shown to people from different cultures, who were asked to identify the emotion conveyed by the facial expressions. Agreement was found cross-culturally. A. Happiness. B. Disgust. C. Surprise. D. Sadness. E. Anger. F. Fear. (From Eckman's Introduction to the revised edition of Darwin's Expression of the *Emotions in Man and Animals*.)[14]

prefer eye-to-eye alignment, and both mothers and infants can be observed tilting their heads to achieve this arrangement (Fig. 7). Of course, things don't always go smoothly, and once a pattern is set in motion it may be self-perpetuating. When I worked with mothers and infants with attachment disorders, I saw infants who struggled to make eye contact with depressed mothers, as well as infants who looked away from their mother's face, apparently overstimulated or distressed by the contact.

This early patterning of psyche-soma is a fundamental problem that we address in analytic work, and we cannot underestimate the possibilities of maladaptive self-regulatory schemata, which

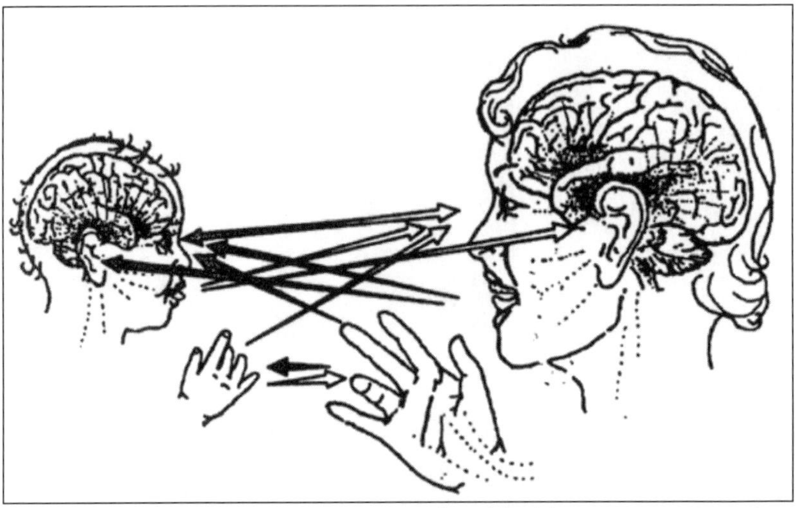

Fig. 7: Face-to-Face Communication is mediated by (1) eye-to-eye orientation, (2) vocalizations, (3) hand gestures, and (4) movements of the arms/head.[17]

unconsciously cause a person to recreate known but overwhelming or depriving states of being. Clinical work suggests to me that the psyche-soma may become set to create a situation or field which matches a pathological set point, around which self-regulation struggles to function.

Affective communications through facial expression can move us into a new state or field. It is a two-way process, at the very least. While the expression of basic emotions is universal, human facial expressions of more complex states can be quite difficult to read, and they may stimulate anxiety or curiosity in the viewer. Moreover, while negative states can be read easily, the interpretation of positive affects is more accurate if voice tone is added to the equation.

Implicit Communication, Symbol, and Paradox Representating a Process of Embodied Transformation

The very first painting of the 22 in the *Splendor Solis* (Fig. 8a) shows the coat of arms of alchemy in the foreground and two men conversing in the background. Let us look more closely at the strange coat of arms, in which there are two suns. The upper sun (Fig. 8b) appears—what?

Fig. 8a: The first illuminated painting of the *Splendor Solis*.

Figs. 8b. (left) & 8c. (right): Details showing the upper and lower suns on the coat-of-arms respectively.

Steady? Serene? Thoughtful? Wise? Slightly sad? This sun sits above three crescent moons, associated in Western alchemy with feminine, lunar consciousness. The lower sun (Fig. 8c) seems to be falling off the banner into three-dimensional space, askew, so that we cannot easily make the eye-to-eye contact that we so innately prefer. What is even more disturbing is that where the eyes and mouth should be, we see three more faces, hence a further fragmentation. Each of these faces has a slightly different expression, as suggested by the gazes and mouths. How are you affected internally when you see these images? When you take into account the two men conversing, does that change your internal response?

So, this painting represents the beginning of the work, or some place in the middle perhaps, when a shield, a second, harder skin, perhaps a *persona* identification begins to dis-integrate. The painting brings us into that emotional field through its implicit contents, including facial expression, as well as by its more explicit contents. In this period of analysis, the patient and the analyst may experience surprising eruptions of affect and confusion. However, the two men conversing provide a compensatory sense that it is possible to discuss and relate at the same time that one is falling apart.

Fig. 9: Detail from the Plate I-4 of the *Splendor Solis*, showing the encounter between the King and Queen.

Now let us go on to another image (Fig. 9), a detail from the fourth painting in the first series (shown in Fig. 1a), where, like the image of the *Rosarium* King and Queen (Fig. 3), we see a meeting of these two symbolic figures. I like to imagine that they have been sitting on their thrones, facing the world, and that they are just now finding themselves outside the royal court, in nature, and facing each other. What do their expressions and gestures tell us? The queen holds up her left palm and points with her forefinger, while the king exposes his right palm. Do the expressions on the sun and moon echo their facial expressions, or perhaps complement them? Can we look at this without some apprehension and curiosity as to what is going to happen in this highly charged meeting of the opposites? Might we see this painting as using implicit communication to tell us about the nature of affect and inner experience, or, to put it another way, to induce a state change in the viewer that we can recognize as something we have experienced when containing rather than acting out a conflict? Might we ask, albeit simplistically, whether this image portrays Jung's two kinds of consciousness? Or perhaps the left and right sides of the brain-body—the analytical left side of the brain associated with speech and the right side of the brain associated with emotion and self-regulation?

In this way, we can use neurobiology to add new dimensions to our imagination, rather than to bracket it. To emphasize this point: I am not suggesting a reductionistic approach. The *reality of the psyche* is paramount for Jungians, and this is receiving affirmation from unexpected quarters, namely from one of the foremost academic experimental psychologists in the United States. For example, Roger Shepard, Emeritus Professor of Psychology at Stanford University, and his colleague, Piet Hut of the Institute of Advanced Study, Princeton University, have suggested:

> Instead of speaking of conscious experience as arising in a brain, we prefer to speak of a brain as arising in conscious experience. From an epistemological standpoint, starting from direct experiences strikes us as more justified. As a first option, we reconsider the "hard problem" of the relation between conscious experience and the physical world by thus turning that problem upside down. We also consider a second option: turning the hard problem sideways. Rather than starting with the third-person approach used in physics, or the first-person approach of starting with individual conscious experience, we consider starting from an I-and-you basis, centered around the second-person.[18]

The Liminality of Transformative States: The Final Series of Four Paintings in the *Splendor Solis*

I now want to consider the final four paintings of the *Splendor Solis*.[19] I believe that they speak to the process of suffering and transformation that I experience in my consulting room and in life. We might think of them as implicit communications, which are listened to by the right side of the brain and through one's entire being, not through words or narrative. Recall that the communication begins even before a conscious process has time to occur. We might ask ourselves whether each of these paintings represents an affect-rich liminal or transitional space.

Fig. 10: Plate III-1 of the Harley *Splendor Solis* (1582). The Dark Sun.

In the first image (Plate III-1, Fig. 10), we see the sun with a human face. We also see a landscape without people but with the personified sun at the horizon and visible below the horizon through earth and water. Its golden rays fill the sky and also seem to travel through the earth to appear in the landscape in the foreground. The sun is black above the horizon, and brilliant golden rays appear to emerge from the blackness. What might this mean? Has a dark sun, or *sol niger*, eclipsed the golden sun? Is the sun rising or setting? What does the human face of the sun convey to you?

We can see signs of death in the blackened stumps of trees but also new growth in the form of delicate plants highlighted with gold. Rivers undulate toward the horizon, where larger trees and a city lit by the sun can be seen. The golden frame holding this scene is filled with flowers and animals, including snails, caterpillars, butterflies, birds, and a frog—reminding us that this process takes place within the diversity and vigor of the life force.

The darkened trees in the foreground suggest that the landscape had recently become desiccated, perhaps by too much heat and too little water. This might suggest feelings of being depressed, dried up, flat, or empty. We are also reminded of the destructive potential of too much analysis, particularly in its reductionistic or overly intellectualized forms. In "Psychology of the Transference," Jung related the phenomenon of soul loss to the loss of libido, as well as a turning-inward that may precede a new conscious attitude.[20] Or, we might ask whether this scene is the aftermath of too much water, a flood, the depletion that follows an immersion into the unconscious. Or has there been a fire? Is this the aftermath of consuming passions? Such is the ambiguity of this image that it thwarts any desire to be correct, to have answers. Our imagination is stirred, our curiosity stimulated—and perhaps the need for mirroring the ineffable in that way feels deeply moving.

The light of the sun has disappeared into the earth, into matter, and a kind of consciousness or intelligence is at work underground, in the watery depths of the unconscious. Or we might say that the light of consciousness has turned its energies away from the activities of life to illuminate what is buried in the unconscious ground of existence.

In this scene we can also see signs of life and hope in the young plants, with green and golden foliage growing from the roots of a dead tree.

This image symbolizes the fundamental inseparability of death and rebirth, a theme often emphasized by Dr. Henderson. The very landscape, as well as the human expression on the face of the sun, suggest a simultaneous death and renewal in nature.

We might also think of this image as representing a state of being in which healing has begun to take place at a very basic (plant) level. This brings to mind the so-called "vegetative" or autonomic nervous system, where our psychosomatic responses can occur completely unconsciously. The absence of humans and other animals suggests that instinctual and intellectual activities have not been fully revitalized in terms of action and will. We might add that, indeed, this should not be rushed.

Mary Jo Spencer, a San Francisco analyst,[21] has noted that there is something very compelling about the actual image of the dark sun looking out over a natural landscape without any human presence. She has suggested that this conveys a feeling that is more like a presence behind the human condition, or even behind the elements. It is perhaps a sense of that presence that informs the capacity of a person in analysis to refrain from unconsciously pursuing familiar activities and from willful problem-solving.

You might be surprised by what follows (Fig. 11), unless you reflect on your own experiences where a dark and nearly unbearable time seems to release energy for humor and play. Perhaps you will also recall how meaningful it is when a patient reaches a point where she or he is able to be genuinely playful. The text which corresponds to this image says,"Wherefore is this Art compared to the play of children, who when they play, turn undermost that which before was uppermost."[22]

Here we see the only image of an interior in the *Splendor Solis*, and it brings to mind what goes on in our consulting rooms symbolically, as well as words such as *potential space*, *transitional space*, and *reverie*. Sunlight filters through beautiful window panes, which are square with circular facets. All the elements are here, Earth, Air, Fire, and Water, and all are contained and in harmony with the needs of humans.

The room is warmed by a tile stove and by the presence of a maternal figure (Fig. 12). She holds an infant who may be self-comforting by sucking his hand while looking out at the older children, who are

Fig. 11: Plate III-2 of the Harley *Splendor Solis* (1582) Children Playing.

mobile and playing. A toddler touches the woman's skirt and elicits eye contact, in what Margaret Mahler called "refueling" before returning to play.

Other children engage in parallel and interactive play, exploring with delight the effect of their own body movements on windmills (turned by the resistance of the air, which is invisible) and imaginatively using the materials at hand.

Fig. 12: Detail from Plate III-2 of the Harley *Splendor Solis*. A maternal figure sits in front of a tile stove, holding an infant while gazing at a toddler who tugs at her skirt.

The perspective of the picture leads the eye toward a doorway (Fig. 13). Above the doorway rest two vessels containing a yellow liquid. For the alchemists, yellow, or *citrinatis*, represented a transitional stage. Why are there *two* vessels? We might think of the number two as denoting something that is just coming into consciousness, or we might think of the two people necessary for a relationship, and of unconscious-to-unconscious communication, since in the second series the alchemical vessels contained the symbols of the interior and perhaps unconscious process. The doorway opens to a dark space, where a girl is carrying something, perhaps a basin, with both hands. What might this mean? What is the link between the room and the dark space, separated by the doorway? Does her

Fig. 13: Detail from Plate III-2 of the Harley *Splendor Solis*. Doorway opening into a deeper interior space.

presence, perhaps carrying water, imply that there is work going on in the darkness, in the unconscious which is accessed in this secure setting full of affectively positive human connections and imaginative play? Could it be an intimation of what is to come, the next *enantiodromia*? Or for those of you who know the *I Ching*, an old *yang* turning into a young *yin*?

The next painting shows a well-known alchemical symbol, women washing (Fig. 14). The women work with nature and with the elements: there is no implication that they have special abilities. The process is represented as the ordinary work of women receiving no special recognition or rewards.

A river runs through a verdant countryside. Neither its source nor its direction is visible. Could this represent the mysterious source and destination of the Self?

As in the previous two images, we see all the elements: earth, air, fire, and water.

Washing clothes and putting them out in the sun to dry is concretely and symbolically a combination of the *solutio* and the *solificatio*, processes of purification. The laying of the cloth on the ground refers to the processes of distillation and sublimation. Water on the earth evaporates into the air during the heat of the day, and then in the coolness of the night, it condenses back onto the surface of the earth as dew. An alchemical text advised, "Gather Dew in the Month of May, with a clean white Linnen Cloth spread upon the Grass."[23] In her commentary on *Aurora Consurgens*, Marie-Louise von Franz referred to alchemical texts which advised that dew must be gathered before sunrise, before "the sun robs it [the earth] of its dew in order to nourish itself, and then the earth is 'a widow and without husband.'"[24] She concluded that, "… the east or dawn was correlated not only with the *rubedo* (blood and life) but also with the feminine, white, 'dewy' substance fertilized by the spirit."[25] However, dew was also associated with the mercurial fiery-water, or spirit, and so can be seen to correspond to the masculine spiritual substance which fertilizes the earth.[26]

The alchemy is no longer in the laboratory. It is found in the humble, daily, repetitive work of life, such as the work we do as analysts. We might note in this context that many spiritual disciplines also use a method of mindful repetition, as in the Zen precept, "Chop wood, carry water."

Fig. 14: Plate III-3 of the Harley *Splendor Solis*. Women Washing.

The final plate in the series, and in the *Splendor Solis*, is of the sun above a gray landscape (Fig. 15). As in the first plate of this final series, the foreground contains blackened tree stumps and delicate foliage. The new growth appears to be a different kind of plant. Patricia Damery, a San Francisco analyst whom I consulted about plant identification, suggested that the newly growing plants might be ones that are better adapted to the bright sunlight of higher altitudes, again pointing to life on a new basis.

A path or stream meanders from the foreground toward a large walled city, with many-spired buildings. A large gated bridge traverses a river, which separates the viewer from the city. In the foreground, to the left, a humble house is nestled among trees. Might this suggest a life closer to nature, with access to collective life but not immersion within it?

The sun's rays do not seem to light the city, to which it is so near, and its lower rays cannot be seen beneath the horizon, as in the first picture in this series (Plate III-1, Fig. 10). The city is in shadow, against the dictates of common sense, since the sun is high in the sky. What is happening here? Even high in the mountains, we see glimmers at sunrise and sunset. Could it be that the sun is not lighting up the world? Once again, this inner, paradoxical landscape can affect us deeply.

How do you read the expression on the human face of the sun? It reminds me of Wolter's description of images of the Greek god Asklepios, as quoted by Kerényi:

> The eyes seem to look upwards and into the distance without definite aim. This ... gives us an impression of a great inner emotion, one might almost say of suffering. This god does not stand before us in Olympian calm: he is assailed as it were by the sufferings of men, which it is his vocation to assuage.[27]

Applied to the process of analysis, the final plate could suggest that the initial loss of soul has lifted—but not into an inflation. The individual is not identified with the archetypal image of the sun in its splendor. Paradoxically, this particular image of the sun, as a symbol of conscious awareness, tells us that becoming more conscious does not promise a state of elation or ecstasy, but rather, a fuller awareness of the human condition. It also reminds me of something Jung wrote in "Two Essays on Analytical Psychology":

Fig. 15: Plate III-4, the final plate of the Harley *Splendor Solis*.

> The unconscious processes that compensate the conscious ego contain all those elements that are necessary for the self-regulation of the psyche as a whole. On the personal level, these are the not consciously recognized personal motives which appear in dreams, or the meanings of daily situations which we have overlooked, or conclusions we have failed to draw, or affects we have not permitted, or criticism we have spared ourselves. But the more we become conscious of ourselves through self-knowledge, and act accordingly, the more the layer [I would say influence rather than layer] of the personal unconscious will be diminished. In this way there arises a consciousness which is no longer imprisoned in the petty, oversensitive, personal world of the ego, but participates freely in the wider world of objective interests. ... At this stage it is fundamentally a question of collective problems, which have activated the collective unconscious because they require collective rather than personal compensation.[28]

In the final series of four, all the royal symbols are absent—no kings, no queens, no princes—no symbols of power or prestige.

These images were painted during the Renaissance in the 16th century, when kingship was still very much alive and the domination of countries by "divine right" of the sovereign was still very much in place (as shown in Figure 2b, Plate II-2 of the *Splendor Solis*). Alchemy was often regarded as heretical by Christianity (since its Christianized versions espoused the Arian heresy) and dangerous to the principle of the vested power of church and state. Alchemy kept bringing in the Earth and the Feminine Principle of embodied and related soul and spirit, expressing values that were not acceptable to cultural attitudes based on power relationships and an inflated view of the values of reason and *logos*. Alchemical images transcend these opposites and suggest the ineffable in their emerging from related, rather than one-sided, development.

This final painting of the *Splendor Solis*, or the *Splendor of the Sun*, leaves us with a final paradox. It contains no splendor and no symbolism in the sense in which we usually use the term symbol. Rather, we see a world of quietly evocative imagery. It is as though the reality of the individual and the imagery come together, and ordinary life now exists in liminal states and is imbued with depth and meaning.

NOTES

1. Joseph L. Henderson, *Shadow and Self* (Wilmette, Illinois: Chiron Publications, 1990), 63.

2. An entire volume of Jung's *Collected Works*, over 600 pages in length, is devoted to *Experimental Researches* (Volume 2).

3. For a superbly sensitive clinical integration of this new material from neurobiology, see Margaret Wilkinson, *Coming into Mind: The Mind-Brain Relationship: a Jungian Clinical Perspective*, Foreword by Allan Shore (London: Routledge, 2006).

4. Joseph L. Henderson and Dyane N. Sherwood, *Transformation of the Psyche: The Symbolic Alchemy of the Splendor Solis* (New York and London: Routledge, 2003).

5. The *Splendor Solis* (1582) belonging to the British Library, MS 3469, is the source of the beautiful illuminated paintings shown throughout this article by permission of the British Library.

6. Adam McLean, "Introduction," in J. Godwin, *Splendor Solis* (Grand Rapids, MI: Phanes Press, 1991), 9.

7. Alan Schore, *Affect Regulation & the Repair of the Self* (New York and London: W. W. Norton, 2003), xvi.

8. Schore, xvi.

9. C. G. Jung, *Collected Works*, 16.

10. C. G. Jung, *Collected Works*, 16 § 410.

11. From J. L. Martin, *Neuroanatomy: Text and Atlas* (New York: McGraw Hill, 1989).

12. The most recent edition: Charles Darwin, *The Expression of Emotion in Man and Animals,* Introduction, Afterword and Commentaries by Paul Ekman (New York and Oxford: Oxford University Press, 1998).

13. Joan Chodorow, "Play, Imagination, and the Emotions," North-South Conference of Jungian Analysts, March 1–4, 2001, np. (from a work-in-progress for the Carolyn and Ernest Fay Series in Analytical Psychology).

14. Eckman in Darwin (1998).

15. S. R. Lehky, "Fine Discrimination of faces can be performed rapidly," *Journal of Cognitive Neuroscience*, 12, 2000, 848-855.

16. U. Dimberg, M. Thunberg, and K. Elmehed, "Unconscious facial reactions to emotional facial expressions," *Psychological Science* 11, 2000, 86-89.

17. From K. J. Aitken & C. Trevarthen, "Self/other organization in human psychological development," *Developmental and Psychopathology*, 9, 653-677, 1997.

18. Piet Hut & Roger Shepard, 1996, "Turning 'The Hard Problem' Upside Down & Sideways," *Journal of Consciousness Studies*, 3(4), 313.

19. Extended and modified from Henderson and Sherwood, 2003.

20. C. G. Jung, *Collected Works,* 16 § 373.

21. Comments made at a videotaped lecture by Dr. Henderson for the Archives for Research in Archetypal Symbolism (ARAS*)* in San Francisco on the *Splendor Solis*, San Francisco, 1987.

22. Henderson and Sherwood. Appendix: English Translation of the Harley text of the *Splendor Solis*, 180.

23. Quoted in John Read, *Prelude to Chemistry* (London: G. Bell & Sons, 1936), 157.

24. Marie-Louise von Franz, ed., *Aurora Consurgens* (New York: Bollingen Foundation, 1966), 206.

25. von Franz, ed., *Aurora Consurgens.*

26. See Alexander Roob, *Alchemy & Mysticism* (New York and London: Taschen, 1997), 47.

27. Wolter, as quoted in K. Kerényi, *Asklepios: Archetypal Image of the Physician's Existence,* trans. Ralph Manheim (New York: Bollingen Series LXV.3 and London: 1959.) (Originally published in German as *Der Göttliche Arzt*, 1947), 22-3.

28. C. G. Jung, *Collected Works*, 7 § 275.

The Un-Refused Feast[1]

TOM CHEETHAM

The Lost Speech

Let me begin by outlining a story that I have treated in detail elsewhere.[2] In his late writings Henry Corbin articulated particularly clearly his vision of the unity of the religions of Abraham. This harmony depends upon a shared story centered on the revelation of the Word of God. Corbin writes,

> The drama common to all the 'religions of the Book' ... can be designated as the drama of the "Lost Speech." And this because the whole meaning of their life revolves around the phenomenon of the revealed holy Book, around the true meaning of this Book. If the true meaning of the Book is the interior meaning, hidden under the literal appearance, then from the instant that

Tom Cheetham lives in rural New England with his wife and two children. He is the author of *The World Turned Inside Out: Henry Corbin and Islamic Mysticism*, New Orleans: Spring Journal Books, 2003 and *Green Man, Earth Angel: The Prophetic Tradition and the Battle for the Soul of the World*, Albany, SUNY Press, 2005. He also prepared the comprehensive bibliography for "Archetypal Psychology: a Brief Account," Vol. 1, *The Uniform Edition of the Writings of James Hillman*, published by Spring Publications, 2005.

> men fail to recognize or refuse this interior meaning, from that instant they mutilate the unity of the Word, of the Logos, and begin the drama of the 'Lost Speech.' [3]

For Corbin much of Judaic, Christian and Islamic history can only be understood if we see it as the theater in which the drama of the conflict between the literal and the hidden meanings of the Word is played out. To the degree that the Word is perceived only literally, to that degree is the true meaning lost.

For Corbin and the mystical theologians for whom he speaks human language is a dim reflection of a spiritual world of images that are at once sensuous and intellectual. The language of the angels is a language of the creative imagination. The language of poetry is as close as we can get to this divine imaginal speech, in which lies the interior meaning of the Word. Corbin's account of Western history traces the progressive loss of the Breath of Compassion that speaks this language and so gives life and soul to the world. The loss of the realm of the *imaginal* inhabited by the Angel of Humanity and the Angel of the Earth occasioned all the schisms that split the West: religion and philosophy, thought and being, intellect and ethics, body and spirit, God and the individual. In this history the place of language and the revealed Word is central, and the quest for the lost language of the angels is the fundamental task. It is *the* drama that underlies the unity of the three branches of the Abrahamic tradition.

Islam, as the last in the sequence of great Revelations in the Abrahamic Tradition, sees itself as the culmination of the present cycle of prophecy. It is, as Martin Lings has put it, "something of a summation," and we might expect that the Qur'an would provide some guidance in our search for the lost language. Henry Corbin and Louis Massignon regarded what they take to be the central episode of Sura XVIII of the Qur'an as pivotal for understanding the Prophetic Tradition.[4] This is the story of the meeting between Moses and Khidr. Khidr is a mysterious figure, who acts as Moses' spiritual Guide and initiator into the mystical truths that Corbin says, "emancipate one from literal religion." It is this Guide who explains the inner and most personal meaning of the Law to Moses. Massignon has translated his name as "The Verdant One." He is the Green Man of Islamic tradition. Corbin tells us that he is associated with every aspect of nature's greenness. He has attained the source of Life and has drunk the water of immortality, and so is the Eternal Youth. He is the archetypal hermeneut whose speech is the lost poetry of Creation. In the Islamic tradition he is linked, and at times identified, with the Old Testament figure of Elija. Khidr is the archetypal figure of the personal spiritual Guide, and Corbin says, equivalent to the Paraclete of the Gospel of John, the Hidden Imam of Shi'ism, and to the Christ of the Cross of Light; he is the *True Prophet*, the inner guide of each person, the Angel Holy Spirit whose appearance to every person is *for each one unique.* The question posed by Islam, at the end of the prophetic tradition, after Moses, Jesus and Mohammad, is What comes after the Prophets? The central questions of Corbin's book on Ibn 'Arabi are *Who is Khidr?* And, *What does it mean to be a disciple of Khidr?*[5] This celestial person, common to all the religions of the Book, is the key to solving the mystery of the Lost Speech.

The inability, or the refusal, to hear the voice of the Verdant One, and so recognize the inner meaning of the Word, severs the link between the human person and the reality of the Imagination. By depriving us of the connection between language and divinity, this incapacity renders us deaf, dumb, blind and lame. In this condition we are so profoundly isolated that all our interactions with the world and the persons who inhabit it are hindered by ignorance, lack of sympathy and the disoriented gropings that arise from a dim, inarticulate desire to restore the lost connection.

The withering of a primordial sympathy, that we can awkwardly call a "poetic or artistic sensibility," is an archetypal phenomenon—that is to say, it is an ever-present possibility inherent in the human condition. The loss marks the beginning of our exile. The drama of the Lost Speech is the story of the quest to return. All of us, at every moment, are balanced between the forces that would silence the inner voices of that forgotten language and the energies that would return us home to a world we dimly recall, and sometimes sense as a longing, the vague fragment of a song, or the memory of a Voice that calls our deepest, most secret Name.

This lost language of Eden is the speech of the Divine Person, of the Angel of Humanity who is unique for each of us. This polymorphic celestial figure guarantees the personal reality of the world. The English language is a bit awkward here. We are speaking of what we might call the "Person-hood" of the world, but that is a bit stilted. Or perhaps we could say the "Person-ality" of the world, but that has the wrong connotations. I tend to favor the term *interiority*, but that misses the underlying theological resonance. However we speak of it, this imaginative reality that is the inner face of things is the source of the personification of the world. To the degree that the language of the imagination is lost, to that degree are people and all the elements of Creation de-personalized, turned into objects, into abstractions. The final result is Hell. The final result is a world without a Face. Everything has a physiognomy: trees and flowers, all animals, buildings and landscapes, chairs, tables... As Corbin asks, "what would a world without face or features—without, that is to say, a look—actually be?"[6] All of reality shares something of the interiority of the Divine Person. For anything to *be* at all, it must fall within the power of this Person. But as our ability to perceive this interiority declines, the richness, variety and complexity of our experience is compromised, our sympathy for the elements of creation withers, our desire to engage in dialogue wanes, and we end with such limited means for interacting with the world and its inhabitants that all we can do is push them around aimlessly in frustration and in anger.

The rationalist account of reality holds that we know about a thing or a person to the degree that we can describe and explain it. This may be true, in Hell. In Hell there are no persons, only objects. But in the approach to Eden, as we learn to discern the inner meaning of the Word and of the World, the more Real, the more *personal*, the beings of Creation become, the more they become *indescribable*. The poetic sensibility always leads towards that which cannot be spoken, yet which is the most Real. The final, paradoxical stage in the drama of the Lost Speech is to attain the freedom of the true Person and to speak a language whose end can only be the silence of contemplation.

To be a disciple of Khidr is to seek for the Speech within the interiority of the World. It requires that we live guided by the Imagination, seeking the primordial poetic sensibility that is necessary to experience the world in all its fullness and complexity. I think D. H. Lawrence's comment on the artistic life is pertinent for all of us: "I always feel as if I stood naked for the fire of Almighty God to go through me—and it's rather an awful feeling. One has to be so terribly religious to be an artist."[7]

But for the most part we don't live by the imagination. We abdicate that responsibility and leave it to others to fill our heads with images and ideas. We abandon ourselves to exteriority and dis-orientation, to be knocked about by our emotions and the manipulations of others, clinging to whatever transient stability we can find in the public world. To wholly abandon the search for the interiority of the Lost Speech is to live a life governed by the multitudinous forms of *idolatry*. Corbin has defined both idolatry and its opposite for us:

> Idolatry consists in immobilizing oneself before an idol because one sees it as opaque, because one is incapable of discerning in it the hidden invitation that it offers to go beyond it. Hence, the opposite of idolatry would not consist in breaking idols, in practicing a fierce iconoclasm aimed against every inner or external Image; it would rather consist in rendering the idol transparent to the light invested in it. In short, it means transmuting the idol into an icon.[8]

This is one way of understanding the function of the Lost Speech: to render the world itself transparent, to reveal the iconic status of Creation. To be a disciple of Khidr is to apprentice oneself in the craft of the transmutation of idols into icons. Transmutation is, of course, an alchemical operation, and alchemical symbolism has the great virtue of combining the material and the spiritual in a dynamic tension which is imaginative and creative to the core. It is one of the central hidden themes of the Abrahamic tradition, and it has, as we shall see, a special relevance to Christianity.

Peacock's Flesh and the Blood of the Lion

Let me recall to you the New Testament parable of the feast. The story is told by both Matthew and Luke. In Chapter 14 of Luke, Christ says, "A man once gave a great banquet, and invited many; and at the time for the banquet he sent his servant to say to those who had been invited, 'Come, for all is now ready.' But they all alike began to make excuses."[9] Being refused by the invited guests, who all have something better to do, the man sends his servants to the city streets to bring in "the poor and maimed and blind and lame," those that is, who have nothing, and who do not refuse. Of this tale Corbin writes, "The Gospel Parable of the Feast means precisely what it says... It would be ridiculous to engage in polemics against men or women who refuse to come to the Feast; their refusal inspires only sadness and compassion."[10]

It is the refusal of the symbolic life, of the imagination, to which Corbin refers. The life to which he calls us implies a radically traditional metaphysics that he spent his life articulating and defending. The compassion he feels is for those who refuse to admit the reality of a cosmos in which it is possible to be transformed, a cosmos in which what you can experience is a measure of who you are. The objectively real world to which the Imagination gives access, that Corbin called the *mundus imaginalis,* is embedded within an infinite creation that has a vertical dimension: there is a kind of hierarchy of levels of being from the less real to the more real. Human beings can, by their actions and passions, become more real, more themselves, more individual; or they can "fall" and lose themselves in what Corbin called "vagabondage and perdition." If we think of this hierarchy as a Ladder or Chain of Being, we are likely to miss the point. Those who count themselves "post-modern" are very rightly suspicious of hierarchic power structures, but this is not a power structure. It has been so misconstrued with great regularity, but it is perhaps better to think of it as a liberating architecture, one that opens the soul and releases the powers of sympathy and compassion. When the lower soul, the *ego*, drops away, even if only for a moment—and this is often the best we can manage—we can see more clearly the beauty and the unselfish, giving love that connects us to the world, and links all beings together. The hierarchy is ascended not so much by going "up," as one does in social hierarchies. In this movement of the soul the motion is inward, or better: outward, but in a new way. We become more intensely real ourselves and so we experience the world as more intensely real, more alive, more pregnant with lives and energies. The invitation to the plenitude of being is our birthright. We have been invited to the Feast, but so many find it so hard to hear that invitation, or to believe such revelry exists.

Why? Corbin's answer to this obvious question is also very traditional: Idolatry. We are all idolators. One reason for this is that being human is the most difficult task there is. Even a privileged life is full of confusion, pain and suffering, and the lives of many are marked by measureless agonies. Sympathy calls us to compassionate action. Sympathy calls us into the world. But the world is complicated in ways we can only dimly comprehend and the best intentions cannot guarantee the consequences of our acts. We become confused, disheartened, angry and despairing. We feel abandoned, exiled and homeless. We lose faith, becoming at best agnostics, at worst, nihilists. And so we *are* the poor, the maimed, the blind and the lame. Isolated and confused, we cling in desperation onto whatever idols promise simple, clear and stable answers to the intractable problems of our lives. But it is the painful state of poverty and abandonment that is the first step on the path of Return. Remember that in the same chapter of the Gospel of Luke, Christ, stunningly, says "whoever of you does not renounce all that he has cannot become my disciple."[11]

We are fragments of God, little embryonic persons, in whose hearts lie the absolute mystery of the divine abyss. Since we are finite we feel this central darkness as both mystery and terror. We fear falling into nothingness and grasp at whatever pseudo-certainties we can. *They are all idols.* Certainties always are. The best among us, those who can still see and feel and think with the heart, do the best they can to stand against the tides of arrogance and fear that sweep so many along into violence and despair. They try to tell us that the world is beautiful: beautiful and terrible and desperate and divine, and that it calls to us to *live* and that this life courses through us at each and every moment whether we feel it or not. And that it is the ability to breathe these winds of life that is the measure of your being.

Henry Corbin's work is an elegant and extended plea that we all commit ourselves to the perpetual struggle to save the Abrahamic religions from idolatry and literalism, and give them back to soul, to Imagination and to Life. The spiritual rebirth of which he speaks is an awakening to the inner, imaginal meaning of the Biblical and Qur'anic symbols that have had such a fundamental influence on so much of human history. It is the tragedy of the prophetic tradition that the disruptive and shocking voices of the prophets are heard only as pronouncements of immutable laws rather than as intensely personal warnings and calls for transformation. The prophets and the angels alike serve to rupture our complacencies and unsettle the fixed and fixating lower self. They fragment the stable constructions of the arrogant and willful *ego*, and in so doing, remind us that we are but shards, bits and pieces of the transcendent hidden God, the Black Light at the center of reality.

At the heart of Corbin's message is this dazzling juxtaposition: *Alchemy is the sister of Prophecy*. The prophets call us to transformation. The visitations of the Angel Holy Spirit, of the Paraclete of the Gospel of John, de-create us by their presence, so that we may learn to live in the state of constant un-doing that defines spiritual poverty and that is necessary for the alchemical opus.

Carl Jung has awakened us to the psychological meaning of alchemy. Corbin shows us the spiritual meaning. But as both well knew, it is also a physical process. Alchemy is concerned with *matter*, with the stuff of creation. Not as a precursor of chemistry or physics, but as a form of psychosomatic and psychospiritual work. The figure of Christ stands as an exemplar of the Stone that the alchemists sought. Christianity's central metaphor is Incarnation. The central project of Christianity is carnal knowing, embodied knowledge.[12] Incarnation is a *verb*. And it is a project for each and every one of us.

Corbin's vision tells us that the Gospel of John holds the heart of the tradition, as does Sura XVIII of the Qur'an. In Chapter 14 Christ says, "he who believes in me will also do the works that I do; and greater works than these will he do..." and later, "the Holy Spirit, whom the Father will send in my name, he will teach you all things, and bring to your remembrance all that I have said to you." Jung comments,

> It is easy to see what happens when the logical conclusion is drawn from the fourteenth chapter of John: the *opus Christi* is transferred to the individual. He then becomes the bearer of the mystery, and this development was unconsciously prefigured and anticipated in alchemy, which showed clear signs of becoming a religion of the Holy Ghost and of the Sapientia Dei.[13]

And yet for this project of Incarnation to "make sense" in the most literal way, that is, to enliven the senses and bring about a new birth, we have to understand "incarnate" as Corbin does. That is, we must learn to perceive with the Active Imagination. The material world and the senses that perceive it are transformed by the imagination. Corbin puts it this way:

> The Active Imagination guides, anticipates, molds sensory perception; that is why it transmutes sensory data into symbols.

> The Burning Bush is only a brushwood fire if it is merely perceived by the sensory organs. In order that Moses may perceive the Burning Bush and hear the Voice calling him 'from the right side of the valley' — in short, in order that there may be a theophany — an organ of trans-sensory perception is needed.[14]

What is true for the visions of Moses is true for the Transfiguration and the Incarnation itself. In the *Acts of Peter* we are told that at the event of the Transfiguration each person present saw the Lord only as each was able to perceive Him.[15] Christ must be there in the flesh, the same flesh that can be Crucified and killed and examined in the laboratories, but each person sees him with a spiritual vision that is personal and unique.

Corbin is proudly and defiantly a "docetist." That is to say, he ascribes to what became one of the fundamental heresies in the Christian tradition, that Christ was not truly human, but an "appearance." To that charge of heresy he responds,

> Yes. But...it is a docetism that is far from degrading 'reality' by making it 'appearance'; on the contrary, by transforming it into appearance it makes this 'reality' transparent to the transcendent meaning manifested in it.[16]

Always he is concerned lest the "raw data" of sensation and the history of material causality trap religious experience on the level of literal, uniform and universal Truth. This is his objection to the dogma of the Incarnation: Christ appeared in material history, once, and the new Covenant was made which applies to everyone identically. Then the Truth can be apprehended publicly, and the guardians of the Church become the mediators between the individual and the Lord. In the end the meaning of the person is degraded into the meaninglessness of statistical truth. Corbin refuses this with passion. We must be the subjects of our own lives, not the objects of some external authority, whether ecclesiastical, political or scientific.

And so we must each accept the challenge given us at birth—and accept the responsibility for our own lives. The only adequate response to the gift of life—to the childbirth struggle endured by the mother of each and every one of us—the only adequate response to this is to make that struggle our own; otherwise we risk being merely the passive recipients of our own lives. We must ourselves become incarnate—we must accept the gift and the challenge that it entails to enter fully alive into the world, by giving birth to ourselves as creative and embodied creatures immersed in the fecundity of the world. In alchemy this means having it out with our passions on the battleground of our own body. As we fight to give birth to our higher self we become our own mother, our own father. And as Jung points out, in the torturous exploration in fecundity which is the alchemical opus, "the pregnancy cravings of the mother are stilled with the peacock's flesh and lion's blood, i.e., with her own flesh and blood."[17] That is to say, the alchemist "*must celebrate a Last Supper with himself*, and eat his own flesh and drink his own blood; which means that he must recognize and accept the other in himself."[18] If we are ever to escape the prison of the lower soul, we have to consume our own passions, obsessions and needs, and so purify them, to discriminate and come to see what belongs to us and what does not. This is how we orient ourselves and escape from "vagabondage and perdition." For in our exile we are not entirely deaf to the call and blind to the figure of the Angel, and it is through the alchemical work of the imagination that we can begin to hear that forgotten Speech and connect to the fullness of the world. Jung's account of the struggle has often been misread as self-centered and isolating. And surely the opus *is* a lonely undertaking. And yet it is only by such a struggle to hear the voice of the True Prophet that the sympathy required for communion with other beings can be developed.

Without the discrimination achieved through the alchemical processes none of the elements of the world can be experienced in their interiority—they will always be contaminated by the chaos and the exteriority of the unconscious lower soul. They will always be objects, never persons. Neither other people, nor even the very matter of creation can be experienced in their plenitude without this process of coming to consciousness. We are filled with the undiscriminated darknesses of Earth, Air, Water and Fire, and we are thus buried underneath them. Najm Kubra, a twelfth century Sufi from what is now Uzbekistan in Central Asia, wrote as follows:

> The only way to separate yourself from [these darknesses] is to act in such a way that every rightful part in you comes together with that to which it rightfully belongs, that is, by acting in such a way that each part comes together with its counterpart: Earth receives the earthly part, Water the watery part, Air the

> etheric part, Fire the fiery part. When each has received its share, you will finally be delivered of these burdens.[19]

And, being delivered of these *as* burdens, we burst open to find that we *are* the microcosm, released into its proper home, returned from exile and full of Persons, full of the otherness, the wild and living diversity of the world. We can sing and shout with that mythic celebrant of the earth, Walt Whitman, who exults:

> I find I incorporate gneiss, coal, long-threaded moss, fruits, grains, esculent roots,
> And am stucco'd with quadrupeds and birds all over...[20]

As in Corbin's vision of an earth where the Word has become flesh not only in the figures of the prophets, but in all the creatures of the Angel of Earth, Whitman sings,

> A song of the rolling earth, and of words according,
> Were you thinking that those were the words, those upright lines?
> those curves, angles, dots?
> No, those are not the words, the substantial words are in the ground and sea,
> They are in the air, they are in you...
>
> Human bodies are words, myriads of words...
>
> Air, soil, water, fire—those are words...[21]

This vision is open to those who are whole in themselves — the interpenetration of the microcosm and the macrocosm can be lived only by those who have transformed themselves. Whitman says:

> I swear the earth shall surely be complete to him or her who shall be complete,
> The earth remains jagged and broken only to him or her who remains jagged and broken.[22]

This is the Alchemy that is the Sister of Prophecy, a Prophecy that is rupture, iconoclasm, and a call to waken from the sleep of the dead and hear the voice of the Verdant One, the Green Man who is the Incarnate One and the Angel of the Earth. The prayer of the fourth century North African Bishop Serapion can stand as *the* great cry of the human heart: "We beg you Lord, make us truly alive!"[23]

And so one great task in our Quest for the Lost Speech is the transformation of our embodiment by means of the imaginative work of the alchemical *opus*. The Lost Speech is creative and "aesthetic" —

it connects us to the Breath of life and enlivens all the senses. This is the transformation of the Word into Flesh. William Blake, that great spokesman for an embodied and free Christianity, states the challenge most simply:

> Jesus & his Apostles & Disciples were all Artists -
> A Poet a Painter a Musician an Architect:
> the Man or Woman who is not one of these
> is not a Christian[24]

The Desert Beyond Language

To transform ourselves and our vision of the world we need forms of perception that are enabled by language that is not burdened with the accumulated idolatries and unconscious assumptions of the past. One function of the Revealed Word is precisely to fragment *human* language and so in this way too, to destroy the idols we erect for ourselves. Dr. Hossein Nasr writes of the Qur'an,

> Many people... who read the Qur'an for the first time are struck by what appears as a kind of incoherence from the human point of view. It is neither like a highly mystical text nor a manual of Aristotelian logic, though it contains both mysticism and logic. It is not just poetry, though it contains the most powerful poetry. The text of the Qu'ran reveals human language crushed by the power of the Divine Word. It is as if human language were scattered into a thousand fragments like a wave scattered into drops against the rocks at sea. One feels through the shattering effect left upon the language of the Qur'an, the power of the Divine whence it originated. The Qur'an displays human language with all the weakness inherent in it becoming suddenly the recipient of the Divine Word and displaying its frailty before a power which is infinitely greater than man can imagine.[25]

In a masterful analysis of the Prophetic Traditon, deeply influenced by Corbin's work, Norman O. Brown has suggested parallels between the language of the Qur'an and, astonishingly, *Finnegan's Wake*. He says that in its structure, its allusiveness, its ambiguities, its imagery and its poetry, it is *more* avant-garde, more *post-modern* than Joyce's merely human text.[26] God's Word unmakes all human meanings, all the proud constructions of civilization, and shocks us out of our complacencies and our belief in all the truths we cling to so tightly. There are two idols in particular that prevent us from opening ourselves to the divinity of the world, and they tend to be mirror images of one another. The two great idols that we must transmute, that we must turn, that is, into *icons*: are God and the *ego*.

I follow Corbin's lead and speak of the *transmutation* of idols into icons, rather than merely of the destructive shattering of idols, and yet we must be quite clear that alchemical transmutation *is* a shattering experience. In order to "render the idol transparent to the light invested in it" a kind of polishing is required. But it is a polishing of the idolator, not the idol. The kinds of polishing are many and diverse, and most of them are in some sense "shattering." Each of the four elements has its own characteristic operation: *Calcinatio* is a fiery immolation; *Solutio* is drowning and dismemberment; *Coagulatio* is fixation in solidity that may lead to imprisonment or crucifixion; *Sublimatio* may grind to a powder that blows away in air. The language of alchemy hints at the difficulty of the soul-work necessary for the journey towards the light that Corbin invites us to begin.

Perhaps all of you will know of the life and work of the Trappist monk Thomas Merton. He was an exemplary figure in what one prominent student of his work has called the "contemplative counter-culture."[27] In one of his last journals, written when he was actively exploring the relation between zen Buddhism and Christianity, he wrote "We are going to have to create a new language of prayer. And this new language of prayer has to come out of something which transcends all our traditions, and comes out of the immediacy of love."[28] It is in just such an attempt to find a language of prayer that unites the religions of the Book into an over-arching *Harmonia Abrahamica* that is a central task of Henry Corbin's work.

Corbin has said that prayer is the highest form of the Creative Imagination.[29] His vision of prayer emphasizes nostalgia and ardent desire for the face of the Beloved Divine. But we must be careful not to take Person in a narrow and excessively human sense. An idolatrous version of the personal God of the monotheistic tradition can stand in the way of our entry into the plenitude of life in which we are immersed. For too many people, "God" has become reduced to the image of an infinite *ego*. The word "God" is so compromised, so covered over with our images and projections, our confused hopes and self-centered desires, that we are blinded to the immensities in which we breathe. The new language of prayer that Merton was searching for beyond all the traditions can perhaps be found by letting go even of the idea of God.

Perhaps it is necessary to be exiles, abandoned in the desert in order to awaken. Here prayer and poverty are complementary. Merton has written:

> [T]he contemplative is… simply he who has risked his mind in the desert beyond language and beyond ideas where God is encountered in the nakedness of pure trust, that is to say in the surrender of our own poverty and incompleteness in order no longer to clench our minds in a cramp upon themselves, as if thinking made us exist.[30]

For this surrender, discipline is required: a discipline of regular, guarded attention, such as one can develop in certain kinds of open-ended prayer, or in the meditation of zen and other forms of Buddhism, or indeed in the intense concentration of the artist and the poet.

Corbin has said that we must learn to "make ourselves capable of God." For this we need practice, we need "a practice," that will enable us to experience those influxes of the divine that exist potentially all around us at each moment. The work of alchemical imagination and the work of artistic creation can be such practices. But more seemingly "public" activities can also serve to disrupt us and reveal our own complacencies and the idols to which we have become blind. In our time these disorienting shocks have included anything that disrupts the powers of the dominant social structure: the revolts of the dispossessed, of minorities, of women, of the poor and the powerless everywhere. We must face squarely the suffering of the innocent, and the destruction of the non-human lives with whom we share the earth. As Brown has suggested, there is much of this at work in certain forms of post-modernism that have as their goal the deconstruction of human certainties and dismantling of oppressive social structures of all kinds.

Yet the postmodern deconstructive project very often leads to nihilism, and political activism can become mired in cynicism and despair. Such failures are a kind of half-way point: even further annihilation of the ego is required of us. If we let go of the idea of God, so too must we let go of any idea of ourselves. Corbin calls the ultimate stage in the struggle in the desert the "annihilation of annihilation."[31] We must go *beyond* nihilism. We must let go of everything—even of our *expectations*. Notice I did not, quite, say "let go of hope." There is a subtle and entirely crucial distinction to be made here. Letting go of expectations and the controlling and defensive "neediness" of the lower soul is not to let go of *hope*, nor to abandon the search for justice and love. For hope is not the same as expectation. We must learn from the radically conservative, even heretical, Catholic social critic Ivan Illich: What expectation expects is the satisfaction of the "needs" of the *ego*, and the claiming of "rights." Hope is something entirely different. If "needs" are childish, then hope is the flowering of maturity. But merely psychological language masks the spiritual meaning of these states of the soul. Hope expresses another order of being altogether. Expectation arises in the world of exteriority, of largely impersonal structures. Hope erupts from within the interiority of the world. Illich writes, "Hope centers on a person from whom we await a gift."[32] Hope is always based upon the possibility of rupture, of unpredictable, uncontrollable gift. Hope, the gift, and the person are all, properly speaking, eschatological. They require open-ness to mystery, and have their source, in the end, in that very desert beyond language where we must go to get beyond the "God" who we "need," "expect," and have constructed. But as we learn from Corbin, such an eschatology can be, indeed must be, realizable in the present, in precisely those ruptures and breaks through which the divine may appear.

We must abandon our childish attachments to everything: to ourselves, to God and to the world. We must discriminate between childish expectations and mature hopes. Until we do, we confuse them all and regard all equally as "desires." Beyond neediness and possessiveness, is a hope that opens onto compassion and to a love that does not split into lover and beloved. Beyond the desert lies awareness of the communion of all beings. But paradoxically this relation is founded on the experience of the otherness of other humans, and the non-human otherness of all beings who live outside the bounds of human concern. The great thirteenth century zen master Dōgen puts it this way:

> To carry yourself forward and experience myriad things is delusion. That myriad things come forth and experience themselves is awakening.[33]

To be present to the world in this way we must free ourselves from the delusions of the "God made in the human image" that so often contaminate our experience. In addition to the negative theology so crucial to Corbin's vision, we also require a strong dose of what the Eastern Orthodox theologian Olivier Clément calls "negative anthropology." Clément writes,

> *An infinite vulnerability is the condition of this unknowing, where the more the known is known, the more it is revealed as unknown.*
>
> No, the God of Christians is not the summit — reassuring and plain to see—of a pyramid of beings. He is the depth who reveals depths everywhere, making the most familiar creature a thing unknown.[34]

Of course only a Fool would want to live in such ignorance, vulnerability and poverty. And there is a long tradition of God's Fools in our heritage. Here we can find vestiges of a vision of spiritual freedom all but covered over by the religion of the theologians, of the councils, of what Corbin called the Doctors of the Law. Clément describes these figures for us:

> Humility and silence are so many aspects of interior poverty and renunciation. A person uprooted from a settled life, heads for the desert, to become God's nomad. The real desert is within us.[35] ...Some men of the desert become pillars of prayer, settled or wandering. They reject all domestication, even that of monastic communities, in order to opt for the untrammelled liberty of the wild animals. 'Men of the hills' on the heights and in freedom.[36] ...The contemplative, like the illiterate person, does without books. Creatures and things in their delicacy and infinite subtlety continually speak to him of God.[37] ...Interior freedom... makes possible that attentive gaze, stripped of covetousness, which perceives the outward appearance of each object and its secret, and honours it.[38]

When our tools, our technologies, our theories, our beliefs about who we are and what the world is, when all of this comes to dominate and control our lives, it is time to head for the hills, to retreat from the systems we have made and that now are making us. To take to the hills, to enter the desert, with compassion, with hope, with humility and the immense discipline of freedom: this is how persons are born. This is how true community is made. For the wilderness is not outside the human city. It grows wherever the strangeness of creation erupts, wherever we come awake to the groundless gift beyond the systems in which we habitually live. This is the "beginner's mind" of zen Buddhism, where everything and anything is cause for pulling up short and wondering "What is this?! Who is this?! What is going on?!" Fools and zen masters, the nomads of God, wander as vagabonds, without destination. But what appears as disorientation when seen from the outside, may be the trail left by the apprentice Person trying to listen to the voice of the angel.

The most important thing is for each of us to find our Voice; the Voice that can articulate the Lost Speech. The quest is a personal one, but the result is communal: the result is compassion and communion. This most personal, most central Voice can be found by those who find a way to heed Christ's call to renounce all that they have, to give up even *need*. In the silence that then descends one can begin to hear the chorus of creation; to find oneself sung into fragments by a music of terrible majesty, and reborn with a love and compassion for creation that passes far, far beyond any human understanding.

NOTES

1. A version of this paper was presented as a lecture for the Temenos Academy, London, October 27, 2004.

2. Tom Cheetham, *The World Turned Inside Out: Henry Corbin and Islamic Mysticism* (New Orleans: Spring Journal Books, 2003) and *Green Man, Earth Angel: The Prophetic Tradition and the Battle for the Soul of the World* (Albany, SUNY Press, 2005), Chapter 5.

3. Henry Corbin, "L'Initiation Ismaèlienne ou l'Esoterisme et le Verbe," in *L'Homme et Son Ange: Initiation et Chevalerie Spirituelle* (Paris: Fayard, 1983), 81.

4. Corbin discusses Khidr in *Creative Imagination in the Sufism of Ibn Arabi,* trans. Ralph Manheim, Princeton/Bollingen Series XCI (Princeton: Princeton Unversity Press, 1969), 53ff.

5. Henry Corbin, *Creative Imagination*, 55.

6. Henry Corbin, *Temple and Contemplation*, trans. by P. Sherrard and L. Sherrard, KPI (London: 1986), 189.

7. Letter 550, in *The Letters of D. H. Lawrence*, vol. 5., ed. James T. Boulton and Lindeth Vasey (Cambridge: Cambridge UP, 1989).

8. Henry Corbin, "Theophanies and Mirrors: Idols or Icons?", trans. Pratt & Donohue, *Spring Journal*, 1983, 2.

9. Lk. 14:16-18.

10. Henry Corbin, *The Man of Light in Iranian Sufism,* trans. Nancy Pearson (New Lebanon, NY: Omega Publications, 1994), 145. See Matt. 22:2-10, Lk. 14:16-24.

11. Lk. 14: 33.

12. Margaret R. Miles, *Carnal Knowing: Female Nakedness and Religious Meaning in the Christian West* (Boston: Beacon Press, 1989), 185.

13. Carl Jung, *CW* 14 § 531.

14. Henry Corbin, *Creative Imagination,* 80.

15. Henry Corbin, *Avicenna and the Visionary Recital*, trans. W. Trask (Princeton: Princeton University Press-Princeton/Bollingen Series LXVI, 1960), 92-93.

16. Henry Corbin, *Creative Imagination*, 244.

17. Carl Jung, *CW* 14 § 512.

18. *Ibid.*

19. Henry Corbin, *Man of Light*, 65-66.

20. Walt Whitman, *Leaves of Grass,* ed. Sculley Bradley and Harold Blodgett (New York: W.W. Norton, 1973), *Song of Myself,* Section 31, lines 669-71.

21. Whitman, *Leaves of Grass, A Song of the Rolling Earth,* Section 1, lines 1-4, 7 & 10.

22. *Ibid.*, 3, 91-2.

23. d. 365-70, Bishop of Thmuis in the Nile delta. Quoted in Margaret Miles, *Fullness of Life: Historical Foundations for a New Ascetism* (Philadephia: Westminster Press, 1981), 9.

24. William Blake, from an engraving of the Laocoön, c. 1818-1820.

25. Seyyed Hossein Nasr, *Ideals and Realities of Islam* (London: Allen & Unwin, 1966); quoted in Norman O. Brown, "The Apocalypse of Islam," in *Apocalypse &/or Metamorphosis* (University of California Press, Berkeley, 1991), 90.

26. Norman O. Brown, "Apocalypse," 90.

27. Inchausti, in Thomas Merton, *Seeds,* edited and introduced by Robert Inchausti (Boston: Shambhala, 2002), xi.

28. Merton, *Seeds*, 76-77.

29. Henry Corbin, *Creative Imagination*, 248.

30. Lawrence S. Cunningham, (ed.), *Thomas Merton: Spiritual Master. The Essential Writings* (New York: Paulist Press, 1992), 426.

31. Henry Corbin, *Man of Light*, 117.

32. Ivan Illich, "The Rebirth of Epimethean Man," in *Deschooling Society* (New York: Harper, 1971), 152. Also helpful is Lee Hoinacki, "Reading Ivan Illich," in Hoinacki and Mitcham (eds.), *The Challenges of Ivan Illich: A Collective Reflection* (Albany, NY: SUNY Press, 2002).

33. Dōgen, *Moon in a Dewdrop: Writings of Zen Master Dōgen,* edited by Kazuaki Tanahashi (New York: North Point, 1985), 69.

34. Olivier Clément, *On Being Human: A Spiritual Anthropology* (New York: New City Press, 2000), 32.

35. Clément, *On Being Human*, 160.

36. Olivier Clément, *The Roots of Christian Mysticism: Texts From the Patristic Era with Commentary* (London: New City Press, 1993), 211.

37. *Ibid.*, 215.

38. *Ibid.*, 222.

ALCHEMICAL LIGHT IN THE KABBALISTIC WORKSHOP

STEVEN M. JOSEPH

I

Both alchemy and kabbalah manifest and represent subterranean Western traditions of inner "self-work" that are at least two millennia old. The roots of these teachings undoubtedly go back to even earlier eras—the traditions themselves ascribe their origins to the earliest emergence of human beings, to the primordial androgynous "*Adam*," in the time before conventional historical time (in *illo tempore*, to use Eliade's phrase).

Alchemists were certainly interested in the transformation of material substances. Yet even the early documents of Western alchemy, such as the accounts of Zosimos of Alexandria and Maria the Jewess, indicate that for many alchemists the work on material "stuff" was primarily a means of working on themselves in a manner that was

Steven M. Joseph is an analyst member of the San Francisco Jung Institute and a board certified psychiatrist, who practices in Tucson, Arizona, and Albany, California (near Berkeley). He is past editor of *The San Francisco Jung Institute Library Journal.* In addition to his ongoing interest in the clinical practice of Jungian analysis and its relationship to its psychoanalytic cousins, he has a deep interest in the teachings and practices of the kabbalistic and Hasidic traditions of Judaism.

overtly *psychical*, more than just a way of changing materials. In other words, some alchemists engaged in a kind of self-work with affectively charged images of stuff in transformation—an ongoing lucid reverie of the sort that Jungians today call active imagination.[1]

Overtly kabbalistic writings appear publicly only in the twelfth century, but they embody esoteric teachings and traditions that are much older—thematically core doctrines of kabbalah reprise archetypal motifs of Neolithic fertility and *coniunctio* ritual and myth. Kabbalistic texts are often theosophical. That is, many kabbalistic texts explicate the workings of intra-divine life through the doctrine of the *sephirot*, the fundamental teaching of ten root emanations from the Infinite which are the inner divine life as it manifests outwards from itself into creation. Sometimes kabbalistic texts are overtly ecstatic and mystical, as in the works of the 13th century kabbalist Abraham Abulafia.[2] Some kabbalists were theurgists. In other words, they attempted to use their knowledge of kabbalistic ritual practice as a kind of magic, to influence directly the flow of divine blessing and abundance into the world.

During the Renaissance, after the expulsion of the Jews from Spain in 1492, a non-Jewish Christian kabbalah (usually spelled "cabala") developed from the studies of Pico della Mirandola, Agrippa von Nettesheim and others, who felt that the doctrines of the Zohar proved the divinity of Christ and the truth of the New Testament. During the same era, yet another occult current of cabala developed, which connected with Hermetic and neo-pagan traditions—Giordano Bruno, Robert Fludd and Thomas Vaughan are representatives of this stream.

In the eighteenth century development of kabbalah in Eastern Europe known as Hasidism, the Ba'al Shem Tov [the "Master of the Good Name"—or, in a better and deeper translation: "The Master of the (Divine) Name 'Good'"], who began the Hasidic movement, taught that the verse from Isaiah (6:3), "the fullness of all the earth is the Presence of the Infinite" (*M'lo Khol HaArets K'vodo*) expresses the core truth of everything that is. He taught that the purpose and meaning of human existence is in the self-work (*sich arbeiten,* in Yiddish) of living in continuous deep awareness of this core truth, and of embodying it in all one's actions in the world. Earlier classical kabbalistic teachings, such as the imaginally rich Book Zohar (thirteenth century) and the sixteenth century teachings of the "Lion" (the *Ari*) Rabbi Isaac Luria, were revisioned through the lens of Hasidism as being about the development and transformations of the inner life of the psyche, and not primarily about theosophy or theurgy.

We might say that the Hasidic masters brought the field-nature of conscious phenomena into the foreground,[3] and in doing so recognized the theosophy of the earlier kabbalists as *projections* of an unconscious psychical background (*kadmut ha-sekhel*)[4] onto the divine realms.[5] This transformed understanding of kabbalistic symbolism and imagery in Hasidic teaching parallels the transformed understanding of alchemy by later Renaissance alchemists such as Gerard Dorn, as Jung explicated in "Paracelsus as a Spiritual Phenomenon"[6] and in *Mysterium Coniunctionis.*[7]

Both alchemy and kabbalah—*as psyche*—that is, as affectively enlivened imaginal systems of symbols and enactive rituals, seek to realize and thereby to liberate the spirit within matter. The spirit *within* matter means: potential images and experiences of light and of life-giving flow (i.e., of illuminated consciousness and of sensuous vitality) *within* the dark opacity and rigidities of conventional, collectively-determined consciousness. Both alchemy and kabbalah, I believe, are less interested in mastering, dominating or suppressing the "matter" of ordinary unconscious complex-ridden conventional life, than they are in realizing the latent untapped potential riches within its apparent opaqueness. We see this in the alchemical idea of the *lumen naturae* (natural light within matter)[8] and in the kabbalistic idea of the *or chozer* (returning, reflected light from the denseness of matter)[9] —which are both gifts from the very heart of matter to spirit. We see it also in the kabbalistic/Hasidic idea of repairing and adorning our finite limited world (*tikkun 'olam*) so that it becomes a vessel and dwelling place for Infinite Oneness (*dirah ba-tachtonim*), as well as in Gerard Dorn's late alchemical idea of the conjunction of the *homo totus* (the whole man) with the *unus mundus* (the unitary world).[10]

Despite what appears to be a similarity of intention (not necessarily conscious) in the work of alchemy and kabbalah, the life contexts and the imagery of these two esoteric traditions are quite different. One way of exploring these differences would be to look at the different social contexts, and then to engage in a comparative study of the two symbol systems. I will not do this here. Instead, I want simply to present a short, accessible text from the Zohar, with a commentary, and to shine a little light on it through the prism of symbolic alchemy.

The "workshop" of the kabbalah, as I have named it here, is found in the *discursive texts* of kabbalah, which are the generative matrix for the kabbalistic opus: the *contemplative discernment* of their explicit and implicit symbolic meanings. The "alchemical light" is the *lumen naturae*, the natural light within the most ordinary matter—within everyday matters. It expresses an aspect of the kabbalistic *or chozer*, the reflected "returning light"—the light that *returns* from the most common, material and mundane to the most sublime, to enliven and infuse the transcendental with immanent meaning.

II

The Zohar itself is the central text of the kabbalah and of the larger Jewish mystical tradition. It attributes itself to the second century Rabbi Shimon bar Yochai. Modern scholarship attributes the book to late thirteenth century Spain (with some parts written in the early fourteenth century). All agree that the main body of the Zohar first entered the public domain after about 1270 in Spain, in the kabbalistic circles of Rabbi Moshe de Leon. The Zohar is arranged as a mystical Midrash on the Torah. It presents its teachings as a kind of peripatetic proto-novel about the meanderings and experiences of Rabbi Shimon and his disciples, known as the Companions (*Chevrayah*), as they wander through the Galilee and discourse on the mysteries of Torah.

The teaching I will translate here is a discussion about the relationship of the human to the Divine, presented through the symbolic image of a candle flame (Zohar 1:50b-51a). I have drawn on two contemporary commentaries to help explicate the text, the new English translation of the Zohar with accompanying notes by Daniel Matt,[11] and the recent Hebrew translation with commentary by Rabbi Daniel Frisch entitled *Matok Mi-D'vash* (Sweeter than Honey).[12]

The teaching follows, interspersed with commentary:

> *The Companions were ready to leave; they stood up. Rabbi Shimon said: There is still a word [a teaching] here with us. Rabbi Shimon then opened and said, Two [apparently contradictory] verses are written:* "For Y-H-V-H your God is a consuming fire" *(Deut. 4:24), and* "You who cleave to Y-H-V-H your God are wholly alive today" *(Deut. 4:4).*

One Talmudic attempt to reconcile these verses (BT Sotah 14a) teaches that we humans can survive the devouring fire of contact with divinity by imitating divine activity—for example, by clothing the naked, visiting the sick, comforting mourners, and burying the dead. The Zohar does not disagree with this outer, action-oriented resolution, but it seeks a deeper, more interior level of holding the opposites.

It is worth noting that for the Zohar and the lexical traditions of Judaism generally, *the written word* is the locus of the numinous—if two verses of Torah seem to contradict each other, there must be a deep secret in this apparent contradiction. In the exoteric traditions of rabbinic Judaism, the resolution may be sought in a third verse that mediates between the two contradictory verses. In the esoteric teaching of the Zohar, however, the resolution is often found in *a visual image* that holds the opposites, as we shall see in our example. Our text continues:

> *Come and see!* "For Y-H-V-H your God is a consuming fire." *This has been discussed among the Companions. There is a fire that consumes fire, that consumes and destroys it—a fire mightier than fire. The Companions have established this.*

The "fire that consumes fire" is the fire of *Shekhinah*, the Lower Mother within Divinity, in her aspect of judgment (*Din*), who consumes the fiery angels who desire to ascend above their fitting level. The fire of *Shekhinah* also destroys those fiery angels that are destined to be destroyed and then renewed on a daily basis. The fire of *Shekhinah* thus consumes and destroys as a function of impartial judgment (everything in its fitting place and at its appropriate level), yet also as a function of destruction as precondition for transformation and renewal.[13]

> *But come and see! Anyone who desires to know (to acquire gnosis of) the secret wisdom of the holy coniunctio should contemplate and meditate upon the flame that ascends from a glowing coal or from a burning candle. For the flame does not ascend except when it is one with a coarse substance (the wick and wax of the candle as the* prima materia).
>
> *So come and see! There are two kinds of luminosity in the ascending flame—one is a luminous white light; the other, attached*

> *to the first, is black or blue. The white light is above and ascends in a straight path. Below it is the blue or black light, which functions as a throne for the white light that dwells upon it. One light embraces the other so that they are fully one (they are in a* coniunctio*). And the black or blue-tinged light below is a throne of Presence for the white light — in this is the secret of blue (alluding to the blue thread in the traditional four-cornered fringed garment, the* tsitsit*).*

This passage is key to the significance of our text. It refers to the *coniunctio* that is made and disrupted between the divine feminine, the *Shekhinah* (the "Lower" Mother, or Daughter, as we shall see when the "Higher" Mother appears at the end of our text), and the divine masculine, known as *Zeir Anpin* (the Small Face, the Small Illumination) and as the Son. This relationship between the masculine and feminine is symbolized by our Zohar passage in the relationship of the white flame to the blue/black flame.

The white flame represents the mystery of the masculine *Zeir Anpin*, which is represented in the Torah by the divine name Y-H-V-H. White is the color of the sephirah *Hesed*, benevolent kindness and generous mercies—the right hand of the Son. Blue and black are colors of *Shekhinah*, the lower feminine who at times executes judgment (black) but who also takes a stand (makes a firm boundary) against the powers of the "shells" of unholiness that wish to unite with her (blue). The blue/black flame thus symbolizes the mystery of the feminine *Shekhinah*. The unity of the two flames, one resting on the other, symbolizes the *coniunctio* of divine masculine and feminine. The white flame's straight ascent goes all the way up to the Higher Mother, *Imma*, as we shall see, who is the true source of the mercies that the Son conveys, via the Daughter, to the lower worlds that we consciously inhabit.

The Father, the higher masculine (*Abba*), does not figure overtly in our Zohar passage, but he is present implicitly with the higher feminine, for they (the Father and Mother) are in a permanent *coniunctio*, unlike the lower masculine and feminine (*Zeir Anpin* and *Shekhinah*, Son and Daughter), symbolized by our candle-flame, whose *coniunctio* is always impermanent and always in flux. This difference is an important dimension of the Zohar's and kabbalah's teaching about unity and diversity. The higher (read: inner, deeper) unification is never disrupted—Father and Mother are known as *Trei Re'in d'Lo*

Mitpardin, "two loving friends who are never apart." This is not yet nonduality, which in the kabbalah is beyond even the unity of Father and Mother. But it is a ceaseless permanent dual unity, in contrast to the impermanence and flux of Son and Daughter, of the white flame and blue/black flame of a candle.

Our text continues:

> *This blue/black flame (Shekhinah) is one with something else below it (the wick and the wax or oil), so that it can ignite and be aroused to unite with the white light (Zeir Anpin). And sometimes the blue/black becomes red! Yet the white light above it never changes, but always remains white. But the blue light changes its color—now blue or black, now red. Moreover, it is pulled in two directions—above by the white light; below by that stuff which is underneath, which is prepared to ignite and give light.*

The commentary *Matok Mi-D'vash* explains the three colors of *Shekhinah* in the following way. "The blue light of *Malkhut/Shekhinah* changes into these other colors according to the kind and severity of judgment that is in her. Everything depends on the degree of awakening of the lower ones [i.e., us!] and on their deeds." *Blue* "is like the sea, and below are the 'shells' (of unholiness) which are like the depths of the sea. So that they will not gaze at *Shekhinah* to be nurtured by her, she clothes herself in a wholly blue garment." Sometimes, the commentary continues, she is *black*, as in the verse from Song of Songs (1:5): *Black am I and beautiful.* Black, physically the absence of light—symbolizing the gateway to the deep unconscious and the world of the objective archetypal psyche, kabbalistically the world of the sephirot—here expresses the real beauty of *Shekhinah*, manifesting forth her true deep unfathomable nature. But sometimes she is *red*, the color of blood symbolizing the most severe judgments.

The *Matok Mi-D'vash* works here from an implicit kabbalistic model of a spectrum of severity of judgment, from blue to red. The blue end of the spectrum represents "mild judgment," which is aimed at creating a separation between us and our unconsciousness and misdeeds, as the blue waters of the sea cover over the depths of the sea—thus the blue of the judgment of *Shekhinah* brings us back into contact with the harmonious flow of divine blessing and vitality. The red end of the spectrum, in contrast, represents "severe judgment," the sephirah *gevurah*, which at times unleashes the bloody destructiveness and disintegrative energies that often pervade our outer and inner worlds.

The "black and beautiful" nature of *Shekhinah* underlies the entire blue-to-red spectrum of judgment that she mediates. Our fundamental inability ever really to comprehend the relationship between our good or bad deeds and the happenings of our lives is like a black flame that mediates a profound mystery. In Michael Fordham's phrase, it is a "not knowing that constellates the self."[14]

We also see *Shekhinah*, our blue/black/red flame in our Zohar passage, as mediating between two realms—the white flame above, and the material stuff below. What is her relationship to the wick and wax (or oil) below—in the Zohar's symbolism, what is her relationship to us? For we are indeed the primordial stuff, the *prima materia*, that the Zohar represents as raw material of a candle or oil lamp—this raw material is, as the *Matok Mi-D'vash* has said, our own degree of awakening and our own deeds. A later Hasidic expansion on the Zohar's image allegorizes the lamp *wick* as our embodied activities (in thought, speech and physical action) and the *oil* of the lamp as the wisdom (awakening) that permeates our active embodiment.[15]

The Zohar continues:

> *This flame (symbolizing Shekhinah) constantly consumes and destroys what is beneath it (the wick and the oil or wax). This blue flame consumes and destroys everything that cleaves to it below, that it dwells upon—its nature is to consume and destroy. For on it depends the destruction of everything, the death of everything. Therefore, it consumes all that clings to it below, while the white flame above it neither consumes nor destroys, nor does its light ever change. . . .*

Shekhinah is identified by the Zohar as the Tree of Knowledge of Good and Evil, from the Garden of Eden—that is, she is the tree of the manifestation of duality, of process and the change of times and seasons, of impermanence. When she is separated from *Zeir Anpin*, when her *coniunctio* is disrupted, she is called the Tree of Death. *Zeir Anpin*, in contrast, is the Tree of Life, always irrigated and nourished by the Higher Mother (*Imma*—the "river that flows out of Eden," Gen. 2:10), even when not in *coniunctio* with his partner *Shekhinah*.

For simplicity I am skipping a small section of the text here, which goes off in a different direction that is not essential to our image. We continue:

> *Come and see! There is no awakening to ignite this blue flame to unite with the white flame, except through Israel who cleaves to it from below.*
>
> *And come and see! Even though the nature of this blue/black flame is to destroy everything that cleaves to it from below, yet Israel cleaves from below and continues to exist! This is what is written: "You who cleave to Y-H-V-H your God are alive . . ." to that blue/black flame that consumes and destroys everything that cleaves to it from below. And yet, you cleave and continue to exist, as is written, "You are wholly alive today."*
>
> *Now, above the white light (of Zeir Anpin, the Son) there dwells an invisible, concealed light that encompasses it like a halo (the light of the Higher Mother, Imma). Here is a supreme mystery! And all of these mysteries are found in the flame that ascends from the candle. The very highest wisdoms are hinted at in it!*
>
> *Rabbi Pinchas approached Rabbi Shimon and kissed him, and he said: Blessed is the Compassionate One that I met with you here today! They walked with Rabbi Pinchas for three miles to send him on his way. Then Rabbi Shimon and the Companions returned.*

In the Zohar's imagery, *Shekhinah* is the principle of impermanence, of inexorable time which changes and consumes whatever is, "that blue/black flame that destroys everything that cleaves to it from below." This is why she is identified with the Tree of Knowledge of Good and Evil (the Tree of Death) in the Garden of Eden. And yet, we who cleave fully to just that consuming flame are the ones who are "wholly alive today," at this very moment! How is this possible? How can cleaving to the Tree of Death unify us with the Tree of Life? The Zohar answers with another image, an image of "an invisible, concealed light" that encompasses the white and blue/black lights of the candle "like a halo." The Zohar calls this resolution of paradox "a supreme mystery."

The encompassing halo is the light of the Higher Divine Mother (*Imma*), who dwells in unceasing *coniunctio* with the Higher Divine Father (*Abba*), "two lovers who never separate." She holds the opposites of Son and Daughter, of *Zeir Anpin* and *Shekhinah*, within her womb. She represents the all-containing vessel of the fullness of being, which resolves the incompatibility of temporal decay and of going-on-being —by encompassing both in an "invisible, concealed" manner. The Higher Mother is the matrix and womb of being and becoming, and both life and death emerge from her and return to her. The "supreme mystery" of our Zohar text is the concealed, encompassing, unconscious possibility of renewal—of being wholly alive today precisely through the paradox of cleaving via consciousness and deeds (contemplation and action) to the divine consuming fires at the cores of our material lives.

III

To understand our text more fully, we will now turn briefly to the sixteenth century physician/alchemist Paracelsus, an important influence on Jung.[16] According to literary scholar Philip Beitchman, Paracelsus (1493-1541) developed a kind of "vitalist-alchemical-cabalistic medicine" that made use of a kabbalistic "multilevel emphasis on the body, both human and divine . . . . [Both Paracelsus' alchemical] medicine and cabala have in common the fact that the individual, through his hygiene, discipline, and habits, intervenes with and tries to alter a natural course of things."[17] In *Elixir of the Brave (Dulcedo de forte sive Elixir)* (1673, 1675) Johann Christoph Steeb describes a life-enhancing healing elixir of "potable gold" made of "equal portions of Alchemy and Cabala" whose origins go back to Paracelsus.[18] By "vitalism" Beitchman refers to a traditional "concept of soul and body as qualitatively homologous entities, energized by a vital force or entelechy, which can be affected and modified by occult techniques." He sees this traditional view as part of the seventeenth century "resistance to Cartesian Cogito—rationalism and the mind-body dualism it fostered" and as "defending a vision of human integration against the threat of incipient scientific fragmentation and mechanical reduction."[19]

Paracelsus' alchemical-kabbalistic approach to healing led to his elaboration of the very important image (and healing experience) of a *lumen naturae* (natural light) which was present within the material nature of the world and of human beings—and which was as important and valid a source of knowledge as was traditional revelation. The *lumen naturae* is closely related, in my view, to the kabbalistic image of an *or chozer*, a light that "returns" as a reflection from the very end of the kabbalistic ray of creation, from within the materiality of the body and the world, to the highest levels of spiritual potential—to infuse the spiritual realms (otherwise abstract and disembodied) with all the healing vitality of instinct and sensuous reality. Paracelsus may well have developed his notion of the *lumen naturae* from his study of kabbalah. According to a teaching of later Lurianic kabbalah (after Paracelsus), the *or chozer* "reflects up from the bottom of the feet of *Adam Kadmon* [the primordial human imago, the *anthropos* image] at the very center of the creative void, to the soul [*neshamah*] of the world and of human beings (i.e. to the world soul, the alchemical *anima mundi*). From there it illuminates that world soul and all creation with a renewed and strengthened light of embodied vitality and existence."[20]

These images of *alchemical natural light* and *kabbalistic returning reflected light* illuminate our Zohar text. Let's see how the natural light within matter, the reflected light from the heart of matter, sheds light on the matter before us, on our contemplation and meditation on the flaming light ascending from a burning candle.

The blue/black/red light consumes the wick and the wax of the candle—i.e., the all-consuming passage of time and the qualities of our consciousness and deeds eat up our lives, consume our existence until, having thoroughly attached ourselves to the Tree of Death, we die. So things go, unless, as the Zohar puts it, there is an "awakening" from below "to ignite this blue flame to unite with the white flame" above it. For this unifying *coniunctio* of blue flame with white flame to occur, as the *Matok Mi-D'vash* says, "everything depends on the degree of awakening of the lower ones and on their deeds." In other words, the matter depends on us, on our self-work (*sich arbeiten*) in the inner world (our "degree of awakening," our consciousness) and in the outer world (our "deeds," meaning ritual and ethical actions, speech and also directed discursive thought).

How can anyone do such self-work unassisted, even with great yearning and desire, even with fitting intention? If it were up to the ego's heroic intentions alone, the answer would of course be that no one could do this self-work, that life consumes us all, and, as Isaac

Bashevis Singer bitterly wrote at the end of his novel of pre-Holocaust Poland, *The Family Moskat*, that "death is the messiah." But the Zohar, in its symbolic image of a burning candle, reminds us that we are *not* unassisted, for "above the white light dwells an invisible, concealed light that encompasses it like a halo." This encompassing halo represents the "supreme mystery" of the Higher Mother—continuously conjoined with the Higher Father—who embraces and contains, sustains and nourishes and generates new possibilities of life at all times, who reveals the deep rootedness of the so-called Tree of Death in the vastly deeper and broader rhizome of the Tree of Life. She is the one whom the alchemists and kabbalists alike invoke when they preface all their work with the prayer, "God willing."

Our Zohar passage does not reveal the secret of the concealed halo, the glow that surrounds the candle's blue and white flame. All it tells us is that "the very highest wisdoms are hinted at in it!" But we have already alluded to at least one of these very highest wisdoms, and the alchemical/kabbalistic *lumen naturae/or chozer* will help us to get the hint.

The light *within* matter, the natural vitality and feeling *within* our complexes, the consciousness *that we bring* to the opaqueness of repetitive suffering of our complexes, reflects through our self-work, God willing, to the very root of our psyches and to the very soul of the world. This reflected, natural light itself becomes the container (or at least a necessary component of the container), which allows us to enter deeply into the life that consumes us, wears us out and ages us, deeply enough to uncover the deep currents and illuminations of life and renewal within. The alchemical natural light reveals how our ongoing self-work—trying to integrate our blue/black/red light of mundane repetitive living with our white light of vital meaning and endurance—is founded on the concealed presence of an encompassing light, which itself is nourished and fed by that natural reflected light of our very mundane existence. There is nowhere we have to go. All we need is right here. As the great Talmudic sage Hillel said, over a millennium before the Zohar was published, at the Festival of Water Drawing (*Simchat Beit HaShoeivah*) during the fall holiday of Sukkot in Jerusalem: "If '*I*' am here, *everything* is here!" [*Avot d'Rabbi Natan* 12; *TB Sukkot* 53a]

Contemplate, in the kabbalistic workshop, the transformative alchemical flame that ascends from a candle!

NOTES

1. Joan Chodorow, ed. & intro., *Jung on Active Imagination* (Princeton, NJ: Princeton University Press, 1997); Elie Humbert, *C.G. Jung: The Fundamentals of Theory and Practice,* tr. Ronald G. Jalbert (Wilmette, IL: Chiron Publications, 1988); Dan Merkur, *Gnosis: An Esoteric Tradition of Mystical Visions and Unions* (Albany, NY: SUNY Press, 1993).

2. Moshe Idel, *The Mystical Experience in Abraham Abulafia* (Albany, NY: SUNY Press, 1988); *Language, Torah and Hermeneutics in Abraham Abulafia* (Albany, NY: SUNY Press, 1989).

3. Erich Neumann, "The Psyche and the Transformation of the Reality Planes: A Metapsychological Essay," in *The Place of Creation* (Princeton, NJ: Princeton University Press, 1989): 3-62; "The Experience of the Unitary Reality," in *The Place of Creation*, 63–130.

4. Sigmund Hurwitz, "Psychological Aspects in Early Hasidic Literature," in *Timeless Documents of the Soul*, ed. James Hillman (Evanston, IL: Northwestern University Press, 1968), 149–240.

5. Alan Brill, *Thinking God: The Mysticism of Rabbi Zadok of Lublin* (New York: Yeshivah University Press, 2002); Yoram Jacobson, *Hasidic Thought*, tr. Jonathan Chipman (Tel Aviv: MOD Press, 1998).

6. C.G. Jung, "Paracelsus as a Spiritual Phenomenon," in *Alchemical Studies, Collected Works,* 13 (Princeton, NJ: Princeton University Press, 1967/1942).

7. C.G. Jung, *Mysterium Coniunctionis, Collected Works,* 14 (Princeton, NJ: Princeton University Press, 1955-1956). See also Arturo Schwarz, *Kabbalah and Alchemy: An Essay on Common Archetypes* (Northvale, NJ: Jason Aronson, Inc., 2000).

8. See Note 6 above.

9. Shneur Zalman of Liady, *Likkutei Amarim (Tanya)*, Part IV, Chapter 20 (Brooklyn, NY: Kehot Publication Society, 1981).

10. See Note 7 above.

11. Daniel Matt, tr. & commentary, *The Zohar*, Vol. 1, Pritzker Edition (Stanford, CA: Stanford University Press, 2004).

12. Daniel Frisch, *Matok Mi-D'vash Ha-Shalem (Sweeter Than Honey)*, in Hebrew (Jerusalem: Machon Da'at Yoel, 5759/1999).

13. Compare *Shekhinah*'s mythic precursor *Inanna*, in Betty De Shong Meador, *Inanna: Lady of Largest Heart* (Austin, TX: University of Texas Press, 2000).

14. Michael Fordham. I have unfortunately not been able to locate the source of this citation in Fordham's writings.

15. DovBer of Lubavich, *Flames: A Chanukah Discourse from Gates of Radiance* (Brooklyn, NY: Kehot Publication Society, 2002).

16. See Note 6 above.

17. Philip Beitchman, *Alchemy of the Word: Cabala of the Renaissance* (Albany, NY: SUNY Press, 1998), 178.

18. *Ibid.*, 185.

19. *Ibid.*, 153.

20. Paraphrasing Shneur Zalman of Liady, see Note 9 above.

Conflict as Creative Act: Psyche's Knife, *Separatio*, and the Feeling Function

ELIZABETH EOWYN NELSON

Those who are experienced in battle know that any naked blade is a threat, which is why opponents attend with particular solemnity to the unsheathing of their weapons. It is a ritual that signals the beginning of the conflict, no matter what ensues or how the conflict is resolved. The moment the weapon slides out of its sheath, with a metallic rasp, a sustained ring, or in stealthy silence, the blade is in play. An unsheathed weapon is a weapon that the combatant is using.

Do you doubt this? Then imagine, for an uncomfortable moment, that you are unarmed and threatened at the point of a knife. Though the knife has not touched your skin, even now the tip wavers slightly

Elizabeth Eowyn Nelson, Ph.D., has degrees in Economics, Political Science, Literature and Depth Psychology and more than 20 years of business experience as a writer/editor for clients in technology, health, and finance. Currently she is a book coach for aspiring authors, on the full-time faculty at the Art Institute of California and adjunct faculty at Pacifica Graduate Institute, teaching depth psychology, philosophy, story writing, and research methodology. She is the co-author (with Joseph Coppin) of *The Art of Inquiry: A Depth Psychological Perspective*, Spring Publications, 2005.

in your opponent's trembling hand. Adrenaline floods your body, making you simultaneously flushed with heat and chilled to the bone, heightening your awareness of every nuance of emotion and movement. Remaining completely still, barely drawing breath, you shift your gaze from the naked blade to the eyes of your opponent. She too feels a rush of adrenaline that renders this moment eternal. She too looks surprised, afraid, even confused. But until the edge of that weapon turns away—whether or not it draws blood—she is an armed antagonist who is using a knife.

It is in the moment before a blade cuts skin that terror reaches its pitch. Film directors and authors of suspense fiction know this, and draw out the moment as long as possible. But there is an ancient source for this truth, the Legend of Damocles.

According to legend, one day Damocles was overheard speaking in extravagant terms about the happiness of his ruler, Dionysius the Tyrant. Dionysius had a different view. To demonstrate what it genuinely felt like to rule, Dionysius invited Damocles to be the guest of honor at a sumptuous banquet. The tyrant had something special in store for Damocles, and seated him beneath a naked sword that was suspended from the ceiling by a single thread. Damocles survived the meal, though he may not have enjoyed the food much, and we can conjecture that he learned an important lesson. The fortunes of men who hold power are as precarious as the predicament in which Damocles found himself. Thus in the Legend of Damocles, the threat of the sword was the use of the sword. The thin thread by which the blade hung over Damocles' head merely enhanced its potency.

I now invite your attention to another legendary blade, used but not blooded, that no one speaks of. In fact, this blade has been almost entirely forgotten for the last 2,000 years, as ignored as the Sword of Damocles is infamous. This blade figures in a tale that has compelled the attention of an entire age, carrying deep symbolic meaning for millions of people, for one clear reason. It is the *only* story we have about the soul. So while it has been read, enjoyed, analyzed, discussed and represented in gorgeous artwork for the last two millennia, there is one part of the story that no one wants to tell: the role of the knife. This knife belongs to a beautiful, vulnerable and loving young woman named Psyche. Her enemy, and her beloved, is Eros. Their story is *Eros and Psyche.*

THE TALE OF EROS AND PSYCHE

In *Eros and Psyche*, Psyche is a mortal woman whose fate is inextricably bound with a god. At a pivotal moment she confronts Eros, committing the transgression that shapes the remainder of the narrative. Without that transgression we would have no story and no Psyche; she would remain a compliant female trapped in a stultifying relationship. Yet the conflict between the lovers can only occur after Psyche begins to imagine the darker possibilities her sisters suggest: that Psyche has fulfilled the prophesied "wedlock dread" and is sleeping with a monster.[1] This possibility allows Psyche to extract herself from an unconscious participation with Eros and take action as an individual against him. For Psyche, separation and confrontation are essential to knowing herself, what she values, and where she stands.

Because *Eros and Psyche* is a story about the soul, not a definition of soul, it is possible to enter the drama and discover how we, like Psyche, are guided and tortured by what we love, lose, and search for without end. We notice which characters fascinate us and who is repellant. If we are alert, we may observe what we dismiss as irrelevant. What aspects of the tale do we simply neglect? I mention this question of neglect because I made a surprising discovery about *Eros and Psyche*. The moment of confrontation between the lovers is stark and dramatic, easily the high point of the first act. All readers easily recall Psyche with a lamp in her hand beholding the beauty of Eros for the first time; almost none recollect the knife. Anthologized versions of the tale[2] for the general reader prominently feature the lamp and scarcely mention the knife. Scholarly studies of the tale[3] explore the symbolism of the lamp in great detail and either dismiss the knife in a few sentences or don't even mention it. Even for experts of myth and symbol, Psyche's knife barely exists. Many of them, I discovered, neglect Psyche's knife because "it was never used." True, the knife is not blooded, but it is unsheathed and in play. Or they ignore Psyche's knife because "it belongs to her sisters." Yes, Psyche's sisters do suggest the motive and the plan to kill the monster, but they leave Psyche alone to decide what to do. It is only after she spends an agonizing day by herself trying to make up her *own* mind that she acts. Psyche alone prepares the lamp, sharpens the knife, and hides them in the bedchamber.

Psyche alone confronts her lover in the dark of night, and discovers the god of love.

Depth psychologists are trained to be acutely aware of what someone forgets or dismisses. In dream analysis, for example, it is often the so-called inconsequential, unimportant, and overlooked element that releases surprisingly profound meanings.[4] I propose two powerful reasons for our collective neglect of Psyche's knife. First, we can imagine a trusting girl holding a lamp to gaze upon her lover, but we recoil from the image of that same girl holding a razor-sharp knife. Not only is knife itself a psychoactive image, knife in the hand of a young woman is even more so: both repugnant and fascinating. Picturing Psyche with a lamp upholds the conventional view of the female as curious, even interfering, but not prepared and powerful. Second, the idea of Psyche wielding the knife disturbs the assumption that the soul is tender and vulnerable without a shred of ruthlessness, autonomy, or purpose. But as *Eros and Psyche* dramatizes, the soul obeys its own inexorable drive toward wholeness with or without the ego's consent.

Digging through Art and Artifacts to Find Psyche's Knife

Just as readers of *Eros and Psyche* forget Psyche's knife, it rarely is represented in paintings or sculptures that depict the two lovers. For example, Canova's marble "Amour et Psyche" at the Musee de l'Ermitage in Saint Petersburg emphasizes the tenderness of the lovers. Another of his marbles, housed in the Louvre, does also. "Cupid and Psyche," by the 19th-century German sculptor Begas, is exceptional.[5] It depicts Psyche bending over the reclining form of Eros, before the god has awakened. She holds the lamp in her left hand and the knife in her right. However, even in this sculpture, Psyche's knife is not the deadly weapon the text describes. It is small and delicate, scarcely larger than Psyche's hand. In another rare illustration of Psyche with both lamp and knife, the weapon is full-sized but cleverly minimized in another way.[6] The reader has to look very closely at the illustration to see the knife at all, since it is hidden within the folds of Psyche's gown.

In the unusual event that Psyche's knife does appear in works of art, it is typically rendered insignificant. But what can we know about the knife Psyche might have used? We have already noted that it is double-edged and razor sharp. For this reason it would more properly be considered a dagger or sheath knife.[7] In a survey of the Bronze Age knives, daggers, and swords housed in the British Museum—the age closest to the time *Eros and Psyche* originated—*every* weapon identified as a dagger had two sharp edges. Moreover, these weapons are far too large to be easily concealed. Two artifacts tell us why. A Mycenean bronze dagger from around 1100 BCE (GR1868.1-10.342) measures approximately 14 inches from pommel to tip and a central Italian dagger from the same period (PRB 1922.11-10.1) measures a full 17 inches. Though this may seem quite large, experts who specialize in classifying weapons point out that any knife longer than 7 inches but shorter than 22 inches is properly considered a dagger. Greek daggers of the period were typically slight and shaped like stilettos, whereas Roman daggers had thick, V-shaped blades and an average length of approximately 16.6 inches.[8] To put this in a human scale, imagine a weapon that extends from the tips of your outstretched fingers to the crook of your elbow with a blade as wide as your wrist.

The only small daggers in the British Museum's collection—similar in size to Psyche's knife depicted in artwork—are not weapons at all. They are votive artifacts from Sardinia (ca 1000 BCE, GR 1856.12 - 23.664 and GR 1974.12 - 1.5) used solely in ritual. Dramatic logic persuades us that Psyche, warned that she may find a monster in her bed, would not approach the sleeper with a votive object. Nor would a votive object need to be sharpened in preparation for the confrontation. She would arm herself with a dagger, which could easily be 16 or 17 inches in length or longer. Thus the combined evidence of historical research, archeological findings, and the logic of the narrative all suggest that Psyche's knife is not a small, dainty implement. It is a sizeable and potent weapon, honed until it is razor-sharp and ready to kill. This is the image we should bear in mind as we reconsider the soul engaged in agon.

The Symbolism of Psyche's Knife

What of the knife's symbolic significance? For millennia, knives and swords have symbolized the discriminating mind or *logos*. This rational capacity includes differentiating one thing from another, focusing attention, discovering structure within chaos, and choosing.[9]

The principal tool of the discriminating mind is language; *Logos* is often translated as "the word." In Western culture, knives and swords have been associated with the discriminating word but, most particularly, with the destroying word, such as the sword emerging from the mouth of Christ in Revelation 19:10.[10] For most people the words *separating* and *discriminating* have negative associations. Perhaps this explains why authors and speakers frequently lump together separating and prioritizing. There is little thought given to the fact that establishing difference does not automatically establish hierarchy. Many kinds of relationship between separated things are possible. Dividing is not always the prelude to conquering.

This brings us to the alchemical process of *separatio*, which, like the logos, also is symbolized by knives, daggers, swords, and cutting implements of all kind.[11] In the context of alchemy, *separatio* is part of a complex transformational process that is fundamentally creative. Jung likened the elusive goal of producing the Philosophers' Stone with the realization of the Self, a psychological journey toward wholeness. And it is in the context of alchemy that the symbolism of Psyche's knife is fully realized. Psyche's knife is an image of the human capacity to differentiate, focus, prioritize, and choose. Since this is the soul's knife, however, it partakes of the qualities we associate to soul, which include warmth, depth, mystery, feeling, and attachment. When we take up Psyche's knife as Psyche did, we make choices with our vulnerable, emotional bodies and not simply with cool, unfeeling intellect. Such decisions are heart wrenching and gut wrenching—as any genuine psychological process is. Little wonder that our pace in such times is slow rather than brisk, we feel confused long before we are clear, and even clarity is evanescent. We don't walk away clean, quick, and easy and alchemy tells us why. *Separatio* is just one of many stages in an ongoing dynamic work of creation—contained in the vessel we call a life—and we live with the consequences of our choices and every choice thereafter.

There is a remarkable precedent for Psyche's knife in the works of the philosopher Philo Judaeus. In an account of creation, Philo speaks of a Logos-Cutter which joins the opposing principles of unity and division. "The Logos was the glue as well as the Cutter; that is, it was the principle of cohesion which made the universe a unit in spite of its manifold divisions."[12] The Logos-Cutter symbolizes the division of the One into its many parts, an idea we see prominently in Western philosophical and religious traditions. Creation myths, for example, consistently provide us with images of separation in service to formation. By following the Orphic maxim *as above, so below*, it is apparent creation occurs at the macrocosmic level (formation of world) and at the microcosmic level (formation of person). As Edinger puts it, "every newly encountered area of the unconscious requires a cosmogonic act of *separatio*."[13] The sharp edge of the knife makes it possible to emerge out of unconscious participation into mature psychological relationship in which we fully perceive the ontology and autonomy of the other. This is true for Psyche; it is equally true for us. Like the Logos-Cutter, Psyche's knife separates within the context of union and destroys in order to create.

Separatio, the Feeling Function, and Identity

Psyche's knife, a symbol of alchemical *separatio*, is closely linked to the feeling function.[14] Like thinking, the other rational function, feeling requires conscious deliberation. In using the feeling function we relate to rather than repress our passions and intuitions and emotions, making heartfelt judgments about the big questions of life. We decide what is alive and worth nurturing in our lives and what is dying and must be let go. The feeling function is so essential that its absence can lead to a grave crisis of identity. The historian Charles Taylor describes this as "an acute form of disorientation, which people often express in terms of not knowing who they are, but which can also be seen as a radical uncertainty of where they stand." As a result, individuals have no "frame or horizon within which things can take on a stable significance, within which some life possibilities can be seen as good or meaningful, others as bad or trivial."[15] To separate the worthwhile from the trivial brings our values into sharp relief so we can know that the ground we stand on is authentically ours. In fact, the dynamic exercise of the feeling function—which is akin to wielding Psyche's knife—fosters meaningful inquiry. Are my values hand-me-downs that I have been taught? Are they embodied in a belief system I unquestioningly have accepted? Or are they values I have weighed in an ongoing dialogue with myself, my community, and my tradition?

Such inquiry goes to the heart of personal identity, as Taylor rightly points out. It also goes to the heart of cultural identity. America's culture war, so prominent in the media in the last 6 years, exemplifies this agon. We are not soaking battlefields with our blood, but we are embroiled in a profound struggle that involves much more than cool, rational logos. This struggle demands the skillful use of Psyche's knife because it cuts to the core, where soul dwells. Neglecting the feeling function is directly related to the malaise of modern and post-modern identity. Rollo May called it "the hollow man."[16] Philip Cushman called it "the empty self."[17] We will see how Psyche's knife reverberates within this hollow, empty self, revealing the associations between *separatio*, the feeling function, and the agon of soul-making as persons and as a society. I will return to this theme later.

Reading Eros and Psyche as a *Separatio* Dream

Eros and Psyche is a collective dream, a text that artists, writers, philosophers, historians, and psychologists have read, analyzed, and rendered in poetry, painting, and sculpture for two millennia. Moreover it is a dream that we have unintentionally misread because we dismiss the apparently inconvenient fact that Psyche confronts Eros with a lamp *and* a knife. When we remember the knife, Psyche's journey reveals itself as a persistent process of sorting, separating and extracting beginning with her use of the lamp and knife and continuing through the four tasks imposed by Aphrodite. We can read the entire story as the development of Psyche's ability to discern and discriminate. Here is a summary of *Eros and Psyche* viewed through the archetypal perspective of knife.

Psyche is the third daughter of a king and queen, yet the community believes Psyche is a fresh incarnation of Aphrodite. Ironically, this failure of *separatio*—confusing girl and goddess—sets the story in motion. Psyche is abducted (extracted) from her community and sequestered in a beautiful palace at the behest of Eros, who has fallen in love with her. (*Extractio* is a variant of alchemical *separatio* and appears again later in the story.) In many ways the abduction is the dreadful fate that the oracle foretold: Psyche is forced to surrender her former life and is deprived of all human contact. Though she eagerly anticipates Eros's nightly visits, the marriage remains a sham of intimacy amounting to no more than long hours in a luxurious prison interrupted by nocturnal visits from a male who refuses to be seen or fully known. The only visible, tangible human contacts for Psyche are two visits with her curious and maleficent sisters. By comparison with the invisible companions of her perfect existence, Psyche's sisters are particularly horrible. But they are real, whole human beings, and Psyche is pining for this kind of companionship—so much so that she hangs on the sisters' every word, indiscriminately adopting their beliefs as her own. Psyche is genuinely ignorant of her sisters' true feelings and motivations, but is she foolishly credulous? *Should* she have known better? It is difficult to say. The story does not tell us that she had any reason to doubt the sisters before this. Psyche's relationship with her sisters demonstrates the cost of deprivation. Denied all human contact, Psyche naïvely accepts whatever crumbs of attention she gets. Her isolation makes her hungry for ordinary human connection regardless of how dangerous it is. It also diminishes her ability to evaluate potential danger. Psyche has long hours by herself but no one to help her reflect on her situation. She cannot discriminate the kindness of her sisters from their cruelty. She also cannot discriminate the objective truths the sisters discuss (the oracle foretold Psyche's marriage to a monster) from the conclusions they draw about that truth (Psyche has never seen her husband; ergo he must be a monster). This is another failure of *separatio* in the story and this time, it is Psyche's failure.

Psyche is afraid and uncertain, but carries out the first part of her sisters' plan without hesitation. At this point in the story, readers become distinctly aware that the lamp and knife are not merely passive tools in the hands of active human beings. They are fully autonomous *dramatis personae* in their own right. "At the sight of [Eros], the light of the lamp burned more brightly and the knife dulled its edge in shame."[18] As Psyche beholds the exquisite beauty of her lover for the first time and realizes that she had intended to kill him, she attempts to turn the knife on herself. The knife prevents it. It is particularly ironic that Psyche's knife, a potentially lethal weapon, ensures that Eros and the erotic relationship between Eros and Psyche does not die. At the dramatic moment of confrontation life prevails, not death.[19] Psyche, irresistibly drawn to Eros' quiver of arrows, tests one of the points with a trembling hand and accidentally wounds herself, falling in love with the god of Love. Symbolically this tells us that injuries we sustain in conflict unite us with our adversary; *separatio* calls forth its complementary alchemical process, *coniunctio*. Many examples drawn from life also show this paradoxical juxtaposition of separation and union, agony and intimacy. Battle is frequently described as heated or passionate; opponents wrestling with one another can resemble partners in the throes of sexual ecstasy; in *Eros and Psyche*, the lovers confront each other but by no means are finished with each other. Though they soon separate and follow different paths, their journey has just begun.

Like the first part of the tale, in which Psyche's family abandons her to wedlock dread, the second part also ends in abandonment. Eros flies away from Psyche, injured and angry that she broke the taboo. Psyche tries to cling to him as he rises above her, making "a pitiable appendage" as he soars aloft before she finally slips, exhausted, down to earth.[20] This moment makes her vulnerable mortality and his arrogant divinity very apparent. Psyche must live with the consequences of her actions. In light of the story as a whole, we can see that the relationship Psyche destroyed is a relationship that needed to end, yet Psyche, a suffering human, does not have our omniscient vantage. She is a paltry human being, as we all are in such moments, overwhelmed with feelings of loss and regret. It is not easy to distinguish what is rotten from what is still good and bravely consent to let go when it is time. Like Psyche, we often cling to the last vestiges of what is dying or dead, and only exhaustion compels us to release our hold.

Psyche's despair after Eros abandons her is so intense that she again tries to commit suicide, but the god Pan tenderly intervenes and tells the grieving girl to seek Eros. She chooses to live, letting her sorrow and despair become an ordeal of faith that will utterly transform her. After making this decision, Psyche begins searching for Eros. Her first important gesture occurs before her encounter with Aphrodite and the often-analyzed trial of four impossible tasks. She accidentally discovers two temples in disarray and spends time restoring them to order. Though she does not know which god she is serving, Psyche possesses the humility needed to serve the divine in all its forms. Her challenge at this point in the story is to seek a particular god because though all powers must be served, not all powers are alike. Psyche intuits this. She demonstrates her power of discrimination—symbolically using the knife—at a key moment. When she asks for sanctuary from Demeter and Hera and the goddesses turn her down for fear of angering Aphrodite, Psyche does not ask why. She realizes she must face her most implacable enemy, symbolically placing love's wound at love's altar. The four tasks Aphrodite imposes on Psyche, though they are quite different, exemplify *separatio* or a variant of it called *extractio*. She completes the first three with helpers who take pity on the sorrowful Psyche. But each is a kind of preparation for the final one, a harrowing journey into the underworld that Psyche must complete alone.

Psyche's first task is to sort a heap of mixed seeds into separate piles by morning. At the moment she is most desperate, assistance arrives in the form of tiny ants, creatures known for their discipline and patience, who take pity on Psyche. Their timely help suggests that when the soul feels overwhelmed and confused, discipline and patience are needed to create order out of the chaos. Psyche's second task is to gather golden fleece from the rams of the sun, fierce and dangerous animals likely to kill anyone who wanders too near. A green reed whispers to Psyche that there is another way to collect the fleece. Instead of approaching the rams directly, in broad daylight, Psyche should wait until the evening when the rams have passed through a grove. There, some of their fleece will catch on the low-hanging branches and Psyche can safely extract the fleece from these. The second task teaches Psyche the delicate and subtle process of *extractio*. She learns to gather the small amount of the fleece she needs and no more. Rather than doing this directly, an element from nature helps her. Psyche's third task is specifically designed to test Psyche's bravery and circumspection. Like the second task, it is also a lesson in *extractio*. Aphrodite hands her a small jug and tells her to collect icy water from the highest point of the fast-flowing river Styx, a river whose waters are even fearful to the gods. As before, Psyche cannot use a direct approach, but once again she doesn't need to. The royal bird of Zeus, the eagle, flies to her assistance. It grasps the jug in its talons and deftly swoops down and fills it with water, then delivers the jug to Psyche.

Psyche's fourth task is more involved and difficult. Like the second and third tasks, it is a lesson in *extractio*, since Aphrodite tells Psyche to descend into the underworld to collect a small amount of a beauty ointment from the dread goddess Persephone. To make this solo journey, Psyche must walk a specific path, turning away from anyone or anything that might tempt her to pause, hesitate, turn back, or wander. And she must learn to choose when, where, and to whom to give the precious resources she brings with her into the underworld, two coins and two barley cakes. Each choice has important consequences. The wrong choice or a faltering commitment means death. The fourth task as an extension of the training she has thus far received because she must not only discriminate one thing from another, she must know that in the act of discriminating, some things are ignored, others are appeased, and still others are left behind. To select one path is not to select others. *Separatio* used in the service of a tangible goal requires choice and sacrifice.

The meaning of Psyche's last task and segue into the ending of the story are hotly debated. Some find the narrative satisfying, some don't. I personally find it unbearably sad. When Psyche does reflect for a moment on her travails, she is primarily concerned with their affect on her appearance. She doesn't notice how she has demonstrated love, courage, faithfulness, endurance, or any number of other exemplary qualities that constitute enduring beauty. She is afraid she has grown ugly, and will only please her "beautiful lover" if she uses some of Persephone's cosmetic.[21] Psyche cannot distinguish between internal beauty and external beauty, nor can she distinguish between what belongs to humanity and what belongs to the gods. Finally, Psyche cannot distinguish among the kinds of beauty conferred by each deity: Aphrodite's beauty is different from Artemis', which is different still from the beauty of an Apollo, Hera, Hecate, or Dionysius. Psyche fails to anticipate the effects of a chthonic cosmetic that is unique to Persephone's realm and falls into a death-like sleep when she opens the box. Thus she survives the journey to the underworld but not the return. As readers of *Eros and Psyche*, we do not know whether Psyche ever learns the difference between internal and external beauty or whether she learns any other lessons. Her swoon sets into motion the train of events in which Psyche is removed from the human world, deified on Mount Olympus, and wed to Eros in a lawful, eternal union.[22] This is, ironically, the final act of *extractio* (*separatio*) in the myth. Psyche is plucked from earth and assumed into the Greek pantheon.

Psyche's inability to complete the final task suggests that she has learned little about *separatio* and wields the knife inconsistently at best. The plot is resolved through an act of god; indeed, through the actions of two gods, Eros and Zeus. In the end, one wonders, doesn't it all come down to the fact that a powerful male ends up rescuing the helpless female once again? Perhaps; Psyche does appear to be a bit of a ninny who caves in at the least whiff of a challenge. Isn't *Eros and Psyche* yet another story that follows the same tedious plot—boy meets girl, boy loses girl, boy rescues girl—reinforcing the same tedious stereotypes? Again, perhaps; for the literal reader, the myth illustrates male-female power dynamics and throws in a few other stock characters such as the vindictive, jealous sisters and evil mother-in-law for good measure. The piece of her story we most need—an answer to the question "how does the soul return from the underworld?"—is the one we don't have. Or do we?

Separatio, Individuation, and Awakening Eros

Psyche's failure to complete the fourth task informs us that learning to separate and choose is an ongoing practice. Once we have taken up Psyche's knife as a symbol of this power, we have commenced the task of becoming conscious through finer and finer discrimination, recognizing what is ours and what is not. The rest has to be left alone.[23] Psyche's challenge is the same one that confronts us all. At some point we must decide between two paths: remaining a *puer aeternus*, the perpetual child, or becoming a substantial individual, unique and irreplaceable. The *puer* is unwilling to relinquish a world of possibilities, which is no genuine existence at all. The individual is one who has sacrificed the *puer* dream of being all things to become something more humbling but infinitely more valuable: a "real fragment."[24] Such individuals commit to a course of action, endure the chaos of feelings this choice brings about, and endure the unforeseeable consequences of their choices. Paradoxically, it is only by becoming a real fragment that we can relate to the eternal whole. Jung says "in knowing ourselves to be unique in our personal combination—that is, ultimately limited—we possess also the capacity for becoming conscious of the infinite. But only then!"[25]

Psyche has this knowledge and this capacity. She sacrifices the unreality of the original relationship with Eros to play a real part in her own story. *Separatio* as a soul task is the exercise of essential discrimination in the context of eros. We struggle to become ourselves, a real fragment instead of a potential whole, without denying what is gained and lost with every choice. Living this tension between real fragment and potential whole is *the* fine art of life, "the most distinguished and rarest of all the arts," according to Jung. "Who ever succeeded in draining the whole cup with grace?"[26] No one; soul making is never complete and never without the fundamental conflict inherent in the creative act.

The scope of Psyche's journey was clearly shaped by the goddess Aphrodite and her son-lover Eros. They are reminiscent of many goddess and son pairs that appear in traditions predating *Eros and Psyche*, which anchors this tale within an ancient tradition. Partly for this reason, it is my thesis that Psyche's real guide is the cosmogonic Eros, the original, primordial force of love and desire who helped engender the cosmos. The cosmogonic Eros is an androgynous being, a unity of the masculine and the feminine symbolizing wholeness, who is neither the terrifying witch-like Aphrodite of this myth nor her childish son-lover. This Eros tortures, guides, challenges, and loves the soul. It awakens Psyche at the perilous edge of the underworld, ensuring the completion of the journey. Moreover, it is this archetypal power that awakens *in* Psyche and refuses to fall back into the death-like sleep of unconsciousness. Psyche's own eros is Psyche's best ally, and has been every step of the way. Psyche's knife is an eros-blade—cutting things together—like the Logos-Cutter of cosmic creation.

Even in agonizing confrontation, the soul's fate is always erotic in the largest sense of that word: dynamic, fluid, and relational. Sometimes eros flows towards another person, or our work, a cause, an object or a place. We feel a tug of longing and desire or a sudden infusion of warmth and contentment. At other times, the flow of eros is inhibited or stuck. Then we feel coolness or melancholy, numb or still or blue. Our task, observes Hillman, is to trust that the movements of eros in our lives are meaningful and right. This is the way to live authentically.[27] If we accept this obligation, we become like Psyche, but it is not a path for cowards. Erotic, soulful life offers alternating periods of peace and conflict, contentment and despair, because it asks us to live the two questions that Psyche faces: "What do I love?" "What must I do on behalf of that love?" These questions stretch the soul and give substance to character. Like Psyche, we must reach within ourselves to decide and then reach beyond ourselves to act, committing our whole life to the adventure.

Consumerism and Character

We do not only reach within for answers; we reach out, too. It is possibly the great myth of individualism that our search for purpose, values, and identity is solipsistic. Philip Cushman says that individualism, an "implicit strategy" that "locates supreme power and agency within the individual," produces the empty self.[28] This strategy fosters the belief that authentic individuals must navigate moral terrain on their own just as we attribute confusion, depression and anxiety to personal brain chemistry and not to culture. Cushman's empty self is reminiscent of the "hollow man" described 50 years ago by Rollo May.[29] Both serve a larger socioeconomic purpose: America's consumer economy depends on filling the emptiness. However much we may be tempted to think of this consumption merely in material terms, it is more than this. We can and do mindlessly consume fast food, video games, trendy clothes, household goods, celebrity trivia, sitcoms, and cell phones. We also consume opinions and beliefs, swallowing them whole without question or criticism. What deserves our attention is the habit of mindless consumption—regardless of the consumable.

I suspect that America's culture war, at bottom, arises from the uneasy feeling that too many people on either side of the divide mindlessly consume an ideology. The blue people think the red people are obsessed with the Christian god; the red people think the blue people are hardened secularists determined to destroy the moral backbone of our nation. *New York Times* columnist Sean Wilentz would argue that red people, that is, the surprisingly strong and resilient Conservative movement in America, would give blue people even less credit than that. The problem with blue people isn't that they are hardened secularists; they have no shape, substance, or spine at all. "Modern conservatism rests on the proposition that Democrats and liberals thrive on a huge, wasteful federal bureaucracy that discourages individual initiative and lavishes public money on the liberals' shiftless political base."[30] One of the common self-criticisms that continually hits home among blue people is precisely this shiftlessness.

I am a blue person and grudgingly I admire what many red people seem to have in great abundance: the willingness to speak on behalf of a tradition and recognize the community that grounds their individual identity. I don't trust the shiftless, which includes people who do not acknowledge a tradition or community. But *having* a tradition is not the same thing as *struggling* with a tradition. Having a tradition veers too closely to mindless consumption, an easy antidote for the hollow empty self in search of certainty. I suspect such people of being like Psyche before she takes up the knife: naïve, ignorant, and untested in the agon of soul-making. A recent article by Howard Fineman in *Newsweek* suggests that I'm not alone. Political strategists "have concluded that any expression of Judeo-Christian devotion, *if seen as genuine*, can reassure culturally traditional voters."[31] It is my belief that genuine humanistic values, Judeo-Christian or not, reassure voters regardless on which side of the cultural divide they see themselves. Genuine values are those we agonize over, not beliefs a person has merely consumed and regurgitated on demand. That is akin to bulimia, a life-threatening eating disorder in which a person digests nothing. Only this is mental bulimia, another life-threatening disease in which character is undernourished and ultimately wastes away, producing a semblance of a self, hollow and empty. We recognize such people. They haven't the substance to be authentic leaders, though they can fool some of the people some of the time.

Can a fast-paced consumer culture support the slow, deliberate pace of thoughtful reflection and in-depth dialogue that produces genuine values? Do we have Psyche's dedication and perseverance no matter what we must endure? I wonder. In the Philosophy and Depth Psychology courses I teach, I ask my undergraduates to *become* philosophers—deep explorers of the psyche—three hours a week. "Question everything," I tell them: the course material, themselves, their beliefs, the culture, and me. When they confess feelings of confusion or disorientation, I tell them "that's great; I'm doing my job." It's my hope that they will take the habit of reflection, inquiry, and struggle with them, carving out of the unconscious meaningful values in the ongoing agon of soul making. I know I'm bringing Psyche's knife into the classroom; it belongs there.

NOTES

1. Apuleius, *The Golden Ass,* trans. P. Walsh (Oxford: Oxford University Press, 1994), 78.

2. See Edith Hamilton, *Mythology* (Boston: Little, Brown and Company, 1942) and P. Monaghan, *The Book of Goddesses and Heroines,* revised ed. (St. Paul, Minnesota: Llewellyn Publications, 1990).

3. See Giselle Labouvie-Vief, *Psyche and Eros* (Cambridge: Cambridge University Press, 1994), Erich Neumann, *Amor and Psyche,* trans. R. Manheim (Princeton: Bollingen, 1956/1971), and Marie-Louis von Franz, *The Golden Ass of Apuleius: The Liberation of the Feminine in Man,* rev. ed. (London: Shambhala, 1980).

4. Freud formalized this idea nearly a century ago in his theory of displacement. See Sigmund Freud, *Introductory Lectures on Psychoanalysis* (New York: W.W. Norton & Co, 1917/1966), 214.

5. J. Williams, *Sex, Portraits of Passion* (New York: The Ivy Press Limited, 1999), 208.

6. A. Murray, *Murray's Manual of Mythology* (New York: Tudor Publishing Company, 1935), 191.

7. G. Stone, *A glossary of the construction, decoration and use of arms and armour in all countries and in all times* (Mineola, NY: Dover Publications, 1999), 198.

8. E. Thompson, *Daggers and Bayonets in History* (Staplehurst, Kent: Spellmount, Ltd., 1999), 14, xii.

9. See C.G. Jung, *Aion,* second edition, *CW* 9 pt. II, Bollingen Series XX (Princeton: Princeton University Press, 1959/1978), 14 and Edward Whitmont, *The Symbolic Quest,* rev. ed. (Princeton: Princeton University Press, 1991), 181.

10. H. Wansborough, (ed.), *The New Jerusalem Bible* (New York: Doubleday, 1990).

11. Edward Edinger, *Anatomy of the Psyche* (Chicago: Open Court, 1985), 191.

12. *Ibid.*, 189.

13. *Ibid.*, 189.

14. C.G. Jung, *Psychological Types, CW* 6, Bollingen Series XX (Princeton: Princeton University Press, 1923/1990).

15. Charles Taylor, *Sources of the Self* (Cambridge: Harvard University Press, 1989), 28.

16. Rollo May, *Man's Search for Himself* (New York: W.W. Norton & Co., 1953).

17. Philip Cushman, *Constructing the Self, Constructing America* (New York: Addison-Wesley, 1996).

18. Diane Wolkstein, *The First Love Stories* (New York: HarperPerennial, 1994), 128.

19. There is one notable exception: the death of Psyche's sisters who rush headlong to the mountaintop for a rendezvous with Eros. Based on Psyche's lie, they expect that he will carry them away safely to a paradise like the one their sister enjoyed. They end up vaulting into empty space rather than the arms of a divine lover, and fall to their deaths, bodies broken by the sharp rocks below.

20. Apuleius, 93-94.

21. Apuleius, 111.

22. Apuleius, 113.

23. Marie-Louis von Franz, *The Golden Ass of Apuleius: The Liberation of the Feminine in Man*, rev. ed. (London: Shambhala, 1980), 256.

24. Edward Edinger, *Ego and Archetype* (Boston: Shambhala, 1992), 14.

25. C.G. Jung, *Memories, Dreams, Reflections* (New York: Vintage Books, 1961/1989), 325.

26. C.G. Jung, *The Stages of Life*, in R. F. C. Hull (trans.), *The Collected Works of C. G. Jung*, Vol. 8 (Princeton, NJ: Princeton University Press, 1930/1981), 400-401.

27. James Hillman, *The Myth of Analysis: Three Essays in Archetypal Psychology* (Evanston, IL: Northwestern University Press, 1972), 80-82.

28. Cushman, 378.

29. Rollo May, *supra*.

30. Sean Wilentz, "The way we live now: Bush's ancestors," in *New York Times*, October 16, 2005. Available online: select.nytimes.com/search/restricted/article?res=F60E13FC3D5B0C758DDDA90994DD404482.

31. H. Fineman, "A faith-based initiative: what the democrats can learn from Kaine's Virginia victory," in *Newsweek*. New York: Newsweek, Inc. November 21, 2005: 37; emphasis added.

FILM REVIEWS

CAPOTE. Philip Seymour Hoffman, Catherine Keener, Chris Copper, Clifton Collins, Jr. Written by Dan Futterman, based on the biography, *Capote*, by Gerald Clark.[1] Directed by Bennett Miller.

REVIEWED BY GLEN SLATER

When *Capote* opens, somewhere in the Midwest, the screen fills with crooked lines cutting through a wheat field. Shortly thereafter we see an impeccably groomed Truman Capote (Philip Seymour Hoffman) take scissors and cut straight lines a little too precisely around a one-column article that appears in *The New York Times*: "Wealthy Farmer, 3 of Family Slain." Both images foreshadow the story about to unfold.

The Clutter family had been found dead the previous day—November 15, 1959—just outside the small town of Holcomb, Kansas. The discovery sent shock waves through the heartland. The manner in

Glen Slater, Ph.D., is a core faculty member at Pacifica Graduate Institute where he teaches in the departments of Mythological Studies and Depth Psychology. He has written articles for various psychology publications including *Spring Journal* and film reviews for Zion's Herald. He recently edited and introduced Volume 3 of the *Uniform Edition* of James Hillman's writings.

Editor's Note: We are very pleased to announce that Glen Slater is the new Film Review Editor of *Spring Journal.*

which Truman Capote removes the article is multivalent: It introduces the dark event at the center of the story while simultaneously conveying an obsessive personal style and sounding the siren call that will alter the course of his life. The short scene exemplifies the taut economy of this film, which consistently manages to neatly fold its thematic layers behind crisp dialogue and stark visuals. The structure of the story is equally elegant. Whereas many screen biographies trace a large horizon of life events and produce poor insight into their subject, this work explores the life of Truman Capote through the episode surrounding these murders, creating a tight vessel in which to cook his character and release its essence. Based upon the expansive biography by Gerald Clarke, the film tracks the six-year period in which the writer-screenwriter researched, wrote and finally published his masterpiece and last book, *In Cold Blood.* It moves with deliberation toward Truman's relationship with one of the two Holcomb killers, Perry Smith. And while the killings themselves draw out the writer's instinct for a story, the killer draws out the dark abyss that exists beneath the glossy outer shell of Truman's psyche, gradually revealing how two outwardly different men share a home in the underworld.

Capote had been writing for *The New Yorker.* With the support of his editors, he boards a train for Kansas with childhood friend and now enlisted research assistant, Nelle Harper Lee (Catherine Keener). She had recently completed her first and only novel, *To Kill a Mockingbird*, but at that point it had yet to be published. As Truman enters the carriage compartment, the black porter gives high praise for his books. Nelle accuses Truman of paying for the tribute. "How did you know?" asks an amused Truman, enjoying the familiarity between them. Nelle sees right through Truman, but her life-long knowing tolerates his immediately apparent grandiosity—a grandiosity that appears so essential and natural it seems to emanate from the pores of his skin. She understands what lies behind the charm, which he uses to adroitly maneuver his way into the lives of New York socialites, small town Kansans and hardened criminals alike. Nelle both underscores and compensates for what emerges as Capote's missing moral compass and lack of any real empathy for those he encounters. Her presence allows the audience to navigate the film's shadows and feel assured that conscience exists somewhere in the picture. Mostly this is accomplished through knowing glances and pregnant silences, until at the end of the film she must confront Truman with the depth of his exploitation.

Once he starts work on *In Cold Blood*, Truman tells his editor, "it could be a kind of masterpiece . . . Sometimes when I think how good it could be, I can hardly breathe." Though prone to this kind of artistic indulgence, Truman also sees the more universal significance of the murders. At one point he says: "Two worlds exist in this country; the quiet conservative life and the lives of these two men—the underbelly, the criminally violent. Those two worlds converged that bloody night." But Truman's insight is always intellectual and cold; his feeling comes across as largely feigned. The more emotional impact of this convergence of worlds is left to characters like lead investigator Alvin Dewey (Chris Cooper), who is devastated by the murders yet goes about his work with a fitting Midwestern stoicism. Truman consistently turns this kind of emotional vulnerability into an opportunity for information. He exploits Perry Smith's recessed feeling life in the same manner, orchestrating legal assistance and offering friendship in order to elicit an account of the killings that would become the pivot of his book. Though there is never any question that Perry's capacity for outer violence far exceeds the dark tendencies in Truman's psyche, we are left sensing their respective inclinations to use others for their own gain share common ground. Peeling off the layers of Truman's wit and genius, we gradually discover his capacity to destroy emotional life—a form of soul-murder.

The core of the story risks overexposure when Capote shares a rare moment of honest self-insight with Nelle after she visits with Truman in Spain. Referring to Perry, he says, "I feel like we grew up in the same house, and one day he stood up and walked out the back door, and I walked out the front." The scene works, I think, because it shows the degree to which Truman sees his interior landscape and yet remains emotionally incapable of understanding its role in his thoughts and actions. Truman is not unaware of the trauma of his own childhood, but the film shows him using his past to manipulate rather than empathize. Towards the end we see Truman's underlying identification with Perry appear in a more subtle way: He lies on a couch in a withdrawn depression, adding Jim Beam to and eating from a jar of the very same baby food he had fed to Perry in prison to ease him out of his refusal to eat.

Moving back and forth between Truman and Perry, faced with their similarities and differences, we become aware there are two kinds of brutality at work in *Capote*. The overt brutality shows itself in the eruption of unprovoked violence and its collective impact is not missed. Poles of repressed darkness and unending fascination become evident whenever a murder shatters American idealism and innocence. Watching Truman stand before a packed house in New York to read excerpts from his unfinished book is an astonishing spectacle of normalized dissociation of these polarized tendencies. Murders of this type take an unconscious grip on American society, but the obsessive and sometimes hysterical reaction conceals an appetite for greed, power, sexual aggression and violence. This grip is rarely traced back to these concealed impulses. The vicious circle at work here is apparent: The repressive tendency blindly invites the tragedy; the superficial fascination obscures its significance; the means to imagine the roots of our darker impulses are never cultivated. A continual denial of human totality is the result and this is, perhaps, the main theme of this film.

Ibsen defined soul murder as "the destruction of the love of life in another human being."[2] And it's clear from both the film and the biography it is based upon that Truman Capote had himself experienced this as a child. This brutality smothers honest reflection, destroys emotional ties and drowns inner truth. Truman hides his real self behind Bergdorf scarves and avoids his shadow by staying in the limelight of New York cocktail parties. It all seems a world away from the scene at the Clutter farmhouse. But it isn't really. *Capote* doesn't flinch when confronting us with the outer slaying, but the power of the film arrives in those moments when the horror of Truman's inner world seems to eclipse the literal bloodbath. Without either condemning or explaining Truman's disposition, *Capote* shows how actual murder and soul murder—these two kinds of brutality—find their meeting point, in both the saga at hand and in the culture at large.

Philip Seymour Hoffman's performance goes far beyond capturing Truman Capote's peculiar mannerisms and high-pitched, affected voice. Although there are moments towards the end of the film when Truman's façade collapses, exposing his inner abyss, Hoffman's achievement is to convey the presence of this profound deficit at the very same time Truman is fully vested in his persona reality. Indications of the full complexity of the character are maintained throughout. Whereas

Truman seems so at home in his grandiosity and self reference, at times to the point of being a caricature of himself, Hoffman's performance is never a caricature of Truman. The Truman we eventually come to see is part genius, part monster and part worm. Each part is there from the start, but Hoffman allows our sense of this to deepen in an incremental way before the revelation is completed in the final act.

Written by Dan Futterman and directed by Bennett Miller (both childhood friends of Hoffman's), *Capote* is a film that contains no grand vistas or spectacular action, yet its look is consistently potent. The effect goes beyond aesthetics; most scenes are crafted with a sense of visual metaphor, often through use of colors—grainy browns, washed grey, whites and baby blue—sometimes placed in vivid contrasts. When Truman is in his world—writing in Spain or driving in Kansas—the lines are clean and the light is clear. Interiors in Kansas—the Clutter's farmhouse, the prison, the courthouse—are muddier and clouded. The film exudes a meticulous care for each and every moment.

Capote portrays the life of a man who reflected the spirit of the times. The film thus always feels larger than the story immediately at hand. *In Cold Blood* was in Capote's mind a new genre of literature, the non-fiction novel, which would employ the techniques of drama to document actual life, turning real persons into rendered characters. Clearly he had practiced this technique in his own life, inventing a persona that would play well in the fabricated social scenes he inhabited, crafting his own celebrity. In doing all this he was also initiating a culture into new way of blurring the lines of fact and fiction, creating a slippery slope that has only become steeper. *Capote* shows these celebrated and shadowed dimensions of the writer's iconic status, providing a penetrating glance into the life of a remarkable individual as well as a portrait of some converging lines of the American psyche.

NOTES

1. Gerald Clarke, *Capote: A Biography* (New York: Carroll and Graf, 1988).

2. Leonard Shengold, *Soul Murder Revisited* (New Haven: Yale University Press, 1999).

BOOK REVIEWS

STANTON MARLAN. *The Black Sun: The Alchemy and Art of Darkness.* College Station: Texas A & M Press, 2005.

REVIEWED BY MURRAY STEIN AND DAVID L. MILLER

BY MURRAY STEIN

Stan Marlan has written a powerful book, richly laced with references and quotations from a myriad of sources, all fused intensely to the theme of darkness, the black sun. It is an unusually dense work. Each page is weighty and deserves long consideration. Marlan gathers images from art and alchemy, texts from literature and philosophy, insights from clinical work and extensive

Murray Stein, Ph.D., is a past president of the International Association for Analytical Psychology (2001-4), a training analyst at the International School of Analytical Psychology in Zürich, and the author of several books including *Jung's Map of the Soul.*

David L. Miller is Watson-Ledden Professor Emeritus at Syracuse University and a retired Core Faculty Member at Pacifica Graduate Institute in Santa Barbara. He is the author or editor of seven books and he has published more than seventy articles and book chapters since 1963. His research and writing works at the intersections of religions and mythologies, literature and literary theory, and depth psychology and culture. Dr. Miller is an honorary member of the International Association of Analytical Psychology.

case material, a host of colorful drawings and paintings, and places them in the context of Jung's writings on alchemy as these are importantly explicated by his two chief mentors, Edward Edinger and James Hillman. This is a book to read more than once, to sit with, to ponder, and to take in deeply and sensitively. Marlan communicates a vision that is important for therapy and for individuation. He ponders the meaning and value of depression for psychological depth. And in the end, he offers a way of looking and living that is deeply Jungian, also post-Jungian (i.e., Hillmanian), and I would add even post-post-Jungian, which is way of saying perhaps neo-Jungian. Marlan is throughout his own man and follows no one slavishly, and repeatedly he comes back to Jung, but with new eyes and greater understanding. So it is a trip well worth taking. I enjoyed reading the book immensely and congratulate Marlan on producing a work of such significance and lasting quality.

Throughout the work, one can see Marlan circling a central paradox like a moth around a flame. He comes close several times, in my view, to getting his wings burned but always recovers his balance exquisitely and flies on. What he wants to avoid is also what Hillman eschews so energetically, i.e., anything pertaining to a notion of linear developmentalism (a straight and forward advance toward individuation through stages like the alchemical colors, black, white, and red); salvationist progressions from lost and pathological states to sane and whole ones; concrete and gross literalisms of subtle psychological states that would put hunks of earth under one's slipping feet and offer sure steps into and out of the darkness and thence into the light of consciousness; leaps out of one alchemical color into another without residue; and so forth. He manages to pull this off remarkably well without getting his wings singed by the fires of radical deconstructionism, which leaves nothing standing in a landscape of cinders. This lies on one side of the ledger, on the left hand, if you will. On the right side, there are strong affirmations of desirable states like health, wisdom, psychological depth, maybe even development of a certain sort, of the Self in some passages (though not without caveats and sophisticated philosophical reservations). These he balances deftly and without seeming preference for one over the other. So he does not disappear into the mist of deconstructionism, nor does he ascend into the fog of a metaphysical essentialism. Marlan practices the art of refusal elegantly with one hand while offering the embrace of generous inclusion with the other. It is a dance: Circling a volatile paradox psychologically, philosophically, and clinically.

It occurred to me that Marlan wants to take a pass on the gold rush. Instead of packing his bags and heading west, he stays in Pittsburgh and searches his own immediate neighborhood for the treasure hard to attain. Not for him the lure of *albedo* out there in Denver, or the *rubedo* of San Francisco. *Nigredo* is where he begins, and *nigredo* is where he ends. He goes down rather than out, vertically and not horizontally. He drills deeply into the world of Black, accustoms his eyes to the darkness, and searches out the most elusive nooks and crannies of this phenomenon. Stubbornly he mines away in his own backyard, and at the end of the day he discovers a kind of light down there that is not known in California. There is gold in Pittsburgh too, but it is not yellow.

Some of what he finds in this venture is horrifying. Black is not a color for beginners. There are accounts of suicide, homicide, crippling depression, agonizing dismemberment. The dead are disinterred as he digs through this territory, and the odors are foul. Dreams of worms and snakes, of worlds collapsing and falling in pieces, of bad food and worse drink. He does not flinch. His clinical stamina is impressive. Not everyone can sit through sessions filled with images like this, in anguish, without hope, delving ever deeper into the pain and fear. No way out, escape routes shut, the only way is further into the dark, until... Well, it does change, at least sometimes. But not in the way one would expect. It's not a light-at-the-end-of-the-tunnel journey. It's a dark light in the dark tunnel, glowing, emanating, illuminating darkness with the light of darkness. It's a trial of transformation.

After a lecture I gave recently, a hand shot up and a man in his 20's offered a dream that he said had changed his life. In the dream, he ascended a mountain and at the top of his trajectory he saw a black sun. From there he fell, and when he stood up again he was changed. He attributed his change to the vision of this black sun. I was not his analyst and did not ask for further details. I only noted that the point of transformation was his confronting the image of a black sun. In a nutshell, this is the message of Marlan's book. If you stay with the darkness long enough, you will see a black sun. And it will change you.

BY DAVID L. MILLER

The Black Sun, by Pittsburgh analyst Stanton Marlan, is the published version of the 2003 Carolyn and Ernest Fay Lectures at Texas A & M University. The book's thematic, *sol niger*, stands in the tradition of Jung's interest in this alchemical motif. Jung not only commented explicitly on the "black sun," but he often evoked the usefulness of this striking image for the practice of psychotherapy. For example, Jung wrote: "Filling the conscious mind with ideal conceptions is a characteristic feature of Western theosophy, but not the confrontation with the shadow and the world of darkness. One does not become enlightened by imagining figures of light, but by making the darkness conscious. The latter procedure, however, is disagreeable and therefore not popular" (*Collected Works* 13 § 335). And in commenting on a particular patient, Jung wrote: "By accepting the darkness, the patient has not, to be sure, changed it into light, but she has kindled a light that illuminates the darkness within. By day no light is needed, and if you don't know it is night you won't light one, nor will any light be lit for you unless you have suffered the horror of darkness. This is not an edifying text but a mere statement of the psychological facts" (*CW* 9.2 § 595).

Not only can Marlan's work be located in relation to Jung—and especially in relation to perhaps the most difficult, if most pertinent, aspect of Jung's work, i.e., alchemy—but it also finds itself in the company of the equally difficult, but hermeneutically useful, critical theory of postmodernism (Adorno, Levinas, Kristeva, Derrida, Heidegger, Foucault, Lacan, etc.). This marks the book as up-to-date philosophically and theoretically, which is not always the case with psychological literature. Marlan's deconstructionist perspective allows him not only to write about the "dark side of light" (the title of the first chapter), i.e., "not only to see blackness," but also to "see by means of black" (190), i.e., to see blackness's light (197, and all of chapter four). The "black sun" is seen through, in every sense: the art of darkness in the heart of darkness (214).

The effect of Marlan's perspective is in the achievement of an "alchemical deconstruction of light" (5), the light whose "historical primacy has infused our understanding of consciousness itself" (12).

The *sol niger* therefore represents an "eclipse of a conscious standpoint" (11). In this shift of a "habit of mind" (185), Marlan manages to argue two important matters.

First, the book problematizes an unconscious soteriological fantasy in Jungian psychology. Again and again, Marlan identifies and resists what he appropriately calls "salvationism" in both analytic theory and its practice (9, 62, 65, 188, etc.). This is in keeping with Jung's oft-quoted statement late in his life: "The experience of the self is always a defeat for the ego" (*Collected Works* 14 § 778, cf. Marlan, 168). For Marlan, this anti-soteriological perspective implies that "the cure for suffering might well be more suffering" (4). It means that there is "no rush to cure," because "perhaps there is no cure" (65). One could even say, with Marlan, that "no one is ever fully analyzed; no deconstruction is ever complete; the unconscious or blackness is never totally eliminated" (189).

A second consistent radicality of this work is a counterpart of the first: namely, an exposé of the obsessive desire of people for light, which becomes an ego-ideal and results in neurotic suffering when not achieved (13). Marlan observes, with David Levin, that a hegemony of the eye and vision and light (ocularcentrism), which is linked with Occidental phallocentrism, logocentrism, and colonialism, may well be driven by a violence of light, i.e., the darkness of light against the light of darkness (16). Thus the phenomenological and epistemological function of the *nigredo* would be to counter the dominance of the perspective of the conscious ego (19). The self could then even find psychological nourishment in wounding and in the dissolution of defenses (22). Indeed, Marlan argues that there are moments in life and in analysis when "the dissolution of the ego is required" (72). This represents a move beyond the humanism of ego psychologies (72), to which much psychotherapeutic theory and practice has regressed, and it situates depth psychology properly in the depths.

There is, to be sure, a risk in all of this. Marlan is aware of this. He asks: "How can we speak about … [the "black sun"]? How can we address that invisible or absent presence that we call the Self or no-Self, Divine Darkness, or Sol niger? … One difficulty is that in every attempt to name the absent presence, there remains a vestige of metaphysical speculation, a transcendental signified (for our purposes read as Self) that is not deconstructed" (183, cf. 213). Marlan—in the postmodern tradition of Derrida, Levinas, and Lacan—wants to avoid "totalization, normalization, domination and essentialism" (16). He wants to "avoid master tropes that appear to refer to some-thing beyond themselves" (186). But just here is the potential problem. What is risked is an obscuring of the sun by the blackness, the light by the darkness. More than a criticism of the work, my concern is for what I take to be a possible misreading or misuse of Marlan's fundamental insight. Let me try to explain this by reference to an argument by Harold Bloom.

In his books *The Anxiety of Influence* and *A Map of Misreading*, Bloom argued that all readings are misreadings, which he called clinamen or misprisions, i.e., they are "mis-takings" because they are inevitably or necessarily "readings" or "interpretations." The task is to accomplish what Bloom called a strong misreading as opposed to a weak one. A weak misreading is a mere doctrinaire repetition. It is mimetic, literal, and wooden. A strong misreading takes off from the texts of others and carries on the reflection. It is not a reproduction, but a production; not mimesis, but poiesis.

I should think that it would be a weak misreading of Marlan to conclude that since the light is in the darkness, the nourishment in the wounding, consciousness in the unconscious, and the cure in the suffering, we should simply leave it all dark, wounded, unconscious and hurt. This is not faithful to Marlan's text (for example, see chapter four), because it is not where Marlan himself leaves it. But this does not allay the risk. Perhaps I can make the point more particular by reference to Marlan's use of the term "paradox."

I have already noted that there is an attempt to "avoid master tropes." But the use of the term "paradox" over and over again in the diction of this book (86-88, 142, 148, 152, 155, 163-164, 174, 185, etc.) makes one wonder whether "paradox" is lurking as itself a master trope. The term seems appropriate to phrases like light in darkness, cure in suffering, neurosis as friend, nourishment in wounding, and black sun. It also seems appropriate to the narratives of the case material so compellingly presented by Marlan. Moreover, there is precedent in analytical psychological theory for the use of the term. Neil Micklem, Adolf Guggenbühl-Craig, Ronald Schenk, and James Hillman—to name only four—have used the term centrally as a sort of objective correlative or root metaphor. Jung, like these others, antecedently had stressed what he called the paradoxical logic of psychology. For example, Jung compares psychological knowing to Gnostic understanding in the following:

> Paradox is a characteristic of the Gnostic writings. It does more justice to the *unknowable* than clarity can do, for uniformity of meaning robs the mystery of its darkness and sets up as something that is *known*. That is a usurpation, and it leads the human intellect into hybris by pretending that it, the intellect, has got hold of the transcendent mystery by a cognitive act and has 'grasped' it. The paradox therefore reflects a higher level of intellect and, by not forcibly representing the unknowable as known, gives a more faithful picture of the real state of affairs (*CW* 11 § 417, cf. the section on "The Paradoxa" in *Mysterium Coniunctionis*, and *CW* 16 § 62-63, as well as the essay on "The Spirit Mercurius").

So, on the one hand, Marlan is in good company.

But, on the other hand, one might have imagined that there is some good reason why "paradox" is a favorite trope, not of Postmodernism, but of Modernism (I am thinking of the work of William Wimsatt, Cleanth Brooks, and Robert Penn Warren). Early Modern and Modernist literature is strewn with poetic paradoxes, such as "loving strife," "joyously shuddering emotions," "deafening and thunderous silence," "sweet sorrow," "cruel kindness," "laborious idleness," "frozen flame," "pointedly foolish," "hot ice," "tragical mirth," "brief and tedious," and—more subtly—"wondrously strange snow." But though "paradox" is the stock and trade of Modernism, it has been largely erased in the lexicon of Postmodern criticism. I suspect that a part of the reason is that "paradox" in the modernist theology of, say, Kierkegaard was a cipher for salvation, the very salvation Marlan wants to avoid, and, even in the modernist prose of Kafka, "paradox" was a norm, a dominating figure, an essence, i.e., the "answer" that stopped discourse.

Psychologically, one could put it this way. To what aspect of the Self is paradox paradoxical? Surely paradoxes are not paradoxical to the objective Psyche or we would not have terms like *sol niger* or *coincidentia oppositorum*, nor in fact any of the poetic instances above. Perhaps paradox is paradoxical only to "me," to the ego consciousness for whom "paradox" conventionally means merely self-contradiction. Perhaps one could modify Jung's saying ("The experience of the self is always a defeat for the ego") and claim that the experience of the black sun is always a paradox for the ego, but it is not a paradox for the alchemy of the deep self. This is to say that to invoke the category of "paradox" centrally runs the risk of placing its perspective back in the economy of ego, against its own intention, rendering the so-called paradoxical perspective possibly Modernist and once again humanistic.

Think of the problem this way. Let us imagine a weak misreader of Marlan's book saying: "Yes, my sufferings, my neuroses, my depressions, my messes, and my dreams and fantasies are paradoxes. They are grotesqueries. They are mysteries. And that's that. One can say no more." In this case, the invoking—even properly—of "paradox" stops the psychological reflection. It stops the psychic processes. It becomes a sort of magical thinking, i.e., non-thinking. To be sure, this is not the case with Marlan's book, which is itself a beginning of a process of many reflections, rather than a stopping of them. The book is, as Marlan properly observes and as the reader will discover, a "continual *solutio*" (187). *Solve et coagula* (188), yes! Paradox? I'm not so sure. It could be that this term, like the Jungian term Self in the book, might well usefully be put under deconstructive erasure.

I realize that another move may also be possible. It is the strategy employed with concepts, like that of "paradox," which utilize the prefix "para-." In true postmodern fashion, and trading on insights from Jacques Derrida, J. Hillis Miller has argued that "para-" is a double antithetical prefix signifying at once proximity and distance, similarity and difference, interiority and exteriority, something this side of a boundary and simultaneously beyond it (See "The Critic as Host," *Deconstruction and Criticism* [New York: Seabury, 1979]). If the concept of "paradox" could function this way, it would make impossible the weak misreading that I have indicated and it would confirm Marlan's psychological alchemy of continual *solutio*. This would be, in my view, a strong misreading, "dissolving" even "paradox." And it would, precisely in the spirit of Marlan's *sol niger*, open the possibility expressed in Octavio Paz' lines ("A Draft of Shadows," *Monte Mora* 6 [1979], 90):

> The black fruit bursts,
> In flesh colored blossoms.

BOOK REVIEWS

KAREN ARMSTRONG. *A Short History of Myth*. Canongate, 2005.

REVIEWED BY ROBERT A. SEGAL

Several decades ago, a professional historian reviewing Barbara Tuchman's best-selling *The Guns of August* dismissed the book not because it was popular history but because it was bad history. Karen Armstrong's *A Short History of Myth* deserves dismissal for the same reason. As the author of *Myth: A Very Short Introduction*, I am hardly in a position to scorn Armstrong's book for its brevity and accessibility. But I believe that, as a specialist in the subject, I am in a position to scorn her book for the ignorance it so breezily displays.

Armstrong, the author of "histories" of subjects as broad as God, Islam, and Muhammed, clearly sees no need to acquire expertise in any of the areas on which she pontificates. As her references to *A Short History of Myth* evince, she relies on books nearly as pop as her own. Her main scholarly authorities are Mircea Eliade and Joseph Campbell.

Robert A. Segal is Professor of Theories of Religion, University of Lancaster, UK, and as of August 2006 will become Chair of Religious Studies, University of Aberdeen. He is the author or editor of *Myth: A Very Short Introduction* (2004), *Theorizing about Myth* (1999), *The Gnostic Jung* (1992), *Jung on Mythology* (1998), *The Myth and Ritual Theory* (1998), and *Hero Myths* (2000).

I blush to disclose that, in one of her few forays into the world of scholarship, she even cites an essay of mine.

Let us consider her pronouncements. Without any evidence or argument she informs us that "the imagination is the faculty that produces religion and mythology" (2). Perhaps so, but what is her rejoinder to E. B. Tylor, who back in 1871 argued that myth in fact arises from observation and reason rather than from imagination—this on the grounds that the similarities among myths worldwide suggest the source to be rigorous thinking rather than untethered imagination? In 1955 Claude Lévi-Strauss first began arguing the same. Neither is even mentioned by Armstrong. I would venture to guess that she is not familiar with the budding use of cognitive psychology to account for recurrences in myth.

Armstrong next tells us that "mythology is usually inseparable from ritual" (3). Now it was William Robertson Smith who, back in 1889, first tied myth to ritual. But the "myth-ritualist" school that subsequently emerged has been subjected to criticisms ever since. Nowadays even the most committed myth ritualists grant that many myths have no connection to rituals. The question is what the connection is whenever one is found. Simply to claim that myth and ritual go together is almost to beg the question, which is *how* they go together. Armstrong writes that "many myths"—no longer most—make no sense outside a liturgical drama that brings them to life, and are incomprehensible in a profane setting" (3). And why is that? She does not say. Multiple answers have been proffered by others: because myths explain rituals, because myths are the script of the rituals, or because myths are ritualistic themselves.

Armstrong then announces that "the most powerful myths are about extremity; they force us to go beyond our experience" (3). "Myth is about the unknown" (4). Really? What of myths about the creation of the known world? What of myths that explain rainfall? Armstrong compares myth with science (2-3), but then myth, as for Tylor and J. G. Frazer, is exactly about the known, not the unknown, world.

Armstrong declares that "all mythology speaks of another plane that exists alongside our own world" (4). This world is "sometimes called the world of the gods" and "is a basic theme of mythology" (4). While for Plato "every earthly reality is only a pale shadow of its archetype" (5), I know of no theorist of myth who holds this view. For

Eliade, whom Armstrong invokes, every present-day phenomenon was created by a god or culture hero in the distant past, but the present is the *product* of that creation, not the *shadow* of it. The relationship is causal, not ontological.

Armstrong declares that "myth is not a story for its own sake. It shows us how we should behave" (4). How myths about physical phenomena like rain shape behavior it is hard to see. Bronislaw Malinowski thus distinguished between myths about physical phenomena such as mortality and myths about social phenomena such as marriage. According to him, the function of myths about physical phenomena is to reconcile humans to unpleasantries of life that cannot be altered, whereas the function of myths about social phenomena is to spur acceptance of them and so to instill behavior. Armstrong, while echoing the uncited Malinowski, fails to make this distinction. She takes all myths to be about the human world.

Armstrong's failure to make this distinction continues with her crude claim that "Today the word 'myth' is often used to describe something that is simply not true" (7). She gives two examples: "A politician accused of a peccadillo will say that it is a 'myth', that it never happened" (7). "When we hear of gods walking the earth, of dead men striding out of tombs, or of seas miraculously parting to let a favoured people escape from their enemies, we dismiss these stories as incredible and demonstrably untrue" (7). When used of social phenomena, a "myth" is far more than a false belief. It is a staunchly held belief, the tenacity of which beckons for explanation. William Rubinstein's *The Myth of Rescue: Why the Democracies Could Not Have Saved More Jews from the Nazis* (1987) challenges the common assumption that the Allies in World War II were indifferent to the fate of European Jews and were indifferent because they were anti-Semitic. He rightly employs the term "myth" to capture the sway of the conviction, which is not merely of something "simply not true." When used of physical phenomena, a "myth" is the "primitive" counterpart to science and therefore refers to beliefs held by our forbears, not by us.

Armstrong's book consists of one simple-minded assertion after another. Myth, we are told authoritatively, does not purport to be true either "objectively" or "historically." Presumably, then, those who have strived to work out the relationship between myth and history—

for example, F. M. Cornford in *Thucydides Mythistoricus* (1907), Lord Raglan in *The Hero* (1936), and Paul Veyne in *Did the Greeks Believe in Their Myths?* (1988)—need not have bothered. Armstrong informs us that myth deals in "make believe," or play. (In my *Myth: A Very Short Introduction,* I myself suggest the same of *some*, by no means all, myths and use the work of D. W. Winnicott on play to do so.) Armstrong is certain that myth was never intended to convey information: "A myth, therefore, is true because it is effective, not because it gives us factual information" (10). No doubt she has since considered Elizabeth Barber and Paul Barber's recent *When They Severed Earth from Sky* (2005), which asserts that myth is exactly the passing on of information about the physical world—information needed by descendants to cope with the travails posed by the world. No doubt she considered but soberly rejected the view of historians of science Giorgio de Santillana and Hertha von Dechand in *Hamlet's Mill* (1969)—the classic effort to find science in myth.

Armstrong asserts that some of the earliest myths were of the sky: "When they gazed at the sky—infinite, remote and existing quite apart from their puny lives—people had a religious experience" (17). No mention is given of the Victorian Indologist Friedrich Max Müller, whose view this is, but instead we are referred to Eliade, who even in the one work of his most focused on natural phenomena, *Patterns in Comparative Religion* (1958), never gives the sky the centrality that Müller does. Not only Müller but the whole school of "nature mythology" goes unmentioned—and so, too, the criticisms of it by theorists ranging from Andrew Lang to Sigmund Freud and C. G. Jung.

Having presented her theses on myth, Armstrong takes us through a history—not just of theories of myth but of myth itself. Her "history," then, is an account both of approaches to myth and of myths themselves—a double feat. Armstrong divides the history of myth into six stages: palaeolithic period, neolithic period, early civilizations, axial age, post-axial age, and the "great Western transformation," or modernity. For the nature of myth in the palaeolithic period, she properly relies on Walter Burkert, who roots myth in hunting. For the neolithic period, in which agriculture arises, she relies once again on Eliade rather than on Frazer—an absurd oversight. In this period we find "the Great Mother"—but not either Jung or Erich Neumann.

The modern age marks the rise of science, or *logos*, which is in conflict with *mythos*. In the "pre-modern world," by contrast, myth and "reason" were deemed "complementary": "Each had its separate sphere, each its particular area of competence" (31). What of attacks on myth by the Presocratics, Plato, and the Sophists? What of the allegorizing of myth by the Stoics to defend it against Plato and others? The opposition of *mythos* to *logos* did not begin in the modern period, as even a hazy familiarity with, say, the work of the French classicist Marcel Detienne (*The Creation of Mythology* [1986]) would show. Armstrong reconciles myth with science in the "pre-modern world" by claiming that "in the pre-modern world, the divine was rarely regarded in the metaphysical terms imposed upon it by Western *logos*, but was usually used to help people to understand their humanity" (141). Again, she cannot fathom myths about nonhuman phenomena such as rain.

The modern period, we learn, is one of "alienation" from traditional, or religious, myth. Following a view that goes back to the Romantics and, among theorists of myth, to Jane Harrison (*Ancient Art and Ritual* [1913]), Armstrong maintains that art has replaced myth, though alternatively she labels mythology one of the arts (see 148). Her citing of famous painters and novelists who present mythic themes hardly clinches her claim that art has come to replace myth, for there have been painters and even novelists since ancient times. At the same time Armstrong asserts that modern art, while containing mythic themes, does not fully substitute for myths of yore. But why not, and especially when she contends that "there is nothing new in the godless mythologies of contemporary novels" (142)? In actuality, there is everything new in the elimination of gods: there is the uncoupling of myth from religion, and it is that uncoupling which above all allows for the retention of myth in the modern world. The presence of mythic themes in literature is but the most superficial aspect of the transformation of myth into literature—the issue considered magisterially by Northrop Frye (*Anatomy of Criticism* [1957]) and many others. Needless to say, neither Frye nor any other theorist garners a mention here.

Doubtless it would come as revelation to Armstrong to learn that theories of myth have shifted sharply *within* the modern period from what I call the nineteenth-century view, in which myth is at odds with science, to what I call the twentieth-century view, in which myth is reconciled with science. Armstrong assumes that the whole of modernity has been one of the rejection of myth and that only now, no doubt partly thanks to her book, can myth again be accepted.

Overall, Armstrong's book is the worst study of myth that I have ever read.

BOOK REVIEWS

SOPHIA HELLER. *The Absence of Myth*. State University of New York Press, 2006.

REVIEWED BY WILLIAM G. DOTY

If the Jungian-oriented evaluations of David L. Miller are correct, then following Jung's refinements of depth psychology, and subsequently those of James Hillman's archetypal psychology, the work of German psychoanalyst Wolfgang Giegerich represents a *third* plateau, essentially a Hegelian sublation of Jung and Hillman ("Introduction" to Giegerich, Miller, and Mogenson, *Dialectics and Analytical Psychology*, 2005, x). Sophie Heller, a recent Ph.D. from Pacifica Graduate Institute, has studied closely with Giegerich and Miller, and this book represents an intensification and refinement of her dissertation (2003). She advocates a "depth psychological appropriation of postmodernism" (114, 235) as she delves into complications of the meanings of myth today.

To prepare for this review, I spent several weeks trying to comprehend the Giegerichian prose—which I find extremely difficult and full of conflicting definitions—and the phenomena of what this

William G. Doty, Ph.D., is professor emeritus in the College of Arts and Sciences at The University of Alabama/Tuscaloosa, and the author of many essays and books in the field of mythological studies.

"third plateau" may represent. I am grateful that Heller's prose is not so impenetrable; she does repeat striking phrases from Giergerich such as "the logical negativity of soul" and "the negation of myth required to know myth" (201), but carefully rather than simplistically—I hope to understand the jargon better some day.

This work will be of interest to persons whose mythography has been influenced by depth psychology as well as those—they are not few, and I admit that I am sometimes in that camp—who question whether such psychology really might or *ought* to be dominant within analytical-interpretive studies of mythology that originate from classics, anthropology, or literary perspectives.

Heller's close attention to the phenomenon represented in the title of her book recognizes right away that the "death of god"—in the work of any of several thinkers to whom it should be attributed—represented a quantum change in recent Western philosophical and theological sensibilities. What, in many ways, did modernism represent but a wrenching cry that the gods and the myths now are absent from everyday experience? Seldom today do we experience them as "the living presentation of the truth of a given people" (132). Certainly the cultures of the world live in a state of despair and anomie that hardly could have been imagined in more stable religious periods. Already the romantics, as well as the modernists, ardently "talked myth" as a sort of social remedy, as seen particularly in the mythopoetic shadings of the poetry of Eliot or the fiction of Joyce and Lawrence, or the filmic work that is postmodernist-fantastic in the auteur's finish, but deeply modernist in Tolkien's attitude, *The Lord of the Rings.*

One may explore attempts to reconstruct or revive or metamorphose myths—particularly of classical antiquity—that sometimes "still" seem redolent with numinosity and inspiring spirituality (ch. 3, "The Lingering of Myth," or mythopoesis). Follow that line unwaveringly enough, and one ends up with "personal mythology," a topic Heller is quite deadly in dismissing, and I am sympathetic to her critique. The issue is largely one of realizing that traditional mythologies have been dedicated to the service of the collectivity, whereas currently personal mythology or "self-writing" most often manifests as somewhat-narcissistic ego-stroking of the individual. This author rejects such "cheap grace" approaches, aware as she is that many contemporary Jungian-oriented proponents of "Live your own myth!" are highly popular and widely published, precisely as they throw into the analytical retort admixtures of psychology, mythology, and developmentalism.

Heller's focus instead is upon important and basic philosophical issues, sometimes negatively trashing projected solutions (as in the work of Elizabeth Baeten and Milton Scarborough), and sometimes more positively affirming, as with respect to works of Hillman, Giegerich, and Miller. She advocates a rationalistic attention to the "positive" aspects of actual lived-experience (Giegerich: sometimes apparently derived from the analytical philosophy of scientific positivism, and other times simply meaning "real," "literal," or "at hand"). She proposes "a *reflective consciousness* [that] assumes the role that myth and the gods once had, enabling consciousness to look inward, and to understand oneself as well as the world through this subjective lens" (181, my emphasis of her key term), and she concludes that "the end of myth makes psychology possible—and necessary" (220).

When the modernists treated "the end of myth or the impossibility of living mythically as a symbolic loss that has to be mourned," they risked "granting myth a specialness that perhaps it [did] not warrant. It was one way of being-in-the-world. Now there is another" (222). And that other is an escape from the protective, yet deceitfully cloaking cocoons of religion and myth that long have searched for special meaning behind or below present existence.

Her concluding sentence: "Because in the moment of living one's life and not just trying to find myth or meaning, one shows without needing to justify that *reality* is, in fact, enough" (223; my emphasis to clarify the point). A rather Zen-like conclusion to her highly-abstract critiques, yet one that might lead to affirmation of a morality of authentic presence, aggressive ecological principles, or a proactive political ethics of care for the world at hand, in all its dimensions (these of course are my own projections).

Heller's book is rich and complex: here I could touch upon only a few of its dense analyses and judgments. Her discussion of myth analysts includes most contemporary theorists and several mythographic movements, especially those that start from "the problem" of the absence of myth. She argues with most of them, in ways that help the reader recognize the substantive underlying intellectual issues at stake as we seek to discern how the long-influential realms of the religious and the mythological—indeed more recently, the psychological—have largely lost their power to enspirit and lead culture.

While often agreeing with her analyses, I am less willing than she to write off the whole mythological enterprise: perhaps we have to restrict our discourse to speaking of "mythoids," but language itself is a witness that terms may continue in common parlance long after they have lost their epiphanic and metaphoric origins. Certainly cultural and pop studies will continue to track the "mythical" ways traditional models, images, and figures recur in human history. The philosophical-theological "god is dead" position has long been, indeed, my own, yet several of my favorite academic cottage industries find it instructive to chart the ways the figure of Superman has been reconfigured as the culture has changed decade by decade, or identifies ideological elements in the super-utopian American Dream, or sexist neuroses in the heroic monomyth of the Western imagination. Heller's book is a brave engagement with positions that may not be stabilized for a long time to come, and it sets the stakes of future arguments quite high.

BOOK REVIEWS

ROSS WOODMAN. *Sanity, Madness, Transformation: The Psyche in Romanticism.* Edited by Joel Faflak. University of Toronto Press, 2005.

REVIEWED BY PAUL BISHOP

Ross Woodman needs no introduction to the readers of this journal; he will be well known to them, both through his personal connection with the Jungian analyst Marion Woodman, to whom he is married (see his contribution to *Spring 72*), and through his professional work, in his capacity as Professor Emeritus in the Department of English at the University of Western Ontario, as a commentator on Romanticism and contemporary art. For the last four decades or so, Woodman has been exploring the work of the English Romantics in a series of studies and articles (notably *The Apocalyptic Vision in the Poetry of Shelley*, 1964), and this volume, *Sanity, Madness, Transformation: The Psyche in Romanticism*, shares their focus on William Blake (1757-1827) and Percy Bysshe Shelley (1792-1822), but also William Wordsworth (1770-1850) and Lord Byron (1788-

Paul Bishop teaches German language and literature at the University of Glasgow. He is the author of various books and articles on the intellectual affinities of C.G. Jung with the German tradition, including *The Dionysian Self* (1995), *Synchronicity and Intellectual Intuition* (2000), and *Jung's 'Answer to Job': A Commentary* (2002).

1824). (According to the book-jacket, what "began as a collection of Woodman's essays assembled by colleague Joel Faflak, quickly evolved into a new book of original compositions.") In theoretical terms, Woodman is indebted to Northrop Frye, as well as Paul de Man, Jacques Derrida, and C.G. Jung. Although he is too frequently relegated to "the lunatic fringe of the academic world," Jung — or, more precisely, his "madness" — "far better serves," Woodman explains in his introduction, "the madness of Romanticism than does the more obvious sanity of Freud or, indeed, the even more logocentric sanity of Frye" (p. 4). Such madness is, Woodman claims, "the inability of man to inhabit himself," that is, the insufficiency of "the logocentric drive towards self-knowledge and self-mastery," a drive that, in Romanticism, "is ironically denied its object by virtue of the steadfast pursuit of it" (p. 3).

In an earlier article on Coleridge and Jung (in *Journal of Analytical Psychology*, 1980), Woodman compared the fate of the Mariner in "The Rime of the Ancient Mariner"— namely, his ability to come to terms with "the Night-mare LIFE-IN-DEATH [...] Who thicks man's blood with cold"— with Jung's encounters with the anima as recorded in *Memories, Dreams, Reflections*. The first chapter, entitled "Jung and Romanticism," develops this reading, so that Woodman can, in chapter 2, argue that, for Jung, creativity did not lie, as in Winnicott's unkind phrase, in "an obsessional flight from disintegration" (p. 48; cf. p. 204), but rather, as it had done for Goethe, Wagner, and Nietzsche, in "a descent into its psychotic core as an archetypal source of new life that had to be analytically channelled into a new understanding of it" (p. 49; cf. p. 201). Himself a pupil of Northrop Frye, Woodman explores the affinities between, first of all, Jung's vision of the turd on the roof of Basel Cathedral and Frye's experience of casting off "that whole shitty and smelly garment," as he called it, of religious fundamentalism, and then, in turn, between those insights and the "dialectical form" of Blake's "apocalyptic vision" in *The Four Zoas* (1797-1804) and *Milton* (1804-1808) (pp. 52, 59, 61). In an autobiographical excursus, Woodman remembers how he spent the Christmas vacation 1948-1949 "struggling" with Blake's *Milton*, "suspended [...] between Locke's empiricism [...] and the autonomy of the imagination" (p. 69); worryingly, perhaps, for anyone involved in university teaching, Woodman has been able to compare his reminiscences of this period with Frye's own (the University of Toronto Press is publishing the notebooks and diaries), and he concludes that "coming to grips with Blake's dreamwork as the figuration of desire rather than the logocentric rationalization of it became the issue that informed my reading of Frye's Blake" (p. 85).

The third chapter constitutes an extended exegesis of the line "The Sexual is Threefold, the Human is Fourfold" from Blake's *Milton* (Book the First, [4], l. 5), in the course of which Woodman contends that "Jung's *Answer to Job* is a psychological account of Blake's prophetic vision in *The Marriage of Heaven and Hell* [1790-1793]" (p. 89). Fusing Blake, Fry, Jung, and Derrida, Woodman's text becomes almost as dense as those on which he is commenting, and the fourth chapter, an explication of Wordsworth with particular reference to *The Prelude* (1798/1789-1805; 1850), is similarly challenging.

In chapter 5, Woodman shifts the focus of his attention to Shelley, suggesting that, "in his own gropingly articulated way, Shelley anticipates not only Jung's work on alchemy, but the entire psychological system that emerged from it," and that "Jung's break with Freud [...] had its prototype in Shelley's and Coleridge's break with the 'mechanical philosophy'" (p. 165). According to Woodman, Jung's psychology, like that of the Romantics, "is not a personal psychology concerned with ego development"; rather, "the sickness of the individual" is understood to be "a cultural sickness" (p. 175). So when, in his letter to Herbert Read of 2 September 1960, Jung spoke of "the great dream which always has spoken through the artist as a mouthpiece," and defined this "great Dream" as "the future and the picture of the new world, which we do not understand yet," he was interpreting the life of the artistic individual in the same way as the Romantics, as poets, perceived their own personal lives (p. 176).

Chapter 6, "The Sanity of Madness: Byron and Shelley", reads the latter's *Adonais* (1821), *Alastor* (1815-1816), and *The Triumph of Life* (1822) in the light of the former's *Cain* (1821), the third Canto of *Childe Harold's Pilgrimage* (1816), and *Beppo* (1818). Woodman contends that "poetry is the sanity of madness" and that "Jung knew this" — "for this reason, until he had restored dialectic to the madness that is its unconscious source, the dialectic governing the life of the psyche was devoid of the meaning he sought to release" (p. 196).

The Romantic poets, Woodman writes, seem "closer" to him "than [his] own life vein" (p. ix), thereby echoing a phrase from Blake's *Milton* about the "Moment" as "a Pulsation of the Artery," but also a well-known part of the Qu'ran (Surah 50: 16). In his Afterword to this volume, Joel Faflak claims that "Woodman has allied Jung with the postmodernism that hopefully contains within it a new humanism capable of embracing a world [....] increasingly polarized"— which may be true. Faflak also suggests, however, that "this study, by gesturing towards Nietzsche's account of the tightrope walker suspended between two towers, rather powerfully evokes this polarization in terms of the terrorist attack on the World Trade Center" (p. 220), and, apropos of the composite Byron/Rousseau figure in *The Triumph of Life* and the lines "But follow thou, and from spectator turn / Actor or victim in this wretchedness" [ll. 305-06], writes that "whether he perishes in the rubble of the World Trade Center collapse or photographs the suicides of those who are about to die—it's all the same thing" (p. 234). At this point, perhaps, some of the dangers of an identification with Romanticism, and a concomitant erosion of critical distance, begin to make themselves felt. That said, anyone concerned with literature, analytical psychology, and archetypal cultural analysis will want to read this brilliant, intriguing, if sometimes frustrating and infuriating, study. You'd have to be mad if you didn't ...

BOOK REVIEWS

CHARLOTTE MATHES. *And A Sword Shall Pierce Your Heart: Moving from Despair to Meaning after the Death of a Child.* Chiron Publications, 2006.

REVIEWED BY KATHRIN ASPER

This is a unique and outstanding book mainly because of the breadth of the various aspects of bereavement it so thoroughly covers. These range from archetypal motifs to a careful and detailed description of the different stages of the mourning process, as well as addressing related spiritual issues and day-to-day practicalities.

The author, who herself lost a son, speaks from the depth of her experience but also broadens it by including many passages from interviews she has done with mothers. All of them experienced the pain Mary suffered and of which she was forewarned by Simeon: "And a sword shall pierce your heart."(*Luke* 2: 35)

Kathrin Asper, Ph.D., is a Jungian analyst and psychotherapist who has been in private practice in Meilen, Switzerland since 1975. She was a lecturer (1978-2004) and training analyst and supervisor (1984-2004) at the C.G. Jung Institute in Zürich, and now serves in those same capacities at the International School of Analytical Psychology, also in Zürich. Her books include *Inner Child in Dreams* and *The Abandoned Child Within: On Losing and Regaining Self-Worth.*

Mathes chose the approach of "qualitative research" in this work and placed herself as a participant observer in connection to other mourning women courageous enough to engage in self-reflection about their "mother-grief."

It is remarkable how Mathes is able to weave together and connect the inner and outer experience of child loss with archetypal themes from many different quarters using the concept of the archetypes to illuminate mothers' struggles. In exploring and discussing this symbolic material she finds ubiquitous and eternal models for one of the most painful of all human experiences. Her meditation upon archetypal texts and artworks has a healing potential because the symbols reflected therein serve as a container for personal experiences of loss and speak directly to the soul.

Childrens' deaths resulting from many causes are explored: death of fetuses and infants, death from AIDS, illness, accident, military casualties, murder and suicide. The author provides detailed and empathic appreciation of each of them and describes carefully their differences and their impact on the mourners.

Besides her own experience of child loss, Charlotte Mathes has had vast experience in working with bereaved clients in her private practice in New Orleans for over twenty years. She is a certified Jungian analyst, has a doctoral degree in psychoanalysis from the Union Graduate School in Cincinnati, is a clinical member of the American Association of Marriage and Family Counselors and a board-certified supervisor for clinical social workers. This entire book mirrors not only her broad expertise but also includes theory and current research on bereavement. Furthermore, she describes the mourning process and its transformation, including the spiritual dimension, and shares helpful insights—practical, spiritual and therapeutic—which are beneficial for mothers who have gone through the same bitter loss that pierced their hearts and cut their lives into distinct periods—before and after.

The death of a child leads mothers through a period of painful struggle to a new sense of identity and transformation stirring the mourner to greater consciousness and a spiritual attitude deeply rooted in the honoring of their subjective experience.

Following a careful study of the different archetypes—child, mother, God and meaning—the author proceeds by linking a detailed description of the way mothers mourn with a rich variety of archetypal texts, for example Isis's mourning after the death of her son Osiris. A chapter then deals with mourning in families, with a special emphasis on the differences in how fathers and siblings grieve. Not excluded also is the estrangement couples may experience after the loss of a child.

Mathes, given her personal experience of child loss and her work with the bereaved, is especially suited to see themes and aspects that one would search for in vain in the vast bereavement literature. For instance, does the loss of a child not only create tremendous mourning and a long process of collecting the pieces of one's own life, but also sometimes lead mothers to a sense of entitlement? "After all I have gone through, I am entitled to have a life free of all discomfort, God owes me this," says a mother. Such residual feelings of omnipotence and entitlement can lead grieving mothers to want more than their share of life's good things and may elicit arrogance and self-absorption; bitterness and heartlessness may also ensue. The reader witnesses here the gentleness of the author whose tone throughout the book is never judgmental but always full of respect, as when she quotes a comment by a mother who says: "I guess everyone is entitled to a little entitlement" (p. 170). Soothing also is Mathes's telling of how a Buddhist story of a mother's grief helped one mother move out of crippling self-involvement and isolation (p. 171).

Another theme explored is based upon the observation that mothers suffer tremendously because they could not protect the child and prevent the death. This painful helplessness may lead mothers to a spiritual attitude which allows them to experience their human limitations and to accept a higher power.

The wealth of Mathes's symbolic material is profound, and there are no emotions explored here that do not find also their symbolic or mythological correspondences, which help to contain the suffering. For example, when a child has been murdered, rage and revenge constellate: this finds symbolic expression in the mythological Furies of Ancient Greece, who mercilessly persecuted murderers and other serious wrongdoers. Can these emotions be overcome, and can the mother find a peace of mind that frees her from toxic entanglement and leads her eventually to forgiveness?

Children who died by suicide may shatter the belief system of their mothers, and the challenge of a suicide is to confront one's own shadow parts, cleansing them, and thus allowing one to keep the middle ground, not trying to be worse or better than one actually is. Mathes looks at suicide from different theological angles and quotes different authors who have also dealt with the topic. From an archetypal perspective she cites the poem of a Sumerian moon priestess of five thousand years ago, where suicide is seen as the will of the Moon God Nanna:

> He gave me a dagger and a sword,
> and said:
> Turn them against your own body,
> They are made for you. (p. 148)

Relating suicide to powers beyond ego consciousness offers a comprehension of suicide that does not narrow it down to a simple action of the ego but as a need of the Self for transformation or as a determination by an archetypal constellation. Passages Mathes quotes from mothers bereaved from the suicide of daughters and sons show that the most painful emotion they experience is that they could not protect their child, that they felt powerless and had to struggle with this human limitation for years along with experiencing shame, guilt, and anger.

In Part Two of her book Mathes presents aids to the mourning process, an assembly of perspectives that is remarkable because it is a distillation of her own bereavement process, a true expression of a lived experience. Help is offered to mourners dealing with shame, guilt, and anger, along with entitlement. This leads to an exploration of how the body can be cleansed and includes archetypal motifs that appear in soul/body healing. An exhaustive chapter is devoted to journaling, dreams, and writing one's life story, including many mothers' writing samples and dreams. Mathes shows how meaningful it can be for bereaved mothers to search for their own myth, the one they have lived before and the one they may find after their child's death. Generously and genuinely she shares her own experience by finding myths that mirror her experience, leading to the conclusion that although death, the great separator, cuts the soul bond between mother and child, it never breaks it and may even make it stronger in another realm.

A further chapter is devoted to creativity by which mourners may find repair and healing in order to keep connection and to create a new home, a safe place for the deceased child. She concludes the chapter by describing creative moves toward transcendence and the importance of honoring one's own subjective experience.

Connection to the outer world is also found in her descriptions of funeral and mourning rituals, sacred journeys, protests and advocacy.

The last chapter of the book is devoted to the Black Madonna and the Pietà, both of whom unite the pain of the child with the pain of the mother: A pain that finds transformation and "compassion born from suffering, detachment born from understanding."

This book is a must for bereaved mothers and for all of us drawn to the subject. It is not a book which teaches but shares in a loving, kind way; a generous gift from the author and from all the mothers who participated in the research. It pays genuine and true tribute to the second part of Simeon's words "and a sword shall pierce your heart," which continues: "[so] that the thoughts of many hearts may be revealed." (*Luke* 2: 34-35) In Mathes's words:

> What we learned from the interviews was that the coming together of women who mourn their child's death creates a transformative power. We recognize the impact each of us had on the other. By sharing intimate parts of ourselves, we deepen our compassion and understanding and derive strength from one another. (p. vii)

To conclude, Charlotte Mathes's book is a jewel among the many books on bereavement. Born from the wellspring of suffering, it leads to new paths and transformation.

BOOK REVIEWS

JEROME S. BERNSTEIN. *Living in the Borderland: The Evolution of Consciousness and the Challenge of Healing Trauma. Routledge,* 2005.

REVIEWED BY SUZANNE WAGNER

This is a groundbreaking book for psychotherapists interested in the extension of Jung's original findings on the dynamics of the ego and the collective unconscious. More broadly, it breaks ground for all people who are reflecting upon the destructive nature of the neurotic, one-sided Western ego. Jerome Bernstein is a man with a unique background of experience, reflection and action. With more than thirty years of experience as a Jungian analyst, he has worked directly with Navajo and Hopi medicine men exploring their healing traditions. He also has worked with the Navajo tribal council in their attempts to sustain healing rituals now in danger of being lost.

Suzanne Wagner, Ph.D., is a Jungian analyst in private practice in Sausalito, CA and a training analyst at the C. G. Jung Institute of San Francisco. She co-created the feature documentary, *Matter of Heart,* 1985 and is Director of *The Remembering Jung Series*: 28 hours of interviews with people who were close to Jung, forthcoming in DVD format.

In this new book, he proposes that we are undergoing a major shift in the nature of consciousness itself. He sees this shift in consciousness as an evolutionary development with its basic source in the mysterious intelligence operating from deep within the psyche and the natural world. He calls this new consciousness *Borderland consciousness*. He defines a new space—*The Borderland*—that is opening up between the Western ego and the deeper dynamics in the body, in the natural world and in the collective psyche. He suggests that there are growing numbers of people who exhibit this new kind of consciousness. The "*transrational*" communications they receive often reflect the problems experienced in other life forms suffering from the destructive effects of industrialized society. The messages are direct, symbolic and linked to events in the body, culture and nature. They are missed if they are referred only to subjective, perceptual reality. Navajo healers would instantly recognize the kinds of phenomena that *Borderland people* report and communicate.

The book is laid out in three major sections. Part I begins as Bernstein describes how he opened up to this new kind of consciousness through his challenging work with a woman artist who had suffered severe trauma in childhood. She experienced a special awareness of nature and direct connection to the feelings of animals in her environment. Bernstein listened more deeply and recognized he could not continue to pathologize her feelings and perceptions as defensive, dissociated experience or as projected material. It took an expansion of his feeling orientation, his empathy and his willingness to listen to this patient without clinical judgment to discover her particular gifts of consciousness. His experiences with her are used as a kind of Ariadne's thread through later sections of the book to help the reader better comprehend the nuances of this new consciousness.

Bernstein then gives a scholarly presentation of the history of the Western ego. He designates the story of the creation myth in Genesis as the source of our orientation to the Word, to logic and to an attitude of total domination over nature. He explores the nature of evolution first explicated by Darwin, and discusses the problems for survival created by "overspecialization". He shows how we developed an "anthropomorphized ego cleaved from nature". This development of a rational, narrowly focused ego, favoring thinking and abstraction, has made possible the wonders of scientific discovery and technological development. This had to happen, but now it must change if we are to survive as a species and if life on planet earth itself is to survive our destructive habits. He brings in his understanding of new developments in chaos theory and the psychological notion of a "fragmentation complex" to illustrate the fact that the Western ego is prone to fear of chaos and enacts a super-determined need to control, assuming god-like omnipotence. This focused ego becomes deaf, dumb and blind to new information and to a "survival intelligence" attempting to reach us through experiences which are "*transrational*" and often appear to the one-sided ego as chaotic, when, in fact, they carry messages of a wider and deeper system of order.

The first section ends with the hopeful idea that human consciousness can change and can begin to cooperate with the larger systems of life intelligence speaking to us in *Borderland experience.* He writes,

> What holds hope for our species is a containing dynamic outside the ego. Reconnection with nature offers that since it does connect the ego—in spite of itself—to the transpersonal dimension...the evolutionary thrust is to have a containing/constraining dynamic outside the ego that can contain its inflation, arrogance, and hubris.(p. 62)

He offers an example of a life-saving decision made by Nikita Krushchev during the Cuban Missile Crisis of 1962,

> which moved him to back down in the face of imminent nuclear mutual annihilation by the United States and the Soviet Union. He was undoubtedly aware that it would cost him his political life, if not his physical survival. In essence, he placed the highest value on the preservation of life above and beyond the value placed on (geographical, political) power. I call this dynamic that gripped Khrushchev in that moment, 'moral consciousness.' (pp. 62-63)

Such consciousness stems from a transcendent place, and "we can choose to behave consonant with it or counter to it." If we can behave in ways consonant with it, we become "co-evolutionary partners" with the forces in the psyche and nature aimed at sustaining life.

All of this follows the outlines of individuation as it proceeds according to Jung's discovery: the conscious ego, opening to the collective unconscious, inevitably comes to a confrontation with the greater intelligence and superior powers of the Self. The ego experiences a defeat as the forces of the deeper Self may overwhelm and fragment it but can as well offer new paths for life which are hidden from it. In my view, Bernstein is giving us fresh examples of this phenomenon as it plays out in both individual lives and in the greater dynamics of our current cultural crises.

In Part II, Bernstein takes pains to describe how *Borderland consciousness* develops out of three different "portals": (1) evolutionary pressures whose source is the deep unconscious, (2) basic 'givens' in personality structure, and (3) the effects of severe trauma. Rational prejudices of most psychotherapists lead them to deal with unconscious material in dreams and symbolic events in reductionistic, categorical and abstract terms. They fail to receive the messages being sent, and they translate them inadequately. This ends up hurting and pathologizing the experiences of *Borderland patients*. They are apt to resist psychotherapy because it can and often does injure them further. He makes a plea to therapists to be more open, to listen more deeply and empathically to the *"transrational"* phenomena that are described by patients. *Borderland people* are carrying grief for the destructive effects of our cultural-shadow and are knowingly and unknowingly doing psychological work toward the transformation of the Western ego. He shows that these people are not necessarily identified with utopian visions, or with a regressive return to a "*participacion mystique*" with Nature. He differentiates the *Borderland person* from both the strongly dissociated trauma patient and from the patient who exhibits patterns of Borderline personality disorder.

Things come alive in Part III with the presentation of material relating to the Navajo world-view and ancient healing rituals. The Navajo recognize that a wound to the environment or the spirit in the natural world surrounding the patient can injure the body and spirit of the patient just as much as would a direct assault upon his body and psyche. This view provides a meaningful link to the *Borderland phenomena* Bernstein has discovered. Both views tell us that our vitality is interdependent with our surroundings at the levels of body, psyche and nature. Healing the individual restores order and brings healing to the environment and *vice versa*. He discusses the ways in which the mind/body split that we experience can be bridged and healed in depth psychotherapy and through Navajo healing practices. He draws parallels and emphasizes the use of *witnessing as a clinical tool* and the *use of story* to reflect new insights into the connection between psyche, body and environment.

Another chapter relates stories of synchronistic phenomena that seem to be attempts to prevent or intervene with untimely death or the onset of destructive diseases. In one impressive example, he tells about his own early detection of cancer in a woman patient using his sensitive reading of the strange qualities in her dreams and the gestalt inherent in a symbolic drawing she did in the course of her therapy. Other examples include stories showing that many people anticipated the World Trade Center attacks in their dreams and imaginative life before it happened. Bernstein also explores issues raised by treatment of Environmental Illness disorders and Attachment disorders. He makes the creative proposal that much could be gained by forming a fully cooperative team effort between Navajo medicine men, analytical psychologists, and environmental physicians to treat such difficult syndromes.

This description gives only the barest outline of the rich, thoughtfully and sensitively presented material in this fine book. It is scholarly as well as anecdotal. There is a wide-ranging bibliography, and there are pithy endnotes for each chapter which illuminate many of the questions that arise in the reader's mind. There are useful diagrams as well as photos of Navajo medicine men in their native habitat. A sense of being with Bernstein in an intimate and elaborate conversation is created by this unusual balance between scholarly thinking, intuition, and passionate feeling. An Epilogue presents a poetic story, expressing from the Native American view how the world of the white man has been experienced. There is humor, and there are touching and refreshing images to be found here. It presents an imagined invitation to sit together on either side of a *Borderland*, to meet each other with respect and openness, to exchange and learn from the different ways and special skills each has developed.

It is deeply moving to read this and to remember Jung's heartfelt wonder when he discovered the depths of spiritual sensibility in the sacred rituals of the Pueblo people and of other Native American cultures. He was moved to realize the close and vital connection with spirit-in-nature shining through all the "life-ways" of the native people.

Jung knew the destructive, shadow aspects of his white man's mentality better than most men of his time. He opened himself to learn from and work with "brown-skinned people" of his dreams, of Africa, of Native America and eventually of many other early indigenous earth cultures. Such experiences were part of Jung's own discovery of the Self and the defeat and transformation of his ego.

This book presents a challenge and a call to the rest of us to listen more deeply and openly and to see more clearly the dynamics between ego and Self. We need not fall victim to depression, panic or despair as we face the powerful forces at work fragmenting our present cultures and our rational views. Our blind and unconscious ways do need to be given up and sacrificed. We do have some hope of bringing ourselves through this terrifying crisis of unconsciousness that we face at the beginning of the twenty-first century. Bernstein has given us a great gift in the form of this book, to read, to discuss and to contemplate together. We can answer this call by paying more attention, using Bernstein's cues and discriminating evaluations as a help to discern better the messages carried in our own "*transrational*" experiences. This is an exciting prospect that offers us the possibility to heal some of the many old wounds we carry as well as to take us into new life-ways as of yet unimagined.

New from Spring Journal Books

Studies in Archetypal Psychology Series

Series Editor: Greg Mogenson

Collected English Papers of Wolfgang Giegerich

THE NEUROSIS OF PSYCHOLOGY
Primary Papers Towards a Critical Psychology

Author: Wolfgang Giegerich
ISBN 1-882670-42-6
Volume 1 ◆ Price $20.00

With its publication of the *Collected English Papers of Wolfgang Giegerich,* Spring Journal Books makes available to the psychological reader the work of one of archetypal psychology's most brilliant theorists. A practicing Jungian analyst and a long-time contributor to the field, Giegerich is renowned for his dedication to the substance of Jungian thought and for his unparalleled ability to think it through with both rigor and speculative strength. The present volume takes its title from Giegerich's groundbreaking paper, "On the Neurosis of Psychology, or The Third of the Two." The "third" referred to in the title is psychology itself as the theory in which the two, patient and analyst, are contained as they engage with one another in the analytic process. By applying to psychology itself the ideas that it draws upon when thinking about the patient, Giegerich establishes the basis for a psychology that defines itself as the discipline of interiority. Topics include Neumann's history of consciousness, Jung's thought of the self, the question of a Jungian identity, projection, the origin of psychology, and more. The product of over three decades of critical reflection, Giegerich's English papers are collected in four volumes: *The Neurosis of Psychology (Vol. 1), Technology and the Soul (Vol. 2), Soul-Violence (Vol. 3),* and *The Soul Always Thinks (Vol. 4).*

Look for Volumes 2,3, & 4 in the Coming Months!

Technology and the Soul

Soul-Violence

The Soul Always Thinks

To order, please visit our online store at
www.springjournalandbooks.com or call *504.524.5117*

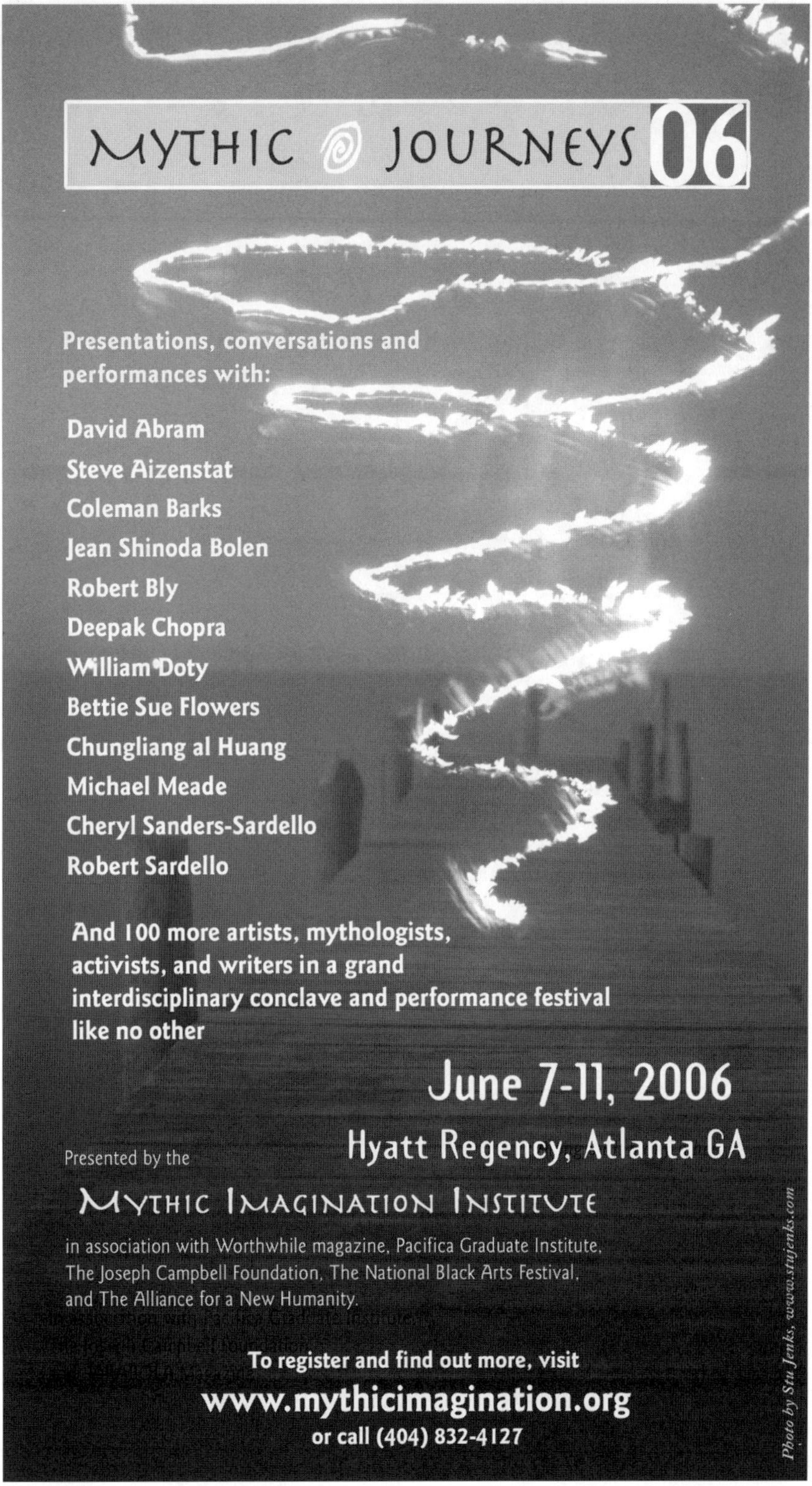
MYTHIC JOURNEYS 06
Presentations, conversations and performances with:
David Abram
Steve Aizenstat
Coleman Barks
Jean Shinoda Bolen
Robert Bly
Deepak Chopra
William Doty
Bettie Sue Flowers
Chungliang al Huang
Michael Meade
Cheryl Sanders-Sardello
Robert Sardello
And 100 more artists, mythologists, activists, and writers in a grand interdisciplinary conclave and performance festival like no other
June 7-11, 2006
Hyatt Regency, Atlanta GA
Presented by the
MYTHIC IMAGINATION INSTITUTE
in association with Worthwhile magazine, Pacifica Graduate Institute, The Joseph Campbell Foundation, The National Black Arts Festival, and The Alliance for a New Humanity.
To register and find out more, visit
www.mythicimagination.org
or call (404) 832-4127
Photo by Stu Jenks, www.stujenks.com